PROLOG AND EXPERT SYSTEMS

Kenneth A. Bowen

Applied Logic Systems, Inc.
and
Syracuse University

McGraw-Hill, Inc.

New York St. Louis San Francisco Auckland Bogotá
Caracas Hamburg Lisbon London Madrid Mexico Milan Montreal
New Delhi Paris San Juan São Paulo Singapore Sydney Tokyo Toronto

This book was set in Times Roman by Publication Services.
The editor was Eric M. Munson.
The production supervisor was Friederich W. Schulte.
The cover was designed by Joseph Gillians.
Project supervision was done by Publication Services.
R. R. Donnelley & Sons Company was printer and binder.

PROLOG AND EXPERT SYSTEMS

1 2 3 4 5 6 7 8 9 0 DOC DOC 9 0 9 8 7 6 5 4 3 2 1

ISBN 0-07-006731-7

Library of Congress Cataloging-in-Publication Data

Bowen, Kenneth A.
    Prolog and expert systems / Kenneth A. Bowen—1st ed.
        p.   cm.
    Includes bibliographical references and index.
    ISBN 0-07-006731-7
    1. Expert systems (Computer science)   2. Prolog (Computer program language)
QA76.76.E95B67   1991
006.3'3—dc20   90-24032

PROLOG AND
EXPERT SYSTEMS

Also Available from McGraw-Hill

Schaum's Outline Series in Computers

Most outlines include basic theory, definitions, and hundreds of solves problems and supplementary problems with answers.

Titles on the Current List Include:

Advanced Structured Cobol
Boolean Algebra
Computer Graphics
Computer Science
Computers and Business
Computers and Programming
Data Processing
Data Structures
Digital Principles, 2d edition
Discrete Mathematics
Essential Computer Mathematics
Linear Algebra, 2d edition
Mathematical Handbook of Formulas & Tables
Matrix Operations
Microprocessor Fundamentals, 2d edition
Programming with Advanced Structured Cobol
Programming with Assembly Language
Programming with Basic, 3d edition
Programming with C
Programming with Fortran
Programming with Pascal
Programming with Structured Cobol

Schaum's Solved Problems Books

Each title in this series is a complete and expert source of solved problems containing thousands of problems with worked out solutions.

Related Titles on the Current List Include:

3000 Solved Problems in Calculus
2500 Solved Problems in Differential Equations
2000 Solved Problems in Discrete Mathematics
3000 Solved Problems in Linear Algebra
2000 Solved Problems in Numerical Analysis

Available at your College Bookstore. A complete listing of Schaum titles may be obtained by writing to: Schaum Division
McGraw-Hill, Inc.
Princeton Road, S-1
Hightstown, NJ   08520

ABOUT THE AUTHOR

Kenneth A. Bowen, founder and President of Applied Logic Systems, Inc., is currently a professor of computer science at Syracuse University, Syracuse, New York, where he was formerly a professor of mathematics. He recieved his B.S.,M.S., and PhD degrees (in mathematics) from the University of Illinois at Urbana, Illinois. Dr. Bowen is a world-wide recognized authority on logic programming and Prolog, and has been an invited speaker at conferences throughout the United States, Europe and Asia. Dr. Bowen was an invited participant in the joint Japanese – U.S. Seminar on the Current State of Logic Programming, sponsored jointly by MITI (Japan) and NSF (USA) at Argonne National Laboratories in October, 1989, and served as the General Chairman for the Joint Meeting of the Fifth International Conference and Symposium on Logic Programming held in Seattle in 1988.

With his extensive experience, he has acted as a consultant to several major computer manufacturers and defense contractors, as well as various agencies of the Federal Government. As a research professor at Syracuse University, Dr. Bowen has directed a large number of government- and corporate-funded projects in the area of logic programming as it relates to knowledge base maintenance. He was one of the principal investigators for the Rome Air Development Command Artificial Intelligence Consortium and was the organizer, and one of the presenters, of a nation-wide live closed-circuit television presentation on Prolog and Expert Systems broadcast in December 1985.

CONTENTS

Part II   MetaLevel Programming and Expert Systems

PREFACE

This book is the result of years of indulgence: indulgence in a love of logic and its computational manifestation in Prolog, indulgence in the joy of teaching Prolog to my students, friends, and family (even when they had reservations about what it was I was leading them into), and indulgence in the delight of using odd and anthropomorphic methaphors and pictures to convey the ideas. I've tried, in the static pages of this book, to capture some of the pleasure I've found in teaching these ideas. I can only hope that some of it comes through.

One of the striking and successful areas of application of Prolog is the implementation of expert systems. I have oriented the presentation of Prolog programming toward the presentation of several approaches to the implementation of expert systems. The exercises utilize information from the everyday and scientific worlds as the basis for developing aspects of such systems. More substantial raw information has been included in the Appendix. There are several sequences of exercises that use the various parts of the Appendix. The following table delineates them.

§	A-TV	B-Enzymes	C-Clouds	D-IRS	E-PhotoEquip	F-AutoRepair
1	1.8,1.9	1.12	1.10,1.11	1.13	1.14	
2	2.8,2.9	2.11	2.10	2.12	2.13	
3	3.8,3.9	3.7	3.6	3.10		3.11
4				4.10		
5	5.12	5.2	5.13			
6	6.15	6.16				
7	7.10	7.8		7.6,7.11-12		
8	8.1		8.5	8.3	8.2	8.6
9	9.1		9.4	9.3	9.2	9.5
10						
11			11.1	11.1	11.1	11.1
12					12.1	12.2

The approach of this book grew out of my approach to the teaching of programming languages at the School of Computer and Information Science at Syracuse University. I usually begin a programming language course with a brisk introduction to the language in question, intending to provide an overall view and appreciation of the language's salient features. I generally omit or brush lightly over the more detailed or obscure aspects of the language during this introduction. Basic competence with the language is reinforced in the students through the use of many small exercises. During the second portion of the course, I usually undertake one or more reasonably large programming problems. As we develop the program(s), I refine the student's understanding and use of the language in the context at hand. I have found this to be a particularly successful approach for several reasons: First, if the large programs are well selected, they are of inherent interest to the students, and hence capture their attention more than sequences of small exercises. Consequently, the students appear much more receptive to discussions of the fine points of the programming language, since these points often have significant bearing on the overall large program. Second, undertaking a reasonably large programming task enables me to discuss and illustrate software design issues, which are all too often glossed over in basic programming language courses. Part I of this book thus reflects the introductory portions of my Prolog programming courses, and Part II, on the implementation of expert systems using Prolog, corresponds to the second portion of my courses. Instructors and students should cover Part I at a brisk pace, and in particular, should just skim Chapter 7. Almost all aspects of Prolog are seriously exercised in Part II during the development of various expert systems. As differing aspects of Prolog are encountered in Part II, readers and instructors should return to the relevant portions of Part I (in particular Chapter 7) for review.

It is a customary statement, yet true, that this book would not have existed without the help of many people. First must come all my many students and friends—together with my family—all of whom entered into the learning process with me, and who taught me what worked (and what didn't) to convey the ideas. More immediately, my colleagues at Applied Logic Systems—Johanna Bowen, Kevin Buettner, Keith Hughes, and Andy Turk, have proven invaluable critics and contributors of ideas. The following reviewers were also helpful in reviewing early stages of the manuscript: Charles Frank, Northern Kentucky University; Forouzan Golshani, Arizona State University; Dennis Kibler, University of California, Irvine; and Kathleen Swigger, North Texas State University. And finally, but not least important, my wife and daughters, Johanna, Melissa, and Alexandra, have been among my sharpest critics and most imaginative contributors. To all, I say thank you. They have improved the book inestimably. The remaining flaws belong only to me.

Kenneth A. Bowen

PROLOG AND
EXPERT SYSTEMS

PART ONE

CORE PROLOG

CHAPTER 1

PROLOG DATABASES

1.1 ELEMENTARY PROLOG DATABASES

The best way to start programming is to write a program. We will start with a simple Prolog program consisting of several facts about drugs and diseases. Let us start by putting down a number of simple assertions: that aspirin relieves headaches, that it also relieves moderate pain, that KO Diarrhea relieves diarrhea, that Noasprinol relieves headache, and so on. Each of these assertions claims that a simple relationship holds:

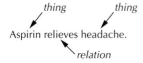

This would be expressed in Prolog by

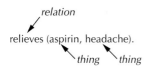

This is an example of a Prolog fact. Facts assert that relationships hold between things. The fact displayed above asserts that the relationship "relieves" holds between the two things "aspirin" and "headache." We will see later that Prolog facts can assert relationships holding between two things, three things, four things, etc. There can even be relations that involve only one thing or no things. We will make sense of that later.

Since relations are very important to Prolog, the name of the relation comes first in the Prolog statement. Then comes the list of things involved in the relationship. The list is enclosed in parentheses, and the things are separated by commas. The entire expression is terminated with a period (.), sometimes called a full stop. Spaces can be used almost everywhere to improve readability with one exception: No space can occur between the relation name and the left-hand parenthesis.

Prolog generally insists that the names of relations and things begin with a lowercase letter. This is why we changed "Aspirin" to "aspirin."

Consider another assertion:

This also asserts that the relation "relieves" holds between two things, but in this case, the expression naming the second thing is a two-word English phrase, namely, "moderate pain." Since Prolog is basically very dumb, it can't handle names made up of more than one word. What can we do? One solution is just to leave out the space:

    moderatepain

But this is hard to read. We can improve things by capitalizing the *p* in *pain*:

    moderatePain

Even though Prolog insists that names begin with a lower-case letter, the rest of the letters in the name can be lower- or upper-case. You can also use digits after the first letter of a Prolog name, and you can use the underbar character (_). Using the underbar character can definitely improve the readability of Prolog names, for example:

    moderate_pain

One can even write

    moderate_Pain

Now that we see how to name "moderate pain" in Prolog, it is easy to see that the Prolog version of the assertion "Aspirin relieves moderate pain" would be

    relieves(aspirin, moderate_pain).

Some other interesting assertions are that "aspirin aggravates asthma," "aspirin aggravates peptic ulcer," "DeCongest aggravates high blood pressure," etc. The assertion that aspirin aggravates peptic ulcer would translate into

    aggravates(aspirin, peptic_ulcer).

The assertion that DeCongest aggravates high blood pressure would translate into

    aggravates(de_congest,high_blood_pressure).

Each of these Prolog facts asserts that a particular relationship holds among several things. A collection of Prolog facts is called a Prolog *database*. Databases are the

FIGURE 1-1
A Prolog database of simple medical facts.

relieves(aspirin, headache).
relieves(aspirin, moderate_pain).
relieves(aspirin, moderate_arthritis).
relieves(aspirin_codeine_combination, severe_pain).
relieves(cough_cure_xm, cough).
relieves(pain_gone, severe_pain).
relieves(ko_diarrhea, diarrhea).
relieves(de_congest, cough).
relieves(de_congest, nasal_congestion).
relieves(penicillin, pneumonia).
relieves(bis_cure, diarrhea).
relieves(bis_cure, nausea).
relieves(noasprinol, headache).
relieves(noasprinol, moderate_pain).
relieves(triple_tuss, nasal_congestion).
aggravates(aspirin, asthma).
aggravates(aspirin, peptic_ulcer).
aggravates(ko_diarrhea, fever).
aggravates(de_congest, high_blood_pressure).
aggravates(de_congest, heart_disease).
aggravates(de_congest, diabetes).
aggravates(de_congest, glaucoma).
aggravates(penicillin, asthma).
aggravates(bis_cure, diabetes).
aggravates(bis_cure, gout).
aggravates(bis_cure, fever).

---

simplest kind of Prolog program. Figure 1-1 shows a Prolog database that includes the elementary facts we've developed above.

These Prolog facts have a natural intuitive translation back into English. Remember that the first part of a Prolog fact is the name of a relation holding between the list of things that follow. Thus,

relieves(de_congest, nasal_congestion).

would translate into

DeCongest relieves nasal congestion.

The fact

aggravates(ko_diarrhea, fever).

translates into

KO Diarrhea aggravates fever.

Besides relations involving just two things, there are many relations that involve more than two things. For example, consider the assertion that

Interstate 81 connects Binghamton and Syracuse.

The relationship here is the "connects" relation. The things involved in the relationship are Interstate 81, Binghamton, and Syracuse. How do we translate this into a Prolog fact? Remember that the name of the relation comes first, followed by the things involved in the relationship, so the corresponding Prolog fact is

connects(interstate_81, binghamton, syracuse).

The assertion

Binghamton and Syracuse are connected by Interstate 81.

conveys the same information as the original, but with a different emphasis. The Prolog version of this is

connected_by(binghamton, syracuse, interstate_81).

Another natural relation involving three things is the "parents of" relation:

Ken and Johanna are the parents of Melissa.

This translates to

parents_of(ken, johanna, melissa).

The original statement can also be phrased as

Melissa's parents are Ken and Johanna.

This version becomes

parents(melissa, ken, johanna).

Notice that we could have also translated the last assertion into the fact

parents_are(melissa, ken, johanna).

Whether or not to include such helping words as *is* and *are* in the names of relations is a matter of personal taste.

In everyday conversation, there aren't very many natural relationships involving four or more things. Of course, one can easily concoct lots of artificial relationships with four or five or more participants. Heres one natural relationship involving four things:

The states of Arizona, Colorado, New Mexico, and Utah meet in a common point.

We can translate this into

common_point(arizona, colorado, new_mexico, utah).

There are many occasions when we must assert that something has a certain property. For example:

Nasal congestion is a mild condition.

Heart disease is a serious condition.

In the first example, the property is "being a mild condition"; in the second, it is "being a serious condition." In English, we usually write the property after the thing for which it holds. However, in the corresponding Prolog facts, the property name occurs first:

mild_condition(nasal_congestion).

serious_condition(heart_disease).

Prolog thinks of properties and relations as being very similar sorts of notions. For this reason, we will use the word *predicate* to refer to either properties or relations. So "relieves," "aggravates," "connects," "parents," "mild_condition," and "serious_condition" are all predicates.

From the examples so far, we can see that the basic form of Prolog facts consists of a predicate name followed by the names of the things involved:

predicate(thing₁name, thing₂name, . . .).

Every Prolog fact must be terminated with a period (full stop). The *predicate name* part of a fact normally appears first, although we will see a few exceptions later. The *things* related to one another by a predicate are called its *arguments*. Thus,

aspirin, headache

is the list of arguments of "relieves" in the fact

relieves(aspirin, headache).

The arguments of "aggravates" in the fact

aggravates(bis_cure, gout).

are

bis_cure, gout.

The names of predicates are made up of letters, digits, and the underbar character (_); but remember, the first character of the name must be a lower-case letter.

The names of things are called *constants* (sometimes called *atomic constants* or simply *atoms*). Like the names of predicates, they are made up of letters, digits, and the underbar character, and must start with a lower-case letter.

If you choose the names of your predicates and constants to be as intuitive as possible, it is very easy to understand the intended meaning of your Prolog facts. The meaning we intended for the first "relieves" fact in Figure 1–1 is that

Aspirin relieves headache.

The meaning of the last fact in the database is that

Bis Cure aggravates fever.

Of course, Prolog doesn't know about aspirin, DeCongest, drugs, or aggravation in any real sense. It only "knows" what we choose to make it do. The sense in which it will "know" that this set of facts is about drugs and aggravation and diseases will arise from what we do with this database. We will ask Prolog to answer questions on the basis of the facts recorded in the database. Later, we will add rules that allow Prolog to make inferences based on the facts in the database.

We will see that the only meaning the database has for Prolog is based on the patterns of the facts and rules, not on the particular names we have used for predicates and constants. Nonetheless, it is a good idea to use your intuition right from the beginning. Recording Prolog facts is just like writing some assertions on a sheet of paper. The graphite or ink marks on paper have no "meaning" in themselves. The meaning comes from our interpretation of them. The same is true of Prolog facts recorded in a computer. The particular recorded Prolog facts might be true or false. In fact, it might be possible to interpret the names of the predicates and constants in two different ways: For one interpretation, the facts might all be true, while for the other, some of them might be false. But if the interpretations of all the facts are true, Prolog guarantees that it will always give true answers to any questions we ask. When we later add rules for making inferences, Prolog also will guarantee that all of the assertions it infers will be true. This is because Prolog is based on logic.

1.2   REPRESENTING A CIRCUIT

Let's consider another example. Figure 1–2 displays a small electrical circuit. (Those of you with no knowledge of electronics should relax. This is only an example. We will supply the few necessary bits of information as we go.)

Our goal is to work out a Prolog description of this circuit. What does this mean? Do we want to somehow describe the *picture* in Prolog? While that could be a possibility, that isn't the goal here. What we want to do is describe the abstract *functionality* of the circuit. We want to write a Prolog description of *what the circuit does*. As such diagrams are ordinarily used, it is understood that abstract electrical signals (on/off, high/low, true/false) enter through the input lines on the left, are transformed in various ways by the circuit components, and exit through the outputs on the right. Thus, to describe the functionality of the circuit is to describe what happens to those signals as they pass through the circuit.

If we take the "what the circuit does" idea very seriously, we will only be concerned with the correspondence between the input and output signals. For example, one can

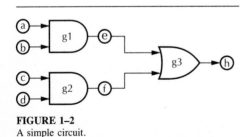

FIGURE 1–2
A simple circuit.

FIGURE 1–3
Overall circuit behavior.

	Input			Output
a	b	c	d $\longrightarrow$ h	
on	on	on	on $\longrightarrow$ on	
on	off	on	on $\longrightarrow$ on	
on	off	on	off $\longrightarrow$ off	

determine that the correspondences indicated in Figure 1–3 would be true for this circuit. (The $\rightarrow$ means that the indicated input on the left side of the arrow produces the output indicated on the right side of the arrow.)

If we select "i_o" as the Prolog predicate to represent the complete version of the table in Figure 1–3, the corresponding Prolog database would include such facts as

i_o(on, on, off, on, on).
i_o(on, off, on, off, off).

The arguments in these facts correspond in order to the columns "a, b, c, d, h".

While this certainly gives a bare-bones description of what the circuit does, it isn't terribly interesting. It's much more intriguing to try to describe the functionality of the whole circuit *in terms of the functionality of its parts*. For instance, what roles do parts *e* and *f* play in the output *g* of the circuit? What is the function of *g2*? The parts of the circuit are the gates and the connecting wires. To describe the functionality of the whole circuit in terms of its parts means that we must build up the description of the circuit's functionality from descriptions of the functionality of the gates and a description of how the gates are connected together. The latter tells us what's connected to what. Such a description of the connections in the circuit is often called the *connectivity* or *topology* of the circuit.

Our goal is now as follows:

Describe the functionality of the whole circuit in terms of descriptions of the functionality of its component gates together with the connectivity of the circuit.

Obviously, we must first construct Prolog descriptions of the functionality of the individual gates, together with a Prolog description of the connectivity of the circuit.

This circuit is a simple example of a *combinational* circuit: The output signals can be described as simple boolean combinations of the input signals. That is, if we are given a particular set of input signals, we can describe the corresponding output signals in terms of the input signals using boolean operators such as and, or, not, etc. The individual circuit elements (the "boxes" in Figure 1–2) represent various boolean functions, as indicated by their labels. Thus, an and-gate represents a logical conjunction. Its output (the signal emerging on the right side) is the logical conjunction of its inputs (the signals entering on the left). Letting $I1$, $I2$, and I stand for the inputs to various gates (or boolean functions), and letting O stand for the output, the action of the gates can be described by standard truth tables, as shown in Figure 1–4.

FIGURE 1–4
Truth tables for circuit gates.

I1 I2	O	I1 I2	O	I	O
on on	on	on on	on	on	off
on off	off	on off	on	off	on
off on	off	off on	on		
off off	off	off off	off		
and_gate		or_gate		not_gate	

The overall function of the circuit is built up out of the functions of its individual elements. To be able to describe the overall function, it is necessary to know two things:

1 The functionality of the individual components (*component functionality*); and
2 The manner in which the individual components are connected (*circuit connectivity*).

Using the tables of Figure 1–4 as a guide, we can construct a set of Prolog facts that describe the input-output characteristics of individual elements. For example, let us use "and_Table" as a predicate for describing the behavior of an and_gate. Since the and_gate has two inputs and one output, "and_Table" should have three arguments. We will assume that the first two arguments of "and_Table" represent the input values, and that the third argument represents the output value. With these assumptions, we can directly transcribe the table for and_gates from Figure 1–4 to these Prolog facts:

    and_Table(on,on,on).
    and_Table(on,off,off).
    and_Table(off,on,off).
    and_Table(off,off,off).

The tables for or_gates and not_gates can be represented in a similar manner. The facts for all three predicates are collected in Figure 1–5.

This solves the first requirement, that of describing the functionality of the individual components. For the second requirement, we must describe the manner in which the components are hooked together. To do this in Prolog, we must give names to all the appropriate circuit pieces. This includes not only the gates, but also the wires connecting them. In Figure 1–2, we provided names for all the appropriate pieces. The gates were named g1, g2, and g3, while the wires were named a, b, c, d, e, f, and h. However, Prolog doesn't have the ability to read the diagram we drew in Figure

    and_Table(on,on,on).   or_Table(on,on,on).   not_Table(on,off).
    and_Table(on,off,off).   or_Table(on,off,on).   not_Table(off,on).
    and_Table(off,on,off).   or_Table(off,on,on).
    and_Table(off,off,off).   or_Table(off,off,off).

FIGURE 1–5
Prolog versions of truth tables.

1–2. Thus, we must use Prolog predicates to describe the nature of all the pieces and the manner in which they are connected. The gates g1 and g2 are "and_gates." The input wires to g1 are a and b, and its output wire is called e. Gate g3 is an "or_gate" with input wires e and f and output wire h. We must decide how to represent this information by means of Prolog facts.

We will see that there is an immense amount of flexibility in the choice of particular ways to describe knowledge in a Prolog program. In this example, there are many different ways of representing the circuit. We have chosen to use a very simple one that clearly lays out the structure of connections in the circuit. We will see later, however, that it has some limitations. However, the representation we will use is easy to appreciate.

Since this simple circuit has two types of circuit elements, we choose to use two basic predicates: and_Gate and or_Gate. The two predicates each have four arguments. The way we intend to use "and_Gate" is schematically indicated as follows:

and_Gate(*Gate_Name, Input$_1$, Input$_2$, Output*).

The predicate "or_Gate" will be used similarly. The first argument of both predicates will be the identity (name) of a particular circuit element. In this example, all circuit elements are gates with two inputs and just one output. The first argument in the description of a gate is the gate's identity (i.e., name). The second and third arguments will be the names of the input wires, and the last argument will be the name of the output wire. With this decision, we can write down three statements that describe the circuit connectivity. The gate labeled g1 in the diagram is an and_gate; it has wires a and b as input and wire e as output. This can be represented by the fact:

and_Gate(g1, a, b, e).

Similarily, g2 is an and_gate with wires c and d as input and wire f as output, and so is represented by the fact:

and_Gate(g2, c, d, f).

Finally, gate g3 is an or_gate with input wires e and f and output wire h. This is represented by the fact:

or_Gate(g3, e, f, h).

To complete our description, there are a few other other assertions we need to make about the structure of the circuit. From the perspective of this problem, we can say that wire a is an input wire to the circuit, and so are b, c, and d. Wire h is the sole output wire for the circuit. If we choose to use the one-place predicates "input" and "output" for this purpose, we can represent these assertions by the following Prolog facts:

input(a).
input(b).
input(c).
input(d).
output(h).

FIGURE 1–6
Prolog description of circuit topology.

    and_Gate(g1, a, b, e).
    and_Gate(g2, c, d, f).
    or_Gate(g3, e, f, h).
    input(a).
    input(b).
    input(c).
    input(d).
    output(h).

Note that "input" and "output" are being used as property names. The entire collection of assertions representing the connectivity of the circuit are listed in Figure 1–6.

The connectivity of the circuit is expressed by its use of the constants naming wires. The letter e appears in the "output slot" of the fact

    and_Gate(g1, a, b, e).

Moreover, e also occurs in one of the "input slots" of the fact

    or_Gate(g3, e, f, h).

The two facts together imply that the output of g1 is connected to an input of g3 via the wire e. Similarly, consider the two facts:

    and_Gate(g2, c, d, f).
    or_Gate(g3, e, f, h).

These jointly imply that the output of g2 is connected to an input of g3 via the wire f.

This completes descriptions of the functionality of the gates and the circuit connectivity. We will combine them in Chapters 4 and 5 to produce descriptions of the functionality of the whole circuit.

1.3 IDENTIFICATION OF HICKORY TREES

Let us consider one more example. Figure 1–7 shows a database of facts representing knowledge about the characteristics or traits of hickory trees.

This database was taken directly out of the book, *Fruit and Twig Key to Trees and Shrubs*, by William Harlow (Dover, 1959.) We are going to return to this problem several times, eventually building a small expert system for identifying types of hickory trees. The system will ask us for characteristics of the branch or bud that we have in front of us and will give us back an identification of the tree. The problem is restricted to hickory trees to keep the scale of the database down.

Harlow's book contains decision tables that take a user through the process of identifying trees. The database in Figure 1–7 extracts the salient traits of branches, twigs, and buds of hickory trees from one of these tables. We have a lot of flexibility in how we choose to represent this knowledge. We choose to use a two-argument predicate "trait." The second argument in each fact is the particular tree that we are

FIGURE 1–7
Prolog facts for traits of hickory trees.

    trait(bud_scales(valvate), bitternut_hickory).
    trait(bud_color(yellow), bitternut_hickory).
    trait(bud_scales(valvate), pecan_hickory).
    trait(bud_color(brownish), pecan_hickory).
    trait(bud_scales(imbricate), pignut_hickory).
    trait(terminal_bud_size(short), pignut_hickory).
    trait(bud_scales(imbricate), mockernut_hickory).
    trait(terminal_bud_size(large), mockernut_hickory).
    trait(outer_scales(persistent), shellbark_hickory).
    trait(twig_color(orange_brown), shellbark_hickory).
    trait(bud_scales(imbricate), shagbark_hickory).
    trait(terminal_bud_size(large), shagbark_hickory).
    trait(outer_scales(persistent), shagbark_hickory).
    trait(twig_color(reddish_brown), shagbark_hickory).

talking about: a shagbark hickory, a pecan hickory, a pignut hickory, etc. The first argument is a representation of the particular trait with which we are concerned. In many cases, traits have the following property:

The trait consists of a generic notion combined with a particular instance of that generic notion.

For example, buds have a color, so one generic notion is "bud_color." That color could be yellow or brownish, hence "yellow" and "brownish" are both particular instances of the generic notion "bud_color." The bud scales can be *valvate*, overlapping, or *imbricate*, just touching each other. Thus, "bud_scale_type"—or simply "bud_scales"—is a generic notion whose particular instances are "valvate" and "imbricate." The terminal buds can be short or large. The outer scales can be *deciduous*, falling in autumn, or *persistent*, staying on through the winter. The table in Figure 1–8 displays the generic notions and their particular instances, as used in the hickory tree database.

The first arguments of the "trait" facts contain a new kind of Prolog term called a *compound term*. Figure 1–7 contains many examples of compound terms. For instance, in the first "trait" fact, the compound term is

    bud_scales(valvate)

In its basic syntactic structure, a compound term has the same appearance as that of a fact but lacks the ending period. A compound term consists of a *functor*, followed by a list of terms enclosed in parentheses. Functors are made up of letters, digits, and the underbar character, and must begin with a lower-case letter. No space is allowed between the functor and the left parenthesis.

The terms in the list following the functor are called the *arguments* of the term. Thus, in bud-scales(valvate), "bud_scales" has just one argument. However, functors can have one, two, three, or more arguments. We will see many examples later.

FIGURE 1–8
Generic characters and their
instances for hickory trees

Notions	Instances
bud_color	yellow
	brownish
bud_scales	valvate
	imbricate
terminal_bud_size	short
	large
outer_scales	persistent
	deciduous
twig_color	orange_brown
	reddish_brown

In constructing the database for hickory trees, we chose to use the generic characteristics—for example, "bud_scales" as functors. We then indicated the actual value for that characteristic, e.g., imbricate or valvate, as a single argument to the functor for the compound term. Thus, you can think of "bud_scales(imbricate)" as a compound term representing a particular quality of "bud_scales." The single argument slot in that compound term is filled in with the actual value "imbricate."

However, there is nothing in the basic structure of the problem that says we must do it this way. There are other ways. We could have flipped it around, using the characteristic as the operator, in effect saying that "yellow applies to bud_color." The compound term in this case would have looked like

yellow(bud_color)

There is nothing in the nature of Prolog that would have stopped us from doing that. We could also have chosen to use "trait" as a three-argument predicate. We could have had the tree as the third argument, the character as the first argument, and the particular value as the second argument. If we had taken this route, the first fact of the hickory database would have been written

trait(bud_color, yellow, bitternut_hickory).

Later, when we learn how to query databases, we'll see exactly what motivated our choice.

1.4 SYNTAX

We can summarize what we have seen so far by saying that the general form of *facts* consists of a predicate name followed by some arguments. The arguments are a sequence of terms that must be enclosed in parentheses. There must be no space between the predicate name and the left parenthesis. Facts must terminate with a period.

In the teminology of Prolog, the part of a fact that includes everything but the period (full stop) is called a (*positive*) *literal*:

predicate_name(term, term, ...)

Literals are the building blocks of Prologs syntax. Notice that literals look just like terms.

It is possible to have a fact or literal in which the predicate has no arguments. There would be zero arguments between the parentheses. In this case, the parentheses are omitted. Thus,

always_True.

would be a fact, with "always_True" being used as a zero-argument predicate.

Predicates can have any number (zero or more) of arguments. The number of arguments for a predicate is called its *arity*. If a predicate has *n* arguments, we describe it as being *n-ary* or *n-place*. Thus, "aggravates" from the drug database is 2-ary or 2-place, while "connected_via" is an example of a 3-ary or 3-place predicate. The predicate "and_Gate" from the circuit database is 4-ary. The predicate "always_True" is 0-place or 0-ary.

When *n* is small, there is some specialized terminology associated with *n-ary* predicates and functors. This is given in Figure 1–9. Thus "relieves" and "aggravates" are binary predicates, while "connected_via" is a ternary predicate. The predicates "input" and "output" from the circuit database are unary.

There is a convenient notation for describing the arity of Prolog predicates. The notation is used when we are talking *about* predicates as opposed to *using* them in facts in a database. The notation

p/n

tells us that *p* is being used as an *n-ary* predicate. Thus "relieves/2" says that "relieves" is being used as a binary predicate, while "expensive/1" says that expensive is being used as a unary predicate.

The arguments of a predicate are called *terms*. They can be *constants*, *numbers*, or *compound terms*. In Figure 1–1, we saw some elementary constants as arguments. These include "de_congest"—the name of a drug—and "cough"—the name of a symptom or disease state. Constants are sometimes called *atomic constants* or *atoms*. Constants are made up of letters, digits, and the underbar character, and must start with a lower-case letter.

Figure 1–7 contains examples of *compound terms*. For instance, in the first "trait" fact, the compound term is

FIGURE 1–9
Terminology for the arities of predicates and functors.

Number of Arguments	Description
1	unary
2	binary
3	ternary

FIGURE 1–10
Determining syntactic roles by context.

trait (bud_color (yellow), bitternut_hickory).

| predicate | functor | constant | constant |

compound term

literal

fact

bud_scales(valvate)

Compound terms have the same appearance as facts, but lack the ending period. A compound term consists of a functor, followed by a list of terms enclosed in parentheses. Functors are made up of letters, digits, and the underbar character, and must begin with a lower-case letter. No space is allowed between the functor and the left parenthesis. The terms in the list following the functor are called its *arguments*. Thus, in the preceding example "bud_scales" has one argument. However, functors can have one, two, three, or more arguments.

Though syntactically all are of the same form, constants, functors, and predicates are always distinguishable by context. That is, the way we use an expression tells us whether it is a constant, predicate, or functor (see Figure 1–10)

Compound terms *look like* the traditional mathematical and computer science notation for the application of a function to its arguments. For example, "bud_color(yellow)" looks just like the notation for application of a function in C or Pascal. Moreover, the name *functor* is similar to the word *function*. This tends to imply the execution of operations. In almost every programming language other than Prolog (and a few of its relatives), this notation really does mean that when the computer focuses on the expression in question (e.g., bud_color(yellow)), the computer will operate on the arguments and produce something new as a value in place of the expression. That does *not* happen in Prolog. Compound terms are complex structures that are used for their patterns. They are best thought of as a way of directly writing a kind of tagged record structure. The functor, such as "bud_color" or "twig_color" is the tag identifying a particular kind of record structure. The arguments are the values that have been put into the slots of the record structure. What Prolog will do when it tries to make use of such a tagged record structure is to look at the pattern expressed by the structure. Sometimes Prolog will use the structure much as we think of a tagged record structure being used in an imperative language, by filling in empty slots or extracting values from full slots and using them for other purposes. Other times, it makes use of the compound term very much as a pattern. We will see how that happens shortly.

Let's review the concept of Prolog *terms*:

- Terms include (individual or atomic) *constants*. Constants are made up of letters, digits, and the underbar character, and must start with a lower-case letter. After the first character, any alpha-numeric character, including upper-case letters and the underbar, can occur. Constants also include any sequence of characters, other than the single quote symbol ('), enclosed in surrounding single quote (') characters, such as:

'This is a funny constant.'

'@..#some junk more &'

If you want to include the single quote symbol (') as one of the characters of such a constant, you must double it. For example

'I don''t like to study.'

- Terms also include *numbers*. Most of the modern Prolog systems allow all of the standard programming representations for numbers, including integers and reals, both in fixed and floating point. In some older Prolog systems, the arithmetic is limited to integers. For example, the following are integers:

    34   −2   +8888

    The following are reals:

    23.5   −0.004   2.3E−12

    Many Prologs identify reals like 23.0 with the corresponding integer 23.

- Terms include *variables*. A variable is an identifier beginning with an upper-case letter or with the underbar character. After the initial upper-case letter or underbar character, it can contain upper- or lower-case letters, digits, and underbars.

- Finally, terms include *compound terms* which are sometimes called *structured terms*. Another example of a compound term is "father(john)," which might intuitively represent the father of John to a program. Any term can be an argument to other compound terms. This nesting can be arbitrarily deep.

Figure 1–11 provides examples of the four kinds of Prolog terms while Figure 1–12 provides a summary definition of Prolog's concept of term.

FIGURE 1–11

Some examples of prolog terms.

Syntactic construct	Example
Constant (Atom)	john
	john_Jones
	'John Jones'
	'some #% funny char^s'
Number	345
	−23.6
	33E−2
Variable	Result
	_2345
	Temporary_Accumulator
Compound term	severe(pain)
	segment(pt(3,−4))
	pt(2.5, 3)

FIGURE 1–12
Summary definitions of Prolog terms.

Syntactic construct	Description
Atom(Constant)	Any identifier beginning with a lower-case alphabetic character Any sequence of characters enclosed in ' signs; embedded ' signs must be doubled
Number	Integer Fixed-point real Floating-point real
Variable	Any identifier beginning with an upper-case alphabetic character
Compound term	A functor followed by "(", followed by a term-sequence, followed by ")"
Identifier	Any sequence of alphabetic characters or digits or the underbar, the first character of which is an alphabetic character
Integer	Any sequence of digits "+" or "−" followed by any sequence of digits
Fixed-point real	An integer followed by a decimal point, followed by any sequence of digits
Floating-point real	A fixed-point real followed by the letter "E" followed by an integer
Functor	Same as Atom
Term-sequence	Any term standing alone A term-sequence followed by a comma in turn followed by any term

1.5   USING PROLOG SYSTEMS

We have introduced the notion of a Prolog database. Now we must begin learning how to use Prolog systems to manipulate these databases. While as yet there is no standard for Prolog systems[1], most are very similar and follow what is called the Edinburg syntax and approach. All of the examples in this book were created on an IBM PC using the ALS Prolog™ Compiler from Applied Logic Systems, Inc.[2] This system is typical of most interactive Prolog systems and will be used for all of the examples in this book.

The first step one must take is to create a file containing the facts that make up the database. This is normally done using a text or program editor for your computer system. Few of the Prolog systems have a built-in text editor. Instead, they allow the user to use any editor that is convenient. Let us assume that we have used some text editor to create a file containing the facts in Figure 1–1. Assume we named the file **medic.pro**. The next step is to invoke the Prolog system. The ALS Prolog system is invoked by typing the command **alspro** to the operating system. When ALS Prolog starts running, it types a greetings banner that looks like this:

---

[1] Prolog standards are currently being developed by committees of the American National Standards Institute (ANSI) and the International Standards Organization (ISO).

[2] ALS Prolog is also available for the Apple Macintosh and various workstations.

FIGURE 1–13
Loading a file.

```
C:>alspro
ALS-Prolog Personal Version 1.0 [1000] Serial Number: 100006
   Copyright (c) Applied Logic Systems

?-consult(medic).
Loading medic...medic loaded.
?-
```
_____

```
ALS-Prolog Personal Version 1.0 [1000] Serial Number: 100006
   Copyright (c) Applied Logic Systems
```

After typing its banner, the system will type a *prompt,* which looks like "?-". This indicates that the system is ready and waiting for the user's instructions. We want to order the system to load the database that is contained in the file "medic". To do this, we will use the built-in command **consult**. This command requires one argument which is the name of the file—in this case **medic**. The command must be terminated with a period. The interaction would look like the interaction shown in Figure 1–13 (using ALS Prolog running on an IBM PC). The system responds to the **consult(medic)** command by typing the message "Loading medic . . . ," and begins searching for the file **medic.pro.** When it finds the file, it begins reading the facts from the file and storing them in its internal Prolog database. When it has read and loaded all the facts from the file, it types the message "medic loaded.", starts a new line on the screen or terminal, and types the prompt. If for any reason, the Prolog system can't find the file to consult (perhaps we made a typing error), it types the message "can't find file medic", starts a new line on the screen, and types the prompt. We can summarize these steps as follows:

- Create a file containing Prolog facts using a text editor.
- Start the Prolog system.
- Type the command
  ```
  consult( filename ).
  ```
  where *filename* is the name of the file containing the facts.
- The system types the message
  ```
  Loading filename...
  ```
  and begins searching for the file.
- If the Prolog system finds the file, it reads the facts in the file, loads them into the internal Prolog database, and types
  ```
  filename loaded.
  ```
- If the Prolog system can't find the file, it types the message
  ```
  Can't find file filename.
  ```
- The system starts a new line on the screen or terminal, and types the prompt.

Once we have loaded a file of facts, what can we do with it? In the next chapter, we will learn how to ask questions about those facts and get responses from the Prolog system. For now, we will content ourselves with listing or typing out the facts that have been loaded into the internal Prolog database. The command to cause the

FIGURE 1-14
Listing the facts in a database.

```
?-consult(circuit).
Loading circuit...circuit loaded.
?-listing.
and_Gate(g1, a, b, e).
and_Gate(g2, c, d, f).
or_Gate(g3, e, f, h).
input(a). input(b).
input(c).
input(d).
output(h).
```

Prolog system to type out the contents of its internal database is called **listing**. It can be used with zero or one arguments. The zero-argument version causes the entire contents of the internal Prolog database to be typed on the screen. For example, suppose that we have used a text editor to create a file named *circuit* which contains the facts from Figure 1–2. The use of **listing** with zero arguments is illustrated in Figure 1–14.

The one-argument version of **listing** requires the name of a predicate for its argument. For example,

```
?-listing(and_Gate).
```

This will cause all the facts about the predicate **and_Gate** to be typed on the screen. Figure 1–15, which extends Figure 1–14, illustrates the use of this version of listing.

Thus far, we have learned how to do the following:

- Start a Prolog system;
- Load a file of facts into the Prolog system's internal database.
- List the entire internal database.
- Selectively list all the facts in the internal database that concern a particular predicate.

```
?-consult(circuit).
Loading circuit...circuit loaded.
?-listing.
and_Gate(g1, a, b, e).
and_Gate(g2, c, d, f).
or_Gate(g3, e, f, h).
input(a).
input(b).
input(c).
input(d).
output(h).
?-listing(and_Gate).
and_Gate(g1, a, b, e).
and_Gate(g2, c, d, f).
```

FIGURE 1-15
Using **listing**.

FIGURE 1–16
Halting a Prolog system.

```
C:>alspro
ALS-Prolog Personal Version 1.0 [1000] Serial Number: 100006
   Copyright (c) Applied Logic Systems
```

      . . . . . . some interactions . . . . . .

```
?-halt.
```

    . . . exits from Prolog to the operating system.

Before we go further, there is an important thing we should learn: how to halt a Prolog system. This is done quite simply with the zero-argument command *halt*, as shown in Figure 1–16.

Assume we have created a file of facts with a text editor, used **consult** to load the file into a Prolog internal database, and used **listing** to examine the contents of the internal database. Moreover, suppose that when we used **listing** we discovered a mistake in one or more of the facts. How do we correct these mistakes? The most primitive way to make the corrections is

- Halt the Prolog system;
- Use the text editor to correct the file;
- Start up the Prolog system again;
- Use **consult** to load the corrected file.

This is somewhat awkward, to say the least. Hence, most Prolog systems provide ways to simplify this process. The essence of the simplification is

- Without halting the Prolog system, you invoke the text editor on the file;
- Using the text editor, you correct the file;
- When you exit from the text editor, you are automatically returned to the Prolog system;
- The (edited) file is automatically *reconsulted*, causing the previously loaded facts to be changed to the versions in the (edited) file.

As can be seen in Figure 1–17, which illustrates the editing process, the editor is invoked using the ALS Prolog command **edit**. (Other Prolog systems have similar commands.) This command has the following effect:

- The Prolog system is suspended, saving the internal database;
- The editor is invoked on the indicated file.

When you exit the editor (presumably having corrected the errors you noticed), the following occurs:

- The suspended Prolog system restarts;
- The file just edited is *reconsulted,* causing the following to occur:
- Any facts about predicates occurring in the file are erased from Prolog's internal database;
- The facts from the (recently edited) file are loaded into Prolog's internal database.

FIGURE 1–17
Using an editor to correct mistakes.

```
C:>alspro
ALS-Prolog Personal Version 1.0 [1000] Serial Number: 100006
   Copyright (c) Applied Logic Systems

?-consult(mine).
Loading mine.pro...mine.pro loaded.

?-listing(my_pred).
 .
 .
 .
my_pred(goerge, tom).   <= erroneous fact that we would like to correct
 .
 .
 .
?-edit('mine.pro').  ...   ALS Prolog suspends & editor is invoked
                           on mine.pro
                           ...use editor to change goerge to george...

                           ...exit from editor...  ALS Prolog resumes
Reconsulting mine.pro...mine.pro reconsulted.
?-listing(my_pred).
 .
 .
 .
my_pred(george, tom).
 .
 .
 .
```

In the next chapter, we will learn how to ask Prolog questions about the database that has been loaded. But before we do that, let us review what we have introduced in this chapter.

CHAPTER SUMMARY

In this chapter, we have dealt with the following topics:

- Prolog facts and databases.
- Predicates, arguments, and literals.
- Terms: Constants, numbers, compound terms, functors and arguments.
- Starting and stopping Prolog systems.
- Loading (consulting) files containing databases of Prolog facts.
- Listing entire databases and particular predicates.
- Editing and reconsulting database files.

EXERCISES

1-1 Design a Prolog database to represent the relations among geographic entities on a map, for example,

west_of(illinois, indiana).

FIGURE 1–18

A company organizational chart.

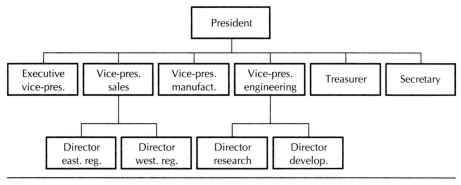

Make use of a vocabulary including the following binary predicates:

north_of   east_of   south_of   west_of
northeast_of   southeast_of   southwest_of   northwest_of

1-2 Design a Prolog database to represent the spatial relationships among the objects in a room. You must specify what objects exist in the room, together with their relations. Make use of a vocabulary that includes the following binary relationships:

is_above   is_on   is_alongside_of
is_below   is_attached_to

1-3 Design a Prolog database to represent the organizational chart of a company. Figure 1–18 provides an example of such a chart.

1-4 Design a Prolog database to represent the structure of the United States government. It should use a vocabulary including the following:

Constants:

executive_arm	legislative_arm	judicial_arm
president	congress	supreme_court
vice_president	senate	house_of_representatives
courts_of_appeal	dept_of_treasury	dept_of_state
budget	bills	laws
veto	suits	override
sec_of_state	sec_of_treasury	

Relations:

head_of	has_veto_power_over	has_review_power_over
can_override_veto_by	must_initiate	
can_impeach	can_invalidate	is_part_of
reports_to		

1-5 Design a Prolog database to represent the food chains in a portion of an environment, such as that shown in the Figure 1–19. The organisms that exist must be specified and a description of which organism feeds on which must be provided.

1-6 Design a Prolog database to represent the speeds, costs, availability, limitations, and suitability of various methods for transmitting and shipping information and documents. The vocabulary should include the following:

FIGURE 1–19
A portion of a lake food chain.

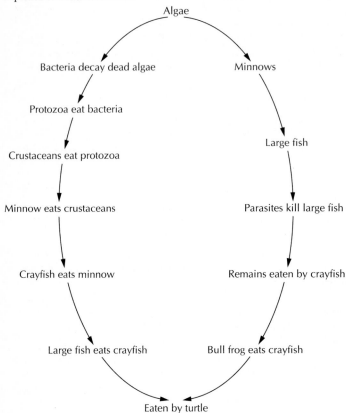

Constants:

short(message)	telephone	all(points)
letter	telegraph	many(points)
short(report)	telex	cities
medium(report)	facsimile	low(cost)
long(report)	bicycle(courier)	moderate(cost)
book	general(courier)	high(cost)
encyclopedia	electronic(mail)	very(fast)
short(program)	government(mail)	fast
medium(program)	short_haul(trucker)	moderate(speed)
long(program)	long_haul(trucker)	slow
rail(shipment)	very(slow)	bus(shipment)
ocean(shipment)	air(shipment)	

Relations:

can_be_used_for	speed_is	cost_is
available_between	suitable_for	unsuitable_for

1-7 Create an alternative representation of the connectivity of the circuit in Figure 1–2. This representation should use only one predicate "gate," yet still be able to distinguish the types of gates.

1-8 Consider the schematic diagram of a television shown in Figure A–1 in Appendix A. Use a binary relation "from_to" in creating a Prolog database representing the immediate component relationships among the parts of the television receiver.

1-9 Consider the simple television trouble-shooting guide displayed in Figure A–2 in Appendix A. Construct a Prolog database encoding the essence of this knowledge. This database should utilize the following relations:

possibly_caused_by   and   possibly_corrected_by

Choose suitable mnemonic identifiers and/or compound terms describing the various malfunctions, symptoms of malfunctions, and corrective actions.

1-10 Consider the general classification of clouds presented in Figure C–1 in Appendix C. Construct a Prolog database that encodes this classification system for clouds.

1-11 Consider the descriptions of group types of clouds presented in Figure C–2 in Appendix C. Combine this information with the information from Figure C–1 to construct a Prolog database, similar to that for hickory trees, which encodes the information on the major group types of clouds.

1-12 Consider the descriptions of food components and digestive enzymes presented in Appendix B. Use the following relations to encode this information:

site_of   acts_on   produces

1-13 Consider the IRS rules specifying who must file an income tax return, as presented in Appendix D. Develop a Prolog database encoding the rows of this table using a four-argument predicate "filing_rule/4."

1-14 Appendix E presents information concerning the diagnosis and correction of problems in photography. Following the style of the hickory database example, develop a Prolog database encoding this information.

CHAPTER 2

SIMPLE QUERIES
AGAINST DATABASES

2.1 CONCRETE QUESTIONS

In Chapter 1, we described several databases of Prolog facts. The first thing one usually wants to do with a database is to ask questions about the information it contains—that is, to ask questions about the predicates and entities that appear in the facts of the database. Referring to the simple database about drugs and diseases in Figure 1–1, suppose we want to ask the simple intuitive question:

> *Does aspirin relieve headache?*

What we must do is translate this English question into a query that Prolog can run against the database. The desired translation is

> ?- relieves(aspirin, headache).

Notice that the Prolog query looks almost exactly like the facts in the database, except that it is prefixed with "?-". The prefix "?-" indicates that what follows should be regarded as a question or query. We provided the Prolog system with a database of facts (via **consult**), and the expression following the "?-" is being submitted as a query to be answered using the database. Like facts, queries are terminated with a period(.). We often say that a query is a *goal to be run*. When Prolog has finished with its solution to the goal, it responds "yes" or "no", telling us the results of its work:

```
C:>alspro
ALS Prolog Version 1.0  Serial Number [xxxxxx]
    Copyright (c) 1986 Applied Logic Systems, Inc.
Loading medic. . .medic loaded.
?-relieves(aspirin, headache).
yes
```

In this example, the system responded "yes" to this query. Why did it respond this way? In the course of this tutorial, we will repeat the process of describing what Prolog systems do and how they do it several times. We will begin with slightly simplified versions of the explanation, focussing on parts of what goes on, either ignoring some other parts or relying on loose intuitive explanations. As the tutorial progresses, we will return to the explanation several times, taking up all of the necessary parts of the explanation making the earlier intuitive explanations precise.

As a first step towards developing this explanation, we can say that when a Prolog system accepts a query, it simply goes off to the database and tries to find an exact match to the query. The notion of an exact match is that

- The predicate name of the query should match the predicate name of some fact in the list of assertions that have been stored in the database;
- The number of arguments to the query should agree with the number of arguments of the fact stored in the database; and
- The arguments of the query and the fact must match exactly, pair by pair.

In the case of the preceding query, Prolog finds that the very first assertion in the database matches the query exactly, so Prolog answers "yes" to this query.

To understand how Prolog works, it is important to know that the database is ordered: The facts are arranged in the order that they were read into Prolog's internal database. When the facts are given to Prolog by consulting a file, this amounts to saying that Prolog arranges the facts in its internal database in the order they appear in the file that was prepared with the editor. The first fact in the file becomes the first element of the database, and so on.

When trying to answer a query, Prolog starts at the top, or beginning, of the database and seeks matches in that order. Consider the question

Does aspirin relieve severe pain?

Some of us might respond to this question with "Yes, that's my experience." Others of us might say it never works. Of course, in order to be able to translate an English query into a Prolog query, we must have a sense of the structure of the facts that we entered into the database. Given what we know of how we entered the facts in Figure 1–1, the Prolog equivalent of this English question is that we are asking about the correctness of the assertion

relieves(aspirin, severe_pain).

As we discussed earlier, Prolog systems don't "know" about drugs or diseases or symptoms. They merely try to find a match for the given goal in the internal database, starting from the beginning of the database. Since the predicates for the goal and the query must match, we can restrict our discussion to those database facts with the same predicate as the goal, in this case "relieves."

Moving through all the assertions for "relieves," Prolog looks at the first argument. In the query, the first argument is "aspirin." That matches the first arguments of each of the first three facts for "relieves." To complete the match, the second argument of the query must match exactly the second argument of one of these three "relieves" facts.

In the first fact, the second argument is "headache," which is different from "severe_pain," so Prolog will say (to itself), "No, those don't match." It will cast the first fact aside and go on to the second "relieves" fact. But here the second argument is "moderate_pain," which is also different from "severe_pain." Prolog doesn't know the meaning of these things, that what is severe for one person may be moderate for another. It simply says that the two constants don't match, discards the second "relieves" fact, and goes on, taking up the third fact. Again, the second arguments don't match.

Prolog will, in effect, sweep through the rest of the database, making sure that there are no other assertions that might match before it says, "no" . This is because the user might have typed some more "relieves" facts after some of the "aggravates" facts — Prolog doesn't care if we mix them up. Prolog systems are organized to perform such searches efficiently. As you would expect, behind the scenes a lot of clever processing is done so that one gets the effect of a sequential search even though only a small number of potential candidates are really considered. Figure 2–1 illustrates Prolog's process of searching for a match to the goal.

In Figure 1–1, we grouped all the assertions for "relieves" and "aggravates" together. That was not necessary. We could have mixed those various assertions together in any order. All that matters is the order in which they appear relative to the predicate name. That is, the only part of the order that counts is the order among facts with the same predicate name. There could have been some "aggravates" assertions intermixed with the "relieves" assertions, but when we have a query about "relieves," we can forget about everything else and just look at the order of the "relieves" assertions.

Returning to the problem of matching, Prolog looks at the representation of the term "severe_pain" and the representation of the term "moderate_pain" and compares them directly. In a naive implementation, Prolog would actually compare the print strings, that is, the actual names of the atoms. In sophisticated implementations, what it really does is very fast comparisons of certain addresses, just like any other symbolic processing language.

Let's consider one more query concerning the drug database:

Does Stomach Calm relieve heartburn?

```
?-relieves(stomach_calm, heartburn).
no.
```

---

relieves(aspirin, headache).
relieves(aspirin, moderate_pain). ↔ *relieves(aspirin, severe_pain)*
relieves(aspirin, moderate_arthritis).
relieves(aspirin_codeine_combination, severe_pain).
relieves(cough_cure_xm, cough).
relieves(pain_gone, severe_pain).

⋮

FIGURE 2–1
Searching for a match.

Once again, Prolog responds "no". It cannot find any matches: The database has no information on stomach_calm or heartburn.

Let's consider a few examples using the hickory tree database from Figure 1–7. The first question is

Do bitternut hickories have yellow buds?

This is a simple factual question, requiring a yes-or-no answer. The database is expressed by the assertions about "trait." The second argument of "trait" is the name of the tree, so "bitternut hickory" becomes "bitternut_hickory" in the Prolog query. We want to know about the particular trait "yellow buds." These traits are represented by compound terms occurring in the first argument of "trait." The way we structured the database specified that the generic property, the bud color, is the functor of the compound term. The particular characteristic, the instance of the generic property—in this case, the particular color—is the value of the slot, so we must use "bud_color(yellow)" to describe the characteristic of having yellow buds. We can formulate the query this way:

```
?-trait(bud_color(yellow), bitternut_hickory).
```

Prolog will answer "yes", since once again, it finds an exact match in the database.
Similarly,

Do mockernut hickories have yellow buds?

is formulated as a Prolog query by

```
?-trait(bud_color(yellow), mockernut_hickory).
```

Prolog's answer will be "no", because there's nothing recorded in the database describing them as having yellow buds.

The examples we've considered show us that the general form of simple queries is

?-<*literal*>.

Most Prolog systems use the symbol "?-" as their query symbol. Some of the older systems use ":-" for the query symbol. At their top-level user interface, most of the systems, like ALS Prolog, assume that you want to submit queries, so they type out the query symbol for you, in the form "?-", as their prompt. You fill in the rest of the query.

2.2 DATABASES AND REALITY

For all the queries we have considered, Prolog has answered as follows:

yes—if it found matching information in the database; or
no—if it couldn't find any matching facts.

The database is all the system knows. The significance of this is straightforward for the "yes" answers: Prolog finds a match for the query in the database and responds "yes" . For the "no" answers though, this raises a concern. Databases are only *representations* of reality, as suggested in Figure 2–2. When one is working with a high-level language (like Prolog) that allows you to suppress many programming details, the distinction between the computer database and the outside world can be blurred.[1] It is tempting to think that the database has really captured the outside world. But we have to be cautious, since the database may be incorrect or incomplete. Even if the statements appearing in the database are correct assertions about the reality being modeled, not all the relevant information may have been included in the database. The last "relieves" query of the previous section is an example of this:

> *Does Stomach Calm relieve heartburn?*

```
?-relieves(stomach_calm, heartburn).
no.
```

In fact, Stomach Calm does relieve heartburn (at least for some people). The fact

> relieves(stomach_calm, heartburn)

is true in the world, even though it hasn't been included in the database. Prolog answered truthfully: It had no information about stomach calm or heartburn in the database, so it had to answer "no". This database is *incomplete*, since there are true assertions that it doesn't include.

Thus, a "no" answer always has to be interpreted carefully. Sometimes the "no" answer may really mean that the query submitted was a false assertion that would remain false no matter what other (correct) information was in the database. For example,

> *Do Vision Drops relieve eye infections?*

```
?-relieves(vision_drops, eye_infection).
no.
```

Prolog answered "no" because it has no information about vision_drops or about eye_infection. As long as we keep our database *correct*, it will always answer "no"

---

[1] This concern applies no matter what language we use for building databases, be it Prolog, LISP, COBOL, etc.

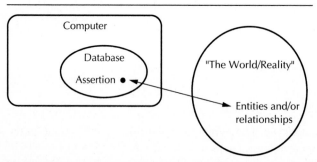

FIGURE 2–2
Computer databases versus "reality."

to this question. A correct database only contains assertions that are true about the reality we are trying to represent. Since Vision Drops do not relieve eye infections (they only relieve irritations), we will never add any assertion that would make this answer become "yes".

Similarly, consider again the query

Do mockernut hickories have yellow buds?
```
?-trait(bud_color(yellow), mockernut_hickory).
no.
```

Prolog's answer was "no" because there is nothing recorded in the database describing them as having yellow buds. Since mockernut hickories don't in fact have yellow buds, our database is correct on this point. Not only did Prolog answer truthfully on the basis of what it knew, but its answer was correct because the database is correct.

We see that sometimes Prolog answers "no" because the query is false about the reality we have (presumably correctly) represented by the database, and no matter how we extended the database with correct information, the query would still produce a "no" answer. At other times, the system responds "no" simply because we failed to provide sufficient information. This is a subtle distinction, one that any programmer has to deal with. Sometimes we write complex programs that, in effect, run queries against other databases and act on the basis of the answers received. Consequently, considerations of both the *correctness* and the *completeness* or *adequacy* of databases (and programs) are very important to programmers.

These distinctions have to be thought out especially carefully when writing Artificial Intelligence (AI) programs, since many AI programs attempt to directly model portions of our external reality. The first step of any AI programming task is to clearly determine the reality to be represented in the database or program. At all stages, the programmer must struggle to ensure that the database remains correct for that program. Whether or not the programmer can also guarantee that the database is complete for that reality depends largely on the precise nature of that reality.

2.3 DOCUMENTATION STYLE AND COMMENTS

We stated earlier that the assertions for different predicates in a database can be mixed up in any order without upsetting Prolog. However, even though Prolog won't get confused if the assertions are jumbled, the *people* who read the program—including the author of the program—can easily become confused. Thus, for the human aspects of software engineering, it is best to keep all the assertions for a given predicate grouped together. Computers and computer time are relatively cheap; it is the creative human beings who read, maintain, modify, and adapt programs that are expensive. Thus, it makes sense to organize programs to maximize the effectiveness of those humans.

For the same reason, it's important to include *comments* in Prolog databases and programs. Even though intelligent choices of names for predicates, functors, and constants can make Prolog programs readable and self-explanatory, the appropriate use of comments can often improve on this. Moreover, comments can convey other useful information that is not inherent in the text of the program or that is not easily inferred from the program text. Such information might include the purposes or limitations of the program, the program's author and owner, the revision and maintenance history, etc. Comments can also be used to convey information about the choices for the use of certain predicates or compound terms, the expected use of the program, the expected forms of queries, etc.

Comments can be added to Prolog program files in two ways: as *block comments* and as *line comments*. Block comments can be any number of lines long—one or more. They must begin with the symbols "/*" and end with the symbols "*/". Between these symbols, almost any text can occur. ALS Prolog allows block comments to be nested. That is, one block comment can occur inside another. For example,

```
/* Here we start the outer comment . . .
    /* This is where the inner comment begins . . . .
       . . . and this is where it ends */
    . . . and this is where the outer comment ends */
```

The most frequent use of such comment nesting is in temporarily "commenting out" some portions of a program. Suppose that for one reason or another (perhaps debugging or experimenting with modifications), you want to remove part of a program without throwing it away—That is, you don't want to delete it from the file or even to move it from its current location. So you simply surround it with the block comment symbols. Prolog can't see this part of the program, since it thinks it is only a comment. If that part of the program includes an ordinary block comment describing some aspect of the program, that descriptive comment is now *nested* inside the block comment symbols you added to comment out the surrounding portion of code. Systems that cannot accept nested block comments would be very confused by this situation. Allowing nested block comments is a pleasant convenience for the programmer.

While nested block comments are permissible, one cannot include the symbols "*/" *by themselves* between a block comment pair

```
/* */.
```

because Prolog will think that the included "*/" really ends the comment and become quite confused.

Line comments are limited to a single line. They begin with the "%" sign and continue to the end of the line on which they occur. *Any* text can follow the "%" sign. The comment can occur on the same line as a bit of program text, but it must start to the right of the program text. Figure 2–3 illustrates the use of both block and line comments.

2.4 QUERIES WITH VARIABLES

Perhaps you can begin to see the potential of building sophisticated factually-oriented databases. We can certainly ask questions of such databases. But so far, this seems rather limited. One apparently has to know basically what information is already present in the database in order to submit queries. Prolog provides simple yes/no answers:

```
/* _____ *
 *                                             *
 *    Title:  Lay Medicine                     *
 *          (c) 1986 Applied Logic Systems, Inc. *
 *    Author:     Kenneth A. Bowen             *
 *                                             *
 *    A database of over-the-counter U.S.      *
 *    medications, their uses and limitations. *
 *                                             *
   * _____ */

/*     Predicate: relieves/2:
               relieves(DRUG,  SYMPTOM).
       SYMPTOM is a manifestation of an underlying disease process,
       but is distinct from the disease process itself.
*/
relieves(aspirin,  headache).
relieves(aspirin, moderate_pain).         %  see  note  below
relieves(aspirin, moderate_arthritis)     %  on compound  terms
relieves(aspirin_codeine_combination,  severe_pain).
relieves(cough_cure_xm,cough).
relieves(pain_gone,severe_pain).
relieves(ko_diarrhea,diarrhea).
relieves(de_congest,cough).
relieves(de_congest,nasal_congestion).
relieves(penicillin,pneumonia).
       relieves(bis_cure,diarrhea).
       relieves(bis_cure,nausea).
relieves(noasprinol,headache).
relieves(noasprinol, moderate_pain).
relieves(triple_tuss,nasal_congestion).
relieves(penicillin,pneumonia).
/*     Predicate: aggravates/2:
                           aggravates(DRUG, CONDITION)


       CONDITION is a single disease process, or a collection of
       disease processes, sometimes called a syndrome.
*/
aggravates(aspirin,asthma).
aggravates(aspirin,peptic_ulcer).
aggravates(ko-diarrhea,fever).
aggravates(de_congest,high_blood_pressure).
aggravates(de_congest,heart_disease).
aggravates(de_congest,diabetes).
aggravates(de_congest,glaucoma).
aggravates(bis_cure,diabetes).
aggravates(bis_cure,gout).
aggravates(bis_cure,fever).
```

FIGURE 2–3
Use of Comments in databases.

Yes, I found it.
No, I didn't find it.

For keeping track of a sizeable body of information, this could be useful. But databases are far more interesting if you can discover information you didn't know before you started asking questions. To do that—as in most programming languages—we use variables. Let's return to our drug database (Figure 1–1) and find out what relieves moderate arthritis. The most direct English form of this question would be

What relieves moderate arthritis?

The query we are going to construct will have almost the same form as the fact that were seeking in the database. However, there is a part of it we don't know yet, specifically, the drug. We proceed almost exactly as we did for the last concrete query. We construct a query that looks exactly like the fact we want to locate, except that at any point where we don't know something, we use a variable. This is quite similar to the *query by example* approaches in some relational database systems.

The names of variables are made up of letters, digits, and the underbar character, and must begin with an upper-case letter or with the underbar character. Thus, "What" is the name of a variable, as are all of the following:

This_Is_A_Variable   X233
Melting_point   Malfunction_Location

In order to find out which drugs relieve moderate arthritis, we will submit the following query:

```
?-relieves(What, moderate_arthritis).
```

Notice that its structure is quite similar to the facts in the database and to the concrete yes/no queries we have used before. But there is one difference: The first argument position contains a variable instead of a concrete term. The best way to think about Prolog variables is that they are like empty boxes in a fact, as this figure suggests:

?-**relieves (** [   ] **, moderate_arthritis).**

Labeling the empty box with the variable name is also useful:

?-**relieves (** [What   ] **, moderate_arthritis).**

How does Prolog react to such a query? Exactly as before! That is, it attempts to match this query with a fact in the database. But now, obviously, Prolog's idea of matching must be more sophisticated, since it must understand the notion of matching a variable. The intuition of a variable as an empty box is still useful in this regard. Imagine the query as being typed on transparent plastic, with the variable box a hole cut in the plastic:

?-**relieves (** [   ] **, moderate_arthritis).**

FIGURE 2–4
Sliding a query template over a database.

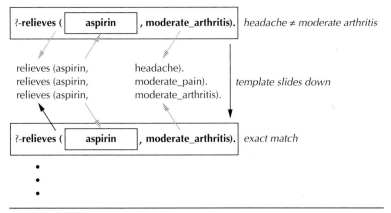

Imagine sliding this plastic template over a copy of the simple medical database, starting at the top, and moving down, as suggested in Figure 2–4.

In this example, there was only one answer in the database for the query. However, sometimes the database will contain more than one answer. Consider the query:

What symptoms does aspirin relieve?

We can easily see that there are in fact three answers. If Prolog databases are to be really useful, we must be able to obtain all of these answers. Fortunately, Prolog was designed to deal with this problem. Very simply, whenever Prolog finds an answer (i.e., an exact match) as it slides a query template through the database, Prolog prints the answer it found (i.e., the matching values of the variables) and keeps track of where the template matched in the database. Intuitively, it holds the template over the matching fact as it prints the answer on the screen. That is, it keeps a place marker pointing to the matching fact. At the same time, Prolog listens carefully to the keyboard, because it will interpret the next character that we type as a command. If we type a semi-colon (;), it interprets this as a command to continue sliding the template through the database looking for another answer. If we type any character other than a semi-colon, Prolog interprets this as a command to abandon the search, to quit sliding the template through the database. This process is illustrated in Figure 2–5.

EXERCISES

2-1 Construct Prolog queries against the simple medical database (Figure 1–1) that interpret the following questions:
   a Does Cough Cure XM relieve coughing?
   b Does Cough Cure XM relieve asthma?
   c Does Cough Cure XM aggravate asthma?
   d What relieves fever?
   e What relieves gout?
   f What aggravates gout?

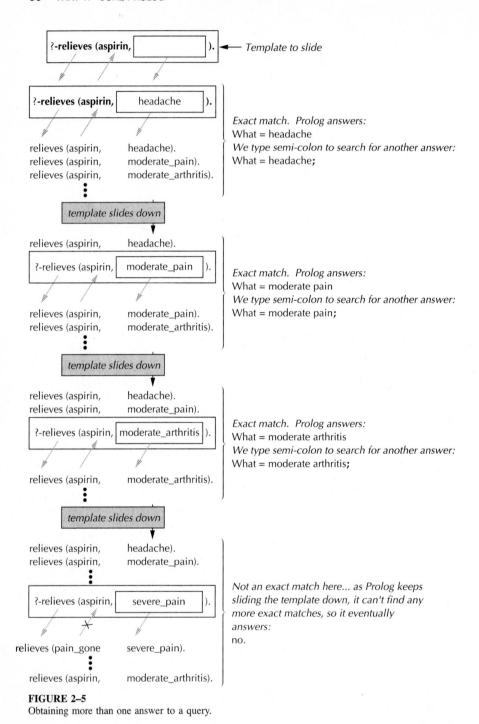

FIGURE 2–5
Obtaining more than one answer to a query.

    g What does DeCongest relieve?

    h What does DeCongest aggravate?

2-2 Create natural English questions corresponding to the following Prolog queries against the simple medical database:

    a ?- aggravates(What, diabetes).

    b ?- aggravates(ko_diarrhea, What).

    c ?- relieves(What, nausea).

    d ?- relieves(triple_tuss, What).

2-3 Using the geographic database constructed for Exercise 1-1, construct Prolog queries interpreting the following questions:

    a What state(s) are west of Ohio?

    b What state(s) is Nebraska south of?

2-4 Create natural English interpretations of the following Prolog queries against the database in Exercise 1-6:

    a ?- available_between(Method, montreal, los_angeles).

    b ?- suitable_for(air(shipment), Item).

    c ?- speed_is(short_haul(trucker), What).

2-5 Using the database constructed for Exercise 1-4, construct Prolog queries interpreting the following questions:

    a Who has review power over laws?

    b What can the House of Representatives invalidate?

    c Who is the head of the Department of Treasury?

    d Who does the Secretary of State report to?

    e Who reports to the President?

Design other similar questions and construct the corresponding Prolog queries.

2-6 Create interesting English questions concerning the food chain database from Exercise 1-5, and construct the corresponding Prolog queries.

2-7 Consider the company organization database constructed for Exercise 1-3. Construct natural English questions corresponding to the following Prolog queries:

    a ?- reports_to (treasurer, who)

    b ?- reports_to (who, director_research).

2-8 Consider the database constructed for Exercise 1-8 that represents a television receiver schematic. Construct Prolog queries interpreting the following natural English questions:

    a What does the video amplifier section feed into?

    b What feeds into the yoke?

    c Is the sync section connected to the video IF section?

2-9 Consider the TV trouble-shooting database constructed for Exercise 1-9. Construct Prolog queries interpreting the following questions:

    a What can cause the picture to be too far to the left?

    b What's probably wrong if the set has a picture on all channels, but no sound?

    c What is the effect of turning the contrast control down?

    d What should you do if the program is a silent movie?

2-10 Consider the clouds description database constructed for Exercise 1-11. Construct Prolog queries for the following:

    a What clouds belong to the Heap (cumulus) family?

    b What kind of cloud is an altostratus?

    c What kinds of clouds occur well separated?

    d What is the color of a Layer (stratus) cloud?

    e How tall can Heap clouds get? How short can they be?

2-11 Consider the enzyme description database constructed for Exercise 1-12. Construct Prolog queries for the following:
  a What is the site of action of lactase?
  b What does lipase act on?
  c What are the products of the action of pepsin?
  d What enzyme produces amino acids?
  e What enzyme(s) act on sugars?
2-12 Consider the IRS filing rules database constructed for Exercise 1-13. Construct Prolog queries for the following:
  a What is the minimum gross income for filing a return for a 41-year-old married person living with her or his spouse, if the person wishes to file a separate return?
  b Must a 72-year-old widow who has not remarried and is living alone file a return if she has a gross income of $5,156?
2-13 Consider the photography problems database constructed for Exercise 1-14. Construct Prolog queries for the following:
  a What is the likely cause of lines along the length of the film? What is the likely remedy?
  b What is the evidence of the presence of static?
  c What is the evidence that would lead one to check the camera wind-on mechanism?

CHAPTER 3

COMPOUND QUERIES

3.1 QUERIES WITH MULTIPLE LITERALS

Thus far, we have only considered simple queries. All of our queries involved a single relation applying to a single sequence of arguments. But it is natural to ask questions that cannot be represented directly by one of the single assertions in the database. For instance,

What drug relieves both coughing and nasal congestion?

We could, of course, ask separately

What drug relieves coughing? (3.1.1a)

and

What drug relieves nasal congestion?, (3.1.1b)

get the two sets of answers, and form the intersection (the common answers) of the two sets ourselves. Here's one way that could be done:

```
?-relieves(Drug, cough).
Drug = cough_cure_xm;
Drug = de_congest;
no.
?-relieves(Drug, nasal_congestion).
Drug = de_congest;
Drug = triple_tuss;
no.
```

The only common element of the two solution lists is DeCongest, the only drug from our database that relieves both cough and nasal congestion.

However, this approach isn't much fun. We would like Prolog to do all the hard work for us. We want to be able to ask a compound query that simultaneously expresses both of these conditions on a drug. Such a compound query would give back the intersection of the sets of answers to the two simple conditions. That is, the answers to the compound question would be just those drugs that satisfied each of the two individual simple conditions.

This can be done very easily with Prolog. We can form *compound queries* made of parts that look exactly like individual single elementary queries, except that we package them together. The individual parts are separated with a comma. The general form of a compound query is

   ?- *literal, literal, ...*

Just like simple queries, compound queries begin with the query symbol (?-) and end with a period. Between the leading query symbol and closing period lie one or more literals separated by commas. Remember

   A literal is that part of a fact consisting of everything but the period.

In a compound query, the comma separating the literals is interpreted as *conjunction*—logical *and*. From a logical point of view, the questions (3.1.1a) and (3.1.1b) are jointly equivalent to

   What drug relieves coughing and relieves nasal congestion?

In Prolog, the corresponding compound query is written

   ?- relieves(Drug, cough), relieves(Drug, nasal_congestion).

Prolog will treat the query this way:

```
?-relieves(Drug,  cough),  relieves(Drug,  nasal_congestion).
Drug = de_congest;
no.
```

Prolog's answers show that the database has information about only one drug that meets both conditions.

Consider another example:

   What drug relieves both headache and moderate pain?

   This translates as

```
?-relieves(Drug, headache), relieves(Drug, moderate_pain).
Drug = aspirin;
Drug = noasprinol;
no.
```

This time there were two drugs that satisfied both of the individual parts of the query.

Consider the question

   What relieves coughs, but aggravates diabetes and glaucoma?

This query contains three individual conditions, so the Prolog version of the query will contain three literals:

```
?-relieves(Drug, cough), aggravates(Drug, diabetes),
               aggravates(Drug, glaucoma).
Drug = de_congest;
no.
```

Three conditions impose three restrictions. The more restrictions there are, the fewer solutions there are likely to be. In this case, we got only one solution.

Just as simple queries can have more than one variable, compound queries can also contain multiple variables. Consider the problem

Name a drug and a condition such that the drug relieves nausea, but aggravates the condition.

The Prolog version of this question would be

```
?-relieves(Drug,nausea),aggravates(Drug,Symptom).
Drug = bis_cure
Symptom = diabetes;
Drug = bis_cure
Symptom = gout;
Drug = bis_cure
Symptom = fever;
no.
```

We received three answers. However, only one drug was involved. By examining the database, we know that we recorded only one drug that relieved nausea. But note that even if the database had other entries for drugs that relieved nausea, we might still have only bis_cure involved in the answers. For example, Stomach Calm relieves nausea, but has no side-effects: It doesn't aggravate any conditions. So even if we entered

relieves(stomach_calm, nausea).

into the database, we would have no entries in the database of the form

aggravates(stomach_calm, *something*).

Therefore stomach_calm would not be able to satisfy *both conditions* of the query. There would be no condition that combined with Stomach Calm to satisfy the "aggravates" requirement. In order for a term to be involved in an answer to a compound query, it must satisfy all individual parts of the query.

Finally, variables can occur inside compound terms in queries. Consider

What are the hickory trees and their bud colors that have valvate bud scales?

This can be formulated as a Prolog query:

```
?-trait(bud_scales(valvate), Tree), trait(bud_color(Bud_Color), Tree).
Tree = bitternut_hickory
Bud_Color = yellow;
Tree = pecan_hickory
Bud_Color = brownish;
no.
```

For a final example, let's try

Name two trees with valvate bud scales.

The corresponding Prolog query template is

?-trait (bud_scales (valvate), | *Tree1* |), trait (bud_scales (valvate), | *Tree2* |).

The interaction with Prolog is shown in Figure 3–1.

We obtained four solutions to our request. But look at them closely: the solutions are a bit repetitive, even a little strange. The second and third are trivial variations of each other: the order of bitternut_hickory and pecan_hickory is simply reversed. But in either order, they are solutions. This underscores how literal-minded Prolog is. Since it interchanges the binding of the variables (Tree1 and Tree2) in the two solutions, it sees them as different solutions, even though they are essentially the same for us.

The first and fourth solutions look even stranger! We asked for *two* hickory trees with valvate bud scales, but we seem to get only one in each solution. Why didn't Prolog give us two *different* trees in these solutions? We used two different variables, so why not two different solutions? Here we encounter a point about variables that is common to Prolog and other programming languages, as well as mathematics and science generally: Even though we utilized two distinct variables, there is nothing inherent in the idea of a variable to force two distinct variables to always assume distinct values when solving problems. The values of two distinct variables in a problem will be forced to be different *only if there is something in the nature of the problem that forces the values to be different.* When we look closely at the problem we posed, we see that it doesn't impose any requirement forcing the values of Tree1 and Tree2 to be different. In fact, it doesn't really impose any relationship between Tree1 and Tree2 at all, other than the requirement that each have valvate bud scales. In later chapters, we will consider ways to force distinct variables to take on distinct values.

```
?-trait(bud_scales(valvate), Tree1),
          trait(bud_scales(valvate), Tree2).
Tree1 = bitternut_hickory
Tree2 = bitternut_hickory;
Tree1 = bitternut_hickory
Tree2 = pecan_hickory;
Tree1 = pecan_hickory
Tree2 = bitternut_hickory;
Tree1 = pecan_hickory
Tree2 = pecan_hickory;
no.
```

FIGURE 3–1
A two-variable compound query.

3.2 SOLVING COMPOUND QUERIES BY BACKTRACKING

Recall the first example in the last section:

What drug relieves both coughing and nasal congestion?

or

What drug relieves coughing and relieves nasal congestion?

The Prolog query expressing this was

```
?-relieves(Drug,cough),relieves(Drug,nasal_congestion).
Drug = de_congest;
no.
```

To satisfy this particular goal or query, Prolog will effectively try to satisfy the individual parts (literals), then combine the two solutions. There are clearly two choices as to how it should proceed:

First, there is the intuitively natural database-oriented choice: Solve the two parts separately, then intersect the solutions.

Second, there is the method actually used by Prolog: Solve the first part and use that solution as a constraint on the solution of the second part.

When Prolog is working on a compound query, it repeatedly selects one of the elementary goals to try to solve. Since the elementary goals are called literals, we can say that Prolog repeatedly selects one of the literals to try to solve. Of course, it tries to solve the selected literal using the database we have provided.

Prolog is lazy and dumb. It does not try to be clever or intelligent about which literal it selects. It simply always chooses the leftmost literal in the whole query. That is, Prolog always selects the first literal in left-to-right order in the compound query, then tries to solve it using the database exactly as we have described in the preceding chapters.

When it begins working on the compound query above, Prolog first selects the literal

relieves(Drug, cough)

and tries to solve it using the Drug database. It finds a solution by matching this selected literal with the fact

relieves(cough_cure_xm, cough).

Having solved this literal, Prolog leaves a place marker for that literal next to the solution fact. When Prolog made this match, it recorded the association between Drug and cough_cure_xm in its scratch work area. By doing this, Prolog has begun building up the substitution that it will compute as the output for the given input (compound) query.

Next, Prolog goes forward to solve the remaining part of the compound query. Since it has taken care of the first literal, it then chooses the first of the remaining literals. In our example, there are only two literals, so it chooses the second of the two original elementary queries. The process of associating the variable Drug with cough_cure_xm can be thought of as composing a constraint on the rest of the elementary queries to be satisfied in the compound query. At the moment that Drug is associated with cough_cure_xm, this information is passed on to the remaining simple queries (literals) in the whole compound goal. They must respect that information. In effect, Drug is immediately replaced by cough_cure_xm throughout the rest of the query. That is, cough_cure_xm is substituted for Drug throughout the compound goal. Put another way, the partial substitution that Prolog is building up is applied to the entire compound goal. At this point, the transformed query would look like

> ?-relieves(cough_cure_xm, cough)
> relieves(cough_cure_xm, nasal_congestion).

To solve the first literal of this query, Prolog matched that first literal against a fact in the database. That's how it got the association between Drug and cough_cure_xm. It has finished working with that first literal. Thus, we can think of Prolog's *current goal* as consisting of those literals (from the original compound goal) that have not yet been solved. Consequently, at this point, Prolog's current goal would be

> ?- relieves(cough_cure_xm, nasal_congestion).

So Prolog goes on and solves this second elementary query using a fact from the database. Since there are no other literals in the original compound query, Prolog's work is done. It gives us the answer

> Drug = cough_cure_xm

Here is an important point about Prolog's database searching when it is working on compound queries. The database search proceeds independently for each elementary query. That is, each time Prolog selects a new literal to work on, it begins the search for facts to match that literal at the beginning of the database. However, the relation between the individual database searches is sequential: One part is done before the other. Specifically, the solution search for any given component literal is carried out before the searches for those literals to the right of the given literal.

The template and place-marker metaphor is quite useful in understanding this process. The template for the original compound query, together with the original state of the database, are shown in Figure 3–2. (Note that we have numbered the two literals making up the compound query with superscripts in square brackets.)

Prolog begins trying to solve the first literal. The template for this problem is

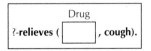

Prolog first slides this template down through the database and finds a solution to the first query at the point of the fact

> relieves(cough_cure_xm, cough).

FIGURE 3–2
Setting out to solve a compound query.

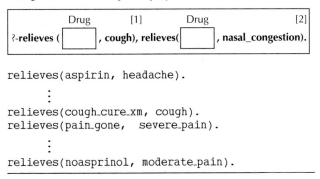

```
relieves(aspirin, headache).
    ⋮
relieves(cough_cure_xm, cough).
relieves(pain_gone,  severe_pain).
    ⋮
relieves(noasprinol, moderate_pain).
```

It positions there a place marker (number [1]) that is associated with this first part of the compound query. In the course of matching the first literal against this fact, the variable Drug was matched (unified) with cough_cure_xm. The transformed query and the new state of the database are shown in Figure 3–3.

Prolog now tackles the second part of the compound query. What was originally a template with a hole in it becomes—because of the matching (unification) of Drug with cough_cure_xm—the following:

?- relieves(cough_cure_xm, nasal_congestion).

Prolog again starts at the beginning of the database with this elementary query. The system tries to find its solution from the top of the database. Eventually, it finds a fact concerning nasal congestion in the database, and the situation is as shown in

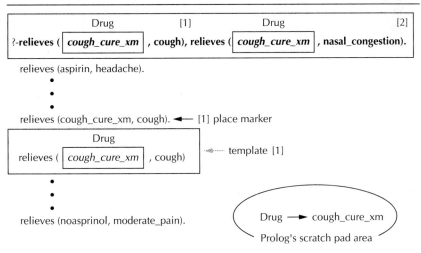

FIGURE 3–3
After solving the first literal.

FIGURE 3–4
Failing to find a solution (again).

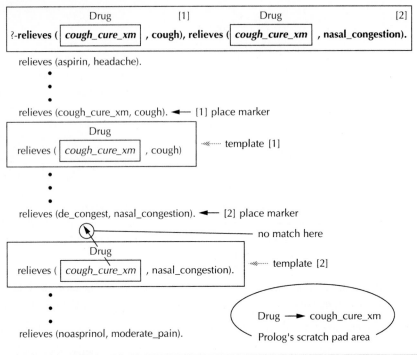

Figure 3–4. However, the current query template doesn't match this fact, so Prolog must continue moving the query template down through the database. After a bit more work, it finds another fact concerning nasal congestion, as shown in Figure 3–5. But the query template also fails to match this fact. Once more, Prolog picks up the place marker [2] and slides the query template further down through the database. It eventually gets to the end of the database without having found a match for this query.

What does Prolog do now? It backs up to the place where it matched the first query template, the place where it set down the place marker [1]. When it set down this place marker, it had found one possible solution to query [1], which caused the variable Drug to be bound to cough_cure_xm, as shown in the scratch pad area of the figures. We have seen that if Prolog accepts this solution to query [1], it cannot find any solution to query [2]. To succeed with the complete compound query, it must find a *joint* solution to both subsidiary queries [1] and [2], so Prolog has no choice but to abandon this initial trial solution to query [1] and to move forward through the database. It keeps the place marker [1] where it is presently located but erases the binding for Drug, which it recorded in the scratch pad area, and moves forward as if it had not encountered the solution it just considered (see Figure 3–6).

After sliding down a bit, Prolog finds a second solution for query [1], and now moves place marker [1] forward as seen in Figure 3–7. Once again, Prolog tackles

FIGURE 3–5
Another failing match.

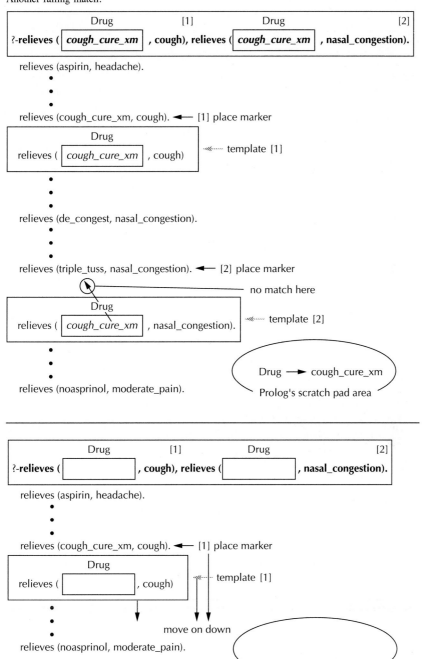

FIGURE 3–6
Moving the first query on down.

FIGURE 3–7
After a second solution for the first literal.

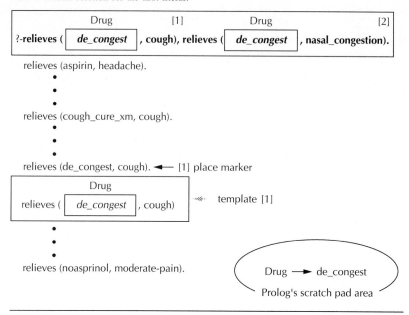

relieves (aspirin, headache).

relieves (cough_cure_xm, cough).

relieves (de_congest, cough). ◄— [1] place marker

relieves (noasprinol, moderate-pain).

the second part (number [2]) of the newly transformed query. Because of the matching (unification) of Drug with de_congest, the second part [2] now appears as:

?- relieves(de_congest, nasal_congestion).

As it did before, Prolog begins at the top of the database with the template for this query, and slides it downward. Before too long, it encounters a fact concerning nasal congestion, and, moreover, this fact matches the query (see Figure 3–8).

Success! By finding the solution to query [2] that still respected the constraint (the binding of Drug to de_congest) created by the solution for query [1], Prolog has found a joint solution to the two subsidiary queries, and hence has found a solution to the complete compound query.

Notice that the two place markers for the two parts of the compound were independently moved through the database.

Suppose we ask, "Are there any other solutions?" by typing a semi-colon. Prolog will set out to look for another drug that solves the problem. But we have two parts to the query. Prolog will try to find more solutions by working strictly backwards. First, it will undo the most recent match that it made and try to move that template forward, searching for another solution. This is the template for the second part (number [2]). If it locates a match, it will tell us. (We know that it will try to match template [2] against the fact

relieves(triple_tuss, nasal_congestion).

But this attempt will fail.) Since it can't find another match for that last problem (query [2]), it will put the template for query [2] temporarily on the shelf, go further

FIGURE 3–8
A solution to query [2] found: success!

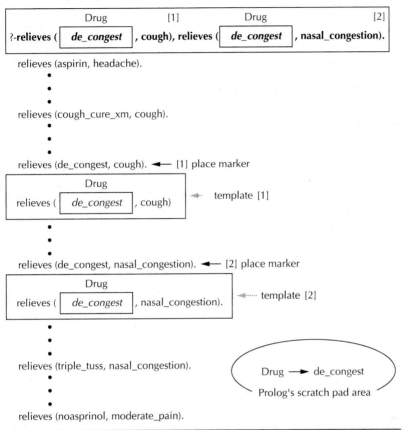

backwards (in time, in its computation), and undo the second most recent match that it made. This is the point where it set down the place marker [1] next to the solution for query [1]. Reversing the match it made at this point means that it erases the binding of Drug to de_congest from the scratch pad area. Then it will move the template for query [1] forward, trying to find another solution for it. We know that it can't find any more solutions. Thus, Drug = de_congest was Prolog's only solution for the original compound query.

The process Prolog used to organize its search for joint solutions is called *strict chronological backtracking*. That is, whenever it cannot complete a joint solution (i.e., cannot solve a second—or third, or fourth, etc.—subsidiary query while respecting the bindings from the first), or whenever it has to try to find more solutions, Prolog will return to the most recent point where it had any choice in behavior and ask if it can redo that choice. If there is an alternative way of making the given choice, Prolog will take that alternative, and then proceed forward trying to solve the rest of the remaining subproblems. If there are no (more) alternatives for the given choice, Prolog will go back further to the next most recent choice point, etc.

In our example above, Figures 3–4 and 3–5 show Prolog in the process of failing to find a solution to query [2] that respects the binding created by its earlier solution to query [1]. But that only means it was unable to find any solution for subproblem [2], as transformed by the substitution (Drug → cough_cure_xm) made when it solved the first literal [1]. So next Prolog walked back in time (really, in its computation record) to the most recent decision point, when it found a solution to the first elementary query. This is the point where it set down the place marker [1]. When this solution was found, Prolog had matched Drug against cough_cure_xm. So its first step in undoing this match was to undo the association of the variable Drug with cough_cure_xm. That is, it erased the association

Drug → cough_cure_xm

from its scratch pad area. Then Prolog picked up the place marker [1] and asked "Can I slide the viewing template [1] further and find any other solutions to subproblem [1] of the compound query, namely,

relieves(Drug,cough)?"

As we saw, it found another solution giving the binding

Drug → de_congest.

Then it proceeded from the top of the database to try to find a solution to the transformed version of query [2]. It found one, so it announced on the screen

Drug = de_congest

When we responded with a semi-colon(;), it backtracked again, as follows:

- First, it undoes the solution to subproblem [2] (since no matches were created by [2], nothing has to be erased from the scratch pad area);
- Next, it slides the template for [2] forward, seeking another solution;
- It fails to find another match (solution) for subproblem [2];
- It goes (further) back to the point where it found the match for subproblem [1] (to the place where it set down the place marker [1]);
- It undoes this match, which means it erases the association
    Drug → de_congest
  from the scratch pad area; and
- It moves the template for subproblem [1] forward from the last position of the place marker [1], trying for another match.

We know that it finally fails to find any further solutions, so its last act (at least for this play) is to say "no" on the screen.

3.3 BACKTRACKING, MULTIPLE VARIABLES, AND MULTIPLE SOLUTIONS

The example in the last section demonstrated the essential nature of Prolog's backtracking search for solutions of compound goals. However, the situation is slightly more complex when there are multiple variables present in the goal and multiple solutions are really possible. In this section, we will follow Prolog at work as it deals with such a goal. Consider the problem

> *Find a drug and a condition such that the drug relieves nausea but aggravates the condition.*

The Prolog rendition of this question is

> ?- relieves(Drug, nausea), aggravates(Drug, Condition).

The initial state of the query template and the database are shown in Figure 3–9.
The template for the first literal in the compound query is

The first match that Prolog can find for this template is the fact

> relieves(bis_cure, nausea).

The state of the query and database are shown in Figure 3–10.
Next, Prolog tackles the second literal. The template for this problem is

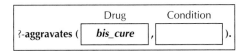

Sliding this template down from the top of the database, Prolog finds the first solution at the fact

> aggravates(bis_cure, diabetes).

The next system state is shown in Figure 3–11.
Suppose that we ask for another solution by typing a semi-colon. Prolog's last match involved template [2], so it returns to place marker [2] and unbinds the vari-

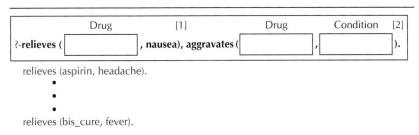

relieves (aspirin, headache).

•
•
•

relieves (bis_cure, fever).

FIGURE 3–9
At the start of the search.

FIGURE 3–10
After subproblem [1] is solved.

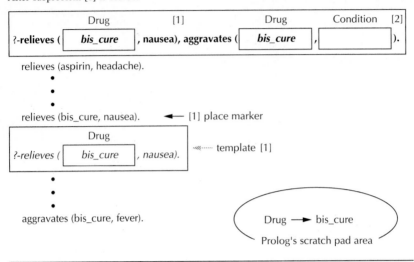

able Condition—i.e., removes Condition → diabetes from the substitution {Drug → bis_cure; Condition → diabetes}. The template for the second condition once again looks like

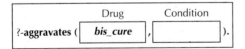

Prolog picks up the place marker [2] and moves this template forward, looking for another match. It finds one at the very next fact

   aggravates(bis_cure, gout).

The system state after this match is shown in Figure 3–12.

Yet again, we ask for another solution. Once more, Prolog returns to where it last left place marker [2] and unbinds the variable Condition, thus removing Condition → gout from the substitution {Drug → bis_cure; Condition → gout}. It then picks up the place marker [2] and once more moves the template for the second literal forward. It finds a match at the fact

   aggravates(bis_cure, fever).

The current system state is as shown in Figure 3–13.

If we ask for yet another solution, Prolog once more returns to place marker [2] and unbinds Condition, thus removing Condition → fever from the substitution {Drug → bis_cure; Condition → fever}. This leaves {Drug → bis_cure} as the current substitution. Then Prolog tries to move the template for the second literal forward again, looking for yet another match. But this time it hits the end of the database without finding any further solutions, so it puts this template on the shelf. Since it had just

FIGURE 3–11
Having found the first solution.

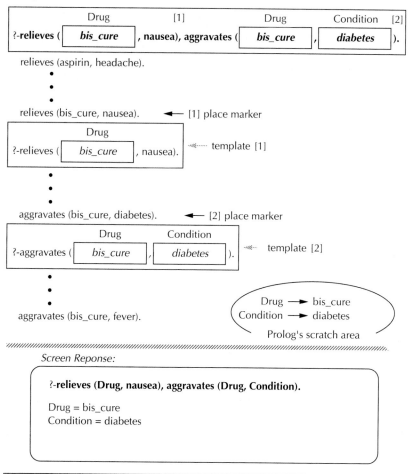

relieves (aspirin, headache).

relieves (bis_cure, nausea). ◄── [1] place marker

aggravates (bis_cure, diabetes). ◄── [2] place marker

aggravates (bis_cure, fever).

Screen Reponse:

?-relieves (Drug, nausea), aggravates (Drug, Condition).

Drug = bis_cure
Condition = diabetes

been carrying around the place-marker [2], it knows that the next place marker to go back to is [1]. Consequently, it returns to place marker [1] and unbinds the variable Drug. This removes Drug → bis_cure from the substitution {Drug → bis_cure}, leaving the empty substitution {}. The template for the first literal is now

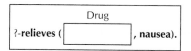

Prolog picks up the place marker [1] and tries to move this template forward, looking for a new solution, but it hits the end of the database without finding any further solutions. Since there are no place markers left in the database, it knows there is no other way to find a solution, so it types "no" on the screen.

FIGURE 3–12
After the second complete solution.

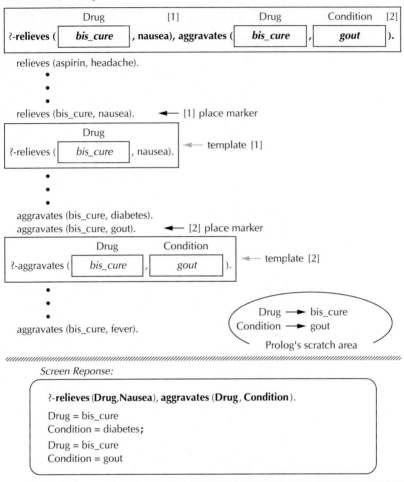

3.4   THE LOGICAL INTERPRETATION OF PROLOG QUERIES

As we discussed in Section 2.2, Prolog databases are *representations* of some reality or state of affairs. The facts appearing in the database are assertions that describe some aspect of that reality. From a logical point of view, such a database is a set of axioms for some subject (i.e., the part of reality of concern to the person building the database). Formal logic can provide a precise definition of what it means for a set of axioms to be true about a part of the world, but we will content ourselves with our intuitive understanding of this notion. However, a few distinctions will be useful.

Under normal circumstances, one begins with a concern for some aspect of the world (e.g., the nature of the relations between genes and DNA, or the state of political relations between countries, or the state of the finances of XYZ company, or methods for diagnosing faulty behavior in diesel locomotives), and then builds a

FIGURE 3–13

After the second complete solution.

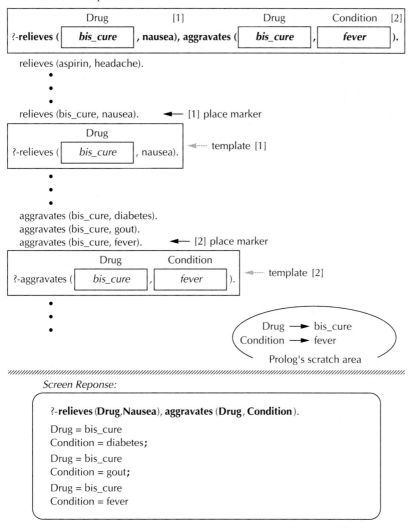

```
          Drug            [1]          Drug       Condition  [2]
?-relieves ( bis_cure , nausea), aggravates ( bis_cure ,   fever  ).
```

relieves (aspirin, headache).
•
•
•

relieves (bis_cure, nausea).   ◄── [1] place marker

```
          Drug
?-relieves ( bis_cure , nausea).    ···· template [1]
```

•
•
•

aggravates (bis_cure, diabetes).
aggravates (bis_cure, gout).
aggravates (bis_cure, fever).   ◄── [2] place marker

```
            Drug      Condition
?-aggravates ( bis_cure ,  fever ).    ···· template [2]
```

•
•
•

Drug ──► bis_cure
Condition ──► fever

Prolog's scratch area

Screen Reponse:

> ?-**relieves (Drug,Nausea), aggravates (Drug, Condition).**
>
> Drug = bis_cure
> Condition = diabetes;
> Drug = bis_cure
> Condition = gout;
> Drug = bis_cure
> Condition = fever

database to represent these concerns. It is clear that the database and its assertions are different things than the aspects of the world being modeled: Whatever we believe genes or countries or numbers or locomotives to be, assertions and databases are linguistic objects and are definitely *not* genes or countries or numbers or locomotives. The database assertions may involve *names* for some of the things in the world, and the database assertions *talk about* the things in the world, but the assertions themselves are different kinds of entities than the things talked about.

When we ask whether the database we have built is correct, we are asking whether the "facts" we put into the database make correct assertions about the entities and relationships in the part of the world we are trying to model. As we all know only too well, it is very easy to become confused and to make assertions that are in fact false. We say that our database is correct when we convince ourselves that all of its facts make correct assertions about the part of the world we are trying to understand.

Of course, one must be very careful to be clear about the part of the world that is being examined. A given assertion might be true about one part of the world but false about another. For example, suppose we were trying to build a database that described the nature of the relationships between genes, chromosomes, and DNA. We would have to be clear whether or not we were discussing human beings, amoebas, plants, or even the notion of genes, etc., in abstraction from particular classes of organisms. A given statement relating genes and chromosomes might be true about humans, monkeys, and pigs, but false about amoebas and hickory trees.

Language, whether it is natural language or computer language, is definitely a different "thing" from the entities we talk about using language. The same "physical" bit of language can be used to talk about very different states of affairs or "pieces of the world," and might be true in one state of affairs and false in another. Whether a statement comes out true or false depends on the particular state of affairs the statement is being used to talk about. That is, the truth of a statement depends on the state of affairs (or "piece of the world") in which the statement in interpreted. For example, the statement

"The United States of America is made up of 48 states."

comes out true in the state of affairs that held in 1949 but false in the state of affairs that held in 1985, as well as the state of affairs that held in 1813. If we were building a Prolog database describing the United States of America, we might have chosen to represent this bit of information by the following Prolog fact:

number_of_states(usa, 48).

Then, a Prolog database that included this fact would be a correct representation of "reality" if we intended to describe the United States as it was in 1949, but the database would be incorrect if we were trying to describe the United States as it was in 1985 or 1813.

Thus, we see that a database (whether or not it is a Prolog database) can be *interpreted* in many possible ways. Under some interpretations, all of the database assertions are true, so the database is *correct relative to the given interpretation*. But under other interpretations, one or more of the database assertions may come out false, and then the database is *incorrect relative to the given interpretation*.

The facts that make up a Prolog database constitute the *explicit* information contained in the database. The *implicit* information contained in the database is made up of all the statements that come out true in all of the correct interpretations of the database. That is, a statement **A** is *implicit* in a database *D* if **A** works out to be a correct assertion about any interpretation of *D* in which all of the facts listed in *D* come out true. Another expression used to describe implicit information is *logical consequence*:

A is a *logical consequence* of the Prolog database *D* if **A** is implicit in *D*; i.e.,

A is a *logical consequence* of the Prolog database *D* if **A** comes out true in all correct interpretations of *D*.

Recall that a query may or may not contain variables. When a query contains *no* variables, we call it a *ground* query. (Sometimes we call it a *fully instantiated* query.) When we submit a ground query **Q** against a Prolog database *D*, we are requesting the Prolog system to determine whether or not **Q** is a logical consequence of the database *D*. If we submit a ground query against a Prolog database, and if the Prolog system responds "yes", the instantiated query is a logical consequence of that database. In fact, Prolog systems are logic engines: They attempt to determine whether queries are logical consequences of databases.

If **Q** is a query that contains variables, when we submit **Q** to a Prolog system, we are asking the system to find instances of those variables such that the resulting ground query is a logical consequence of the database. For example, suppose that **Q** contains just one variable, say **V**. Submitting **Q** as a query roughly has the meaning of the following question:

Is there something *x* such that if **Q*** is the result of replacing *V* by *x* in **Q** , then **Q*** comes out true?

Let's make this a bit more precise. Suppose that **Q** is a query containing the variable **V**, and suppose also that **t** is any term. If we replace every occurrence of **V** in **Q** by **t**, we get a new query (or statement). This new query is called the *result of substituting* **t** *for* **V** *in* **Q**. Since this phase is a little bit unwieldy, we'll abbreviate it by the notation

Q{V/t } .

That is, **Q{ V/t }** simply describes the new query that is obtained by running over **Q** and replacing every occurrence of **V** by **t**.

We can now be more precise about what it means to submit a query containing a variable. Again, suppose that *D* is a Prolog database and that **Q** is a query containing just the variable **V**. The submission of **Q** as a query against *D* is equivalent to asking the following question:

Is there a term **t** such that **Q{ V/t }** is a logical consequence of *D*?

It is worth noting here that Prolog is reasonably sophisticated in its attempts to answer this question. One simplistic method for trying to answer such a question would be the following:

1 Systematically generate every possible term **t**;
2 As each term **t** is generated, create **Q{ V/t }** and set out to determine whether **Q{ V/t }** is a logical consequence of *D*;
3 If **Q{ V/t }** is a logical consequence of *D*, stop the process and answer "yes"; otherwise, go on to the next term for **t**.

Since there are lots and lots of terms **t**, this approach would attempt step 2 for many, many terms **t** that don't have any possibility of leading to success before it actually came upon a suitable candidate for **t**.

However, Prolog's matching process interleaves the problem of finding the term **t** with the problem of determining whether **Q** { **V/t** } is a logical consequence of *D*. In essence, the process of matching elementary queries against the database facts, together with the treatment of variables as *windows* that match against terms occurring in the facts of the database, means that Prolog attempts step 2 only for those terms **t** that have some chance of leading to success.

3.5 FACTS CONTAINING VARIABLES

Thus far, we have only used variables in queries that we submit for processing. However, Prolog allows us another very powerful use of variables, namely in the facts of a database. If we add a fact containing a variable to a database, we must interpret that variable as being universally quantified. For example, consider the expression

relieves(aspirin, Symptom).   (3.5.1)

Notice that the second argument of this expression is a variable, namely Symptom. Prolog allows us to add such an expression to a database. But then, what is the meaning of this assertion? The logical reading of this assertion is this:

For any symptom, "relieves" holds of "aspirin" and that symptom.

Thus, when used as an assertion in a database, the expression (3.5.1) is really an abbreviation of

For all Symptom, relieves(aspirin, Symptom).   (3.5.2)

Whether or not this is an appropriate assertion to add to a database depends on the reality one is trying to model. Some people certainly act as if they believed (3.5.2), so it might be an appropriate assertion in the database of what such a person believed. On the other hand, it would not be an appropriate assertion for what doctors generally believe.

How does Prolog utilize such assertions when we submit queries? Suppose that we have added the assertion

relieves(aspirin, Symptom)   (3.5.3)

to our Drug database, and that we submit the query

?-relieves(aspirin, itching)

We can understand how Prolog will use the assertion (3.5.3) by extending our view of windows and templates just a little bit. Variables in queries were thought of as clear windows through which one can look at the database. Variables in assertions in the database are like mirrors: They reflect back whatever is at that position in the query. As usual, Prolog will create a query template

relieves (aspirin, itching)

and start sliding it down the facts of the database. None of the facts that were in the original version of the database will match this template. However, when Prolog gets the template to the database assertion

relieves(aspirin, Symptom)

the predicates of the query and assertion match since they are both "relieves". Moreover, the first arguments of each match since they are both "aspirin". The second argument of the query is "itching", while the second argument of the database assertion is the "mirror variable, Symptom". That "mirror variable" will match anything occurring in the corresponding position of the query. So in particular, it matches "itching". Figure 3–14 suggests what happens. Consequently, Prolog's reponse to this query will be "yes".

Submit the queries "Does aspirin relieve high blood pressure?" and "Does aspirin relieve asthma?" and Prolog will respond "yes" to each. This is so even though the Drug database includes the knowledge that aspirin aggravates asthma. This is weird! The database *seems* to be responding inconsistently. Doesn't everyone know a drug can't both relieve and aggravate a symptom? Obviously, Prolog is so dumb that it doesn't know this.

What happened? The database seems to be behaving inconsistently. On the other hand, most of us know that a collection of assertions such as a database is inconsistent precisely when it leads to a contradiction. That is, a database is inconsistent if and only if there is some assertion **A** such that both **A** and not-**A** are logical consequences of the database. But now we have a real problem: So far, we have not discussed any notion of negation ("not") in connection with Prolog. In fact, there really is no primitive notion of negation connected with Prolog. So how can the database be inconsistent? It turns out that all pure Prolog databases are indeed consistent! Yet our extended Drug database seems to be behaving in an inconsistent manner. We seem to be in a real tangle.

The way out of the difficulty is to return to the question of what Prolog can really know, and what information is really contained in a database. It is important to remember that we have been using English words for the names of Prolog predicates, constants, variables, etc. However, nothing in the notions of logic or Prolog requires this. The names of predicates, constants, variables, etc., can all be meaningless symbol strings if we choose. All that Prolog can know is what follows from the form and structure of the assertions that we include in the database. In particular, Prolog has

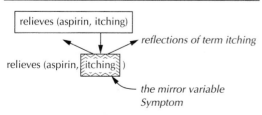

FIGURE 3–14
Variables in database assertions as "mirrors."

no knowledge of any meaning we attach to the English (or French or Japanese, etc.) words we use in expressing the database *unless* that meaning is somehow conveyed by the structure of the assertions in the database. The apparent inconsistency of our extended Drug database is due to the extra meaning we attach to the words relieves and aggravates, but which we have not in fact reflected in the form and structure of the database assertions. Prolog is able to derive both of the assertions

relieves(aspirin, asthma) and aggravates(aspirin, asthma)

from the extended Drug database. This appears improper to us because of the meaning that English attaches to the words relieves and aggravates. This additional meaning is sometimes called *semantic knowledge*. It is knowledge about the *intended* interpretation of the database, where the intended interpretation of the database is that piece of reality that the designer of the database intended to model. However, nothing in the structure of the assertions in the extended Drug database conveys any incompatibility between "relieves" and "aggravates". In order to convey this incompatibility, additional structure must be imposed on the database. We will examine methods for doing this in later chapters.

From the preceding discussion, it is clear that one can build databases that are semantically inconsistent in the sense that the database is not correct for the piece of reality that it was intended to model. This is a very important point. From a logical point of view, adding the assertion (3.5.3) to the Drug database does not make the extended database inconsistent. One cannot derive a contradiction from the extended database because a contradiction involves negation, and Prolog has no primitive notion of negation. We say that the database was semantically inconsistent because we load semantic, intuitive knowledge onto the words "aggravates" and "relieves." There really is nothing in Prolog that will let it deduce that there is any conflict between the notions of "relieves" and "aggravates." One has to be very, very cautious about the intuitive load we add onto a logical database. On the one hand, I advocate using mnemonic words that convey the intended interpretation of the database. However, as we have seen, using mnemonic words can sometimes lead one down a garden path. The notion that "relieves" and "aggravates" are contradictory is a semantic, intuitive notion that has not been added to the database. If we want to have the program understand that "aggravates" and "relieves" are two conflicting notions, we must add rules reflecting that conflict. This is an example of one of the most difficult problems of current work in Artificial Intelligence: the problem of dealing with common-sense reasoning. Common sense suggests that "relieves" and "aggravates" are two notions that are antithetical: If we say, on one hand, that "aspirin relieves asthma," and on the other hand, "aspirin aggravates asthma," we know we're in trouble. However, expressing that kind of knowledge in a general, yet efficient, way is one of the hardest parts of current-day Artificial Intelligence programming.

Let's return to the mirrors and windows metaphor. What happens if we have variables in the same positions in a query and in a matching database assertion? We have a piece of window looking at a mirror. There are two variables. They each will match against anything. What should Prolog do? It adopts the simplest solution and just lets them match. How should we interpret this? One way is the following. Suppose that in the process of solving a query **Q**, Prolog causes two uninstantiated variables, say **U** and **V**, to match. This means that if Prolog is eventually able to solve **Q**, whatever term it uses to replace **U** must be the same as whatever term it uses to replace **V**.

The notion of two variables matching is entirely natural. You can think of it this way:

> "Whatever problem the user gave me, successful solution of the problem requires that the two things at the **U** and **V** positions must come out to be the same. I (Prolog) don't know what they are yet, but I will internally identify them. Then, if one of these variables later gets bound to something specific, so will the other variable."

A more complex query actually might identify three or four more variables with those original two, then later determine the constraint these variables all had to obey. In fact, this is a very natural and powerful way to program in Prolog. You write out your set of constraints in the form of assertions in the database, together with a possibly complex query. As Prolog goes about solving the elementary literals in the query, quite often they initially have big gaping holes in them in the sense that some of the elementary literals are solved with variables matching variables, but no concrete instantiation for those variables. However, Prolog keeps working through the elementary queries, finally imposing enough constraints or conditions so that, via the matching process, it can say exactly what all the unknown items are. We will see many examples of this approach to programming in the succeeding chapters.

3.6 DIFFERENCE

Consider the following problem to be solved with the Drug database:

Find two distinct drugs that relieve severe pain.

We know that to find some drug that relieves severe pain, we should use the following:

?- relieves(Drug, severe_pain).

This suggests that we could solve the problem using the following query:

?-relieves(Drug1, severe_pain),relieves(Drug2, severe_pain).

However, here's what happens when we ask Prolog to solve the query:

```
?-relieves(Drug1, severe_pain),relieves(Drug2, severe_pain).
Drug1 = aspirin_codeine_combination
Drug2 = aspirin_codeine_combination
```

This is not what we expected! Why is Prolog being so stupid? Didn't we use two different variables? So shouldn't we get back two different values? The problem we have run into lies in the difference between a variable and the value of the variable. Although any variable can have at most one value, it is possible for two different variables to have the same value. We have just discussed this in the preceding sections. Consequently, simply using different variables (e.g., Drug1 and Drug2) does not require Prolog to assign them different values. In the case of our compound query, after Prolog solves the first query (matching Drug1 with aspirin_codeine_combination), it begins its search for a fact to match against the second "relieves" at the beginning of the database (as it should), so it first encounters the same matching fact involving aspirin_codeine_combination. Even though the two variables Drug1 and Drug2 are different, nothing in the query forces Prolog to assign them different values. Consequently, it returns the solution assigning aspirin_codeine_combination to both Drug1 and Drug2.

Thus, to solve the original problem, we must be able to impose an additional constraint on Drug1 and Drug2 that forces them to be different. Fortunately, Prolog provides a facility for doing this by supplying a *built-in predicate* called *difference* or *inequality*. The symbol \== is used to name this predicate. The expression

Drug1 \== Drug2

expresses the requirement that Drug1 must be different from Drug2. Thus, we can solve the original problem with the query

```
?relieves(Drug1, severe_pain),
    relieves(Drug2, severe_pain),
    Drug1 \== Drug2.
```

Running this query, we obtain the following results:

```
?relieves(Drug1, severe_pain),
    relieves(Drug2, severe_pain),
    Drug1 \== Drug2.
Drug1 = aspirin_codeine_combination
Drug2 = pain_gone
```

In outline, here is what happened when Prolog solved this query:

1 Beginning at the top of the database, Prolog solved the first component of the query by matching it against the fact
    relieves(aspirin_codeine_combination, severe_pain).
   This caused Drug1 to be assigned the value
    Drug1 = aspirin_codeine_combination.

2 Once again starting at the top of the database, Prolog solved the second component of the query by also matching it against the same fact, causing Drug2 to be assigned the value
    Drug2 = aspirin_codeine_combination.

3 Prolog then set about trying to solve the third component of the query. Since Drug1 and Drug2 had been assigned values at this point, the third component of the query was equivalent to
    aspirin_codeine_combination \== aspirin_codeine_combination.
   But this goal fails, since the two elements are identical. Prolog can't solve the third component using the current values for Drug1 and Drug2.

4 Consequently, Prolog backtracks and tries to find another solution to the second component of the query. It finds such a solution by matching against the fact
    relieves(pain_gone, severe_pain).
   This causes Drug2 to be assigned the value
    drug2 = pain_gone.

5 Prolog next tries to solve the third component of the query (again). With the current values of Drug1 and Drug2, the third component is equivalent to

aspirin_codeine_combination \== pain_gone.

Since the two elements of this goal are in fact distinct, Prolog succeeds in solving the (current version of the) third goal, and thus succeeds in solving the entire query.

Consider another query:

Find a drug that relieves two distinct symptoms.

This can be solved as follows:

```
?-relieves(Drug, SymptomA), relieves(Drug, SymptomB),
     SymptomA \== SymptomB.
Drug = aspirin
SymptomA = headache
SymptomB = moderate_pain;
Drug = aspirin
SymptomA = headache
SymptomB = moderate_arthritis;
Drug = aspirin
SymptomA = moderate_pain
SymptomB = moderate_arthritis;
no.
```

Finally, consider one more problem:

Find two different drugs that each relieve at least two symptoms.

We can combine our solutions to the two previous problems as follows:

```
?-relieves(Drug1, SymptomA), relieves(Drug1, SymptomB),
     SymptomA \= = SymptomB,
     relieves(Drug2, SymptomC), relieves(Drug2, SymptomD),
     SymptomC \= = SymptomD.
Drug1 = aspirin
SymptomA = headache
SymptomB = moderate_pain
Drug2 = de_congest
SymptomC = cough
SymptomD = nasal_congestion;
Drug1 = aspirin
SymptomA = headache
SymptomB = moderate_pain
Drug2 = bis_cure,
SymptomC = diarrhea
SymptomD = nausea
```

and so on.

EXERCISES

3-1 Using the drug database from Chapter 1 (Figure 1–1), construct Prolog queries interpreting the following questions:

    a What drug relieves coughs, but aggravates diabetes?

    b Is there a drug that relieves both nausea and diarrhea?

    c Is there a condition that is aggravated by a drug that relieves severe pain?

    d Are there any conditions that are relieved by a drug that aggravates both gout and fever?

3-2 Formulate natural English questions corresponding to the following Prolog queries against the Hickory tree database (Figure 1–7) in Chapter 1.

    a ?-trait(outer_scales(persistent), Tree), trait(terminal_bud_size(short), Tree).

    b ?-trait(X, mockernut_hickory), trait(X, pignut_hickory), trait(X, shagbark_hickory).

    c ?-trait(terminal_bud_size(What), mockernut_hickory).

3-3 Using the database of Exercise 1-1, express the following as Prolog queries:

    a Find a state that is west of Indiana and north of Kentucky.

    b Is there a state that is north of New Mexico and south of Utah?

    c Is there a state between Pennsylvania and Indiana?

    d Is there a state between New Jersey and Indiana?

    e Find a state that is one state away from Illinois.

    f Find a state that is west of New York and one state away from Illinois.

3-4 Formulate Prolog queries for the Hickory tree database corresponding to the following:

    a Are there any traits common to two hickory trees?

    b Are there any traits common to three hickory trees?

    c Are there any hickory trees having three traits?

3-5 Use the database formulated to solve Exercise 1-7 and formulate queries corresponding to the following:

    a What line (wire) connects gate g1 and g3?

    b Is there a line connecting g1 and g2?

    c Find a gate that has one gate between it and an input wire.

3-6 Formulate queries corresponding to the following problems for the cloud database constructed for Exercise 1-11:

    a Find a cloud that occurs in two different tiers.

    b Are there any clouds that occur in all three tiers?

    c What is the name of the Heap (cumulus) family cloud(s) that occur above 7 km?

3-7 Formulate queries corresponding to the following problems for the enzyme database constructed for Exercise 1-12:

    a Find an enzyme which produces two different products?

    b Find a site at which two distinct enzymes act.

3-8 Formulate queries corresponding to the following problems for the TV trouble-shooting database constructed for Exercise 1-9:

    a Find a problem that produces two distinct symptoms.

    b Find a symptom that may be caused by more than one problem.

3-9 Formulate queries corresponding to the following problems for the TV schematic database constructed for Exercise 1-8:

    a Determine what component lies between the video amplifier section and the video detector.

    b Find a component with output to more than one section.

    c Find a component with input from more than one section.

    d Find a pair of components that have more than one section lying between them.

3-10 Using the IRS filing rules database constructed in Exercise 1-13, determine whether there are any distinct marital status categories that have the same gross income value for determining whether to file a return. Are there two distinct combinations of marital status and filing status that use the same gross income value?

3-11 Consider the information concerning automobile fuel system problems contained in Appendix F, Section 15. Develop a database for this information in the style of the Hickory tree database. Formulate queries for this database corresponding to the following questions.

a Are there symptoms with more than one probable cause?

b Are there causes (problems) that are involved in more than one symptom?

CHAPTER 4

QUERIES AND RULES

4.1 ABBREVIATING QUESTIONS BY RULES

In the last chapter, we learned how to construct compound questions. As we saw by the end of that chapter, we can build complex questions with multiple parts. The typing involved in constructing one of these questions is somewhat tedious. Moreover, we may want to use the question more than once. Consequently, it would be nice to be able to package and store the question. Fortunately, Prolog provides such an ability, using the idea of a *rule*. A rule can be thought of as defining an abbreviation of a question. Use of rules will allow us to submit questions by typing the abbreviation instead of the complete question.

Just as we used variables in Section 2.5 to abbreviate many ground facts by one general fact that contained variables, we will often use variables to help us abbreviate queries. Let me start with some examples. Consider the first compound query from Chapter 3:

?- relieves(Drug, cough), relieves(Drug, nasal_congestion).

Any drug that relieves both cough and nasal_congestion is certainly good treatment for colds, so we will use relieves_colds as part of our abbreviation for this query. The statement that tells Prolog about the abbreviation is

relieves_colds(Drug) :- relieves(Drug,cough), relieves(Drug,nasal_congestion).

This is an example of a *rule*. Rules consist of two parts: a *head* and a *body*. The two parts are separated by the arrow symbol:

The head is the part on the left of the arrow, and the body is the part on the right of the arrow:

Prolog arrow symbol

relieves_colds (Drug) :- relieves (Drug, cough), relieves (Drug, nasal_congestion).

‾‾‾‾‾‾‾‾‾‾‾‾‾‾‾‾‾   ‾‾‾

Head   *Body*

As you can see in this example, the body of the rule is just the original query that is being abbreviated without the usual query symbol (?-) in front of it.

The head by itself is a literal. The predicate of the head literal is the name re-lieves_colds that we chose for this abbreviation or rule. The name is always selected by the programmer. In the example above, the only argument in the head literal is the variable Drug. Notice that Drug was the sole variable that occurred in the original query, which has now become the body of this rule. The arguments of the head literal are usually the variables that occur in the body, that is, the variables that occur in the query being abbreviated.

The rule is written by placing the arrow symbol ":-" between the head and the body, and terminating the entire expression with a period, thus,

Head :- *Body* .

In such rules, the head portion specifies a relation. The rule states that the relation specified by its head can be proved true (for some values of its variables) by proving all the problems in its body are true. Put another way, if we regard the head as a question, the rule provides a method for answering that question. The method is to find answers to all the questions following the "if" (i.e., the ":-").

Prolog makes it very convenient to add abbreviations. We can simply add them to the file containing the original database. (Alternatively, we can place the rules in a separate file, then load—i.e., consult—both the fact file and rule file into Prolog. The result is one combined Prolog database.) It doesn't matter where in the database we add the rule or abbreviation. Prolog can easily tell the difference between a fact and a rule, so it doesn't need any special instructions to tell it which is which. Suppose that we have used the editor to add the rule at the end of the file containing the original Drug database and that we have consulted that file into our Prolog system. At that point, Prolog will think that the database looks like Figure 4–1.

```
relieves(asprin, headache).
    . . .
relieves(noasprinol, moderate_pain).
aggravates(aspirin, asthma).
    . . .
aggravates(bis_cure, fever).
relieves_colds(Drug) :- relieves(Drug,cough), relieves(Drug,nasal_congestion).
```

FIGURE 4–1
The drugs database with a rule added.

FIGURE 4–2
Replacing a query by a rule body.

*Replacement step: Prolog replaces
the original query by the rule body
that the query abbreviates*

?-**relieves_colds** (**Drug**).
?-relieves (Drug, cough), relieves (Drug, nasal_congestion).

Drug = de_congest;
no.   *Any more solutions?*

How do *we* make use of such abbreviations? Our motivation for introducing these abbreviations was to be able to use them instead of the complicated compound queries they abbreviate. To use the abbreviation or rule, we submit a query that consists of the head of the rule:

```
?-relieves_colds(Drug).
Drug = de_congest;
no.
```

As this shows, we get the same answer(s) we got when we typed the complete original query.

How does *Prolog* actually make use of these abbreviations? It treats them as real abbreviations; That is whenever Prolog encounters the literal "relieves_colds(Drug), it replaces this literal by the body on the right side of the arrow in the definition, as illustrated in Figure 4–2. (Note: Prolog doesn't type the replacement step on the terminal. The figure shows the replacement step for illustrative purposes.)

Prolog actually makes very sophisticated use of abbreviations (i.e., rules). We'll work up to it by means of another example. Suppose that we wish to check whether some drug, say Relieve Nose, relieves coughs and nasal congestion. The full query to check this would be

?- relieves(relieve_nose, cough), relieves(contact, nasal_congestion).

Do we have to type out this query to find out? No. We can make use of the abbreviation. Recall that the abbreviation looks like this

relieves_colds(Drug) :- relieves(Drug,cough), relieves(Drug,nasal_congestion).

Notice that the variable Drug appears on both sides of the arrow (:-). Here is how Prolog really uses such abbreviations. Whenever it selects a literal from the current working query for processing, this chosen literal might correspond to a fact or might correspond to the head of some abbreviation rule. We saw earlier, that the literal chosen doesn't have to correspond exactly to a fact in the database in order for Prolog to be able to use the database fact to solve the problem posed by the literal. All that is required is that the chosen literal and the fact *match* in the sense we described earlier. Similarly, the chosen literal doesn't have to correspond exactly to a rule head in order for Prolog to be able to use the rule to process the chosen literal. Once again, all that is required is that the chosen literal and the head of the rule *match*. That is,

FIGURE 4–3
Match a chosen literal with a rule head.

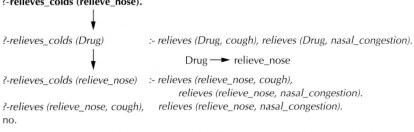

?-**relieves_colds (relieve_nose).**

?-*relieves_colds (Drug)*   :- *relieves (Drug, cough), relieves (Drug, nasal_congestion).*

Drug ⟶ relieve_nose

?-*relieves_colds (relieve_nose)*   :- *relieves (relieve_nose, cough),*
                                                    relieves (relieve_nose, nasal_congestion).
?-*relieves (relieve_nose, cough),*   *relieves (relieve_nose, nasal_congestion).*
no.

when Prolog tries to use a rule to process a chosen literal, it tries to match (unify) the chosen literal with the head of the rule. So if it chooses a literal whose predicate name is relieves_colds, it will try to match that literal with either facts about relieves_colds or with the head of any relieves_colds abbreviation rule. Since our current database has no facts concerning relieves_colds and only one rule about relieves_colds, Prolog will immediately try to use that rule, as illustrated in Figure 4–3.

As the diagram illustrates, when Prolog matched the goal literal

?-relieves_colds(relieve_nose).

with the head of the abbreviation rule, it associated the variable Drug with the constant relieve_nose:

Drug ⟶ *relieve_nose*

Before Prolog replaces the literal

relieves_colds(relieve_nose)

by the body of the rule, it *first* replaces Drug everywhere in the rule body by relieve_nose. Then it makes the transformed body of the rule its new current goal and goes on to try and solve it.

Here is another example:

Tell me the pairs of drugs and conditions for which the drug aggravates asthma and relieves the condition.

We might name this query asthma_involved. We're going to be interested in a Drug and a Condition, so the head of the rule would be

asthma_involved(Drug, Condition).

The body is the actual query that we want to run, namely,

?-aggravates(Drug, asthma), relieves(Drug, Condition).

Thus, the rule looks like:

asthma_involved(Drug, Condition) :- aggravates(Drug, asthma),
                                                    relieves(Drug, Condition).

FIGURE 4–4
Using a rule with two variables.

?-*asthma_involved (Drug, pneumonia).*

↓

asthma_involved (Drug, Condition) :- aggravates (Drug, asthma), relieves (Drug, Condition).

↓   ↓

asthma involved (Drug, pneumonia) :- aggravates (Drug, asthma), relieves (Drug, pneumonia).

?-aggravates (Drug, asthma), relieves (Drug, pneumonia).

....

Drug = penicillin

We could submit the query

?- asthma_involved(Drug, Condition).

and receive all the pairs of Drug and Condition that satisfy the body. However, we can also use the abbreviation in the following way:

?-asthma_involved(Drug, pneumonia).

Drug = penicillin

This new query causes Condition to be instantiated to pneumonia, as seen in Figure 4–4.

Although when we wrote the rule, we might have thought of the variables appearing in the head as output variables (i.e., they were the variables we were using to extract information from the database), nothing about this aspect of our intentions was conveyed to Prolog: A variable is a variable is a variable. As we indicated in the figure, when Prolog sees the query,

?-asthma_involved(Drug,pneumonia)

it searches its file of abbreviations for one whose head matches this query. The notion of matching that Prolog uses for this is exactly the same as that used in matching queries against facts. Consequently, this query will match the head of the rule for asthma_involved. As part of this match, the variable, Condition is bound to pneumonia. The transformed rule body is then run as a goal with Condition replaced by pneumonia.

Just as we saw for databases (where many facts can be recorded for a given predicate), there can also be more than one rule for a given predicate. For example, suppose we want to define a predicate that classifies those drugs that are pain killers. One approach would be to define pain_killer using the following clauses:

pain_killer(Drug) :- relieves(Drug, moderate_pain).

pain_killer(Drug) :- relieves(Drug, severe_pain).

FIGURE 4-5
Matching multiple rules.

?-pain_killer (Drug).

Prolog selects the first rule for 'pain_killer' to use:

pain_killer (Drug) :- relieves (Drug, moderate_pain).

?-relieves (Drug, moderate_pain).

Drug = aspirin;
Drug = noasprinol;

No more facts match relieves (Drug, moderate_pain)
so Prolog selects the second rule for 'pain_killer' to use:

pain_killer (Drug) :- relieves (Drug, severe_pain).

?-relieves (Drug, severe_pain).

Drug = aspirin_codeine_combination;
Drug = pain_gone;

There are no more facts which match relieves (Drug, severe_pain),
and no more rules for 'pain_killer', so Prolog now answers:

no.

(Note that we did not include two more potential rules for pain_killer, namely those that would assert that a drug is a pain killer either if it relieves headache or relieves moderate_arthritis. This is simply because some drugs may relieve these conditions directly, thereby indirectly reducing pain due to these conditions, but having no effect on pain due to other conditions.)

Prolog makes use of multiple rules for a given predicate the same way it uses multiple facts for the same predicate. When first dealing with a query involving the predicate, it will try to use the first fact or rule for the predicate in the order in which they are listed in the database. If the first fact or rule it tries matches the chosen literal, Prolog goes on with any further work. Otherwise, Prolog goes on to the next fact or rule for the predicate. It will continue this way until it finds a fact or rule that will provide a solution or until there are no more facts or rules for this predicate that it can try to use. Figure 4-5 suggests how this would work for the predicate pain_killer.

Thus far, we have only made use of the definitions (i.e., abbreviations) provided by rules directly in the queries we submit. However, we noted that the matching (or unification) that Prolog uses to match a rule head with a query is exactly the same as the matching it uses to match facts with the literals in a general compound query. This is a very important observation, since it is the ultimate basis of much of Prolog's power. It makes no difference whether the query (simple or compound) on which Prolog is working at any given moment is the original query submitted by the user or is the result of a previously applied abbreviation. In either case, Prolog chooses the first (leftmost) literal in the query and tries to find either a fact that matches the literal or a rule whose head matches the literal. If Prolog finds a fact matching the literal, it removes it from further consideration, since the match has solved that literal. On the other hand, if Prolog finds a fact whose head matches the literal, Prolog replaces the literal in the query by the body of the matching rule, since the rule body is regarded as an abbreviation of its head.

Suppose we had approached the problem of determining pain killers differently. Instead of defining pain_killer directly, let us first use some facts to define the notion of a painful condition:

form_of_pain(moderate_pain).

form_of_pain(severe_pain).

We now can define pain_killer with just one rule:

pain_killer(Drug) :- form_of_pain(Condition), relieves(Drug, Condition).

Figure 4–6 illustrates how Prolog would use these facts and rules to solve the problem of finding pain killers.

Let us summarize what we have learned about rules thus far:

- The general form of rules for abbreviating queries is:
    Head :- Body .
- The symbol ":-" is called an arrow; it points leftward. To the right of the arrow is the query.
- To the left of the arrow is a literal that has in it variables that represent the information we are trying to extract from the compound query.
- We can freely choose the predicate name for this literal.
- The rule can be thought of as an abbreviation statement saying that the literal on the left is an abbreviation for the compound query on the right.
- We can effectively submit the original compound goal by simply typing the left-side literal; that is, the head can be used as a query.
- When Prolog selects a literal on which it is going to work, it looks through both the abbreviations and the facts in the database for one that matches the selected literal, where a rule matches the selected literal if the head of the rule matches. Prolog makes matches using true matching (unification).
- If the unification between the target literal and the rule head succeeds, Prolog rewrites the current goal by replacing the target literal with the body of the abbreviation. It does this by first replacing any variables in the body by any values that were associated to them by the match of the head with the target literal.
- Prolog then runs the transformed current goal.

Prolog operates by pattern matching and is entirely neutral with regard to matching (unifying) queries and database facts or rules. That is, it doesn't care where a variable lives, whether it is in the query or in a fact or rule from the database. If it is matching two items and encounters a variable, it associates the variable with whatever the corresponding term is.

Since queries are made up from one or more literals, the bodies of abbreviation rules contain one or more literals. However, suppose that we extend the definition of

FIGURE 4–6

Matching with multiple rules.

?-pain_killer (Drug).

       ↓   *Prolog selects the rule for 'pain_killer' to use:*

  pain_killer (Drug) :- form_of_pain (Condition), relieves (Drug, Condition).

?-form_of_pain (Condition), relieves (Drug, Condition).

       ↓ |

  form_of_pain (moderate_pain).⤸ *matching database fact*

                          Prolog crosses off form-of-pain (Condition),

?-relieves (Drug, moderate_pain).   *leaving:*

     ↓|

  relieves (aspirin, moderate_pain).⤸ *matching database fact*

drug = aspirin;

     ↓

  relieves (noasprinol, moderate_pain). ⤸ *another matching database fact*

Drug = noasprinol;

        There are no more facts which match relieves (Drug, moderate_pain),
        so Prolog now returns to the query where it matches the query literal
        form-of-pain (Condition) with the fact form-of-pain (moderate-pain),
        and looks to see if there are any other matching facts:

               ↓

?-form_of_pain (Condition), relieves (Drug, Condition).

       ↓

  form_of_pain (severe_pain). ⤸ *matching database fact*

                        Prolog crosses off form_of_pain (Condition),

?-relieves (Drug, severe_pain).   *leaving:*

     ↓|

  relieves (aspirin_codeine_combination, severe_pain).⤸ *matching database fact*

     ↓

  relieves (pain_gone, severe_pain).⤸ *another matching database fact*

                No more facts match relieves (Drug, severe_pain), and
                no more facts match form_of_pain (Condition),
                so Prolog now answers:

no.

---

the body of a rule to allow zero or more literals. Suppose we also drop the rule arrow (:-) when there are zero literals. What's left in this case is something that looks just like a fact. Thus, the idea of a rule includes the idea of a fact. That is, the class of rules includes the class of facts. A fact can be thought of as a degenerate rule that has no body. Alternatively, a rule can be thought of as a conditional fact in which the head is a fact that is solvable under the conditions expressed in the body.

The process Prolog uses to respond to such queries is a combination of database search and rewriting. The rewriting occurs when an elementary part of a query is replaced by the body of a matching rule.

FIGURE 4–7

Part of George Washington's family tree.

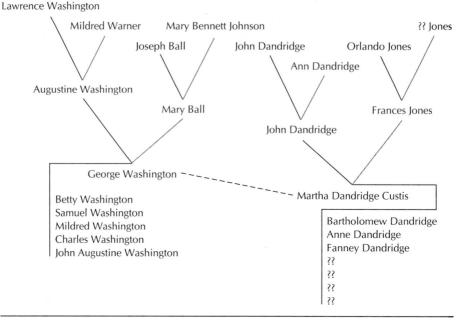

4.2 DEFINING RELATIONSHIPS WITH RULES

Let's look at another example, one of my favorites. An intuitive application of Prolog is to describe family trees and family relationships. The family we will consider is that of George Washington. Figure 4–7 sets out part of George Washington's family tree. The solid black lines represent a parent who is a father, the solid gray lines represent a parent who is a mother, and the dashed lines represent marriage relationships. We will use this tree as the raw information for constructing a database.

To represent the knowledge embedded in this tree, we have some choices to make. These choices are independent of our use of Prolog. Whether we are building this database using LISP or FORTRAN or Prolog, we have the same basic kinds of choices to make. These choices will be partially dictated by our intuitions of what we want to express with the database. The choices will also be affected by what we want to get out of the database.

The principal choice concerns which basic primitive predicates we will use. Should we use *mother* and *father* as primitive predicates? Or perhaps we should use *parent* together with unary predicates determining sex as the primitive predicates. There are no absolute criteria for determining which alternative to choose. Often, one must explore the consequences of choosing various alternatives before a final decision can be made. Such an exploration often involves constructing at least part of a database according to one of the alternatives. Then one poses various queries to the database in order to see just how easy or difficult it is to obtain information from a database built in the manner being explored.

FIGURE 4–8
A database corresponding to Washington's family tree.

> parent('Augustine Washington', 'George Washington').
> parent('Mary Ball Washington', 'George Washington').
> parent('Lawrence Washington', 'Augustine Washington').
> parent('Mildred Warner Washington', 'Augustine Washington').
> parent('Joseph Ball', 'Mary Ball Washington').
> parent('Mary Johnson Ball', 'Mary Ball Washington').
> parent('John Dandridge', 'Martha Washington').
> parent('Frances Jones Dandridge', 'Martha Washington').
> male('George Washington').
> male('Augustine Washington').
> male('Lawrence Washington').
> male('Joseph Ball').
> male('John Dandridge').
> female('Mary Ball Washington').
> female('Mildred Warner Washington').
> female('Mary Johnson Ball').
> female('Martha Washington').
> female('Frances Jones Dandridge').

Suppose we explore the latter of the two choices above. That is, we will take the parent relationship together with the *male* and *female* relationships as primitive. Each solid link in the tree, whether black or gray, represents a parent-child relationship. Thus, for each such link in the tree, we will need a parent assertion relating the two people at either end of the link. For example, Mary Ball Washington is connected to George Washington by a gray, line meaning that Mary Ball Washington is the mother of George Washington. Certainly then, Mary Ball Washington is a parent of George Washington. Thus, our Prolog database for George Washington's family will need to have an assertion

> parent('Mary Ball Washington', 'George Washington').

The sex of the people in the database will be expressed by the two unary predicates, female and male. For example, since Mary Ball Washington is the mother of George Washington, she is certainly female. Thus, the database must contain the assertion

> female('Mary Ball Washington').

A portion of the Prolog database corresponding to the family tree in Figure 4–7 is shown in Figure 4–8. Let's use this database to answer some questions. To determine George Washington's father, we must find someone who is a parent of George Washington and who is also male. Thus, we have two conditions to impose:

1 The unknown person is a parent of George Washington;
2 The unknown person is male.

These two conditions translate to the following two Prolog conditions or literals:

parent(Who, 'George Washington')
male(Who)

Combining these into a single compound query gives us:

```
?-parent(Who, 'George Washington'), male(Who).
Who = 'Augustine Washington'.
```

A simple direct abbreviation of this query would be:

father_of_George_Washington(Who) :- parent(Who, 'George Washington'),
male (Who).

We can use this abbreviation to determine George Washington's father, rather than typing the entire original query, as follows:

```
?-father_of_George_Washington( Who ).
Who = Augustine Washington.
```

However, it is not too often that we must ask just about George Washington's father. In general, we are curious about various people's fathers. Thus, we want to write a rule that has two variables in it. One variable will be for an arbitrary person, and one variable will be for that person's father. The arbitrary person replaces George Washington. In English, the rule will read

Someone is the father of a person
if *that someone is a parent of the person* **and** *that someone is male.*

Lets use "father" for the predicate name of this rule. Let's also use the variable "Child" for the arbitrary person, and use the variable "Dad" for the unknown father we are seeking. The rule will look like Figure 4–9.

The body of this rule looks almost exactly the same as the compound query for finding George Washington's father, except that we have replaced 'George Washington' by the variable Child, and we used the variable Dad in place of the variable Who. We could still use this rule to find George Washington's father:

```
?-father(Who, 'George Washington').
Who = Augustine Washington
```

The head of this rule is a literal that expresses the relationship in which we're interested. We can think of the rule as defining that relationship. The predicate name in the head of the rule is used as a name of the relationship. The rule, as a totality, defines the relationship—at least partially. In this example, the rule says that

Dad is the father of *Child*
if *Dad* is the parent of *Child*
and *Dad* is male.

```
father(Dad, Child) :- parent(Dad, Child), male(Dad).
```
FIGURE 4–9
A Prolog rule defining the father relationship.

FIGURE 4–10
A rule defining the grandfather relation.

grandfather(GrandDad, Kid) :- parent(GrandDad, Person), parent(Person, Kid),
male(GrandDad).

One common question concerning family relationships is the determination of grandfathers. Somebody is going to be a grandfather of George Washington if that somebody is the male parent of one of George Washington's parents. That is,

Somebody is a grandfather of George Washington
   if *Somebody* is the parent of *Person*
   and *Person* is a parent of George Washington
   and *Somebody* is male.

If we use P for the intermediate person, the query to find a grandfather of George Washington can be written

```
?-parent(GrandDad,P), parent(P,'George Washington'), male(GrandDad).
GrandDad='Lawrence Washington'
P = 'Augustine Washington';
GrandDad='Joseph Ball'
P = 'Mary Ball Washington';
no.
```

The answers returned are determined by the database of George Washington's family tree. Since the variable P occurred in the query, we also learn who the intermediate parent is.

As in the case of fathers, we are sometimes interested in grandfathers other than the grandfathers of George Washington. We can define the general grandfather relationship by proceeding just as we did in the case of the father relationship. That is, we replace the name of George Washington by a variable for an arbitrary person. The rule defining the general grandfather relation now appears as Figure 4–10.

We can determine George Washington's grandfathers as follows:

```
?-grandfather(GrandDad, 'George Washington').
GrandDad = 'Augustine Washington';
GrandDad = 'Joseph Ball';
no.
```

Notice that in contrast to the original query, since the variable (Person) used for the intermediate parent does not occur in the query we submitted, Prolog does not print out its value when it returns the answers. Prolog is lazy: It only tells us what we asked—no more.

4.3 TWO INTERPRETATIONS OF RULES

Even though we introduced the notion of rules as a simple method of abbreviating questions, they have much more substantial interpretations and uses. As we indicated at the beginning of Chapter 1, we use databases to record knowledge about the world around us. In this context, rules can be viewed as providing methods of solving problems concerning the knowledge stored in the database. This view of rules is called the *problem-solving interpretation*. When we use a statement concerning a relation or a property in a database, we regard it as a fact. But when we use the same sort of statement in a question, it can be regarded as a problem to be solved. If such a statement is concrete (i.e., has no variables), solving the problem consists simply of showing that it is true in the database—that it matches a fact recorded in the database. When the statement has variables, the problem is to find values for its variables so that the resulting concrete statement is also true in the database. Again, this amounts to matching it against a fact in the database. A compound question can be regarded as a compound problem. That is, it is made up of subproblems. Solving the compound problem consists of jointly solving all of the simple component problems. The sense in which the solution must be joint is this: if a variable occurs in more than one part of the *and statement*, it must receive the same value from each of the matches of the simple problems against facts in the database. From this point of view, a rule

> *head :- body*

provides a method for solving simple problems of the form described by the head of the rule. What the rule says is

> *In order to solve problems of the form head, it suffices to solve the problem(s) posed by body.*

Or, to phrase it slightly differently,

> *Whenever you have a problem of the form head to solve, you can find a solution by solving the problem(s) posed by body.*

Thus, the rule for "father" given in Figure 4–9 can be interpreted to say

> *Whenever you have a problem of the form*
>
> father(Dad, Kid)
>
> *to solve, you can find a solution by solving the problem*
>
> parent(Dad, Kid), male(Dad).

There is an important point to notice about this interpretation: It does not say that the *only* way to solve the problem posed by the head is to solve the given body. All it says is that *one* way to solve the problem posed by the head is to solve the problem posed by the body. In view of this, Prolog allows us to add more than one rule with the same relation name in the head. In such a situation, it simply regards the different rules as alternative ways of solving the common problem posed by their heads. This is illustrated by the two rules for pain_killer considered in Section 4.1:

> pain_killer(Drug) :- relieves(Drug, moderate_pain).
>
> pain_killer(Drug) :- relieves(Drug, severe_pain).

Together, these two rules provide us with two methods of determining that some Drug is a pain killer—namely, determining whether the Drug relieves moderate pain or whether the Drug relieves severe pain.

The second principal interpretation of rules treats them as logical definitions. This interpretation is called the *logical interpretation* of rules. In this context, we make a distinction between explicit and implicit definitions. A collection of concrete facts in a database—all of which concern some relation R—are thought of as *explicitly defining* R. Each separate fact is one case of the definition. On the other hand, consider a collection of rules stored in a database and suppose that all of their heads concern the relation R. This collection of rules is then thought of as *implicitly defining* R. Rather than telling us specifically the cases for which R holds, this sort of definition gives us rules for proving that a given case of R holds. The methods for proving the given case of R holds lie in examining combinations of other relations. By using the rules, we have indirectly or implicitly defined R rather than simply listing the cases for which R holds. Finally, we can mix the two approaches to specifying a relation R. That is, we can use some facts to explicitly list some of the cases for which R is true, and we can use some rules to implicitly specify the remaining cases for which R is to be true.

To be precise, the logical interpretation of an individual rule

head :- body

is

> *For all possible values of all the variables occurring in the rule, if the body of the rule is true, then the head of the rule must be true.*

From this point of view, the rule for father presented earlier can be seen as a logical definition of the notion of fatherhood, given that we already have available the relations parent and male. Thus, the logical meaning of the father rule is

> For all values of the variables Dad and Child,
> **if** parent(Dad, Child) is true and male(Dad) is true,
> **then** father(Dad, Child) is also true.

Suppose that a database contains several rules for a relation R and that the heads are all of exactly the same form. For example, suppose the rules are

head :- body$_1$
head :- body$_2$

. . . . .

head :- body$_n$

The logical interpretation of this collection of rules is

> *For all possible values of all the variables occurring in any of the rules*
> **if** *body$_1$ is true, or body$_2$ is true, or . . . or body $_n$ is true,*
> **then** *head must be true.*

Consequently, the logical interpretation of the two rules for pain_killer is

> For all possible values of the variable Drug,
> **if** relieves(Drug, moderate_pain) is true
> **or** relieves(Drug, severe_pain) is true,
> **then** pain_killer(Drug) is true.

We initially took the notion of a rule to simply be an abbreviation for a compound query. But now we have moved to the position that a rule can be a definition of a relationship. A rule is (part of) a logical definition of a relationship. For the purposes of a program dealing in family relationships, the rules in Figures 4–9 and 4–10 define the notion of father and grandfather.

4.4   HOW PROLOG WORKS

It's time to take a closer look at what really happens inside a Prolog system. As we've indicated, a Prolog program is a collection of facts and rules. The Prolog system collects all the rules and facts that you supply it (possibly by consulting several files) into one monolithic database. That database is organized according to the predicates for the facts and for the heads of the rules. It is possible for a Prolog program to have both facts and rules for the same predicate—in fact, it is very common. For example, we might want to add the following rule to the Drug database:

aspirin relieves *Disease* **if** *Disease* is inflammatory.

This is a rule for relieves, but the Drug database also contains some facts for relieves. This creates no problem if you take the point of view that facts are really just degenerate rules—that is, that facts are rules with unconditional bodies (i.e., with no conditions in their bodies). Then, the database is simply a collection of rules for predicates. (Alternatively, we can view rules as conditional facts and view a database as a collection of generalized facts.)

What happens when we submit a goal? As we have seen, Prolog tries to solve it and answers "yes" or "no", depending on whether or not it could find a solution. If there were variables in the query and Prolog succeeds in solving the query, Prolog returns the values of those variables. These are the values that enabled Prolog to find a solution. Here is roughly what it does. Prolog maintains at all times a notion of the *current goal*. Prolog transforms that current goal in the process of its action, but at any point in time, there is a current goal to be solved. If at any point that goal becomes empty (there is nothing more to do; it has solved all the problems remaining), Prolog has *succeeded*. In this case, Prolog responds by typing out the current values of the variables that occurred in the original query. On the other hand, if the current goal is not empty, there is more work to be done. There will be one or more literals occurring in the current goal, which we can think of as a compound query that is being continuously transformed. Prolog will select one of the literals from current goal (the leftmost one) and ask whether there is anything in its database that is applicable to the selected literal. The notion of *applicability* is that there are clauses (rules or facts) in the database that have the same predicate and the same number of arguments as the literal and that might match the chosen literal. (We'll go into the notion of matching and applicability in a bit more detail later.) If there is an applicable clause, Prolog applies it. The process of application transforms the current goal. After applying the clause and transforming the goal, Prolog once again asks if the current goal is empty

FIGURE 4–11
The basic cyclic action of a prolog processor.

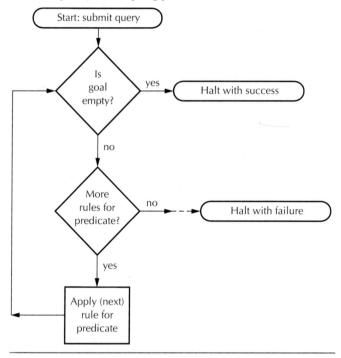

or not, etc. This is the basic cycle of a Prolog processor. The cycle is illustrated in Figure 4–11.

Given the current goal, the processor looks to see if there is anything in the database—either a fact or a rule—that it can use to transform that goal. If the processor finds something useful in the database—possibly, more than one useful item—it chooses a fact or goal from the database to try to use to transform the leftmost literal in the current goal. If the chosen fact or rule from the database matches the leftmost literal of the current goal, the processor applies the database fact or rule to the current goal and goes around the loop. If at any point in time the current goal is not empty but the processor cannot find any applicable clauses, we think of that as being a failure. The processor has no way of moving forward. However, because Prolog databases allow more than one rule or fact for a given predicate, at each point in the main cycle the Prolog processor may actually have to make a choice of which fact or rule to apply: There may be more than one applicable clause. When the processor encounters a failure, it undoes the effects of the most recent such choice and chooses some other clause instead for possible application. After making this alternate choice, it tries to work forward again. (This is called chronological backtracking.) Figure 4–12 extends Figure 4–11 by adding the backtracking action.

FIGURE 4–12
Basic processor cycle with backtracking.

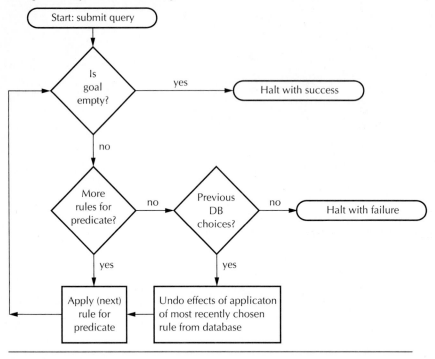

4.5 TRACING PROLOG COMPUTATIONS

Let's consider another example family tree;, this one from the mythological Greek gods, as seen in Figure 4–13.[1] Due to the proclivities of the gods, this tree has somewhat more complexity than that for George Washington's family. If we choose parent, male, and female as the basic predicates with which to express this tree, the corresponding Prolog database will be as shown in Figure 4–14.

Let's add the rules for father and grandfather to this database and submit some queries. Asking for Zeus's father, we get

```
?-father(Dad, zeus).
Dad = cronus;
no.
```

Asking for Zeus's grandfathers, we get

---

[1] The knowledge embodied by this tree, being shrouded in the mists of time, is incomplete and at best conjectural. For a fuller discussion of these tangled relationships and some alternative conjectures, see the following excellent books: Robert Graves, *The Greek Myths, Vols. One and Two*, Penguin Books, Baltimore, 1955, and Edith Hamilton, *Mythology*, Little Brown, New York, 1940 (reprinted as a Mentor Book by New American Library, New York, 1955). A delightful presentation of the basic information can be found in Ingri and Edgar Parin d'Aulaire, *Book of Greek Myths*, Doubleday, Garden City, NJ, 1962.

FIGURE 4–13
A partial family tree for the Greek gods.

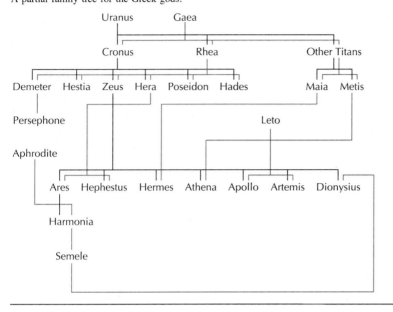

```
?-grandfather(GrandPop,  zeus).
GrandPop = uranus;
GrandPop = uranus;
no.
```

Hold on! Something looks wrong here! George Washington had two grandfathers (as do the rest of us), but Zeus appears to have only one, namely Uranus. Is there something wrong with Prolog? Is it so in awe of the inhabitants of Mount Olympus that it got confused? Not at all. Prolog is only being its truthful self and reporting to us what it finds in the database. If we look at the family tree of the Greek gods, we see that indeed, Zeus only has one grandfather, Uranus. If we submit the body of the grandfather rule as a query, we can get some more information on what happened:

```
?-parent(GrandDad,P), parent(P,zeus), male(GrandDad).
GrandDad=uranus
P = cronus;
GrandDad=uranus
P = rhea;
no.
```

To arrive at Zeus's grandfathers, Prolog has to climb up from Zeus via one of Zeus's parents. But in either case, whether Prolog proceeds via Cronus or Rhea, it arrives at the same male grandparent, namely Uranus. A diagram showing Prolog's internal action conveys this even more clearly (see Figure 4–15).

This kind of picture of the computation is so useful for understanding what is happening that almost all Prolog systems provide methods of generating *traces* that

FIGURE 4–14
The Greek gods family tree database.

parent(uranus, cronus).
parent(gaea, cronus).
parent(uranus, rhea).
parent(gaea, rhea).
parent(rhea, zeus).
parent(cronus, zeus).
parent(rhea, hera).
parent(cronus, hera).
parent(cronus, hades).
parent(rhea, hades).
parent(cronus, hestia).
parent(rhea, hestia).
parent(zeus, hermes).
parent(maia, hermes).
parent(zeus, athena).
parent(zeus, ares).
parent(hera, ares).
parent(zeus, hephaestus).
parent(hera, hephaestus).
parent(zeus, apollo).
parent(leto, apollo).
parent(zeus, artemis).
parent(leto, artemis).
parent(zeus, dionysius).
parent(semele, dionysius).
parent(aphrodite, harmonia).
parent(ares, harmonia).
parent(harmonia, semele).
parent(demeter, persephone).

female(gaea).
female(rhea).
female(hera).
female(hestia).
female(demeter).
female(athena).
female(metis).
female(maia).
female(persephone).
female(aphrodite).
female(artemis).
female(leto).

male(uranus).
male(cronus).
male(zeus).
male(hades).
male(hermes).
male(apollo).
male(dionysius).
male(hephaestus).
male(poseidon).

approximate the picture. The methods for generating the traces are incorporated into the debugger. Figure 4–16 shows such a trace generated by ALS Prolog.

The debuggers provide a variety of services that we will learn about in the course of this book. In the trace Figure 4–16, the debugger is being used in *single-step mode*, which means that we are walking through the computation, stopping at each individual step. The debugger types the given line, ending with a question mark (?), and pauses. It is waiting for us to type a single character to indicate what it should do next. In this trace, we typed a simple <return> at the end of each line. This tells the debugger to go on to the next step of the computation, type it out, and wait and see what we want to do after that.

Let us explain some of the details of the notation that appears in Prolog traces. The typical trace line appears in Figure 4–17. We will disuss the trace notation further in later chapters. Such traces are very, very useful in coming to understand how Prolog

FIGURE 4–15
Computing Zeus's grandfathers.

?-grandfather (GrandPop, zeus)

  grandfather (GrandDad, Kid) :- parent (GrandDad, Person),
                                  parent (Person, Kid),
                                  male (GrandDad).

?-parent (GrandPop, Person), parent (Person, zeus), male (GrandPop).

?-parent (GrandPop, Person), parent (Person, zeus), male (GrandPop).

  parent (uranus, cronus).

?-parent (uranus, cronus), parent (cronus, zeus), male (uranus).

  parent (cronus, zeus).

?-parent (uranus, cronus), parent (cronus, zeus), male (uranus).

  male (uranus).

GrandPop = uranus;

?-parent (uranus, cronus), parent (cronus, zeus), male (uranus).

        No other ways to solve this problem.

?-parent (uranus, cronus), parent (cronus, zeus), male (uranus).

        No other ways to solve this problem.

?-parent (GrandPop, Person), parent (Person, zeus), male (GrandPop).

  parent (uranus, rhea). ◄— *Another way to solve this problem*

?-parent (uranus, rhea), parent (rhea, zeus), male (uranus).

  parent (rhea, zeus).

?-parent (uranus, rhea), parent (rhea, zeus), male (uranus).

  male (uranus).

GrandPop = uranus

```
>alspro
ALS Prolog Version 1.12 [nnnn]
    Copyright (c) 1987 Applied Logic Systems, Inc.
?-[greeks].
Consulting greeks...greeks consulted.
?-grandfather(Who, zeus).
Who = uranus;
Who = uranus;
no.
```

FIGURE 4–16
A trace of ?-grandfather(Who,zeus).

FIGURE 4–16—*Continued*

```
?- trace grandfather(Who, zeus).
Consulting debugger....debugger consulted.
    (1)   1 call: grandfather(_2,zeus) ?
    (2)   2 call: parent(_2,_126) ?
    (2)   2 exit: parent(uranus,cronus)
    (3)   2 call: parent(cronus,zeus) ?
    (3)   2 exit: parent(cronus,zeus)
    (4)   2 call: male(uranus) ?
    (4)   2 exit: male(uranus)
    (1)   1 exit: grandfather(uranus,zeus)
Who = uranus;                                        Found uranus first time
    (4)   2 redo: male(uranus) ?
    (4)   2 fail: male(uranus)
    (3)   2 redo: parent(cronus,zeus) ?
    (3)   2 fail: parent(cronus,zeus)
    (2)   2 redo: parent(_2,_126) ?
    (2)   2 exit: parent(gaea,cronus)
    (4)   2 call: parent(cronus,zeus) ?
    (4)   2 exit: parent(cronus,zeus)
    (5)   2 call: male(gaea) ?
    (5)   2 fail: male(gaea)
    (4)   2 redo: parent(cronus,zeus) ?
    (4)   2 fail: parent(cronus,zeus)
    (2)   2 redo: parent(_2,_126) ?
    (2)   2 exit: parent(uranus,rhea)
    (5)   2 call: parent(rhea,zeus) ?
    (5)   2 exit: parent(rhea,zeus)
    (6)   2 call: male(uranus) ?
    (6)   2 exit: male(uranus)
    (1)   1 exit: grandfather(uranus,zeus)
Who = uranus;                                        Found uranus 2nd time
    (6)   2 redo: male(uranus) ?
    (6)   2 fail: male(uranus)
    (5)   2 redo: parent(rhea,zeus) ?
    (5)   2 fail: parent(rhea,zeus)
    (2)   2 redo: parent(_2,_126) ?
    (2)   2 exit: parent(gaea,rhea)
    (6)   2 call: parent(rhea,zeus) ?
    (6)   2 exit: parent(rhea,zeus)
    (7)   2 call: male(gaea) ?
    (7)   2 fail: male(gaea)
    (6)   2 redo: parent(rhea,zeus) ?
    (6)   2 fail: parent(rhea,zeus)
    (2)   2 redo: parent(_2,_126) ?
        works through all instances of parent . . . . . .
   (31)   2 call: parent(semele,zeus) ?
   (31)   2 fail: parent(semele,zeus) ?
    (2)   2 redo: parent(_2,_126) ?
    (2)   2 exit: parent(demeter,persephone)
   (32)   2 call: parent(persephone,zeus) ?
   (32)   2 fail: parent(persephone,zeus) ?
    (2)   2 fail: parent(_2,_126)
    (1)   1 fail: grandfather(_2,zeus)
no
```

FIGURE 4–17
A typical line of a Prolog trace.

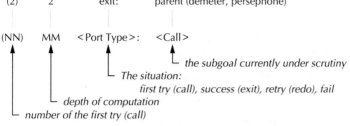

works. You should regularly load the example databases and trace the various goals that we consider in the book.[2]

*4.6 HOW PROLOG APPLIES RULES

Before we go further, let's look more closely at the notion of applicability. What does it mean to apply a rule or a procedure? Suppose the current goal is

$$?\text{-}\mathbf{D_1}, \mathbf{D_2}, \ldots, \mathbf{D_{i-1}}, \mathbf{D_i}, \mathbf{D_{i+1}}, \ldots, \mathbf{D_k}.$$

It consists of literals $\mathbf{D_1}$ through $\mathbf{D_k}$. Lets suppose that Prolog has solved the first i-1 literals $\mathbf{D_1}, \mathbf{D_2}, \ldots, \mathbf{D_{i-1}}$. Moreover, suppose $\mathbf{D_i}$ has predicate $\mathbf{p}$, with n arguments. Perhaps $\mathbf{D_i}$ looks like

$$\mathbf{p(b_1, b_2, \ldots, b_n)}.$$

Here the arguments to $\mathbf{p}$ are the terms $\mathbf{b_1}$ through $\mathbf{b_n}$. These might be big, compound, nasty terms, containing variables and constants and numbers and all sorts of things. The situation might be as seen in the Figure 4–18.

Finally, suppose the database contains a rule whose head has the predicate with *n* arguments:

$$\mathbf{p(a_1, a_2, \ldots, a_n)} \text{ :- } \mathbf{C_1}, \ldots, \mathbf{C_m}.$$

This rule is a candidate for possible application to the chosen literal.

We know the possible application of the rule to the chosen literal is actually going to work only if the arguments of the head of the rule pairwise match the arguments of the chosen literal. Thus our problem is one of understanding what it means for

---

[2] Most of the example databases and programs are available on the program disks supplied with ALS Prolog from Applied Logic Systems.

$$?\text{-}\mathbf{D_1}, \mathbf{D_2}, \ldots, \mathbf{D_{i-1}}, \mathbf{p(b_1, b_2, \ldots, b_n)}, \mathbf{D_{i+1}}, \ldots, \mathbf{D_k}.$$

FIGURE 4–18
A current goal with selected and complete subproblems.

terms to match. We have informally examined the notion of matching already. We have seen that two constants match only if they are identical and that variables match against anything. Two compound terms match if they have the same operators and the same number of arguments and (recursively) their arguments match pairwise. To summarize

Successful Matches:
- Constant $\leftrightarrow$ Constant $\Rightarrow$ Constants are identical
- Variable $\leftrightarrow$ Anything $\Rightarrow$ Variable matches anything
  $\mathbf{f}(\mathbf{a_1}, \ldots, \mathbf{a_r}) \leftrightarrow \mathbf{g}(\mathbf{c_1}, \ldots, \mathbf{c_s}) \Rightarrow r = s$ and (recursively):

$$\mathbf{a_1} \leftrightarrow \mathbf{c_1} \ldots$$

$$\mathbf{a_r} \leftrightarrow \mathbf{c_s}$$

Since what interests us in matching is the resulting values of any variables that are present, you can think of the point of matching as trying to find a substitution that will make the match work. A substitution which makes the match work is called a *unifier* of the two expressions being matched. Let's write Greek letters θ or σ for substitutions (including unifiers). Remember that unifiers are just substitutions, and that when substitutions are applied to an expression they produce a new expression obtained by replacement of variables. To show the result of applying a substitution θ to some expression $\mathbf{E}$, we'll write θ after the expression $\mathbf{E}$, like this:

$$\mathbf{E}\theta$$

In particular, if θ is a unifier of two expressions $\mathbf{D}$ and $\mathbf{E}$, then $\mathbf{D}\theta$ and $\mathbf{E}\theta$ will be identically the same expression.

Thus, the matching process is best thought of as computing a unifying substitution, if one exists. The matching or unifying process is summarized by the informal algorithm given in Figure 4–19. Keep in mind that there might be variables in both of the terms we are trying to match. Consequently, we must think of applying the substitution evenhandedly to both. Some examples of successful and unsuccessful attempts at unification are shown in Figure 4–20.

Let's return to the problem of applying a rule to the selected literal $\mathbf{D_i}$. Our problem has become that of matching the expressions

$$\mathbf{p}(\mathbf{b_1}, \mathbf{b_2}, \ldots, \mathbf{b_n}) \quad \text{and} \quad \mathbf{p}(\mathbf{a_1}, \mathbf{a_2}, \ldots, \mathbf{an}).$$

If these expressions won't match, there is no way we can apply the rule to the selected literal. So suppose that these two expressions will in fact match. That means that there is a unifier θ for these expressions. Then, by definition,

$$\mathbf{p}(\mathbf{b_1}, \mathbf{b_2}, \ldots, \mathbf{b_n})\theta \quad \text{is identical with} \quad \mathbf{p}(\mathbf{a_1}, \mathbf{a_2}, \ldots, \mathbf{a_n})\theta.$$

Thus, the rule

$$\mathbf{p}(\mathbf{a_1}, \mathbf{a_2}, \ldots, \mathbf{a_n}) \text{ :- } \mathbf{C_1}, \ldots, \mathbf{C_m}.$$

can be used to solve the selected subproblem

$$\mathbf{p}(\mathbf{b_1}, \mathbf{b_2}, \ldots, \mathbf{b_n}).$$

FIGURE 4–19
The unification algorithm.

Given: Two expressions E_1 and E_2;

Find: A unifier for E_1 and E_2 if one exists.

Procedure: Build up the unifier θ piece by piece, according to the following cases:

1. If E_1 and E_2 are both constants, then:
   1a) If E_1 and E_2 are identical, then θ can be the trivial or empty unifier;
   1b) If E_1 and E_2 are not indentical, no unifier will work, so quit;
2. If E_1 is a variable, match E_1 with E_2 by adding the requirement that E_1 map to E_2 to the part of θ built up thus far—now you are done;
3. If E_1 is not a variable, but E_2 is a variable, match E_2 with E_1 by adding the requirement that E_2 map to E_1 to the part of θ built up thus far—now you are done;
4. If neither E_1 nor E_2 is a constant or variable, assume that E_1 is $f(a_1, \ldots, a_n)$ and E_2 is $g(b_1, \ldots, b_m)$; then:
   4a) If $m \neq n$, quit—no match is possible;
   4b) If $m = n$, but $f \neq g$, quit—no match is possible;
   4c) If $m = n$ and $f = g$, then proceed as follows:
       4c.1) Apply the θ built up thus far to a_1 and to b_1, yielding c_1 and d_1, respectively; now try to match c_1 and d_1;
       4c.2) If step 4c.1 succeeded (was not forced to quit), then apply the θ built up thus far to a_2 and to b_2, yielding c_2 and d_2, respectively; now try to match c_2 and d_2;
       $\cdots$
       4c.m) If step 4c.$(m - 1)$ succeeded (was not forced to quit), then apply the θ built up thus far to a_m and to b_m, yielding c_m and d_m, respectively; now try to match c_m and d_m;
       4c.m + 1) If step 4c.m succeeded (was not forced to quit), you may stop now; the θ built up at this point is a unifier of E_1 and E_2.

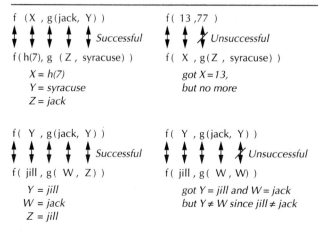

FIGURE 4–20
Some examples of successful and unsuccessful matches.

The problem-solving interpretation of Prolog rules would seem to indicate that we should replace the selected subproblem by the body of the rule, and continue working. However, it is clear that there must be a restriction. For the selected subproblem matches the head of the rule only under the assumptions embodied in the substitution (unifier) θ. One way to enforce the assumptions embodied by the matching unification is to apply it to both the rule and the current goal, like this:

$$\left\{ \text{?-}D_1, D_2, \ldots, D_{i-1}, \overbrace{p(\ b_1, b_2, \ldots, b_n)}, D_{i+1}, \ldots, D_k \right\} \theta$$

$$\left\{ p(a_1, a_2, \ldots, a_n) \text{ :- } C_1, \ldots, C_m \right\} \theta.$$

Substitutions do their work by replacing variables. Moreover, all the variables in each of these expressions lie in one of the parts of the expression. Thus is it clear that another way of writing the same two expressions would be

$$\text{?-}D_1\theta, D_2\theta, \ldots, D_{i-1}\theta, \overbrace{p(\ b_1, b_2, \ldots, b_n)\theta}, D_{i+1}\theta, \ldots, D_k\theta.$$

$$p(a_1, a_2, \ldots, a_n)\theta \text{ :- } C_1\theta, \ldots, C_m\theta.$$

But since the expression $p(a_1, a_2, \ldots, a_n)\theta$ is identical with the expression $p(b_1, b_2, \ldots, b_n)\theta$, the first can replace the second in the current goal, yielding:

$$\text{?-}D_1\theta, D_2\theta, \ldots, D_{i-1}\theta, C_1\theta, \ldots, C_m\theta, D_{i+1}\theta, \ldots, D_k\theta.$$

But this is just the same expression as:

$$\left\{ \text{?-}D_1, D_2, \ldots, D_{i-1}, C_1, \ldots, C_m, D_{i+1}, \ldots, D_k \right\} \theta$$

We can summarize this discussion as follows.
To apply the rule

$$p(a_1, a_2, \ldots, a_n) \text{ :- } C_1, \ldots, C_m.$$

to the goal

$$\text{?-}D_1, D_2, \ldots, D_{i-1}, \overbrace{p(\ b_1, b_2, \ldots, b_n)}, D_{i+1}, \ldots, D_k.$$

proceed as follows:

1 Attempt to compute a matching unifier for

$$p(b_1, b_2, \ldots, b_n) \quad \text{and} \quad p(a_1, a_2, \ldots, a_n).$$

2a If the two expressions cannot be matched, the rule cannot be applied to the goal;

2b If the two expressions match, let θ be the unifier and replace the old goal by

$$\left\{ \overbrace{\text{?-}\mathbf{D_1, D_2, ..., D_{i-1},}}\ \overline{\underline{\mathbf{C_1, ..., C_m,}}}\ \mathbf{D_{i+1}, ..., D_k} \right\}\ \theta$$

There is one final observation we need to make about how Prolog carries out the application of a rule to a goal. Before it begins to try to match the selected subproblem (literal) with the head of the candidate rule, it makes a change in the rule. The problem it is worried about is this: there might be variables in common between the goal and the candidate rule, and these common variables could pose difficulties when attempting the match. Since Prolog sees the rule as completely independent of the goal, it takes the rather cavalier approach of immediately replacing all the variables in the rule by new variables that have not been used yet in the computation. (Since there are infinitely many variables, Prolog has no problem in finding such new variables.) This is called *renaming the variables*. After this replacement, there will be no variables in common between the goal and the rule since all the variables in the new rule have never yet appeared in the computation, so in particular they can't occur in the goal. But is Prolog justified in doing this? Prolog claims to perform logical deductions. Will this renaming mess up these claims? The answer is no, based on the logical interpretations of rules. Recall that the logical interpretation of a rule

head :- *body*

is this:

> *For all values of variables occurring in the rule, if the result of replacing the variables in the body by their values is true, then the result of replacing the variables in the head by their values is also true.*

For example, consider the following compact form of the grandfather rule:

grandfather(GF, K) :- parent(GF, P), parent(P, K), male(GF).

The logical interpretation of this rule is expressed briefly by:

> For all GF, P, and K,
>   **If** parent(GF, P) and parent(P, K) and male(GF) is true,
>   **then** grandfather(GF, K) is true.

The expression "For all GF, P, and K" is called a *universal quantifier* and is said to *bind* the variables occurring in the rule proper. It is clear that the actual names of variables used in such a logical interpretation have no effect on its overall truth or falsity. The example version means exactly the same thing as the following version:

> For all X, Y, and Z,
>   **If** parent(X, Y) and parent(Y, Z) and male(X) is true,
>   **then** grandfather(X, Z) is true.

Thus, it is safe for Prolog to rename the variables in rules. In this effect, the universal quantifier is quite similar to the variable of integration in a calculus integral. Universal quantifiers are also similar to local binding operators in block-structured languages such as C or Pascal. When you define a Pascal procedure or a C procedure, you use parameters in the procedure definition. It doesn't matter what you name them because what the compiler guarantees for you is that at run-time, if you invoke this procedure, the computer will dynamically allocate new storage locations—at that moment—to each of those parameters. You can repeatedly invoke this procedure, and each time you'll get new storage locations for each of those parameters. The successive storage locations have nothing to do with one another. In Prolog the same thing has to happen, only it is a little more subtle because Prolog is just a big syntax game. All we are doing is using a computer to help us organize the problem of writing down long proofs. Our computations are the process of trying to prove something, to prove that the query we've submitted is a logical consequence of the database. That means that each time we pick up one of these universally quantified rules and want to use it, we are really using it in the problem reduction sense. But the variables in that rule were universally quantified, so we have to guarantee fresh instances of the variables each and every time we use the rule, just as a Pascal compiler or a C compiler does. That means that every time the grandfather rule is used, what the system really does is give you a new instance of all the variables. Such renaming guarantees that the variables of the rule won't tangle with the variables of the goal during the matching process.

If you pursue the consequences of the use of universal quantifiers in the logical interpretation of Prolog rules, it follows that there is nothing in Prolog analogous to the notion of global variables such as occur in most other computer programming languages. *There is no such thing as a global variable in Prolog.*

The scope of a variable is defined to be that part of the program in which the use of that variable is meaningful. In Prolog, the scope of a variable is strictly limited by the quantifiers to be the rule in which the variable occurs. There is no way for one rule to communicate with another through any sort of global variable. The only way for communication between rules to take place is for one rule to invoke the other by calling on the head of the second rule. This is the proper block-structured way for one procedure to communicate with another.

Compare the two definitions of grandfather in Figure 4–21. They look almost the same. The heads are virtually identical, and the last calls of the bodies are the same. But if you look closely at the first two calls in the bodies, the two calls have been interchanged.

The first definition of grandfather can be intuitively described as saying

Starting from the grandfather, find a child of the potential grandfather and then show that the child of the grandfather is a parent of the target child.

The second version, grandfather2, says,

```
grandfather(GrandDad, Kid) :- parent(grandDad, Person),
                              parent(Person, Kid),   male(GrandDad).
grandfather2(GrandDad, Kid) :- parent(Person, Kid),
           parent(GrandDad, Person),    male(GrandDad).
```

FIGURE 4–21
Two definitions of a grandfather.

Starting from the grandchild, find a parent of the grandchild and show that the target grandfather is a parent of that intermediate parent.

Logically there is no difference between the two definitions, However, computationally there is a significant difference in the two definitions. The difference is apparent when we try to find grandfathers of Zeus using each of the definitions, then examine the traces of the computations.

The trace of grandfather, as shown in Figure 4–16, effectively says

If you want to find somebody who is a grandfather of Zeus, youve got to find somebody Z, such that the target grandfather is a parent of that Z.

This leads to a call on parent where both variables are uninstantiated: We don't know the grandfather, and were looking for a child of this unknown grandfather. For Prolog, this is no particular problem, because it just starts working its way through the parent relationship in the database. Since at this point in the computation, there are no constraints on the solutions of the call on parent, Prolog will return the first solution it finds. It happens that the first solution in the database is

parent(uranus,cronus).

Prolog then tries to see if cronus is a parent of zeus. This succeeds, leaving the last subgoal—showing that uranus is male. That fact is present in the database, so Prolog is able to show that uranus is a grandfather of zeus.

After we type a semi-colon, Prolog sets out to find whether there are any other solutions to the original problem. But, as we've discussed earlier, it carries out this reexamination by systematic backtracking. It goes back and tries to redo the last subproblem (subgoal) that it solved, showing that uranus was male. But there is no other way to solve that, so Prolog goes back further and says, "Is there any other way to redo finding a solution to the most recent parent goal that I solved?" That is, "Are there are other ways to show that cronus is a parent of zeus?" The answer is "No," because there is no other information for this problem in the database. Prolog goes back to the most recent goal before that. This is the totally unconstrained problem of finding one person who is a parent of another. The first person is to be the target grandfather that we seek, and the other person is to be the intermediate "stepping-stone" parent. Previously, Prolog used the first solution from the database, which was

parent(uranus,cronus).

It now uses the second solution,

parent(gaea,cronus).

Then it charges forward, having redone the first subgoal. Once more, this leads to the goal

parent(cronus,zeus),

which Prolog solves easily, just as it did before. This leaves the goal of showing that Gaea is male:

> male(gaea).

But this subgoal isn't solvable, so Prolog backtracks from this position, back all the way to the first open-ended parent problem again and finds another solution for it, using the third entry in the database,

> parent(uranus,rhea).

Since the database has entries indicating that rhea is a parent of zeus, and also that uranus is male, we come out with a second way of showing that uranus is a grandfather of zeus.

We hit semi-colon again, and Prolog attempts to find yet another way of solving the original problem. Proceeding by backtracking, Prolog finds that the two most recent subgoals,

> male(uranus)   and   parent(uranus,rhea),

fail on retry since there are no other ways to solve them. We find ourselves with Prolog back to retrying the open-ended call on parent,

> parent(Grandfather, SteppingStone).

Advancing forward in the database, Prolog tries parent(gaea,rhea), then parent(rhea,zeus), etc. But none of the remaining database entries will lead to a solution of the entire goal. Prolog will keep cycling back to the open-ended parent problem, advancing through the entire database (that is, the parent part of the database) until it exhausts all the remaining parent facts. Clearly, Prolog is systematic in its explorations but dumb.

On the other hand, when we use grandfather2 we can solve the same problem of finding a grandfather of zeus, but the details of the computation are somewhat different. The definition of grandfather tries to go from the grandfather to the grandchild by finding an intermediate stepping-stone person. The definition of grandfather2 tries to go from the grandchild to the grandfather via a stepping-stone person. These are logically equivalent but computationally different. We trace the use of grandfather2 in Figure 4–22.

In this case, the first subgoal is a call to find a parent of zeus:

> parent(SteppingStone, zeus).

This is partially specific, or *partially instantiated*. Consequently, as we try to find multiple solutions to the original problem, every time we fail back all the way to this initial subproblem; the call on parent is not an open-ended call anymore. It is only partly open-ended, saying "I'm only interested in parents of zeus." so it doesn't cycle through the entire database of assertions about parent. As the trace shows, it fails very quickly after using the first two solutions.

However, grandfather2 also has its problems. Consider the problem, "Find me a grandchild of uranus:"

> grandfather2(uranus, GrandKid).

The first subcall to parent will be open-ended:

FIGURE 4–22

A trace of ?-grandfather2(Who,zeus).

```
?-trace grandfather2(Who, zeus).
(1)   1 call: grandfather2(_2,zeus) ?
(2)   2 call: parent(_1020,zeus) ?          Partially instantiated call
(2)   2 exit: parent(cronus,zeus)
(3)   2 call: parent(_2,cronus) ?
(3)   2 exit: parent(uranus,cronus)
(4)   2 call: male(uranus) ?
(4)   2 exit: male(uranus)
(1)   1 exit: grandfather2(uranus,zeus)
Who = uranus;                              Found first solution
(4)   2 redo: male(uranus) ?
(4)   2 fail: male(uranus)
(3)   2 redo: parent(_2,cronus) ?
(3)   2 exit: parent(gaea,cronus)
(5)   2 call: male(gaea) ?
(5)   2 fail: male(gaea)
(3)   2 redo: parent(_2,cronus) ?
(3)   2 fail: parent(_2,cronus)
(2)   2 redo: parent(_1020,zeus) ?
(2)   2 exit: parent(rhea,zeus)
(4)   2 call: parent(_2,rhea) ?
(4)   2 exit: parent(uranus,rhea)
(5)   2 call: male(uranus) ?
(5)   2 exit: male(uranus)
(1)   1 exit: grandfather2(uranus,zeus)
Who = uranus;                              Found second solution
(5)   2 redo: male(uranus) ?
(5)   2 fail: male(uranus)
(4)   2 redo: parent(_2,rhea) ?
(4)   2 exit: parent(gaea,rhea)
(6)   2 call: male(gaea) ?
(6)   2 fail: male(gaea)
(4)   2 redo: parent(_2,rhea) ?
(4)   2 fail: parent(_2,rhea)
(2)   2 redo: parent(_1020,zeus) ?         Call is partially instantiated,
(2)   2 fail: parent(_1020,zeus)                so doesn't go through
(1)   1 fail: grandfather2(_2,zeus)            entire database
no
```

parent(SteppingStone, GrandKid).

On the other hand, if we use the original definition of grandfather to find a grandchild of uranus, the first subcall on parent is now partially instantiated:

parent(uranus, SteppingStone).

Thus, the original definition will behave more efficiently for this problem.

The moral of the story is this:

Rules or definitions can exhibit interactions between their computational behavior and the input data used for particular problems.

Of course, that's not a big discovery in computing: One can define procedures whose behavior will be dependent on the exact nature of the input data. Here it suggests that there are alternative ways of defining a relation that are logically equivalent, but whose computational behavior differs. We can't say that one is absolutely better than the other, but rather that one is better for certain purposes than the other. Sometimes you must reason about your programs and their actual behavior in particular situations. You may have to be concerned with how the patterns of the input and output behavior interact relative to the searching through databases.

EXERCISES

4-1 Construct Prolog rules defining the following human kinship relations:

mother	father	son
daughter	child_of	grandmother
grandfather	grandson	granddaughter
grandchild	aunt	uncle
niece	nephew	cousin
second cousin	sibling	

Test your definitions out with George Washington's family database, a database of your own family, and the Greek gods database. Do you notice any anomalies in your definitions, even when you use them with ordinary human family tree databases? Conjecture about the cause of these anomalies, and suggest facilities Prolog should have to cure them.

4-2 Use Prolog rules to define a three-place predicate for use in kinship databases. Call this predicate "relationship." Its first two arguments are intended to be persons from the database, while its third argument is intended to be the name(s) of relationships that hold between the two people. For example, in George Washington's family database, we would have the following:

```
?-relationship('George Washington', 'Lawrence Washington',
               grandfather).
yes.
```

4-3 Using the Greeks database, trace the goals

```
?-grandfather(uranus, GrandKid).
```

and

```
?-grandfather2(uranus, GrandKid).
```

Compare the results in detail.

4-4 Construct a number of additional variations on the definition of grandfather by further changing the order of the subgoals in the body. For example, consider

```
grandfather3(GrandDad, GrandKid) :- male(GrandDad), parent(GrandDad, Intermed),
                                     parent(Intermed, GrandKid).
```

Trace the computations when trying to find a grandfather of zeus as well as a grandchild of uranus, and carefully compare the computational behavior of these new definitions with the traces of the earlier definitions of grandfather (cf. Exercise 4-3).

4-5 Consider the Greek gods family tree. Develop an alternative way to represent the original family tree with a database (Greeks2) of clauses as follows. Instead of choosing *parent, male,* and *female* as the primitive predicates, chose to make *mother* and *father* the primitive predicates. In our original (Greeks) representation, once we had chosen parent, male, and female as the primitives, we were able to define rules that captured father and mother as implicitly defined by the primitive database. In the new Greeks2 database, attempt to define rules that capture parent, male, and female. Do you encounter any difficulties? If so, conjecture the sources of these difficulties and suggest facilities Prolog should have to overcome them.

4-6 Below are simplified versions of four rules from the MYCIN expert system for diagnosing blood infections. Create Prolog rules for each of them.

Rule A
> If: 1) The morphology of the organism is coccus, and
>   2) The stain of the organism is unknown,

Then: There is evidence that the stain of the organism is Grampos.

Rule B
> If: 1) The morphology of the organism is rod, and
>   2) The stain of the organism is unknown,

Then: There is evidence that the stain of the organism is Gramneg.

Rule C
> If: 1) The stain of the organism is Grampos, and
>   2) The morphology of the organism is unknown,

Then: There is evidence that the morphology of the organism is coccus.

Rule D
> If: 1) The stain of the organism is Gramneg, and
>   2) The morphology of the organism is unknown,

Then: There is evidence that the morphology of the organism is rod.

4-7 Consider the game of tic-tac-toe. For terminology, define a *slice* to be either a row, a column, or a diagonal:

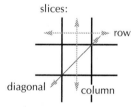

slices:

a Devise a representation for the tic-tac-toe board using compound terms.

b Define the relation
two_down(B,S)
which holds if and only if S is a slice of board B that has two squares the same (either X or O) and the third square blank.

c Devise predicates to determine when the game has been won.

4-8 Use compound terms of some sort to represent the various hands of cards in five-card poker. Devise predicates to classify the hands in standard poker fashion. (Variations: use any other card game with hands such as bridge, gin rummy, or hearts, provided there is a reasonable notion of ranking hands.)

4-9 Using the TV trouble-shooting database constructed for Exercise 1-9 (cf. also Exercises 2–9 and 3–8), develop rules that relate a TV problem to both its possible cause and a possible remedy.

4-10 Appendix D contains an extract from the U.S. Internal Revenue Service instruction booklets describing the rules determining who must file an income tax return. In Exercise 1–13, you developed a database using a four-argument predicate. For the following, you may choose to use this database, or to reorganize it using predicate(s) of different arities.

Analyze the IRS filing rules and produce a collection of predicates that can be used to define the unary predicate

must_file(Person)

which holds if and only if Person must file an income tax return. You will need to make simple arithmetic comparisons in these definitions. Arithmetic is treated in detail in section 7.7. For this problem, it will suffice to know that arthmetic comparisons can be made with the following operators:

Expression 1	$<$	Expression 2	less than
Expression 1	$>$	Expression 2	greater than
Expression 1	$=:=$	Expression 2	equal
Expression 1	$=\backslash=$	Expression2	not equal
Expression 1	$=<$	Expression 2	less than or equal
Expression 1	$>=$	Expression 2	greater than or equal

Thus, to require that Income is at least \$4,950, one would use

Income $>=$ 4950.

4-11 The IRS allows taxpayers to deduct the costs of moving under certain circumstances. A simplified version of their rules follow. Analyze them and develop a definition for a predicate

may_deduct_moving(Person)

that holds if and only if Person may deduct moving expenses under the IRS rules. The rules are

- **Who May Deduct.** If you moved to a different home because of a change in the location of your job, you may be able to deduct your moving expenses. You may qualify for a deduction whether you are self-employed or an employee. However, you must meet certain tests explained below.
- **Distance Test.** Your new workplace must be at least 35 miles farther from your old home than your old workplace was . . . If you did not have an old workplace, your new workplace must be at least 35 miles from your old home . . .
- **Time Test.** If you are an employee, you must work full time for at least 39 weeks during the 12 months right after you move. If you are self-employed, you must work full time for at least 39 weeks during the first 12 months and a total of at least 78 weeks during the 24 months right after you move . . .
- **Exceptions to the Distance and Time Tests.** You do not have to meet the time test in case of death, if your job ends because of disability, if you are transferred for your employer's benefit, or if you are laid off or discharged for a reason other than willful misconduct . . .

CHAPTER 5

RECURSION ON PREDICATES

5.1 THE ANCESTOR PROBLEM

Consider the problem of writing a definition of the ancestor relationship. Imagine working with George Washington's family database (Figure 4–8), where our primitive predicate is the relationship of parenthood. Given that we have parenthood available, how can we define ancestor? It is certainly the case that

> *A is an ancestor of D* **if**
>   *A is a parent of D*. (5.1)

This describes the simplest instance of what it is to be an ancestor.

    Another way that we can see that A is an ancestor of D is

> *A is an ancestor of D* **if**
>   **there is** *a parent P of D (the descendant)* (5.2)
>   **such that** *A is an ancestor of P.*

That is, we find a *stepping-stone* person, P, who is a parent of the proposed descendant and who is such that the proposed ancestor is an ancestor of P. The sketches in Figure 5–1 illustrate several uses of rules (5.1) and (5.2) to establish an ancestor relationship.

    A definition presented in the style of (5.1) and (5.2) is called a *recursive definition* of a relation. What is distinctive about such definitions is that they appear to be circular. In (5.2), it looks as though we are defining ancestor in terms of itself—and indeed, we are. But there is a subtlety that makes such a definition logically sound. For the moment, let us think about the definition from the procedural point of view. Rule (5.1) tells us how to establish certain instances of the ancestor relation by using the parent relation. Given that we already have the parent relation available, this is certainly acceptable. On the other hand, rule (5.2) tells us how to establish *certain* instances

FIGURE 5–1
Determining ancestors.

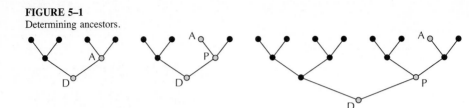

(a) Rule (5.1)   (b) Rule (5.2)   (c) Rule (5.2)

of the ancestor relation in terms of some *other* instances of the ancestor relation. If we can show that these other instances of ancestor could always be established *before* the certain instances we are presently trying to establish, the apparent circularity of the definition will disappear.

The sketches in Figure 5–1 suggest how we can do this. In such an ancestor tree, it is intuitively the case that A is an ancestor of D if there is a path traveling upward from D to A. In tree (*a*), the path consists of one link. In tree (*b*), the path consists of two links, while in (*c*), it consists of three links. In trees (*b*) and (*c*), the intermediate node P lies on the same path from D to A. However, in tree (*b*), the path from D to A has two links, while the path from P to A has only one link. In tree (*c*), the path from D to A has three links, while the path from P to A has only two links. In each case, the path from P to A is shorter than the path from D to A. We will see that the recursive definition (5.1) and (5.2) attempts to establish the ancestor relationship between a pair D and A by finding a path upward from D to A. In rule (5.2), when we define

A is an ancestor of D

in terms of

A is an ancestor of P

we could interpret this as

There is a path upward from D to A **if**
   there is *a parent P of D*   (5.3)
   such that *there is a path upward from P to A.*

But P is also required to be a parent of D, so that P will be above D in the tree. Thus, any path from P to A *must* be shorter than any path from D to A. Consequently, the ancestor relationship between P and D can be established *before* the ancestor relationship between D and A, so it will be available to us when we set out to establish the ancestor relationship between D and A. Loosely put, (5.2) can be phrased as

   Any ancestor A of a parent P of D is also an ancestor of D.   (5.4)

The rule (5.1) is called the *basis case* of the recursive definition. It allows us to establish the basic cases of the ancestor relationship without reference to any other instances of the ancestor relation. The rule (5.2) is called the *recursive case* of the definition.

The rules (5.5) and (5.6) are straightforward Prolog statements of the English versions (5.1) and (5.2) of the ancestor rules.

ancestor(A, D) :- parent(A, D).   (5.5)

ancestor(A, D) :- parent(P, D), ancestor(A, P).   (5.6)

The first clause (5.5) is called the *basis clause* of the procedure. The second clause (5.6) is called the *recursive clause,* or *recursive rule,* of the procedure. Thus, the ancestor procedure is defined in terms of itself, recursively.

This is a sound definition. If we set out to determine whether any A and D are in the ancestor relation using the recursive clause, what we're doing is trying to step up from the descendant D to a parent P and then ask the same question about two people, P and A, between whom the chain is potentially shorter. At each step of the recursion, as we apply that recursive rule, the distance between the proposed descendant and the proposed ancestor gets shorter and shorter, until sooner or later, either the first rule will apply (yielding success), or we reach the top of the tree and can no longer apply the second rule. For example, we can ask whether or not Uranus is an ancestor of Apollo. The computation is shown in Figure 5–2.

```
?-ancestor(uranus, apollo).
      Try (5.5)
?-parent(uranus, apollo).
      Fail; backtrack and try (5.6)
?-parent(P1, apollo), ancestor(uranus, P1).
      1st goal succeeds: P1 = zeus
?-ancestor(uranus, zeus).
      Try (5.5)
?-parent(uranus, zeus).
      Fail; backtrack and try (5.6)
?-parent(P2,zeus), ancestor(uranus, P2).
      1st goal succeeds: P2 = rhea
?-ancestor(uranus, rhea).
      Try (5.5)
?-parent(uranus, rhea).
      1st goal succeeds
?- .
      Success!
```

FIGURE 5–2
Establishing that Uranus is an ancestor of Apollo.

Let's follow the computation through, rewriting the goals according to the procedure used by Prolog. We start with the first goal,

?-ancestor(uranus, apollo).   (5.7)

The first thing Prolog will do is to try to use the first rule (5.5) for ancestor because its head matches this goal: it can match A → uranus and D → apollo. Prolog will rewrite the original goal into the simple goal:

?-parent(uranus, apollo).   (5.8)

But when it checks the database, it will be unable to satisfy (5.8). Thus, Prolog will fail the subsidiary goal (5.8) and will backtrack, seeking an alternative way to solve goal (5.7). Since the head of the second rule (5.6) also matches the original simple goal, Prolog will set out to use (5.6), rewriting (5.7) into (5.9), where A1, D1, and P1 indicate the new variables renaming the original variables of the rule:

?-ancestor(uranus, apollo).   (5.7)
ancestor(A1, D1) : - parent(P1, D1), ancestor(A1, P1) —renamed rule (5.6)
?- parent(P1, apollo), ancestor(uranus, P1).   (5.9)

The match between the head of the renamed rule (5.6) and the selected subproblem was

A1 → uranus   *and*   D1 → apollo.

Note that during the head matching, the variable P1 in the body of (5.6) didn't get a value. It will have to be instantiated during later steps of the computation.

We now face the problem (5.9) of finding some P1 that is a parent of apollo and then showing that uranus is an ancestor of that P1. Focusing on the first subgoal of finding a P1 that is a parent of apollo, Prolog finds the matching fact

parent(zeus, apollo).

Note that when this fact is matched against parent(P1, apollo), the variable P1 is instantiated to zeus when the matching unifier is applied. Since the same unifier is applied to the entire current goal, the other occurrence of P1 is also replaced by zeus, yielding the new goal

?-ancestor(uranus, zeus).   (5.10)

Thus, we have reduced the original problem ancestor(uranus, apollo) to the problem of showing ancestor(uranus, zeus). (Of course, we expect Prolog to solve this, since we long ago learned that Uranus is the grandfather of Zeus.) Once more, the head of the first ancestor rule (5.5) matches the current goal, yielding the new goal

?-parent(uranus, zeus)   (5.11)

But since there is no entry in the database corresponding to this Prolog will fail this goal and backtrack, once again looking for alternative ways to solve (5.10). Since the second ancestor rule is a likely candidate, Prolog creates a brand-new renamed version of the rule and sets out again to match the head with the current subproblem, of course succeeding:

?-ancestor(uranus, zeus). (5.11a)

   ancestor(A2, D2) :- parent(P2,D2), ancestor(A2, P2). —renamed rule (5.6)

?-parent(P2, zeus), ancestor(uranus, P2). (5.12)

We now face the problem of finding a P2 that is a parent of zeus (and such that uranus is an ancestor of P2). Going to the database again, we find the fact

   parent(cronus, zeus). (5.13)

Matching this with the selected subproblem causes P2 to match cronus, so the resulting new goal is

   ?-ancestor(uranus, cronus). (5.14)

Once more (perhaps wearily), we attempt to use the first ancestor rule, transforming the goal into:

   ?-parent(uranus, cronus). (5.15)

But, lo and behold! Finally, this fact is recorded in the database, so the last step reduces (5.15) to the empty goal, and the computation succeeds.

We will encounter many examples of exactly this order: recursive definitions based on a relation such as parent. The definition of ancestor we gave earlier is a recursive definition based on the basic parent connection relationship. Parent is available as a primitive single-link connection between people. We define ancestor relative to this as saying, in essence,

> *Count an arbitrary number of links of parenthood from the particular starting person; if you can find an arbitrarily long chain connecting the two people, then they are in the ancestor relationship.*

There are many instances of such clean and simple recursions in the application of Prolog: Recursive definition is a fundamental tool of the Prolog programmer.

5.2   PATH FINDING IN GRAPHS

Many applications of artificial intelligence, as well as general computer science, directly or indirectly involve the notion of a *graph*. For example, the graph in Figure 5–3 illustrates the routes of a fictitious regional airline.

Any graph is made up of *nodes*; (also called vertices) and *edges*. In Figure 5–3, the nodes are the large black dots corresponding to cities, while the edges are the lines connecting the nodes. In addition, the nodes of Figure 5–3 are *labeled*, in this case with the names of cities. Sometimes the edges of a graph are also labeled, as in Figure 5–4, in which the edges of the graph in Figure 5–3 have been labeled with flight numbers.

Figures 5–3 and 5–4 are examples of *undirected graphs*. By this we mean that none of the edges carry any sense of direction: It is possible to travel in either direction along an edge. In contrast, some graphs are *directed graphs*. In these graphs, each edge carries a definite sense of direction, and one can only travel along an edge in

FIGURE 5–3
Regional airline routes graph.

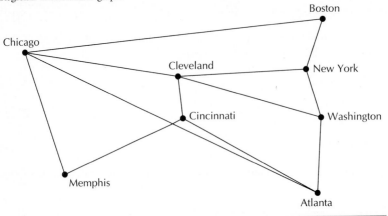

the direction assigned to that edge. When one presents a two-dimensional picture of a directed graph, the edges are drawn with arrowheads indicating the sense of direction. Figure 5–5 is an example of a directed graph that portrays the so-called nitrogen cycle, which traces the chemical pathways of nitrogen in the terrestrial environment.

Intuitively, most of us would agree that the examples in Figures 5–3 through 5–5 are *connected* graphs, in the sense of the nodes all "hanging together." However, there are applications of graphs in which it is important to consider graphs that are *disconnected*. Figure 5–6 illustrates a disconnected graph. Clearly, it is not possible to get from Tucson to Atlanta by flying only on the fictitious airline whose flight graph is presented in Figure 5–6.

This raises a simple, yet common, question: Given nodes A and B in a graph G, is it possible to get from A to B by traveling along the edges of the graph G? If

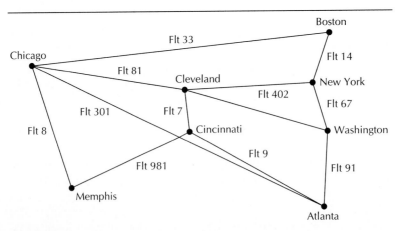

FIGURE 5–4
An airline flight graph with labeled edges.

FIGURE 5–5
A directed graph representing the nitrogen cycle.

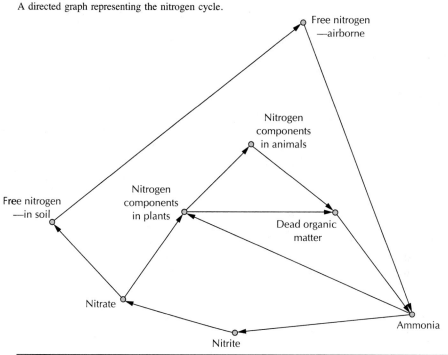

the answer is yes, we say that there is a *path* from A to B in G. Thus, there is no path from Tucson to Atlanta in the graph of Figure 5–6. If G is a directed graph, it is understood that the path must follow the indicated direction along each edge.

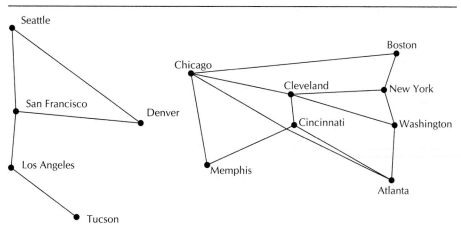

FIGURE 5–6
An airline flight graph that is disconnected.

FIGURE 5–7

A directed graph in which some nodes cannot be reached from others.

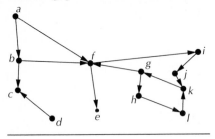

In Figure 5–7, there is no path from *a* to *d*. Also, there is no path from *j* to *a*, while on the other hand, there is a path from *a* to *j*. Let's call this question the *path-finding problem*.

Quite often, an application problem can be viewed as the problem of determining whether or not a path exists between two specific nodes in a certain graph. So it is of interest to develop useful methods for dealing with graphs in Prolog. There are many methods for representing graphs in Prolog, but they divide into two fundamental groups. The first represents a graph by means of a collection of assertions in the database, while the second represents a graph by means of a (complex) compound term. We will study the first method in this chapter, leaving the second method for Chapter 6.

Let's start with the graph in Figure 5–7. It is very natural to represent the nodes of the graph by the atoms labeling the nodes; then we can represent the edges by means of assertions. Lets use the binary predicate *edge* for this purpose. The directed edge from *b* to *f* can be represented by the assertion

    edge(b, f).

Since we are working in a directed graph, we interpret such assertions as saying that there is an edge *from* its first argument *to* its second argument. Thus, the graph of Figure 5–5 can be represented by the collection of assertions in Figure 5–8.

The facts making up *edge* in Figure 5–8 represent the graph in Figure 5–7 in a manner quite similar to the way that the facts making up *parent* in Figure 4–8 represented George Washington's family tree. This shouldn't be too surprising, since every tree is clearly a graph. However, it is also clear that traveling a path between two nodes in a graph is quite similar to tracing from a person to an ancestor in a family tree. We can use this observation to guide us in developing a recursive predicate that

---

edge(a, b). edge(f, i). edge(h, l).
edge(b, c). edge(f, e). edge(l, k).
edge(d, c). edge(g, f). edge(j, k).
edge(a, f). edge(g, h). edge(i, j).
edge(b, f). edge(k, g).

FIGURE 5–8

A prolog database representing Figure 5–5.

can solve path-finding problems. We broke the problem of determining whether the ancestor relation holds into two parts:

- A is an ancestor of B if
    A is a parent of B
- A is an ancestor of B if
    there is a C
    such that A is a parent of C and
    C is an ancestor of B.

Given a graph G with nodes A and B, we can attack the problem of finding a path from A to B in a manner directly analogous to the solution to the ancestor problem:

- There is a path from A to B if
    there is an edge from A to B.
- There is a path from A to B if   (5.16)
    there is a node C
    such that there is an edge from A to C and
    there is a path from C to B.

This approach to path-finding uses the same stepping-stone approach that was used to solve the problem of finding ancestors: Either A is directly linked to B or there is an intermediate node C, the stepping stone, that is directly linked to A and such that there is a path from C to B. We can express this with the following Prolog clauses:

path(A, B) :- edge(A, B).   (5.17)
path(A, B) :- edge(A, C), path(C, B).   (5.18)

Figure 5–9 shows how this predicate answers the problem of finding a path from *a* to *j* in the graph of Figure 5–7.

On the other hand, both the problem

?-path(j, a).

and

?-path(a, d).

will fail. It is instructive to follow the detailed traces of Prologs attempts to solve these goals. Figure 5–10 shows a compressed version of such a trace.

Examination of this trace shows that the attempt to search out a path is caught in a never-ending loop:

j, k, g, f, k, j, k, g, f, k, j, k, g, f, k, j, k, g, f, k, . . .

In fact, if you submit the goal **?-path(j,a)** to Prolog, it will eventually quit, complaining that it has exhausted an internal computational space called the *stack space*. Once again, we see that Prolog is sometimes rather dumb: Prolog itself has no way of knowing it is in such a loop. However, we will see in Chapter 6 how to organize our path-finding programs so that they will be able to recognize and avoid such loops. For the present, we will explore some other aspects of graphs.

FIGURE 5–9
A compressed trace of the action of *path*.

```
?-path(a,j).
?-edge(a,f), path(f, j).
?-path(f, j).
?-edge(f, i), path(i, j).
?-path(i, j).
?-edge(i, j).
```

Underlying any undirected graph, one can always imagine a number of different directed graphs. For example, the directed graph in Figure 5–7 can be thought of as underlying the undirected graph in Figure 5–11.

One can think of the edges in Figure 5–11 being obtained from the edges in Figure 5–7 by erasing the arrowheads. Note that some directed graphs will have arrows in each direction between two nodes. When the arrowheads are erased to obtain the corresponding undirected graph, any extra undirected edges must be erased. Figure 5–12 illustrates this situation. Conversely, of course, any undirected graph can

```
?-trace path(j,a).
(1) 1 call: path(j,a)?
(3) 2 exit: edge(j,k)
(4) 2 call: path(k,a)?
(6) 3 exit: edge(k,g)
(7) 3 call: path(g,a)?
(9) 4 exit: edge(g,f)
(10) 4 call: path(f,a)?
(12) 5 exit: edge(f,i)
(13) 5 call: path(i,a)?
(15) 6 exit: edge(i,j)
(16) 6 call: path(j,a)?
(18) 7 exit: edge(j,k)
(19) 7 call; path(k,a)?
(21) 8 exit; edge(k,g)
(22) 8 call; path(g,a)?
(24) 9 exit; edge(g,f)
(25) 9 call; path(f,a)?
(27) 10 exit; edge(f,i)
(28) 10 call; path(i,a)?
(30) 11 exit; edge(i,j)
(31) 11 call; path(j,a)?
(33) 12 exit; edge(j,k)
(34) 12 call; path(k,a)?
(36) 13 exit; edge(k,g)
(37) 13 call; path(g,a)?
(39) 14 exit; edge(g,f)
(40) 14 call; path(f,a)?
(42) 15 exit; edge(f,i)
(43) 15 call; path(i,a)?
(45) 16 exit; edge(i,j)
(46) 16 call; path(j,a)?
```
FIGURE 5–10
Tracing a looping path.

FIGURE 5–11
A undirected version of Figure 5–7.

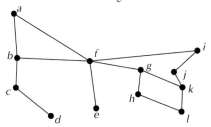

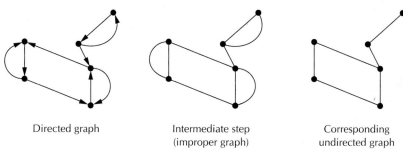

Directed graph

Intermediate step
(improper graph)

Corresponding
undirected graph

FIGURE 5–12
Undirected graphs corresponding to directed graphs.

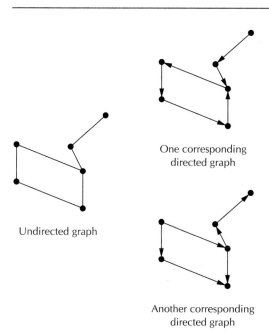

One corresponding
directed graph

Undirected graph

Another corresponding
directed graph

FIGURE 5–13
Two directed graphs corresponding to an undirected graph.

FIGURE 5–14
Directed and undirected graphs with databases.

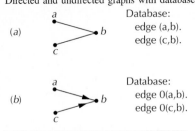

Database:

    edge (a,b).
    edge (c,b).

Database:

    edge 0(a,b).
    edge 0(c,b).

be turned into a directed graph simply by assigning a sense of direction to to each edge, as suggested by Figure 5–13.

Many graphs used in applications are often undirected, such as travel or communication links, relationships (e.g., married), etc. Unfortunately, our earlier approach to path-finding encounters some problems in handling undirected graphs. Consider the very simple graph in Figure 5–14. Visual inspection shows that a path from *a* to *c* exists. However, consider using the path-finding rules (5.17) and (5.18) together with the database from Figure 5–14(a). A simple trace of the attempt to search for this path is shown in Figure 5–15.

Even though there clearly is a path from *a* to *c,* in Figure 5–14(a), Prolog can't find it using the simple database and path-finding program. The difficulty is that edge(b,c) is needed, but the database only contains edge(c,b). One cure would be to add the rule

    edge(X, Y) :- edge(Y, X).

But then we get the behavior traced in Figure 5–16.

This is the simplest sort of cycle, bouncing back and forth between the same two points. One approach to curing this problem is to make use of one of the directed

```
?-trace path(a,c).
(1) 1 call: path(a,c) ?
(2) 2 call: edge(a,c) ?
(2) 2 fail: edge(a,c)
(1) 1 redo: path(a,c) ?
(3) 2 call: edge(a,_1032) ?
(3) 2 exit: edge(a,b)
(4) 2 call: path(b,c) ?
(5) 3 call: edge(b,c) ?
(5) 3 fail: edge(b,c)
(4) 2 redo: path(b,c) ?
(6) 3 call: edge(b,_1382) ?
(6) 3 fail: edge(b,_1382)
(4) 2 fail: path(b,c)
(3) 2 redo: edge(a,_1032) ?
(3) 2 fail: edge(a,_1032)
(1) 1 fail: path(a,c)
no.
```

— intuitively, should succeed here, but the database doesn't exactly match this fact

FIGURE 5–15
Failing to find a path.

FIGURE 5–16
Failing to find a path, again.

```
?-trace path(a,c).
(1) 1 call: path(a,c) ?
(2) 2 call: edge(a,c) ?
(3) 3 call: edge(c,a) ?
(4) 4 call: edge(a,c) ?
(5) 5 call: edge(c,a) ?
(6) 6 call: edge(a,c) ?
(7) 7 call: edge(c,a) ?
(8) 8 call: edge(a,c) ?
(9) 9 call: edge(c,a) ?
       ...  etc......
```

graphs that underlies the undirected graph in which we are searching for a path, for example, as illustrated in Figure 5–14(b). Let edge0 represent the edges of one such (fixed) underlying directed graph, then we can represent the edges of the directed graph by

edge(X, Y) :- edge0(X, Y).

edge(X, Y) :- edge0(Y, X).

In essence, this says that an undirected edge connects X and Y if there is a directed edge from X to Y or from Y to X. Using this approach, we obtain the behavior traced in Figure 5–17.

```
?- trace path(a,c).
(1)  1 call: path(a,c) ?
(2)  2 call: edge(a,c) ?
(3)  3 call: edge0(a,c) ?
(3)  3 fail: edge0(a,c)
(2)  2 redo: edge(a,c) ?
(4)  3 call: edge0(c,a) ?
(4)  3 fail: edge0(c,a)
(2)  2 fail: edge(a,c)
(1)  1 redo: path(a,c) ?
(5)  2 call: edge(a,_228) ?
(6)  3 call: edge0(a,_228) ?
(6)  3 exit: edge0(a,b)
(5)  2 exit: edge(a,b)
(7)  2 call: path(b,c) ?
(8)  3 call: edge(b,c) ?
(9)  4 call: edge0(b,c) ?
(9)  4 fail: edge0(b,c)
(8)  3 redo: edge(b,c) ?
(10) 4 call: edge0(c,b) ?
(10) 4 exit: edge0(c,b)
(8)  3 exit: edge(b,c)
(7)  2 exit: path(b,c)
(1)  1 exit: path(a,c)
yes
```

FIGURE 5–17
Avoiding cycling when searching for a path.

5.3.   REPRESENTING SYSTEMS WITH STATE

A *system* is almost any complex object imaginable, from mechanical and electronic devices to collections of people and things in space and time. Almost by definition, systems can assume different states. The states of a system are generally determined by the properties or states of its components. Thus, for example, the states of a computer are determined by the states of such components as memory, cpu, disks, etc. The states of a collection of people are determined by the states (positions, motions, internal states) of the individual people. As a simple example, consider the following variation on the classic *missionaries and cannibals* puzzle. This version is called the *Russian farmer* puzzle.

> A Russian farmer is on his way to market, taking a goat and a huge cabbage to sell. As in all Russian fairy tales, there is a wolf following the farmer, hoping for a quick meal. At length, the farmer arrives at a river with no bridge, but finds a small boat by the shore. The boat is so small that the farmer can only squeeze himself and one passenger in at a time. (The cabbage really is huge.) Moreover, the farmer has grown accustomed to the wolf's company, so he wants to take the wolf across too. However, because the boat is so small, the farmer has a problem. If he leaves the wolf alone with the goat, the wolf will eat the goat. If he leaves the goat alone with the cabbage, the goat will eat the cabbage. However, the wolf abhors cabbage, so the wolf could be safely left alone with the cabbage. The problem is, can the farmer get all of the travelers safely across the river?

Assuming the river runs east to west and the farmer is traveling from north to south, Figure 5–18 illustrates the puzzle.

From the point of view of the puzzle, the states of this system are determined simply by the location of the players: which side of the river (north, south) they are on, or whether they are in the boat crossing the river. Thus, the state of the system could be represented by using a small table whose columns correspond to the players and whose entries are north, south, or boat, as in Figure 5–19.

Note that as far as this particular puzzle is concerned, there is no essential difference between the states in which the farmer is in the boat and those in which he is on shore,

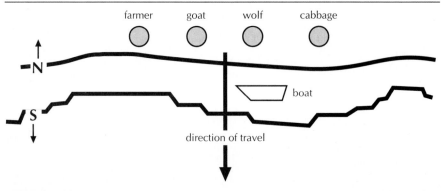

FIGURE 5–18
The Russian farmer puzzle.

FIGURE 5–19

A representation of the Russian Farmer puzzle states.

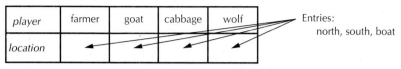

player	farmer	goat	cabbage	wolf
location				

Entries:
  north, south, boat

since once he is in the boat, some combination of the rest of the players is left alone, independent of whether he is in the boat or on the opposite shore. Thus, we really need to record only those states in which each player is on one shore or the other, as illustrated in Figure 5–20.

This approach provides a basic method of representing the states of the Russian farmer system. As the sample lines of the table in Figure 5–20 suggest, each line of the table will correspond to a possible state of the system. Note that in more complex problems, the relationship between the possible states according to the representation (e.g., lines of our table) and actual states of the system (e.g., actual configurations of the players in the Russian farmer problem) may be more complex, and that in particular, there may be possible states according to the representation that do not correspond to actually realizable system states. In such problems, it will be important to specify precise rules relating the representation to the system, and delineating the realizable states.

As noted, each line of our table does indeed correspond to a possible configuration of the farmer, goat, cabbage and wolf. However, although each configuration is possible, the puzzle asks a more precise question: Can the configuration corresponding to the second line of the table (south, south, south, south) be reached from the configuration corresponding to the first line of the table (north, north, north, north) by changes corresponding to use of the small boat with the farmer rowing? So the puzzle concerns

player	farmer	goat	cabbage	wolf
location				
state1	north	north	north	north
state2	south	south	south	south
state3	north	north	north	south
state4	south	north	south	north
state5	south	south	north	north
etc				

Entries:
  north, south

FIGURE 5–20

A simpler representation of the Russian Farmer puzzle states.

FIGURE 5–21
An acceptable state transition.

farmer	goat	cabbage	wolf		farmer	goat	cabbage	wolf
north	north	north	north	→	south	south	north	north

not only individual states of the system but also the allowable transitions or changes between system states. The allowable state transitions are those that correspond to the farmer's use of the boat but that do not lead to any of the players being eaten. Thus, for example, starting from the original configuration of all players on the north shore of the river, the farmer can row the goat across the river since both goat and farmer can fit in the boat, and the wolf and cabbage can be left alone on the same side of the river since the wolf abhors cabbage. This would correspond to the transition between rows of the table shown in Figure 5–21. This corresponds to moving from *state1* in Figure 5–20 to *state5*. If we fix the columns corresponding to the various players, the transition can be more compactly represented as

state(north, north, north, north) → state(south, south, north, north).

The allowable transitions of our system can be compactly represented by a directed graph in which the nodes correspond to system states and the directed edges correspond to allowable state transitions, as shown in Figure 5–22, where for compactness, we have used "n" for north and "s" for south.

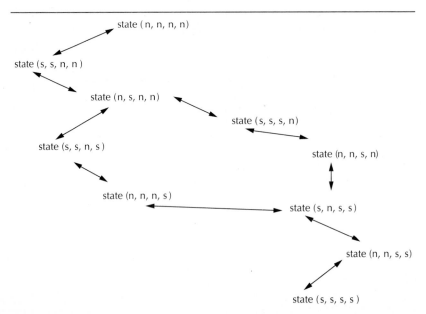

FIGURE 5–22
State transition graph for the Russian farmer puzzle.

Each edge in this graph is marked as a double arrow, since each state transition of this particular system is immediately reversible. This may not be the case for other problems.

This graphical representation of the state transitions of the system suggests that the solution of the puzzle corresponds to the path-finding problem considered in the previous section. That is, the question as to whether there is a sequence of legal state transitions leading from state(n, n, n, n) to state(s, s, s, s) corresponds exactly to the problem of finding a path in the state transition graph from node state(n, n, n, n) to node state(s, s, s, s). Consequently, we can adapt our Prolog path-finding program to finding a solution of this puzzle. If we adapt it as directly as possible, we would need to construct a database of assertions of the form

```
edge(state(n, n, n, n), state(s, s, n, n) ).
edge(state(s, s, n, n), state(n, n, n, n) ).
edge(state(s, s, n, n), state(n, s, n, n) ).
        etc.
```

However, since we ought to use predicate names that intuitively suggest the nature of the problem, we might use *transition* instead of *edge:*

```
transition(state(n, n, n, n), state(s, s, n, n) ).
transition(state(s, s, n, n), state(n, n, n, n) ).
transition(state(s, s, n, n), state(n, s, n, n) ).
        etc.
```

We would also modify the path-finding program:

```
path(A, B) :- transition(A, B).

path(A, B) :- transition(A, C), path(C, B).
```

While this is all quite sound, it does seem a bit silly, since this approach requires us to figure out all the allowable state transitions *by hand* as we construct the database! It would be much more attractive if we could reorganize the program so that it not only searched for a path of transitions between the desired start and stop states, but also implicitly calculated the allowable state transitions as it proceeded. How can we achieve this? Our earlier approach explicitly listed all of the allowable state transitions in the database defining the graph. It would seem that we could achieve the desired goal if we replaced the definition of transition used above (the explicit listing) by a definition using rules. Intuitively, such a rule should be of the form

The transition from state A to state B is allowable provided that . . .

For example, one such rule would be

The transition from state(F0,G0,C0,W0) to state(F1,G1,C1,W1) is allowable provided that the following conditions hold:
- F1 is opposite to F0;
- F0 = G0 and F1 = G1;
- C0 = C1 and W0 = W1.

This rule describes those transitions in which the farmer moves the goat from one side of the river to the other. It clearly has a direct Prolog form:

```
transition(state(F0,G0,C0,W0), state(F1,G1,C1,W1) )
    :-
    opposite(F0,  F1),
    F0 = G0,   F1 = G1,
    C0 = C1,   W0 = W1.
```

Of course, we must define *opposite*, which is done simply:

opposite(n, s).
opposite(s, n).

Here are the rest of the necessary rules:

The transition from state(F0,G0,C0,W0) to state(F1,G1,C1,W1) is allowable provided that the following conditions hold:
- F1 is opposite to F0;
- F0 = W0 and F1 = W1;
- G0 = G1 and C0 = C1;
- G0 is opposite to C0, and G1 is opposite to C1.

```
/* Farmer crosses with cabbage */
transition(state(F0,G0,C0,W0), state(F1,G1,C1,W1) )
    :-
    opposite(F0,  F1),
    F0 = C0, F1 = C1,
    G0 = G1,   W0 = W1,
    opposite(G0, W0), opposite(G1, W1).
```

The transition from state(F0,G0,C0,W0) to state(F1,G1,C1,W1) is allowable provided that the following conditions hold:
- F1 is opposite to F0;
- F0 = W0 and F1 = W1;
- G0 = G1 and C0 = C1;
- G0 is opposite to C0, and G1 is opposite to C1.

```
/* Farmer crosses with wolf */
transition(state(F0,G0,C0,W0), state(F1,G1,C1,W1) )
    :-
    opposite(F0,  F1),
    F0 = W0, F1 = W1,
    G0 = G1,   C0 = C1,
    opposite(G0, C0), opposite(G1, C1).
```

The transition from state(F0,G0,C0,W0) to state(F1,G1,C1,W1) is allowable provided that the following conditions hold:
- F1 is opposite to F0;
- G0 = G1 and C0 = C1 and W0 = W1;

- G0 is opposite to W0, and G1 is opposite to W1;
- G0 is opposite to C0, and G1 is opposite to C1.

```
/* Farmer crosses alone */
transition(state(F0,G0,C0,W0), state(F1,G1,C1,W1) )
    :-
    opposite(F0,  F1),
    G0 = G1,  C0 = C1,  W0 = W1,
    opposite(G0, C0), opposite(G1, C1),
    opposite(G0, W0), opposite(G1, W1).
```

We can simplify each of the rules by utilizing the equality statements involved. The resulting definition for transition will then appear

```
/* Farmer crosses with goat */
transition(state(F0,F0,C,W), state(F1,F1,C,W) )
    :-
    opposite(F0,  F1).
```

```
/* Farmer crosses with cabbage */
transition(state(F0,G,F0,W), state(F1,G,F1,W) )
    :-
    opposite(F0,F1),

    opposite(G, W).
```

```
/* Farmer crosses with wolf */
transition(state(F0,G,C,F0), state(F1,G,C,F1) )
    :-
    opposite(F0,  F1),

    opposite(G, C).
```

```
/* Farmer crosses alone */
transition(state(F0,G,C,W), state(F1,G,C,W) )
    :-
    opposite(F0,  F1),
    opposite(G, C),
    opposite(G, W).
```

Unfortunately, if we trace the use of this program for solving the puzzle, we observe the same sort of looping behavior we observed in our basic path-finding program. Figure 5–23 shows the trace.

Fortunately, the method for avoiding path-finding loops to be developed in Chapter 6 will also work for this program.

Before proceeding to Chapter 6, let us consider another puzzle problem and develop representation techniques for it. This puzzle is sometimes called the *eight-puzzle* or the *nine-puzzle*. The puzzle consists of a 9×9 grid on which eight tiles, numbered 1 through 8, can be placed, as illustrated in Figure 5–24.

The tiles can slide vertically and horizontally. Since only one tile can occupy a grid square, it is clear that the allowable moves are those that move a tile onto the single adjacent empty square. Typically, one is presented with a random starting

FIGURE 5–23
Looping in the Russian farmer program.

```
?-trace path(state(n,n,n,n),state(s,s,s,s)).
(1) 1 call: path(state(n,n,n,n),state(s,s,s,s)) ?
(2) 2 call: transition(state(n,n,n,n),state(s,s,s,s)) ?
(2) 2 fail: transition(state(n,n,n,n),state(s,s,s,s))
(1) 1 redo: path(state(n,n,n,n),state(s,s,s,s)) ?
(3) 2 call: transition(state(n,n,n,n),_182) ?
(4) 3 call: opposite(n,_302) ?
(4) 3 exit: opposite(n,s)
(3) 2 exit: transition(state(n,n,n,n),state(s,s,n,n))
(5) 2 call: path(state(s,s,n,n),state(s,s,s,s)) ?
(6) 3 call: transition(state(s,s,n,n),state(s,s,s,s)) ?
(6) 3 fail: transition(state(s,s,n,n),state(s,s,s,s))
(5) 2 redo: path(state(s,s,n,n),state(s,s,s,s)) ?
(7) 3 call: transition(state(s,s,n,n),_744) ?
(8) 4 call: opposite(s,_864) ?
(8) 4 exit: opposite(s,n)
(7) 3 exit: transition(state(s,s,n,n),state(n,n,n,n))
(9) 3 call: path(state(n,n,n,n),state(s,s,s,s)) ?
(10) 4 call: transition(state(n,n,n,n),state(s,s,s,s)) ?
(10) 4 fail: transition(state(n,n,n,n),state(s,s,s,s))
(9) 3 redo: path(state(n,n,n,n),state(s,s,s,s)) ?
(11) 4 call: transition(state(n,n,n,n),_1306) ?
(12) 5 call: opposite(n,_1426) ?
(12) 5 exit: opposite(n,s)
(11) 4 exit: transition(state(n,n,n,n),state(s,s,n,n))
(13) 4 call: path(state(s,s,n,n),state(s,s,s,s)) ?
(14) 5 call: transition(state(s,s,n,n),state(s,s,s,s)) ?
(14) 5 fail: transition(state(s,s,n,n),state(s,s,s,s))
(13) 4 redo: path(state(s,s,n,n),state(s,s,s,s)) ?
(15) 5 call: transition(state(s,s,n,n),_1868) ?
(16) 6 call: opposite(s,_1988) ?
(16) 6 exit: opposite(s,n)
(15) 5 exit: transition(state(s,s,n,n),state(n,n,n,n))
(17) 5 call: path(state(n,n,n,n),state(s,s,s,s)) ? a
```

configuration. The goal is to arrive at the standard solution configuration seen in Figure 5–25.

To develop a representation, let us consider two methods of providing coordinates for the grid squares, as shown in Figure 5–26.

We can specify a particular configuration by specifying which tile is on which square. If we think reasonably abstractly, we can see that this is a symmetric problem: Either we specify which tile is on which square (keeping the squares fixed, as in the normal physical setting) or we can specify which square is on which tile (being rather abstract in this case). Figures 5–27 and 5–28 suggest several approaches.

In Figures 5–27 and 5–28, we have suggested several options: First, the alternative between viewing the squares as fixed, with the tiles moving or vice versa. In each figure, the first two representations take the squares as fixed (as is physically the usual case) and allow the tiles to be moved among the squares. The difference between

FIGURE 5–24
A typical configuration of the eight puzzle.

FIGURE 5–25
Standard eight puzzle solution.

the first and second representations is simply that in the second, we use the 0 tile to represent the empty space. In each figure, the third and fourth representations take the tiles as fixed and allow the squares to move among the tiles. The difference between the third and fourth representations is that the fourth utilizes the 0 tile, while the third does not. Finally, the difference between the two figures lies in which style of grid coordinates is used. Figure 5–27 uses the sequential numbering of grid cells, while Figure 5–28 uses pairs of numbers as is standard in cartesian coordinates.

These figures suggest that at least eight possible representations may be used in writing a program to solve the eight puzzle. These map rather directly onto Prolog terms. For example, the second representation of Figure 5–27 corresponds to a nine-place Prolog term *squares*. The configuration shown in the figure would correspond to the term

squares(8,1,3,2,4,0,7,5,6).

Similarly, the third representation of Figure 5–28 might correspond to the term

tiles(s(1,2), s(2,1), s(1,3), s(2,2), s(3,2), s(3,3), s(3,1), s(1,1)).

Such configurations are the states of the eight puzzle. The moves of the eight puzzle are the acceptable state transitions. Thus, the primary effort remaining to encode the eight puzzle is to develop a complete set of rules specifying the legal moves. The exact form of the rules will ,of course, depend on the particular state of representation you choose. In general, they will be of one of the two forms

1	2	3		1		1,2	
4	5	6		2			2,3
7	8	9		3			

FIGURE 5–26
Two types of grid coordinates for the eight-puzzle.

FIGURE 5–27
Four ways of matching squares and tiles.

Squares:	2	4	3	5	8	9	7	1
Tiles:	1	2	3	4	5	6	7	8

Squares:	6	2	4	3	5	8	9	7	1
Tiles:	0	1	2	3	4	5	6	7	8

move(squares(ST1,ST2,ST3,ST4,ST5,ST6,ST7,ST8,ST9),
squares(FT1,FT2,FT3,FT4,FT5,FT6,FT7,FT8,FT9))
:-
<conditions>.

or

move(tiles(s(X1,Y1),s(X2,Y2),s(X3,Y3),...,s(X8,Y8)),
tiles(s(U1,V1), s(U2,V2), s(U3,V3), ...,s(U8, V8)))
:-
<conditions>.

EXERCISES

5-1 Consider the ecological database developed for Exercise 1-5. Using this database, define
the notion that one organism depends on another in the sense that a decline in the population
of the second organism would ultimately cause a decline in the population of the first.

5-2 Consider the enzyme database developed for Exercise 1-12. Define the notion that one
component (item acted upon) leads to (leads_to/2) another in the sense that several steps
of enzymatic chemical action may be necessary. Similarly, define the notion that an enzyme

FIGURE 5–28
Four more ways of matching squares and tiles

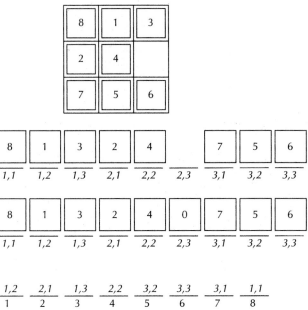

Tiles:	8	1	3	2	4		7	5	6
Squares:	1,1	1,2	1,3	2,1	2,2	2,3	3,1	3,2	3,3

Tiles:	8	1	3	2	4	0	7	5	6
Squares:	1,1	1,2	1,3	2,1	2,2	2,3	3,1	3,2	3,3

Squares:	1,2	2,1	1,3	2,2	3,2	3,3	3,1	1,1
Tiles:	1	2	3	4	5	6	7	8

Squares:	2,3	1,2	2,1	1,3	2,2	3,2	3,3	3,1	1,1
Tiles:	0	1	2	3	4	5	6	7	8

E may affect (affects/2) a compound C in the sense that E is involved in a chemical interaction with a compound D, which leads to C.

5-3 Assume that the nodes of the graph in Figure 5–7 may be colored either red or blue.

a Modify the database of Figure 5–7 so that it will indicate the color of the node.

b Modify the path-finding program of (5.17) so that it selects only the paths consisting of red nodes.

c Modify the path-finding program of (5.17) so that the paths selected consist of alternating color nodes. (Consider an extra argument to "path" that is used to "remember" the color of the previous node.)

5-4 In contrast to Exercise 5-3, assume the edges of the graph in Figure 5–7 can be colored either red or blue.

a Modify the database of Figure 5–7 so that it will indicate the colors of the edges.

b Modify the path-finding program of (5.17) so that it selects only paths all of whose edges are blue.

5-5 Combine the work done in Exercises 5-3 and 5-4 to produce a path-finding program that selects paths consisting of red nodes and blue edges.

5-6 Develop a state representation for the simple monkey and banana problem. A monkey and a box are in a room where a bunch of bananas is hanging from the ceiling. If the monkey carries the box under the bananas and climbs on the box, he can reach the bananas. Moreover, the monkey wants the bananas.

5-7 Project planning and management is a complex activity in a wide range of industries, including construction and software development. Consider the table in Figure 5–29, which describes the principal components of a project to develop the software for a product stock control system for a manufacturing company.
  a Create a graph representing this information.
  b Develop a database to represent this information. Use three predicates: activity_name/2, precedes/2, and duration/2.
  c Define a predicate depends_on/2 such that
      depends_on(Activity_1, Activity_2)
    holds if and only if Activity_1 must be finished before Activity_2 can be started. Note that this is like ancestor/2.

5-8 A simple computer consists of an accumulator (acc) and some unspecified number of registers, reg 1, reg2, etc. The instructions it obeys are specified as follows. Let R be a register, and let expressions such as "acc" or "reg 3" be understood to refer to their contents:

plus R	—	acc: = acc + reg R
subtract R	—	acc: = acc − reg R
load R	—	acc: = reg R
store R	—	reg R: = acc

  a Devise a compound term that has two parts: one part is one of the machine instructions and the other part represents the contents of the accumulator after execution of the instruction (obviously in terms of parameters that represent contents of various things before execution).
  b Using **a**, write clauses representing the preconditions under which the terms of part **a** can be understood as making a correct assertion about the machine state.

5-9 a Consider the simple circuit discussed in Section 1.2. Using the predicates and_Table/3 and or_Table/3, use one clause to define the predicate circuit/5 specified as follows, where the values of A–H are the atoms "on" or "off":

  circuit(A,B,C,D,E,H) holds if and only if
      when the inputs **a–d** of the circuit of Figure 1–2 are given input A–D, respectively, the output **h** produces value H.

  b Consider arbitrary circuits made up of and-gates and or-gates, as in Section 1.2. Assume that the topology of such circuits is specified in the style presented in Figure 1–6. Define the predicate precedes/2, which is specified as follows:

FIGURE 5–29

Activity	Immediate predecessors	Duration (weeks)
A. Design stock control model	—	4
B. Develop stock control program	A	13
C. Design forecasting model	—	4
D. Develop forecasting program	C	15
E. Collect product data	—	12
F. Design product database	A	4
G. Set up product database	E,F	2
H. Train staff	B,D	2
I. Test system	G,H	2

precedes(G1, G2) holds if and only if
>the output of gate G1 is connected, possibly via intervening gates, to an input of gate G2.

>Note that this will be similar to the definition of ancestor.

5-10 Consider the eight puzzle discussed at the end of this chapter. Use the second form of the squares representation of the state of the puzzle wherein a 0 tile is used to represent the empty square. For each possible position of 0, specifying the legal moves will involve exchanging 0 with the contents of an adjacent square.

a Write the clauses for move/2 for the case in which 0 occupies square 1.

b Write the clauses for move/2 for the case in which 0 occupies square 5.

5-11 Consider the eight puzzle discussed at the end of this chapter. Use the second form of the tiles representation of the state of the puzzle wherein a 0 tile is used to hold the empty square. For each possible square s(X,Y) occupying the 0 tile, specifying the legal moves will involve exchanging the square s(X,Y) occupying the 0 tile with an adjacent square occupying some other tile.

a Write several clauses for move/2 for the case in which s(1,1) occupies the 0 tile.

b Compare these clauses with the clauses written for part **a** of Exercise 5–10 with regard to conceptual clarity.

5-12 Using the TV schematic database developed in Exercise 1-8, define a predicate connected/2 that holds between two sections if and only if there is a path lead from the first argument to the second. Does this predicate ever loop? Could it loop for another schematic?

5-13 Using the clouds databases developed in Exercises 1-10 and 1-11, define a predicate higher_than/2 that holds if and only if its first argument is a kind of cloud that occurs at a higher level than the type of cloud in the second argument.

5-14 The diagram in Figure 5–30 presents a more complete version of the Nitrogen cycle than the one presented in Figure 5–5.

a Create a database encoding all of the information in this figure.

b Develop a predicate that traces paths in this graph.

5-15 The diagram in Figure 5–31 presents a schematic design for an industrial chemical process plant.

a Create a database encoding all of the information in this diagram.

b Develop a predicate that traces paths in this graph.

FIGURE 5–30
The nitrogen cycle. (From Edward J. Kormondy, *Concepts of Ecology*, 3d ed., © 1984, p. 59. Reprinted
by permission of Prentice Hall, Inc., Englewood Cliffs, NJ.

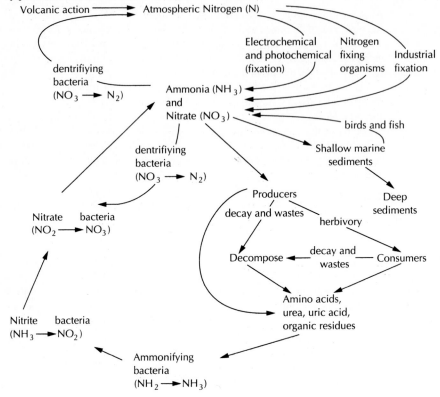

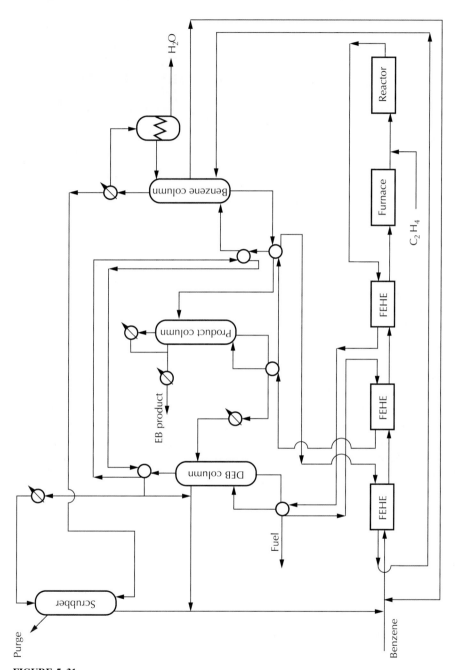

FIGURE 5–31
Energy-integrated ethylbenzene process. (After J. M. Douglas *Conceptual Design of Chemical Processes*, McGraw-Hill, New York, 1988, p. 19.)

CHAPTER 6

RECURSION ON TERMS

6.1 ELEMENTARY LIST PROCESSING

In Chapter 5, we studied recursion based on predicates. There, recursive predicates were binary relations defined in terms of certain other more primitive relations. This sort of recursion is best thought of as iteration of the process of walking along links between entities, the links being provided by the basic primitive relations. In this chapter, we will study another type of recursion: one based on the notion of compound term.

So far, we have largely used either constants or variables as the arguments for Prolog predicates. However, Prolog also allows *compound terms* as arguments to predicates, including lists as a special case. Syntactically, compound terms look just like literals. They consist of a *functor* applied to arguments, as described in Chapter 1. Thus,

    date(12, october, 1981)
    course(dept (cis), number(661))

are both acceptable examples of compound terms. As the second example indicates, compound terms can appear as arguments to other compound terms, as can constants and variables. The nesting of compound terms within other compound terms can be arbitrarily deep. It is this nesting that provides the basis for the sort of recursion we will study in this chapter.

A compound term that involves much subsidiary nesting is certainly more complex than another term involving little such nesting. Let's try to make this idea precise by developing some sort of measure of complexity of terms. One possible approach would be to count the total number of primitive symbols occurring in the term. While this can be done, there is another approach that turns out to be more useful. In this latter approach, what is significant is not the absolute number of primitive symbols, but rather the extent of the nesting. Here again, two approaches are possible. Given a term **t**, we can

- Count the total number of occurrences within **t** of the nesting of any term inside another (including **t** itself);
- Determine the maximal depth of *towers* of terms nested within one another inside **t**.

Figure 6–1 illustrates these two ideas.

As the left term in the figure illustrates, the two approaches can produce quite different results. It turns out that the *depth of nesting* (or *height of tower*) approach is the most useful for our purposes. Here is one way of making the idea precise: To define the *nesting depth* (or simply, *depth*) of a term **t**, proceed as follows:

- If **t** is a constant or variable, the *depth* of **t** is 0;
- If **t** is of the form $f(a_1, \ldots a_n)$, then the *depth* of **t** is 1 plus the maximum of $s \ldots, s_n$, where for $i = 1, \ldots n$, s_i is the *depth* of a_i.

The table in Figure 6–2 provides some examples.

In Prolog, *lists* are simply certain compound terms: No special machinery has to be added to Prolog to handle them. However, if they are written in normal compound term notation, they become somewhat clumsy to read and write. So most Prolog systems allow them to be written with their own specialized notation, as shown in Figure 6–3.

The first list consists of the elements a, b, and c, the second list is the empty list, and the third is the list with *head* H and *tail* T: H is the called first element of the list and T is the sublist consisting of everything following the first element. The fourth list begins with the elements a and b, followed by the tail T. We will return to the question on writing lists in the ordinary compound term notation later. However, it will turn out that the nesting depth of a list is closely related to its intuitive length, so we will begin our study of recursion with terms with lists, since most of us are quite familiar with the idea.

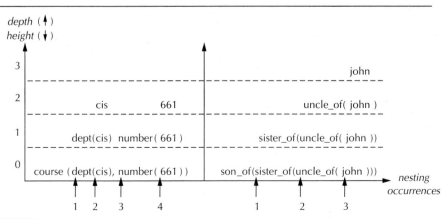

FIGURE 6–1
Term nesting complexity.

FIGURE 6–2

Example nesting depths of terms.

Term	Depth
f(g(h(i(j(k(l(m)))))))	7
q(r(s),t(u),v(w),x(y(z)))	3
keybd_of(wk_stn_on(st(at,id(56)),lan(ether,id_3)))	4

   Predicates that process lists provide excellent examples of the manner in which Prolog provides for recursive definitions over terms. Just as in the last chapter, such recursive definitions give the appearance of defining a predicate in terms of itself. However, as before, these definitions are not circular, as we shall see. Consider a predicate for determining whether or not a given item is a member of a list. We can analyze it as follows:

> *An Item is a member of a List if either the Item is the first element of the List or it is a member of the tail of the list (the part after the first element).*

We can reflect this analysis with the following Prolog rules:

   member(Item, [Item | Tail]).   (6.1)
   member(Item, [Anything | Tail])
      :-   (6.2)
      member(Item, Tail).

We can read these rules procedurally:

> *In order to show that an Item is a member of a List, show that the Item is identical with the head of the list (by using a list pattern) or show that it is a member of the tail of the list (again, making use of a list pattern).*

The second rule is not circular, since the problem

   member(Item, Tail)

in its body involves a list (Tail) that is shorter than the corresponding list in the problem expressed in the head. The rule reduces the problem in its head to the simpler one in its body. Figure 6–4 traces the execution of a goal concerning *member*.
   Another very interesting relation on lists is the length relation. While we have not yet studied Prolog's approach to arithmetic, we can anticipate it just enough to provide what we need for the definition of the length of a list. If N is a number and X is a variable, the subproblem

   X is N+1

   [a,b,c]   [ ]   [H | T]   [a,b | T]

FIGURE 6–3
Examples of lists.

FIGURE 6–4

Executing a goal concerning the member relation.

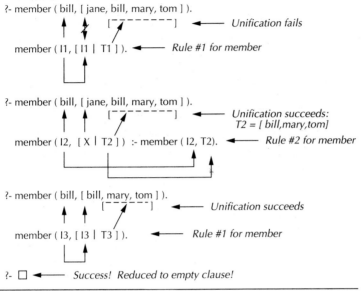

causes X to be bound to the value of N plus 1. With this in hand, let us analyze the length relation:

The length of the empty list is 0.
The length of any nonempty list is the length of its tail plus 1.

This is reflected in the following two Prolog rules:

length([ ] , 0).

length([Head | Tail], M) :- length(Tail, N), M is N + 1.   (6.3)

Figure 6–5 is a sample goal involving length.

Finally, we will consider one of the well-worn examples from list processing. We will define the three-place relation

append(List1, List2, Result).

Intuitively, Result is obtained by sticking List2 on the right end of List1. For example, both of the following are true:

append([a, b] , [c, d, e] , [a, b, c, d, e]),

append ([], [a, b, c, d, e, f] , [a, b, c, d, e, f]).

We can analyze this problem as follows:

- If List1 is empty, the work is trivial: Result is just List2, since sticking List2 on the end of the empty list will leave just List2.

FIGURE 6–5

Finding the length of a list.

?- length ([a, b, c], W).

⟍ ⟵ *Unification fails*

length ([ ] , 0). ⟵ *Rule #1 for length*

?- length ([a, b, c], W).

W = M1   *Rule #2 for length*

length ([H1 | T1], M1) :- length (T1, N1), M1 is N1 + 1.

?- length ([b, c], N1), W is N1 + 1.

⟍ ⟵ *Unification fails*

length ([ ] , 0). ⟵ *Rule #1 for length*

?- length ([b, c], N1), W is N1 + 1.

N1 = M2   *Rule #2 for length*

length ([H2 | T2], M2) :- length (T2, N2), M2 is N2 + 1.

?- length ([c] , N2), N1 is N2 + 1, W is N1 + 1.

⟍ ⟵ *Unification fails*

length ([ ] , 0). ⟵ *Rule #1 for length*

?- length ([c] , N2), N1 is N2 + 1, W is N1 + 1.

N2 = M3   *Rule #2 for length*

length ([H3 | T3], M3) :- length (T3, N3), M3 is N3 + 1.

?- length ([ ] , N3), N2 is N3 + 1, N1 is N2 + 1, W is N1 + 1.

↑ ↑ ⟵ *Unification succeeds: N3 = 0*

length ([ ] , 0). ⟵ *Rule #1 for length*

?- N2 is 0 + 1, N1 is N2 + 1, W is N1 + 1.

?- N1 is 1 + 1, W is N1 + 1.

?- W is 2 + 1.

W = 3

- On the other hand, suppose List1 has at least one item, so that List1 is of the form [Head | Tail] (though Tail might be the empty list if List1 had just one element). In this case, we reduce the problem to a simpler one as follows: pop the Head off of List1 (using the list pattern), execute the simpler problem of sticking List2 on the Tail of List1, and then paste the Head of List1 back on the front of this Result_Tail (again using a list pattern).

The rules (6.4) and (6.5) provide a Prolog expression of this analysis.

append([], List2, List2).   (6.4)

append([Head | Tail], List2,[Head | Result_Tail])   (6.5)

:-

append(Tail, List2, Result_Tail).

Here is a goal involving append:

```
?-append([a,b,45],[c,7,e], Result).
Result = [ a, b, 45, c, 7, e ]
```

However, Prolog sees such definitions as logical relations and normally does not accord any special role to any of the arguments. Although we intuitively thought of the first two arguments of append as *inputs* and the third as *output*, Prolog doesn't think in these terms. Instead, no matter what arguments it is given, it tries to solve the problem by proving the relation true using the facts and rules it has been given. For example, we could invoke it with the first and third arguments given (instantiated), and Prolog will calculate the required second argument:

```
?-append([a, b], List2, [a, b, c, d, e]).
List2 = [ c, d, e]
```

We can even submit an append goal with only the third argument instantiated, thereby obtaining all the possible ways of decomposing that third argument:

```
?-append( List1, List2, [a, b, c]).
List1 = []          List2 = [a,b,c] ;
List1 = [a]         List2 = [b,c] ;
List1 = [a,b]       List2 = [c] ;
List1 = [a,b,c]     List2 = [] ;
no.
```

There is a fundamental sense in which everything one needs for list processing is available to us in Prolog with no special provisions being necessary. If we don't want to use any nice, humanly-readable syntax, we can define a notion of list and carry out list processing on the basis of the pure Prolog machinery we have developed previously. Let us give an indication of how this would work because it is fairly important to realize that no special facilities for doing list processing must be added to Prolog. Keep in mind the way we really deal with lists in almost any programming language, be it LISP, Pascal, or C, etc. Consider the list consisting of the numbers 6,4, and 9. One organizes the data structures for this list in a way that is best pictured with little boxes or cells. The cells are split in half, with the list elements 6, 4, and 9 in the left halves of the boxes. In the right halves of the boxes, one stores pointers from one box to the next, as shown in Figure 6–6.

The pointer to the very first box is regarded as being the desired list. The second (lower) picture is just an abbreviation of the first. In almost any approach to list processing, including LISP, if you look inside, these are the sorts of data structures you really find. This suggests that lists are composed using a primitive pairing operation (called *cons* for constructor) together with a primitive null entity, often written *nil*, which is also used to represent the empty list. We can think of the final right hand entry as being a pointer to the empty list in effect saying,"I've hit the end." Let us

FIGURE 6–6
The box representation of lists.

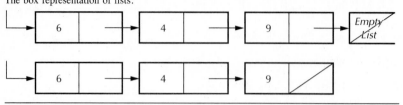

write "c" with two arguments to indicate the result of putting together one of these boxes. For instance, the last box could be symbolically represented as c(3,nil). The letter c represents *constructor* (or, briefly, *cons*). The entire picture of Figure 6–6 could be symbolically represented as in Figure 6–7.

But look at it: The expression in the Figure 6–7 is a Prolog term! Consequently, if we were willing to read horrible-looking things like that, we could directly represent lists by Prolog terms with no modification at all. Figure 6–8 compares the examples from Figure 6–3 with their versions in the present notation.

We have discovered Prolog terms we can use to represent lists. The question is, can we process them? Using this representation, can we write Prolog definitions of the standard list-processing functions, such as appending two lists together, or determining whether something is a member of a list? Let's consider append. This, of course, is a classic list-processing problem: We have two lists A and B, and we want to obtain a list consisting of the elements of A followed by the elements of B, as suggested in Figure 6–9.

As is now usual, to define append in this notation we break it down into a recursive definition. The recursive definition has two cases, depending on whether or not the list A is empty—that is, whether or not A is *nil*. In the first case, the left-hand list is empty: The output should be the elements of the empty list followed by the elements of B. But whatever the right-hand list is, no matter what we try to paste on to the right end of the empty list, when we're done, what we get is just B again. This is the basis case for this recursion. This is implemented by the following Prolog fact:

append (nil, B, B).

Next, the recursion case must say what happens when the left-hand list A is a nonempty list. If A is a nonempty list, it has to have at least one entry, a first element. So the left-hand list must take the form c(H,T), where H is the first element

```
c( 6, c( 4, c( 9, nil))).
```
FIGURE 6–7
A Prolog term representing the cons cell version of a list.

[a,b,c]	[]	[H	T]	[a,b	T]
c(a,c(b,c(c,nil)))	nil	c(H,T)	c(a,c(b,T))

FIGURE 6–8
List terms in "cons" and "sweetened" notation.

FIGURE 6–9
Appending lists in box representation.

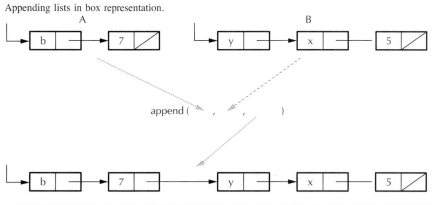

and T is the remainder. We don't know whether T is an empty list or a nonempty list: T is just whatever is there. We are trying to stick some other list onto c(H,T). What does the result look like? Of course it is hard to tell entirely in detail what the result looks like, because we don't know entirely what the input looks like. But we do know what the first element of the left-hand list is — it is H. But if H is the first element of the left-hand list, and we put something (i.e.,B) onto the right end of the left-hand list, the result is going to have the same first element — namely, H. So we can at least say that the result is going to look like c(H,Z), where Z is the rest of the result list following H. What is the relationship between Z, the tail of the result, and T, the tail of the original left-hand input list? If we drop the original H off both the left-hand input list and the result, the tail Z of the result should be the result of appending B to the tail T of the left-hand list. The second clause for append says just that:

    append(c(H, T), B, c(H, Z)) :- append(T, B, Z).

Figure 6–10 illustrates the computation of an append goal in this notation.

Figure 6–11 compares the definitions of append using this cons notation with the standard *sweetened* notation.

```
?-append( c(a,c(b,c(45,nil))), c(d,c(7,c(e,nil))), Result).
Call: append( c(b,c(45,nil)), c(d,c(7,c(e,nil))), Result ).
Call: append( c(45,nil), c(d,c(7,c(e,nil))), Result ).
Call: append( nil, c(d,c7(,c(e,nil))), Result ).
Exit: append( nil, c(d,c(7,c(e,nil))), c(d,c(7,c(e,nil))) ).
Exit: append( c(45,nil), c(d,c(7,c(e,nil))),
                    c(45,c(d,c(7,c(e,nil)))) ).
Exit: append( c(b,c(45,nil)), c(d,c(7,c(e,nil))),
                    c(b,c(45,c(d,c(7,c(e,nil))))) ).
Exit: append( c(a,c(b,c(45,nil))), c(d,c(7,c(e,nil))),
                    c(a,c(b,c(45,c(dc(7,c(e,nil)))))) ).
Result  c(a,c(b,c(45,c(d,c(7,c(e,nil)))))))
```

FIGURE 6–10
Computing append in cons notation.

FIGURE 6–11
Append in two rotations.

```
append( [ ], B, B ).
append( nil, B, B).
append([H | T], B, [H | Z]) :- append(T,B,Z).
append(c(H,T), B, c(H,Z)) :- append(T,B,Z).
```

Finally, let us compare the notion of the length of a list with the notion of its nesting depth. While they are related, they are not the same, as shown in the table of examples in Figure 6–12. As is evident from examination of the cons notations, the length of a list is similar to the nesting depth, *provided we ignore the contribution from the first argument of the cons term.* Both provide a measure of complexity of the terms, in that terms with smaller complexity are definitely simpler in some regard than terms of larger complexity. This is the key ingredient that any measure of complexity must have in order to be useful for recursive definitions. So long as the terms of smaller complexity measure have some aspect that is simpler than the corresponding aspect of the terms of larger complexity measure, we can use the measure to guide recursive definitions, for then the recursive case of the definition is sound: It reduces a computation on a more complex object to a similar computation on a less complex object.

6.2 REVERSING AND SORTING LISTS

Suppose we want to reverse a list L. Once again, a direct recursive definition will do the job. If L is the empty list, there is nothing to it: The reversal of [] is just[]. Otherwise, if L is a list that has a head H and a tail T, just remove the head H, reverse the tail T, and use append to paste the head H at the end of the reversed tail. This can be defined clearly in terms of append, as shown in Figure 6–13.

While this method is certainly clear and correct, it's fairly ineffecient. It does a lot of extra work, because the multiple calls to append start at the beginning of the reversed list being built up and run down to the end each time. A much faster way to reverse a list is to use an algorithm you would use for reversing a stack of plates, as seen in Figure 6–14.

FIGURE 6–12
Lengths and nesting depths of lists compared.

List	Cons Form	Length	Depth
[a,b,c]	c(a,c(b,c(c,nil)))	3	3
[h(k(x(y))),r]	c(h(k(x(y))),c(r,nil))	2	4
[]	nil	0	0
[tom]	c(tom,nil)	1	1
[h(k(x(y))),r,s,t,u]	c(h(k(x(y))),c(r,c(s,c(t,c(t,c(u,nil))))))	5	5

FIGURE 6–13
Definition of naive reverse.

```
naive_reverse([],[]).
naive_reverse([Head | Tail], Result)
    :-
    naive_reverse(Tail, Reversed_Tail),
    append(Reversed_Tail,[ Head ], Result).
```

If we have a stack of plates that we want to reverse, we could of course just turn it upside down. But that would be cheating. What we need to do is to get the plates facing up, in reversed order. Suppose you are at a table. The input stack of plates is on your left and the output stack is at the right end of the table. Between the two piles of plates there is space for a temporary stack. You remove the plates one by one from the input pile, and stack them on the temporary work space. When you have transferred the whole input stack to the temporary stack, you just shove it down to the output stack space—hoping it doesn't slide off the end of the table! Notice that this is a very quick way to work, because if the input stack is N plates deep, you only have to do N simple operations. We can represent that idea very directly in Prolog. This approach is a standard technique, not special to Prolog at all. It is ideal for speeding up many algorithms. It operates by using an extra scratch variable to accumulate work as you go. It is a useful technique that is very common in Prolog programming. What we do to reverse L yielding R is to call a subsidiary predicate that has L and R as arguments, but also has an additional parameter that is going to be used as our scratch space, or as we might call it, our *accumulator*, thus,

reverse(L, R) :- rev0(L, [], R).

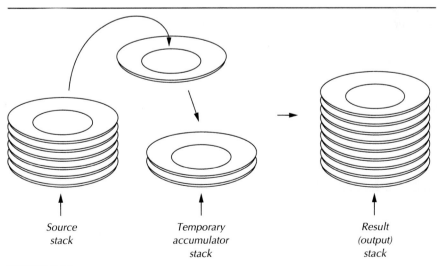

Source
stack

Temporary
accumulator
stack

Result
(output)
stack

FIGURE 6–14
Reversing a stack of plates.

The predicate rev0 will implement the temporary stacking idea. When you start out, your scratch space is empty: in the example, there were no plates in the scratch space, so the accumulator was initially set to the empty list. Typically that's the way one initially invokes the scratch space idea.

Our problem is to work out a definition for rev0. If we've gotten down to the end of the input stack so that there are no more input plates, the output we originally wanted what is now stacked up on the accumulator. In this case we simply say the output is the same as the accumulator, as in the second clause of Figure 6–15.

On the other hand, if there is still something on the original input stack of plates— so our input list is of the form [H|T]—then we can say that the final result R is going to be the same result that you would get if you moved the top plate from the input over to the accumulator, and continue working on the rest of the input, as seen in the third clause in Figure 6–15. Notice that result variable R doesn't change at all in this clause. The only place in this set of rules where R—the output variable—is affected is in the first clause of rev0, where we have reached the bottom of the input stack. Then it is expressly defined to be the same as the accumulator variable. Through the whole recursion, the result variable R is unaffected until the recursion gets down to the basis case, when R is identified with the value in the accumulator. We've used the accumulator to compute what the result is, and we just pass things back out to the user through the result variable R, which has been carried along unchanged. Figure 6–16 shows a trace involving rev0.

At each recursive step, you peel the top element off the input stack and place it on top of the accumulator. We are just taking things off one stack and putting them on another. Thus, we see that lists can be used as stacks by pushing things on the front of the list.

I like to think of Prolog programs such as those for append and reverse as a kind of *programming with pictures*—not icons in the sense of the Apple Macintosh, but by using Prolog terms. We're "drawing pictures" of what we want at various places. In the case of rev0, at the input, we drew a picture of what the input looked like; we showed what the new accumulator looked like at the next step, etc. The general idea of using Prolog terms for drawing pictures of what you get as input at various places, and what you want to get out at other places, is a useful way to approach Prolog programming. It is not an approach that works in all settings, but it works in quite a few.

Thus far in our examples of list processing, the elements of the list have been atoms, either numbers or symbolic constants. But there is nothing in the notion of lists to restrict the elements in this way. Anything that the language can talk about can

---

```
reverse(L, R)
     :- rev0(L, [], R).
rev0([], Accum, Accum).
rev0( [Next | RestInput], Accum, Output)
     :-
     rev0( RestInput, [ Next| Accum], Output).
```

FIGURE 6–15

FIGURE 6–16

```
?-reverse( [a, b, c], R).
?-revᗅ( [a, b, c], [], R).
?-revᗅ( [b, c], [a], R).
?-revᗅ( [c], [b, a], R).
?-revᗅ( [], [c, b, a], R).
R = [c, b, a].
```

be an element of a list. Elements could be compound terms, and they could also be other lists, which are just a special kind of a compound term. In many applications, particularly applications written in LISP, lists whose elements are other lists are used to represent complex structures, conceptual structures of various sorts. Some examples are shown in Figure 6–17.

Sometimes it is of interest to take a list that might have other lists as elements and produce a simple list of all the atomic items occurring in the list, in its elements that are lists, in lists that are elements of lists that are elements, etc. Figure 6–18 shows that we can view such lists as big complicated tree structures.

If you stood up at the top of this tree structure and jumped up and down on it, it would flatten out on the floor. All the intermediate list structure is removed and just the atoms that occurred are left, as Figure 6–18 shows, but there is a sense of left-to-right order that will be preserved. Writing a program to do this is an interesting problem to solve. If we look at the structure as a tree, with atoms as the leaves, we want to traverse that tree in left-to-right order. We want to traverse those leaves in left-to-right order and produce the list of the leaves in the order we encounter them.

The predicate flatten(ComplexList, FlatList) will be one version of doing that. Its intended definition is that the left-hand argument is the structured input list, and its right-hand argument is the flattened version, the list of atoms that occur in the input in the order that one would get by traversing the leaves of the input. Certainly, if the input is the empty list, the output is going to be the empty list—there is nothing to get back if there is nothing put in. Thus, the first clause of the definition of flatten will be

flatten([], []).

On the other hand, if the input is a nonempty list, it has a head H and a tail T. Certainly the tail T is itself a list. The head H might be an atom or it might be one of the lists that was an element of the original. What we have to do is call flatten on the head H: It might be a list. But then we also must guarantee that flatten is prepared

```
[ person(jones, john), person(smith, mary)]
[ [2, 3, [4, [5, 6], 7], 8, [9, [10], 11] ]
person( [tom, smith]).
[person(thomas, mark), [ [boston, mass], [los_angeles, calif]
```

FIGURE 6–17

FIGURE 6–18

Flattening a list.

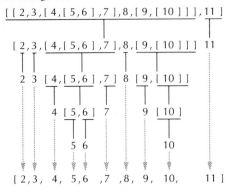

to deal with getting an atomic object in its first argument, so we flatten the head H getting a flat head FlatHead. We also flatten the tail getting a flat tail FlatTail. Thus far, the second clause of flatten will look like this:

```
flatten( [ Head | Tail ], FlatList )
    :-
    flatten( Head, FlatHead ),
    flatten( Tail, FlatTail ),
    ??
```

But look at the order: The head H came before the tail T, so the atoms we get out of H have got to come before the atoms we get out of T, so we simply append FlatTail to FlatHead to get the result FlatList of flattening the whole list, as follows:

```
flatten( [ Head | Tail ], FlatList )
    :-
    flatten( Head, FlatHead ),
    flatten( Tail, FlatTail ),
    append( FlatHead, FlatTail, FlatList).
```

Finally, we need one more clause that deals with the case that the input entity is an atom. The complete definition is shown in Figure 6–19.

Whenever someone has a list in hand, they are often tempted to sort it according to some criteria. We'll consider several instances of sorting lists as done in Prolog. The first is a definition of insertion sort based on the intuitive notion of sorting a hand of playing cards. You have the unsorted cards on the left side of your hand, and in the right end of your hand you build up the sorted collection (see Figure 6–20). You do this by simply going through the unsorted cards in order and putting them in the right place among the sorted cards. At the top level, sort would be defined by a recursion on that unsorted pile. If the unsorted pile is empty, the output is going to

FIGURE 6–19
```
flatten( [], []).
flatten( [ Head | Tail ], FlatList )
:-
    flatten( Head, FlatHead ),
    flatten( Tail, FlatTail ),
    append( FlatHead, FlatTail, FlatList).
flatten( Item, [ Item ] ).
```

FIGURE 6–20
Sorting playing cards.

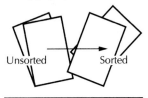

be the empty list too:

insert_sort([], [])

On the other hand, if the unsorted pile is nonempty, the sorted result could be obtained by first sorting the rest of the unsorted input list, then putting that first card in the right place. The model for this kind of sorting is to skip over the first card (the head), produce the sorted result for the tail, and put that first card in the right place. Figure 6–21 represents that model with a Prolog clause.

It is instructive to consider a variant model: Put the first card in its proper place, then recursively put the rest in the right places (Figure 6–22). The small hint here is

```
insert_sort([Head | Tail], Sorted_Result)
    :-
    insert_sort( Tail, Sorted_Tail ),
    insert( Head, Sorted_Tail, Sorted_Result).
```
FIGURE 6–21

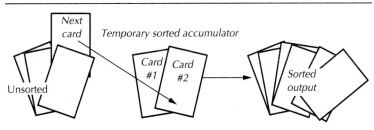

FIGURE 6–22
Insertion sorting cards with an accumulator.

FIGURE 6–23

```
insert_sort2(Unsorted, Sorted_Result)
    :-
    insert_sort3(Unsorted,[], Sorted_Result).

insert_sort3([], Accumulator, Accumulator).

insert_sort3([Head_Unsorted_Tail, Accumlator, Sorted_Result)
    :-
        insert(Head, Accumulator, New_Accumulator),
        insert(Unsorted_Tail, New_Accumulator, Sorted_Result).
```

that it's best to use the accumulator idea from the efficient version of reverse: Use an extra argument that is accumulating the sorted pile, with the third argument outputting the result after you get all the way to the end of the unsorted pile. This model is represented in Figure 6–23.

Figures 6–21 and 6–23 define two models of insertion sort at the top level. To complete them, we have to give you a definition of *insert*. This is a three-argument relation. It takes a card as its first argument: That's the thing to be inserted. The second argument is the current sorted collection into which that card is to be inserted. These are the inputs. The third argument—the output—is the result of carrying out that insertion. As you would suspect, by now, this is going to be organized by a recursion on that middle argument. It is a recursion on that current sorted pile to find the right place to insert the new card, as illustrated in Figure 6–24.

If the current sorted pile is empty, the result of doing that insertion is just the list whose only element is that card:

insert(Item, [], [Item]).

If the pile of previously sorted things is nonempty, there are two cases: the card comes before the first element of the current sorted list, or else after it (assuming no duplicates). In the first case, the thing to be inserted has to go at the front; so the result is going to be the list starting with the item to be inserted, followed by the

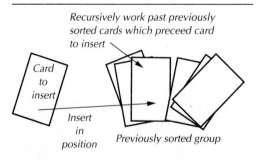

FIGURE 6–24

previously sorted items:

> insert(Item, [Head | Tail], [Item, Head | Tail])
> :-
> comes_before(Item, Head).

Again, this clause draws a picture of the situation. In the remaining case, the card comes after the current head of the sorted list; that is, the head is *before* the thing to be inserted. That means you must insert it somewhere deeper in the list: It will at least go beyond the head. So the result will have the current head as its head, followed by some tail that is the result of inserting the card in the tail of the current sorted pile. That is, skip over the current head and insert the card or number in that tail producing the result tail. Of course, you better keep the current head of the list in place. So again, it's done with pictures:

> insert(Item, [Head | Tail], [Head | Result_Tail])
> :-
> comes_before(Head, Item),
> insert(Item, Tail, Result_Tail).

We've drawn a picture of what the sorted pile looks like and a picture of what the output pile is going to look like. We can't tell where in the tail the card is going to go because we don't have any information about it. But we can state a constraint that expresses the relationship between the result tail, the sorted tail, and the thing to be inserted.

That's a basic insertion sort. Some other models of sorting are considered in the exercises. If you have lots of lists to sort though, or very long lists, it's nice to sort them as fast as possible. The fastest sort around is Hoare's quicksort. It is worthwhile to see how one can sort a list very quickly. But no matter whether your sorting is slow or fast, if you sort the empty list, you will get back the empty list:

> quicksort([], []).

It's at the recursive case that Hoare's quicksort diverges very sharply from what we would normally do if we were sorting cards in our hand. Hoare's quicksort is a divide and conquer approach. It's roughly the sort of notion that you can get work done fast if you can somehow keep dividing the work in half. If the work to be done can roughly be split in half and the two new sub-jobs tackled the same way—the work they have to do can be split in half, and so on—then the depth of the recursion is log base two ($\log_2$) of the input rather than quadratic in the length of the input. That is the basic philosophy under which quicksort is going to operate. The basic problem is finding some notion of splitting in half the work to be done. Hoare's idea is, suppose you have a nonempty list to sort. It must have a head H and a tail T. Use that head H in some way to split the the tail T into two parts—we'll call them T_Left and T_Right. This is where the notion of dividing in half the work to be done occurs. We call it *partition*. Let's not worry just yet about how partition works. All we need to know for the moment is that T_Left and T_Right have the following property: as individual lists, they are not in general sorted—not yet. But they have the property that every number that occurs in T_Left is smaller than every one of the numbers that occurs in

FIGURE 6–25

```
quicksort([H | Tail], Result)
  :-
  partition(Tail, H, T_Left, T_Right),
  quicksort(T_Left, Sorted_Left),
  quicksort(T_Right, Sorted_Right),
  quicksort(T_Right, [H | Sorted_Right], Result).
```

T_Right. As individual lists they may be very jumbled, but they have the property that the numbers in T_Left are less than or equal to the numbers in T_Right. Moreover, the head H is a number right in the middle between the two lists. This is the notion of partitioning. If we can do the partitioning, we can go ahead and quicksort the left list T_Left, getting a Sorted_Left, and quicksort the right list, getting a Sorted_Right, then put them back together with append. This is shown in Figure 6–25.

Finally, we must define *partition*. When we start out with an unsorted input list, everything is a total jumble. However, partition will act to guarantee that the ordering property between the two clumps holds. We have a *wedge* number N in our hands, together with a list L, and we want to split up L into two clumps using the wedge. The left clump numbers are all to be less than or equal to the wedge number, and the right clump numbers are all to be greater than or equal to the wedge number. At the basis case, no matter what wedge number you have in your hand, if you are trying to split up the empty list, you can say right away that the resulting clumps are both empty lists:

partition(Wedge, [], [], []).

This certainly preserves the property that partition has to guarantee, that everything in the left list is less than or equal to everything in the right list, because there are no counter examples to the property. (Try to find a pair of counter-example numbers in the empty list!) The rest of the work lies in the case where the list L to be split is not empty. Again, there are two cases. In the first case, the head H of the list is smaller than or equal to the wedge element, so H is supposed to go into the left-hand list. You can say that the left hand list is going to consist of H followed by some tail. You can't say much about the right-hand list at all, only that there will be one. But we can state that the tail of the left-hand list together with the right-hand list are the result of using the wedge element to partition the tail of L:

partition(Wedge, [H | Input_Tail], [H | Left_Tail], Right)
  :-
  H = < Wedge,
  partition(Wedge, Input_Tail, Left_Tail, Right).

In the other case, H would be put into the right-hand list. Thus, partition is just peeling each element off L, comparing it with the wedge element, and putting it in either the left or right box, accordingly. The complete definition appears in Figure 6–26.

FIGURE 6–26

```
partition(Wedge, [], [], []).
partition(Wedge,[H | Input_Tail], [H | Left_Tail], Right)
    :-
    H =< Wedge,
    partition(Wedge, Input_Tail, Left_Tail, Right ).
partition(Wedge, [H | Input_Tail, Left [H | Right_Tail])
    :-
    Wedge > H,
    partition(Wedge, Input, Left, Right_Tail).
```

If the input list is actually sorted, quicksort is no faster than doing an insertion sort. But in the general case, the expected behavior when the list is randomly ordered is a lot faster because you will get genuine chunks on both sides after splitting, so there is real work to be done on both sides. You split L in half, you split the two chunks in half, etc. There are two recursive calls in the top level of quicksort. However, the two calls are independent. It doesn't matter in what order they appear in the body of the rule.

6.3   ASSOCIATION LISTS

Many applications require components that simulate *associative retrieval*. The simplest form of the problem is as follows. The program makes use of a list of pairs of entities for various purposes. The first element of the pair is regarded as a *key*, while the second is the *value* associated with that key. The program requires two fundamental facilities:

- It must be able to store newly generated *key-value* pairs;
- Given a *key*, the program must be able to retrieve the associated *value*.

Figure 6–27 suggests some possible applications of these tools.

Obviously, the range of possible applications is quite wide. Notice that these examples can be divided into two classes: Those that associate a *unique* value with each key, and those that may associate more than one value with a key. Another way of classifying these examples is to divide them up into *static* and *dynamic* applications. In static applications, associations are set up once and for all (usually when the program starts running), and the program only performs retrievals from the data. In dynamic applications, not only does the program perform associative retrievals, but it also dynamically adds new key-value entries or modifies the values of existing entries.

There are many methods of implementing such associative retrieval facilities. We have already encountered one: use of binary relation facts in Prolog's database. The *relieves* predicate in the Drug database (Figure 1–1), as well as the *parent* predicate in the family tree databases, implement, such key-value associations, as indicated in Figure 6–28.

Let us introduce another technique for managing associative retrieval, this one based on the use of lists. Any collection of key-value pairs can be regarded as a

FIGURE 6–27

Examples of Possible Uses of Associative Retrieval.

Key	Value
Persons/organizations	Phone numbers
Diseases	Causes of the disease or treatments
Diseases	Severity ranking
Diagnoses	Likelihood rankings
Social Security numbers	Persons
Computer CPUs	Appropriate bus
Vitamins	Food sources
Financial transactions	Appropriate contracts
Financial investments	Suitability ranking
Books	Authors
Automobiles	Manufacturers
Leaf/stem/twig types	Associated trees
Program execution steps	Difficulty or priority rankings

list. The entries on the list are pairs: the key-value pairs. The list might be ordered according to either the keys or the values, or it might be unordered. In either case, we must create predicates that enable us to do the following:

- Retrieve values or key-value pairs according to the key; and
- Insert new key-value pairs in the list.

Our first problem is to decide how we shall represent such key-value lists. Obviously, the overall structure is a list. But what structure shall we use to represent the key-value entries? Just as obviously, we can use any structure that has two slots: one for a key and one for a value. Thus, we can make use of Prolog terms with two arguments. Here are some examples:

```
book(bob_kowalski, logic_for_problem_solving)
ssn(mary_smith, 123456789)
likelihood(asthma, 0.45)
suitability( silver_contract, high)
bk(person(kowalski,bob), ['Logic',for,'Problem','Solving'])
ssn(person(smith, mary), 123-45-6789)
[aspirin, pain(moderate) ]
relief(aspirin, symptom(pain, moderate) )
[auto(chevrolet), ['General', 'Motors'] ]
```

FIGURE 6–28

Associative predicates.

Predicate	Key	Value
relieves	Drugs	Symptoms that the drug relieves
parent	Persons	Children
trait	Leaf/twig traits	Hickory trees

The particular choice of structure will depend on the nature of the given application. In particular, the nature of the entries will weigh heavily.

Assume that we have settled on a choice of structures for the entries in the list, and that such a list is available to the program. How can we retrieve items from the list based on their keys? What we need is a three–argument predicate. Lets's call it *lookup*:

> *lookup(List, Key, Value) holds if and only if the key-value pair consisting of Key and Value is entered on List.*

We must provide Prolog rules that logically implement this specification. The secret is to adopt a recursive analysis similar to the approaches in the two preceding sections. First, note that if List is empty, there can be no key-value pairs entered on List. Consequently, our rules must *fail* whenever List is empty. When List is nonempty, there are two cases:

- The key of the first element on the list matches the key being looked up. In this case, extract Value from the first entry on the list;
- The key of the first element on the list does not match the key being looked up. In this case, skip over the first entry and go on looking for Key in the tail of the list.

It is clear that we must have some means of matching a given key against the key of a list entry, and that we must also be able to extract the value portion of a list entry. The details of this will depend on the structures we have chosen for the list entries. For the moment, let's adopt an abstract approach (or top-down approach) and assume that we have such predicates available. That is, assume that we have the following predicates available:

- key_of(Key, Entry) holds if and only if Key is the key of Entry;
- value_of(Value, Entry) holds if and only if Value is the value of Entry.

We can create Prolog rules corresponding to this analysis as follows:

```
lookup ( [ Entry | Tail ], Key, Value)
    :-
    key_of(Key, Entry), value_of(Value, Entry).

lookup( [ Skip | Tail ], Key, Value)
    :-
    lookup( Tail, Key, Value).
```

To examine a concrete example, let's suppose that we are building a financial advisory system. Among the actions the system will perform, one of its prime goals will be to determine the suitability of different kinds of investments for a particular investor. Thus, the form of the association list used for this will be

Key	Value
Financial Investments	Suitability ranking

Perhaps the suitability rankings would be

unsuitable, neutral, low, high,

and the entries on the association list would take the form

suitability(silver_contract, high).

In this case, the definitions of key_of and value_of can be given by simple Prolog facts, as follows:

key_of(suitability(Key, Ignore), Key).

value_of(suitability(Ignore, Value), Value).

With these definitions, we can run the following query:

```
?-SuitList = [suitability(mutual_fund, low),
            suitability(silver_contract, high),
            suitability(hog_belly_contract, high),
            suitability(ibm, unsuitable) ],
lookup(SuitList, hog_belly_contract,  Evaluation).
Evaluation = high
```

As a second example, consider the problem of hickory tree identification. In this case, the association list will have the form:

Key	Value
Leaf/stem/twig types	Associated trees

The entries on the association list might take a form that looks just like the facts we used in the Hickory database:

trait(bud_color(brownish), pecan_hickory)

(Recall that facts without the trailing period are just literals, and that literals are just terms.) The definitions of key_of and value_of will become

key_of(trait(Key, Ignore), Key).
value_of(trait(Ignore, Value), Value).

Finally, suppose that we also have the following assertion in the database:

trait_list([trait(bud_scales(valvate), bitternut_hickory),
            trait(bud_color(yellow), bitternut_hickory),
            trait(bud_scales(valvate), pecan_hickory),
            trait(bud_color(brownish), pecan_hickory),
            trait(bud_scales(imbricate), pignut_hickory),
            trait(terminal_bud_size(short), pignut_hickory),
            trait(bud_scales(imbricate), mockernut_hickory),

```
         trait(terminal_bud_size(large), mockernut_hickory),
         trait(outer_scales(persistent), shellbark_hickory),
         trait(twig_color(orange_brown), shellbark_hickory),
         trait(bud_scales(imbricate), shagbark_hickory),
         trait(terminal_bud_size(large), shagbark_hickory),
         trait(outer_scales(persistent), shagbark_hickory),
         trait(twig_color(reddish_brown), shagbark_hickory) ] ).
```

We can execute the following query:

```
?-trait_list(TL), lookup( terminal_bud_size(large), TL, Tree).
TL = ...
Tree = mockernut_hickory ;
TL = ...
Tree = shagbark_hickory ;
no.
```

Note that, as is typical with Prolog definitions, we can use lookup in ways different from those we originally intended:

```
?-trait_list(TL),  lookup( Trait, TL, shellbark_hickory) .
TL = ...
Trait = bud_scales(imbricate) ;
TL = ...
Trait = terminal_bud_size(large) ;
TL = ...
Trait = outer_scales(persistent) ;
no.
```

We could avoid seeing the value for the trait list in our answers by packaging our queries thus:

```
   hickory(Trait, Tree) :- trait_list(TL), lookup(Trait, TL, Tree).
```

Then:

```
?-hickory(bud_color(Color),  HickoryTree).
Color = yellow
Tree = bitternut_hickory ;
Color = brownish
Tree = pecan_hickory ;
no.
```

We must now work out how we can add new entries to an association list. In general, we must define a predicate *insert* with three arguments, such that

insert(List, Entry, NewList) holds if and only if NewList is the result of (properly) inserting Entry into List.

First, let's consider the simplest case in which the association list is totally unordered. The solution here is quite simple: just put the new entry onto the front of the old list to produce the new list, as the following fact indicates:

insert(List, Entry, [Entry | List]).

Now for something a little harder: Assume that we have a binary predicate precedes, which orders the keys. To maintain the association list with the keys in order, we would proceed as follows:

insert([OldEntry | OldTail], NewEntry, [NewEntry, OldEntry | OldTail])
:-
key_of(NewKey, NewEntry),
key_of(OldKey, OldEntry),
precedes(NewKey, OldKey).

insert([OldEntry | OldTail], NewEntry, [OldEntry | NewTail])
:-
insert(OldTail, NewEntry, NewTail).

insert([ ], NewEntry, [NewEntry]).

A variation on this that avoids repeatedly extracting the new key as it steps down the list would run as follows:

insert(OldList, NewEntry, NewList)
:-
key_of(NewKey, NewEntry),
insert0(OldList, NewKey, NewEntry, NewList).

insert0([OldEntry | OldTail], NewKey, NewEntry,
                              [NewEntry, OldEntry | OldTail])
:-
key_of(OldKey, OldEntry),
precedes(NewKey, OldKey).

insert0([OldEntry | OldTail], NewKey,
              NewEntry, [OldEntry | NewTail])
:-
insert0(OldTail, NewKey, NewEntry, NewTail).

insert0([ ], NewKey, NewEntry, [NewEntry]).

Finally, let us note that when key_of and value_of are defined by simple pattern-matching facts, we can avoid the use of separate accessing predicates of this sort. Instead, we use the patterns contained in the definitions of key_of and value_of directly in the definition(s) of insert, as follows for the Hickory tree example:

insert(OldList, trait(Key, Value), NewList)
:-
insert0(OldList, NewKey, NewValue, NewList).

insert0([trait(OldKey, OldValue) | OldTail], NewKey, NewValue,
      [trait(NewKey, NewValue), trait(OldKey, OldValue) | OldTail])
  :-
   precedes(NewKey, OldKey).

insert0([OldEntry | OldTail], NewKey, NewValue, [OldEntry | NewTail])
  :-
   insert0(OldTail, NewKey, NewValue, NewTail).
insert0([ ], NewKey, NewValue, [trait (NewKey, NewValue)]).

Recall that the definitions for key_of and value_of were

key_of(trait(Key, Ignore), Key).
value_of(trait(Ignore, Value), Value).

Obviously, the same devices can be applied to the definition of lookup. It is worth noting the advantages and disadvantages of using these devices. The advantage is that in most Prolog systems, the definitions that utilize these techniques (essentially moving as much pattern-matching into rule heads as possible) will execute more quickly than the original definitions. This is due to the way in which Prolog systems are implemented, whether they are interpreters or compilers. On the other hand, use of these and other such devices entails the following (often severe) disadvantage for program development and maintenance. When predicates such as key_of and value_of are utilized in defining the higher-level predicates, all of the information concerning the exact nature of the structures in the list is sealed inside the definitions of key_of and value_of. Consequently, if changes must be made (and it is surprising how often they must for real programs), the process of changing the structures on the association list is extremely simple: one only needs to change the definitions of key_of and value_of. On the other hand, if the devices we have just studied are used, when changes to the structure of the association list are required, the effort is often substantial, since information about the structure of the association list is now scattered throughout the code of the program and is not often easy to identify. (Which patterns deal with the association list and which deal with other aspects of the program? What are all the predicates that do things with or to the association list? There may be more predicates beyond just lookup and insert.)

The practice of utilizing such predicates as key_of and value_of is a simple form of the programming notion of abstract data types. Some languages, such as Ada, provide direct language support for the use of abstract data types. Most, like Prolog, do not. However, the nature of Prolog is such that one can have one's cake and eat it too: One can gain all the advantages of abstract data types as a programming discipline (practiced not-quite-religiously by the programmer) and avoid paying the price of slower execution speed of the program. The secret lies in realizing that it is possible to construct program transformers that can convert Prolog programs utilizing an abstract data type discipline to equivalent, but more efficient, Prolog programs in which the patterns expressed in such definitions as key_of and value_of are propagated throughout the appropriate places in the program, just as we did above by hand. When a change to one of the abstract data types is necessary, the original (source) program is modified, and the program transformer is applied again to generate a new, equivalent, and more efficient version of the modified program. What is surprising is that such transformers are not overly difficult to construct using Prolog itself! We will explore such techniques in Part II.

6.4   TREES

The association lists in the previous section are a very useful technique for implementing the idea of associative retrieval. However, if an association list is very long and the key being sought is near the end, it may take a long time to work down the list and retrieve the associated value (or insert a new entry if the list is ordered). Fortunately, there are more sophisticated techniques—related to the ideas underlying the development of the quicksort program in Section 6.2—that we can use to implement more efficient associative retrieval schemes. These techniques are based on the idea of trees.

Trees are familiar to all of us, both the living kind and the abstract kind. For example, we have already extensively used the idea of family trees. Like lists, trees can be created and manipulated as data structures through the use of Prolog terms. Like graphs (see Section 5.2), abstract trees are made up of nodes and links, as suggested in Figure 6–29.

Nodes normally have entries attached to them, while the links in most trees are uniform and have no associated entities. Often, one identifies nodes with their entries. The *root* of a tree is the only node with no ancestors. Nodes that have no descendents are called *leaves*. Trees are often classified according to the number of descendents a node may possess. The tree in Figure 6–29 is called a *binary tree*, since each node can have at most two descendents; *ternary tree* allows each node to have at most three descendents; and so on. Note that a *unary tree*, in which each node has at most one descendent, is just a list: The root is the first element of the list, and the only leaf is the last element of the list. Any node N determines a subtree, called the *subtree rooted at N*, which consists of the node together with all of its descendents, as shown in Figure 6–30.

Since there are many, many varieties of trees utilized in programs, Prolog does not provide any special notation for trees. Instead, we simply use structured terms that

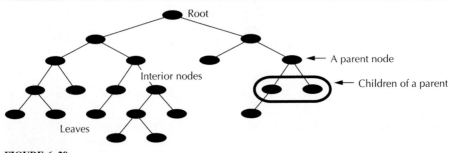

FIGURE 6–29
A binary tree.

FIGURE 6–30
A subtree rooted at a node.

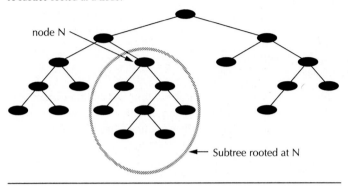

node N

Subtree rooted at N

provide a quite adequate picture of the situation. We will consider binary trees for the purposes of exposition, but everything we will develop can easily be modified to deal with other classes of trees. The subtree rooted at a node N breaks naturally into two parts: the portion hanging off the left side of N and the portion hanging off the right side of N. Together with the label L of N, these completely determine the subtree. This suggests that one way to represent trees is to follow the pattern developed for lists and recursively build up representations of trees. Thus, we could represent binary trees by terms of the form

tr(Left, Label, Right)

where Left and Right are (smaller) terms representing trees, and Label is an appropriate term serving as a label in this particular tree. Note that Label could itself be a complex structured term, including a list. Since leaf nodes have no descendents, it is clear that we will also need to employ the notion of an *empty tree*. We will use *nil* to represent the empty tree. Then, under these conventions, the following Prolog term would represent the simple tree with atomic labels shown in Figure 6–31:

tr(tr(tr(nil, n4, nil), n2, nil), n1, tr(nil, n3, nil)))

As mentioned earlier, one of the uses of trees is to implement efficient associative retrieval schemes. In that case, the labels for nodes will usually be some sort of complex term with (at least) two arguments. For example, if we were to build a tree storing the suitabilities of various kinds of investments (as described in Section 6.3),

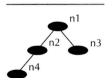

n1

n2   n3

n4

FIGURE 6–31
A simple tree.

we might label the nodes with terms of the form

suitability(Key, Value),

for example,

suitability(stock(preferred), medium),
suitability(futures(silver), low).

To hide the details of the tree labels, it is useful to define access predicates and construction predicates. The access predicates might be called key_of/2 and value_of/2. In the case of our investments example, they would be defined by

key_of(suitability(Key, _), Key).

value_of(suitability(_, Value), Value).

The construction predicate might be called make_entry/3 and would be defined for the investments tree by

make_entry(Key, Value, suitability(Key, Value)).

If the tree were to have a different kind of labels, one would simply change these definitions.

What makes trees useful for information retrieval is that under the proper usage, one never has to search more than a small fraction of the tree to perform a retrieval. This doesn't work for arbitrary trees, but only for organized trees called *search trees*. The notion of a search tree presupposes that the keys of the labels can be ordered by some linear ordering. Let's suppose that precedes/2 is a binary predicate that linearly orders the keys of the search tree we might be working with. For our investments example, we will assume that precedes is defined by Prolog's standard order on terms (see Section 7.4), as follows:

precedes(Item1, Item2) :- Item1 @< Item2.

A tree T is called a *search tree* provided that for every node N = tr(Left, Label, Right) in T, if K is the key of Label (i.e., key_of(Label, K) holds), the following are true:

- For any descendent node M = tr(_, MLabel, _) occurring in Left, if KM is the key of MLabel (i.e., key_of(MLabel, KM) holds), then KM precedes K;
- For any descendent node P = tr(_, PLabel, _) occurring in Right, if KP is the key of PLabel (i.e., key_of(PLabel, KP) holds), then K precedes KP.

Thus, in a search tree, to locate a node with a given key K, one starts at the root and "bounces down" left or right by comparing K with the key of each tree node encountered, as suggested in Figure 6–32. We can define a predicate locate/3 according to this idea, as follows:

locate(tr(Left, Entry, Right), Key, Value)
　:-
　key_of(Entry, Key),
　value_of(Entry, Value).

FIGURE 6–32
Locating a node with a given label in a tree.

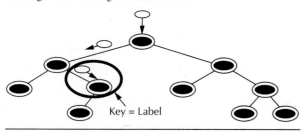

Key = Label

---

locate(tr(Left, Entry, Right), Key, Value)
:-
key_of(Entry, EntryKey),
precedes(Key, EntryKey),
locate(Left, Key, Value).

locate(tr(Left, Entry, Right), Key, Value)
:-
key_of(Entry, EntryKey),
precedes(EntryKey, Key),
locate(Right, Key, Value).

The process of inserting a node with a new label is similar. In essence, we bounce through the tree in the same manner as locate/3 does until we reach a point where no further descent is possible. This might be a leaf node or might be an interior node with only one descendent branch and the comparison with the label of that node insists that we should follow the other (empty) branch. At that point, we insert a new leaf node carrying the new label we were to insert. Figure 6–33 suggests how this might go. We can define insert/4 to accomplish this as follows:

insert(nil, Key, Value, tr(nil, NewEntry, nil))
:-
make_entry(Key, Value, NewEntry).

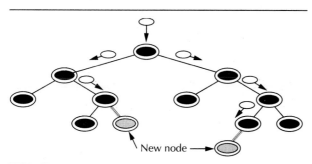

New node ⟶

FIGURE 6–33
Inserting a new node with a given label in a tree.

insert(tr(OldLeft, Entry, Right), Key, Value, tr(NewLeft, Entry, Right))

:-

key_of(Entry, EntryKey),

precedes(Key, EntryKey),

insert(OldLeft, Key, Value, NewLeft).

insert(tr(Left, Entry, OldRight), Key, Value, tr(Left, Entry, NewRight))

:-

key_of(Entry, EntryKey),

precedes(EntryKey, Key),

insert(OldRight, Key, Value, NewRight).

To put this to work, suppose we specify a list of suitability labels as follows:

```
suitability_list([
                suitability(loans(bankers_acceptance),low),
                suitability(savings_account(certificate_of_deposit),high),
                suitability(loans(commercial),low),
                suitability(savings_account(commercial_bank),medium),
                suitability(stock(common),low),
                suitability(bonds(corporate),high),
                suitability(retirement_plan(corporate),high),
                suitability(savings_account(credit_union),medium),
                suitability(futures(gold),low),
                suitability(retirement_plan(ira),high),
                suitability(retirement_plan(keogh),high),
                suitability(mutual_fund(load),high),
                suitability(bonds(municipal),high),
                suitability(mutual_fund(no_load),high),
                suitability(limited_partnership(oil_and_gas),low),
                suitability(stock(preferred),medium),
                suitability(limited_partnership(real_estate),low),
                suitability(savings_account(savings_and_loan),low),
                suitability(retirement_plan(section_401k),high),
                suitability(futures(silver),low),
                suitability(life_contract(single_payment),high),
                suitability(annuity(single_premium),high),
                suitability(bonds(state),high),
                suitability(life_insurance(term),medium),
                suitability(loans(treasury_bills),high),
                suitability(bonds(us_government),high),
                suitability(life_insurance(whole_life),high)
]).
```

Our goal will be to build a search tree labeled with the entries in this list. The top level of a predicate to accomplish this runs as follows:

test(ResultTree)

:-

suitability_list(Items),

do_inserts(Items, nil, ResultTree).

The intent of do_inserts/3 is to recurse down the list of Items, building up the tree that it accumulates in its second argument, and returning the final result through the variable ResultTree in its third argument. The definition is

FIGURE 6–34
The investment suitability tree.

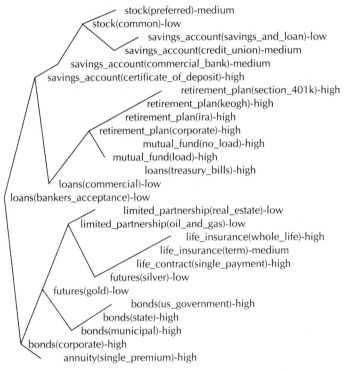

```
do_inserts([], Tree, Tree).
do_inserts([Item | RestItems], CurrentTree, FinalTree)
    :-
    key_of(Item, Key),
    value_of(Item, Value),
    insert(CurrentTree, Key, Value, NextTree),
    do_inserts(RestItems, NextTree, FinalTree).
```

Execution of the goal

?-test(Result).

will produce the tree that is illustrated in Figure 6–34. The exercises for Chapter 7 consider methods of printing out related representations of trees.

6.5 GRAPHS REVISITED

What we want to do next is to consider a totally different way of representing graphs. Instead of using a set of assertations, as we did in Chapter 5, we will represent graphs by terms. The term representing the graph is a list containing one entry for each of the vertices. Each entry is a binary term v(_, _). The left-hand element is the vertex, and the right-hand element is a list containing the other vertices to which this one is connected by an edge. We adopt the following proviso: as you move from left to right through the master list, if you've already listed a connection between two vertices you won't repeat it here. Figure 6–35 presents a term that would represent the undirected graph in Figure 5–11 in Chapter 5.

In order to work with graphs in this representation, we must define some basic predicates. First, we must be able to determine the vertices in the graph. What we have to do is write a predicate vertex that has two arguments, one that is the representation of the graph and the other the vertex in question. The predicate tells us whether the vertex is contained in the graph. What is it to be a vertex in this graph? It is to be the left-hand element of one of the terms on the list. But this is simply a lookup problem similar to what we did for association lists, except that we don't have to extract a value. Figure 6–36 presents the definition of vertex.

We must also be able to determine the edges in a graph. Suppose we are given X and Y and we want to know whether or not there is an edge between X and Y in the graph G. Recall that each term v(N, L) on the list specifies that N is a vertex and lists some of the other vertices connected to N on the list L. Since the (undirected) edge between X and Y might be listed either with X or with Y, we have two cases to consider:

1 Look up X, then look up Y in the list associated with X;
2 Look up Y, then look up X in the list associated with Y.

We can implement this using *member*, as shown in Figure 6–37.

With these two definitions in hand, we can revise the definition of path from Chapter 5 as follows:

```
path(A, B, G) :- edge(G, A, B).
path(A, B, G) :-
    edge(G, A, C), path(C, B, G).
```

The representation of graphs using assertions in Chapter 5 and the present representation using terms are very different representations, having different virtues. The first one is rigid in the sense that if the program database is fixed, the graph is fixed by the program. (We will see that it is possible to modify the program database *on the fly* in Part II). However, because of that, lots of things can be done very quickly. Path finding in the graph can be done very, very quickly. If your application uses a fixed graph that is not going to change, but that asks many questions about paths in

---

[v(d, [c]),	v(c, [b]),
v(b, [f,a]),	v(a, [f]).
v(f, [i,g,e]),	v(e, []),
v(g, [k,h]),	v(i, [j]),
v(k, [l]),	v(l, [h]),
v(h, [])	]

FIGURE 6–35

FIGURE 6–36
Definition of vertex.

    vertex([v(Entity, Connects) | GraphTail], Entity).

    vertex([Skip | GraphTail], Entity)
        :-
        vertex(GraphTail, Entity).

---

the graph, it is worth considering representing the graph directly in the program as a set of assertions. On the other hand, in many applications the graph changes. The graph is actually dynamic in time as the program executes. In that case, you'll want to consider the second approach, representing the graph as a term, since new terms can always be made out of old terms.

When we developed our path-finding program in Chapter 5, we observed that it had a fatal weakness: it couldn't avoid looping in circular paths in the graph. If you think of the program as a small, dumb mouse running around in a maze, the mouse can only see its immediate surroundings. It cannot view the graph globally as we do when we look at a two-dimensional picture of the graph. Our original program is a very dumb mouse since it also can't remember where it has been previously. One way of dealing with the looping problem would be to allow the mouse to remember the nodes it has previously visited. Then each time it set out to try an edge to a node, it would make sure the node it was heading toward had not been visited before. The problem is to devise a means of allowing the path-finding program to remember the nodes it has previously visited. One simple method is to cause the program to keep a list of the previously visited nodes. It could do this by adopting the accumulator approach used in the efficient list reversal program. If we follow this approach, we will define path/2 in terms of another predicate, smart_path/3, which can remember the nodes previously visited. Figure 6–38 presents the definition.

The third argument of smart_path is to be a list of the previously visited nodes. Thus, at the outset, path calls smart_path with the third argument set to the empty list, since there are no previously visited nodes when the path search begins. In general, smart_path first looks to see if there is an edge from the Current node to the Target node. If so, the search is finished. On the other hand, if there is no edge from the Current node to the Target node, smart_path tries to find a SteppingStone node that is connected to the Current node and that is not a member of the list of previously visited

---

    edge(G,X,Y)
        :-
        member(v(X,L),G), member(Y,L).
    edge(G,X,Y)
        :-
        member(v(Y,L),G), member(X,L).

FIGURE 6–37
Definition of edge.

FIGURE 6–38
Definition of smart_path.

```
    path(Start, Finish)
        :-
        smart_path(Start, Finish, []).

    smart_path(Current, Target, Previous)
        :-
        edge(Current,Target).

    smart_path(Current, Target, Previous)
        :-
        edge(Current, SteppingStone),
        non_member(SteppingStone, Previous),
        smart_path(SteppingStone, Target, [Current | Previous]).
```

nodes. If it finds such a SteppingStone, smart_path adds the Current node to the list of previously visited nodes, and makes SteppingStone the current node by recursively calling itself. This is exactly the pattern of the original path program, except for the test that SteppingStone is not a member of the list of previously visited nodes.

How do we define the *non-member* predicate? The basic intuition is

> *An entity X is a non_member of a list L if and only if X is different from every element of L.*

Thus, one way of defining non_member(X, L) is to sweep through every element Y of L, checking whether or not X is different from Y. Of course, we do this recursively, as follows:

```
    non_member(X, []).

    non_member(X, [ Y | Tail_L] )
        :-
        X \== Y,
        non_member(X, Tail_L).
```

Figure 6–39 shows a trace of this new path predicate for a path-finding problem that causes the previous "dumb" version to fall into a loop.

```
?-trace path(j,a).
(1) 1 call: path(j,a) ?
(2) 2 call: smart_path(j,a,[]) ?
(3) 3 call: edge(j,a) ?
(3) 3 fail: edge(j,a)
(2) 2 redo: smart_path(j,a,[]) ?
(4) 3 call: edge(j,_376) ?
(4) 3 exit: edge(j,k)
(5) 3 call: non_member(k,[]) ?
```

FIGURE 6–39
A trace of path(j, a).

FIGURE 6–39 (*Continued*)

```
(5) 3 exit: non_member(k,[])
(6) 3 call: smart_path(k,a,[j]) ?
(7) 4 call: edge(k,a) ?
(7) 4 fail: edge(k,a)
(6) 3 redo: smart_path(k,a,[j]) ?
(8) 4 call: edge(k,_930) ?
(8) 4 exit: edge(k,g)
(9) 4 call: non_member(g,[j]) ?
(10) 5 call: g\==j ?
(10) 5 exit: g\==j
(11) 5 call: non_member(g,[]) ?
(11) 5 exit: non_member(g,[])
(9) 4 exit: non_member(g,[j])
(12) 4 call: smart_path(g,a,[k,j]) ?
(13) 5 call: edge(g,a) ?
(13) 5 fail: edge(g,a)
(12) 4 redo: smart_path(g,a,[k,j]) ?
(14) 5 call: edge(g,_1882) ?
(14) 5 exit: edge(g,f)
(15) 5 call: non_member(f,[k,j]) ?
(16) 6 call: f\==k ?
(16) 6 exit: f\==k
(17) 6 call: non_member(f,[j]) ?
(18) 7 call: f\==j ?
(18) 7 exit: f\==j
(19) 7 call: non_member(f,[]) ?
(19) 7 exit: non_member(f,[])
(17) 6 exit: non_member(f,[j])
(15) 5 exit: non_member(f,[k,j])
(20) 5 call: smart_path(f,a,[g,k,j]) ?
(21) 6 call: edge(f,a) ?
(21) 6 fail: edge(f,a)
(20) 5 redo: smart_path(f,a,[g,k,j]) ?
(22) 6 call: edge(f,_3080) ?
(22) 6 exit: edge(f,i)
(23) 6 call: non_member(i,[g,k,j]) ?
(24) 7 call: i\==g ?
(24) 7 exit: i\==g
(25) 7 call: non_member(i,[k,j]) ?
(26) 8 call: i\==k ?
(26) 8 exit: i\==k
(27) 8 call: non_member(i,[j]) ?
(28) 9 call: i\==j ?
(28) 9 exit: i\==j
(29) 9 call: non_member(i,[]) ?
(29) 9 exit: non_member(i,[])
(27) 8 exit: non_member(i,[j])
(25) 7 exit: non_member(i,[k,j])
(23) 6 exit: non_member(i,[g,k,j])
(30) 6 call: smart_path(i,a,[f,g,k,j]) ?
(31) 7 call: edge(i,a) ?
(31) 7 fail: edge(i,a)
(30) 6 redo: smart_path(i,a,[f,g,k,j]) ?
(32) 7 call: edge(i,_4600) ?
```

FIGURE 6–39   (*Continued*)

```
(32) 7 exit: edge(i,j)
(33) 7 call: non_member(j,[f,g,k,j]) ?
(34) 8 call: j\==f ?
(34) 8 exit: j\==f
(35) 8 call: non_member(j,[g,k,j]) ?
(36) 9 call: j\==g ?
(36) 9 exit: j\==g
(37) 9 call: non_member(j,[k,j]) ?
(38) 10 call: j\==k ?
(38) 10 exit: j\==k
(39) 10 call: non_member(j,[j]) ?
(40) 11 call: j\==j ?
(40) 11 fail: j\==j
(39) 10 fail: non_member(j,[j])
(38) 10 fail: j\==k
(37) 9 fail: non_member(j,[k,j])
(36) 9 fail: j\==g
(35) 8 fail: non_member(j,[g,k,j])
(34) 8 fail: j\==f
(33) 7 fail: non_member(j,[f,g,k,j])
(32) 7 redo: edge(i,_4600) ?
(32) 7 fail: edge(i,_4600)
(30) 6 fail: smart_path(i,a,[f,g,k,j])
(29) 9 redo: non_member(i,[]) ?
(29) 9 fail: non_member(i,[])
(28) 9 fail: i\==j
(27) 8 fail: non_member(i,[j])
(26) 8 fail: i\==k
(25) 7 fail: non_member(i,[k,j])
(24) 7 fail: i\==g
(23) 6 fail: non_member(i,[g,k,j])
(22) 6 redo: edge(f,_3080) ?
(22) 6 exit: edge(f,e)
(30) 6 call: non_member(e,[g,k,j]) ?
(31) 7 call: e\==g ?
(31) 7 exit: e\==g
(32) 7 call: non_member(e,[k,j]) ?
(33) 8 call: e\==k ?
(33) 8 exit: e\==k
(34) 8 call: non_member(e,[j]) ?
(35) 9 call: e\==j ?
(35) 9 exit: e\==j
(36) 9 call: non_member(e,[]) ?
(36) 9 exit: non_member(e,[])
(34) 8 exit: non_member(e,[j])
(32) 7 exit: non_member(e,[k,j])
(30) 6 exit: non_member(e,[g,k,j])
(37) 6 call: smart_path(e,a,[f,g,k,j]) ?
(38) 7 call: edge(e,a) ?
(38) 7 fail: edge(e,a)
(37) 6 redo: smart_path(e,a,[f,g,k,j]) ?
(39) 7 call: edge(e,_4656) ?
(39) 7 fail: edge(e,_4656)
(37) 6 fail: smart_path(e,a,[f,g,k,j])
```

FIGURE 6–39 (*Continued*)

```
(36) 9 redo: non_member(e,[]) ?
(36) 9 fail: non_member(e,[])
(35) 9 fail: e\==j
(34) 8 fail: non_member(e,[j])
(33) 8 fail: e\==k
(32) 7 fail: non_member(e,[k,j])
(31) 7 fail: e\==g
(30) 6 fail: non_member(e,[g,k,j])
(22) 6 redo: edge(f,_3080) ?
(22) 6 fail: edge(f,_3080)
(20) 5 fail: smart_path(f,a,[g,k,j])
(19) 7 redo: non_member(f,[]) ?
(19) 7 fail: non_member(f,[])
(18) 7 fail: f\==j
(17) 6 fail: non_member(f,[j])
(16) 6 fail: f\==k
(15) 5 fail: non_member(f,[k,j])
(14) 5 redo: edge(g,_1882) ?
(14) 5 exit: edge(g,h)
(20) 5 call: non_member(h,[k,j]) ?
(21) 6 call: h\==k ?
(21) 6 exit: h\==k
(22) 6 call: non_member(h,[j]) ?
(23) 7 call: h\==j ?
(23) 7 exit: h\==j
(24) 7 call: non_member(h,[]) ?
(24) 7 exit: non_member(h,[])
(22) 6 exit: non_member(h,[j])
(20) 5 exit: non_member(h,[k,j])
(25) 5 call: smart_path(h,a,[g,k,j]) ?
(26) 6 call: edge(h,a) ?
(26) 6 fail: edge(h,a)
(25) 5 redo: smart_path(h,a,[g,k,j]) ?
(27) 6 call: edge(h,_3136) ?
(27) 6 exit: edge(h,l)
(28) 6 call: non_member(l,[g,k,j]) ?
(29) 7 call: l\==g ?
(29) 7 exit: l\==g
(30) 7 call: non_member(l,[k,j]) ?
(31) 8 call: l\==k ?
(31) 8 exit: l\==k
(32) 8 call: non_member(l,[j]) ?
(33) 9 call: l\==j ?
(33) 9 exit: l\==j
(34) 9 call: non_member(l,[]) ?
(34) 9 exit: non_member(l,[])
(32) 8 exit: non_member(l,[j])
(30) 7 exit: non_member(l,[k,j])
(28) 6 exit: non_member(l,[g,k,j])
(35) 6 call: smart_path(l,a,[h,g,k,j]) ?
(36) 7 call: edge(l,a) ?
(36) 7 fail: edge(l,a)
(35) 6 redo: smart_path(l,a,[h,g,k,j]) ?
(37) 7 call: edge(l,_4656) ?
```

FIGURE 6–39 *(Continued)*

```
(37) 7 exit: edge(l,k)
(38) 7 call: non_member(k,[h,g,k,j]) ?
(39) 8 call: k\==h ?
(39) 8 exit: k\==h
(40) 8 call: non_member(k,[g,k,j]) ?
(41) 9 fail: call: k\==g ?
(41) 9 exit: k\==g
(42) 9 call: non_member(k, [k,j]) ?
(43) 10 call: k\==k ?
(43) 10 fail: k\==k
(42) 9 fail: non_member(k,[k,j])
(41) 9 fail: k\==g
(40) 8 fail: non_member(k,[g,k,j])
(39) 8 fail: k\==h
(38) 7 fail: non_member(k,[h,g,k,j])
(37) 7 redo: edge(l,_4656) ?
(37) 7 fail: edge(l,_4656)
(35) 6 fail: smart_path(l,a,[h,g,k,j])
(34) 9 redo: non_member(l,[]) ?
(34) 9 fail: non_member(l,[])
(33) 9 fail: l\==j
(32) 8 fail: non_member(l,[j])
(31) 8 fail: l\==k
(30) 7 fail: non_member(l,[k,j])
(29) 7 fail: l\==g
(28) 6 fail: non_member(l,[g,k,j])
(27) 6 redo: edge(h,_3136) ?
(27) 6 fail: edge(h,_3136)
(25) 5 fail: smart_path(h,a,[g,k,j])
(24) 7 redo: non_member(h,[]) ?
(24) 7 fail: non_member(h,[])
(23) 7 fail: h\==j
(22) 6 fail: non_member(h,[j])
(21) 6 fail: h\==k
(20) 5 fail: non_member(h,[k,j])
(14) 5 redo: edge(g,_1882) ?
(14) 5 fail: edge(g,_1882)
(12) 4 fail: smart_path(g,a,[k,j])
(11) 5 redo: non_member(g,[]) ?
(11) 5 fail: non_member(g,[])
(10) 5 fail: g\==j
(9) 4 fail: non_member(g,[j])
(8) 4 fail: edge(k,_930)
(6) 3 fail: smart_path(k,a,[j])
(5) 3 redo: non_member(k,[]) ?
(5) 3 fail: non_member(k,[])
(4) 3 redo: edge(j,_376) ?
(4) 3 fail: edge(j,_376)
(2) 2 fail: smart_path(j,a,[])
(1) 1 fail: path(j,a)
```

no

We know from global examination of the graph (Figure 5.7) that there is no path from *j* to *a*. However, the original dumb path-search program fell into an infinite loop, so it could not prove that there was no path. However, as the trace in Figure 6–39 shows, our smart path program correctly examines all the possible routes and correctly indicates that no path is possible.

The trace in Figure 6–39 is rather lengthy. It is possible to obtain more compressed traces. One way is to use the *skip* command with the debugger. Instead of typing Enter after every line, you can type an "s" instead (for *skip*) after a *call* port (line). The system will attempt to execute the indicated call (as usual) but will skip showing any trace information for this call (and any of its subcalls). It will print the matching "exit" or "fail" line, but nothing in between. Figure 6–40 shows how the trace would look if we skipped all the non-member calls.

```
?-trace path(j,a).
(1)  1 call: path(j,a) ?
(2)  2 call: smart_path(j,a,[]) ?
(3)  3 call: edge(j,a) ?
(3)  3 fail: edge(j,a)
(2)  2 redo: smart_path(j,a,[]) ?
(4)  3 call: edge(j,_284) ?
(4)  3 exit: edge(j,k)
(5)  3 call: non_member(k,[]) ?  s
(5)  3 exit: non_member(k,[])
(6)  3 call: smart_path(k,a,[j]) ?
(7)  4 call: edge(k,a) ?
(7)  4 fail: edge(k,a)
(6)  3 redo: smart_path(k,a,[j]) ?
(8)  4 call: edge(k,_856) ?
(8)  4 exit: edge(k,g)
(9)  4 call: non_member(g,[j]) ?  s
(9)  4 exit: non_member(g,[j])
(12) 4 call: smart_path(g,a,[k,j]) ?
(13) 5 call: edge(g,a) ?
(13) 5 fail: edge(g,a)
(12) 4 redo: smart_path(g,a,[k,j]) ?
(14) 5 call: edge(g,_1670) ?
(14) 5 exit: edge(g,f)
(15) 5 call: non_member(f,[k,j]) ?  s
(15) 5 exit: non_member(f,[k,j])
(20) 5 call: smart_path(f,a,[g,k,j]) ?
(21) 6 call: edge(f,a) ?
(21) 6 fail: edge(f,a)
(20) 5 redo: smart_path(f,a,[g,k,j]) ?
(22) 6 call: edge(f,_2726) ?
(22) 6 exit: edge(f,i)
(23) 6 call: non_member(i,[g,k,j]) ?  s
(23) 6 exit: non_member(i,[g,k,j])
(30) 6 call: smart_path(i,a,[f,g,k,j]) ?
(31) 7 call: edge(i,a) ?
```

FIGURE 6–40
Tracing path(j,a) using skips.

FIGURE 6-40   *(Continued)*.

```
(31) 7 fail: edge(i,a)
(30) 6 redo: smart_path(i,a,[f,g,k,j]) ?
(32) 7 call: edge(i,_4024) ?
(32) 7 exit: edge(i,j)
(33) 7 call: non_member(j,[f,g,k,j]) ?  s
(33) 7 fail: non_member(j,[f,g,k,j])
(32) 7 redo: edge(i,_4024) ?
(32) 7 fail: edge(i,_4024)
(30) 6 fail: smart_path(i,a,[f,g,k,j])
(29) 9 redo: non_member(i,[]) ?  s
(23) 6 fail: non_member(i,[g,k,j])
(22) 6 redo: edge(f,_2726) ?
(22) 6 exit: edge(f,e)
(30) 6 call: non_member(e,[g,k,j]) ?  s
(30) 6 exit: non_member(e,[g,k,j])
(37) 6 call: smart_path(e,a,[f,g,k,j]) ?
(38) 7 call: edge(e,a) ?
(38) 7 fail: edge(e,a)
(37) 6 redo: smart_path(e,a,[f,g,k,j]) ?
(39) 7 call: edge(e,_4080) ?
(39) 7 fail: edge(e,_4080)
(37) 6 fail: smart_path(e,a,[f,g,k,j])
(36) 9 redo: non_member(e,[]) ?  s
(30) 6 fail: non_member(e,[g,k,j])
(22) 6 redo: edge(f,_2726) ?
(22) 6 fail: edge(f,_2726)
(20) 5 fail: smart_path(f,a,[g,k,j])
(19) 7 redo: non_member(f,[]) ?  s
(15) 5 fail: non_member(f,[k,j])
(14) 5 redo: edge(g,_1670) ?
(14) 5 exit: edge(g,h)
(20) 5 call: non_member(h,[k,j]) ?  s
(20) 5 exit: non_member(h,[k,j])
(25) 5 call: smart_path(h,a,[g,k,j]) ?
(26) 6 call: edge(h,a) ?
(26) 6 fail: edge(h,a)
(25) 5 redo: smart_path(h,a,[g,k,j]) ?
(27) 6 call: edge(h,_2782) ?
(27) 6 exit: edge(h,l)
(28) 6 call: non_member(l,[g,k,j]) ?  s
(28) 6 exit: non_member(l,[g,k,j])
(35) 6 call: smart_path(l,a,[h,g,k,j]) ?
(36) 7 call: edge(l,a) ?
(36) 7 fail: edge(l,a)
(35) 6 redo: smart_path(l,a,[h,g,k,j]) ?
(37) 7 call: edge(l,_4080) ?
(37) 7 exit: edge(l,k)
(38) 7 call: non_member(k,[h,g,k,j]) ?  s
(38) 7 fail: non_member(k,[h,g,k,j])
(37) 7 redo: edge(l,_4080) ?
(37) 7 fail: edge(l,_4080)
(35) 6 fail: smart_path(l,a,[h,g,k,j])
(34) 9 redo: non_member(l,[]) ?  s
(28) 6 fail: non_member(l,[g,k,j])
```

FIGURE 6-40   *(Continued)*

```
(27)  6 redo: edge(h,_2782) ?
(27)  6 fail: edge(h,_2782)
(25)  5 fail: smart_path(h,a,[g,k,j])
(24)  7 redo: non_member(h,[]) ?  s
(20)  5 fail: non_member(h,[k,j])
(14)  5 redo: edge(g,_1670) ?
(14)  5 fail: edge(g,_1670)
(12)  4 fail: smart_path(g,a,[k,j])
(11)  5 redo: non_member(g,[]) ?  s
(9)   4 fail: non_member(g,[j])
(8)   4 fail: edge(k,_856)
(6)   3 fail: smart_path(k,a,[j])
(5)   3 redo: non_member(k,[]) ?  s
(5)   3 fail: non_member(k,[])
(4)   3 redo: edge(j,_284) ?
(4)   3 fail: edge(j,_284)
(2)   2 fail: smart_path(j,a,[])
(1)   1 fail: path(j,a)
```

no

It is possible to produce even more compressed, but still useful, traces with the debugger. This involves shifting our point of view from tracing the entire computation (perhaps with some skips) to letting the computation run normally but causing selected portions to be shown. The key notion is that of *spying on a predicate*. One indicates that one wishes to spy on a predicate by *setting a spy point* on that predicate. For example, suppose that we want to spy on smart_path/3. We would accomplish this with the command

```
?-spy smart_path/3.
```

The effect of setting a spy point on smart_path/3 is that whenever a call to smart_path/3 is made the debugger will "wake up" and start tracing. Thus, if we had a more complex program that did lots of computation before calling smart_path, we would not see any of that preceding computation before the call to smart_path. One can also *leap* between spy points, by typing "l" (for "leap") to the debugger. Figure 6–41 shows how the trace would look if we set a spy point on smart_path/3 and leapt from one call to the next.

The same technique can be used with state-space programs to keep them from looping: Simply add an extra argument to accumulate the previously visited states and test for membership in that list each time a transition to a new state is attempted. To add some spice, suppose we also wished to return the path through the state space when the program succeeded. We would need to add two additional variables: One to function as the accumulator, and one to return the final path, just as with the efficient list reversal program. Here is how we would modify the main part of the program:

```
(path(A, B, FinalPath)
   :-
   path(A, B, [], ReversedFinalPath),
   reverse(ReversedFinalPath, FinalPath).
```

FIGURE 6–41
Spying on smart_path/3, and leaping between spy points.

```
?-< spy smart_path/3.
Spy point set on user: smart_path/3
yes
?-path(j,a).
(1) 1 call: smart_path(j,a,[]) ?  1
(1) 1 redo: smart_path(j,a,[]) ?  1
(5) 2 call: smart_path(k,a,[j]) ?  1
(5) 2 redo: smart_path(k,a,[j]) ?  1
(11) 3 call: smart_path(g,a,[k,j]) ?  1
(11) 3 redo: smart_path(g,a,[k,j]) ?  1
(19) 4 call: smart_path(f,a,[g,k,j]) ?  1
(19) 4 redo: smart_path(f,a,[g,k,j]) ?  1
(29) 5 call: smart_path(i,a,[f,g,k,j]) ?  1
(29) 5 redo: smart_path(i,a,[f,g,k,j]) ?  1
(29) 5 fail: smart_path(i,a,[f,g,k,j])
(28) 8 redo: non_member(i,[]) ?  1
(36) 5 call: smart_path(e,a,[f,g,k,j]) ?  1
(36) 5 redo: smart_path(e,a,[f,g,k,j]) ?  1
(36) 5 fail: smart_path(e,a,[f,g,k,j])
(35) 8 redo: non_member(e,[]) ?  1
(19) 4 fail: smart_path(f,a,[g,k,j])
(18) 6 redo: non_member(f,[]) ?  1
(24) 4 call: smart_path(h,a,[g,k,j]) ?  1
(24) 4 redo: smart_path(h,a,[g,k,j]) ?  1
(34) 5 call: smart_path(l,a,[h,g,k,j]) ?  1
(34) 5 redo: smart_path(l,a,[h,g,k,j]) ?  1
(34) 5 fail: smart_path(l,a,[h,g,k,j])
(33) 8 redo: non_member(l,[]) ?  1
(24) 4 fail: smart_path(h,a,[g,k,j])
(23) 6 redo: non_member(h,[]) ?  1
(11) 3 fail: smart_path(g,a,[k,j])
(10) 4 redo: non_member(g,[]) ?  1
(5) 2 fail: smart_path(k,a,[j])
(4) 2 redo: non_member(k,[]) ?  1
(1) 1 fail: smart_path(j,a,[])
no
```

path(CurState, GoalState, PrevStates, [GoalState | PrevStates])

:-

transition(CurState, GoalState).

path(CurState, GoalState, PrevStates, FinalPath)

:-

transition(CurState, NextState),
not(member(NextState, PrevStates)),
path (CurState, GoalState, [CurState | PrevStates], FinalPath).

The representation of the system state that we used in the Russian farmer problem was direct and simple:

s(F,G,C,W).

This permitted a quite direct statement of the allowable transitions, such as

    transition(state(s,s,n,n), state(n,s,n,n)),

or

    transition(state(F0,G0,C0,W0), state(F1,G1,C1,W1))
        :-
        opposite(F0, F1),
        F0 = C0, F1 = C1,
        G0 = G1, W0 = W1,
        opposite(G0, W0), opposite(G1, W1).

However, for more complex systems, such simple representations are not always possible. There may be more components to the system, there may be properties of the components that can change in time, there may be more complex relations between the components, etc. In complex settings, it is often not possible to adopt the uniform sort of representation we used above. One approach is to represent the state by a collection of intuitive assertions about the system components and their relations. Applying this idea to the Russian farmer problem (even though we don't need to), we might represent the state s(n,s,s,n) by this collection:

(The) farmer (is) located north (of the river).
(The) goat (is) located south (of the river).
(The) cabbage (is) located south (of the river).
(The) wolf (is) located north (of the river).

We could use a compressed form:

    loc(farmer, north).
    loc(goat, south).
    loc(cabbage, south).
    loc(wolf, north).

Since the system state is continually changing, we do not want to use these intuitive assertions directly as Prolog facts. Rather, we will view them as terms and represent the system state by the list of terms:

    [loc(farmer, north), loc(goat, south), loc(cabbage, south), loc(wolf, north)]

Even with this change in the representation of state, the top-level of the path-finding program can remain the same. What must change is the definition of transition/2. Recall one of the clauses from the previous definition of transition:

    transition(state(F0,G0,C0,W0), state(F1,G1,C1,W1))
        :-
        opposite(F0, F1),
        F0 = C0, F1 = C1,
        G0 = G1, W0 = W1,
        opposite(G0, W0), opposite(G1, W1).

One intuitive reading of this transition rule is:

There is an acceptable transition from state S0 to state S1 provided that

1 The locations of the farmer and the cabbage are the same in S0;
2 The locations of the goat and wolf are opposite in state S0;
3 The locations of the farmer and the cabbage in S1 are the opposite of what they were in S0; and
4 Everything else stays the same.

Note that 4 implies that the locations of the goat and wolf are opposite in state S1 since they were opposite in state S0. Moreover, since we start the search problem in a state that is acceptable, if we assume that only acceptable transitions are made, we know that the resulting state will always be acceptable. Consequently, item 2 can be regarded as redundant.

We can determine the location of one of the players under our new state representation by using member/2:

    holds(loc(Player, RiverBank), State)
      :-
      member(loc(Player, RiverBank), State).

Thus, we can rewrite the transition rule above as:

    transition(S0, S1)
      :-
      holds(loc(farmer, F0), S0),
      holds(loc(cabbage, C0), S0),
      C0 = F0,
      opposite(F0, F1),
      C1 = F1,
      change(loc(farmer, F0), S0, loc(farmer, F1), S_Inter),
      change(loc(cabbage, C0), S_Inter, loc(cabbage, C1), S1).

As usual, we can state this more simply by applying the equality statements:

    transition(S0, S1)
      :-
      holds(loc(farmer, F0), S0),
      holds(loc(cabbage, F0), S0),
      opposite(F0, F1),
      delete(S0, loc(farmer, F0), S0_A),
      add(S0_A, loc(farmer, F1), S_B),
      delete(S_B, loc(cabbage, F0), S_C),
      add(S_C, loc(cabbage, F1), S1).

The auxiliary predicates add/3 and delete/3 have rather obvious specifications, and can be formally defined as follows:

    add(State, Assertion, [Assertion | State]).

    delete([], Assertion, []).

delete([Assertion | Remainder], Assertion, Remainder)
:-!.

delete([Item | Remainder], Assertion, [Item | ResultRemainder])
:-

delete(Remainder, Assertion, ResultRemainder).

Note that our definition of delete assumes that no item is repeated in the list, so that after it locates the item, delete/3 does not check further for any other occurrences. On the other hand, add/3 does not check to see whether the new item to be added is already present on the list. Thus, it is up to the discipline of the program using these particular add/3 and delete/3 to ensure that no items become duplicated on the list.

EXERCISES

6-1 a Define the predicate delete/3, which is specified as follows:
delete(InList, Item, OutList) holds *if and only if*
OutList is the result of deleting the first occurrence of Item from InList.
b Define delete/3 when the specification is changed to require that every occurrence of Item in InList be deleted.
6-2 Consider lists of integers. Define the predicate insert/3, which is specified as follows:
insert(InList, Item, OutList) holds *if and only if*
InList is an ordered list of integers, Item is an integer, and OutList is the result of inserting Item in the correct position in InList.
Arithmetic is discussed in detail in Section 7.7. For the purposes of this problem, you
need only note that when X and Y are integers, the expression
X =< Y
holds if and only if X is less than or equal to Y.
6-3 Consider lists of integers (see Exercise 6-2). Define the predicate boundedCollect/3, which is specified as follows:
boundedCollect (InList, Bound, ResultList) holds *if and only if*
InList is a list of integers, Bound is an integer, and ResultList consists of all integers occurring on InList which are less than or equal to Bound.
6-4 Define copy/2 such that copy(InList, OutList) holds if and only if OutList is a copy of InList.
6-5 a rotateUp/2 moves the head of the input list to the end and leaves everything else in its original order. Thus, for example, the following would hold:
rotateUp[a, b, c, d], [b, c, d, a]).
Define rotateUp/2.
b Similarly, rotateDown/2 moves the last element of the input list to the head. Define rotateDown/2.
6-6 The predicate interleave/3 is defined as follows:
interleave(InList1, InList2, OutList) holds *if and only if* InList1 and InList2 are lists of the same length N, and OutList is a list of length 2N consisting of the elements of InList1 interleaved with the elements of InList2, with the elements of InList1 preceding the corresponding elements of InList2.
Thus, for example, the following would hold:
interleave([a, b, c], [x, y, z], [a, x, b, y, c, z]).

Define interleave/3.

6-7 *Bubble Sort.* Imagine that the cards (which will just be numbers for this illustration) are arranged vertically:

$$3$$
$$1$$
$$7$$
$$4$$
$$2$$
$$5$$

The approach is to make repeated passes through the list, at each pass letting the least element bubble up to its correct position in the list:

Define bubble_sort/2 to implement this approach to sorting.

> (*Hint:* Define comes_before/2 on some atoms representing cards. The primary part of the definition runs. Extract the least element from the current list, leaving a remainder. Paste the least element on the head of the output list and recursively bubble sort the remainder to produce the tail of the output list. To extract the least element from a list, use two arguments in addition to the list, one for the current least element, and one for the final least element. Recursively walk through the list comparing the head of the list with the current least element; if the head comes before the current least element, replace the current least element with the head at the next recursive call; return the current least element through the final least element when the end of the list is reached. Start with the current least element set to *infinity* and extend the definition of comes_before/2 to make anything different from infinity come before infinity).

6-8 Define predicates for a variant of association lists that can deal with the situation in which more than one value can be associated with a single key (e.g., grades on an exam (keys) and students (values)). The actual data item associated with a key will be a list of the associated values.

a Define one version in which lookup returns the list associated with a key.

b Define another version in which lookup first returns the first element of the list associated with a key, and upon backtracking, lookup successively returns the second, third, etc., values associated with a key.

6-9 To traverse a tree is to start at the root and successively visit each and every node of the tree. A *left-to-right depth-first traversal* proceeds by a depth-first search, following the left-most branch to the bottom (leaf) first, then backtracking to the first node with a right branch and continuing from there down to the next lower node and continuing from the left-most search for the bottom, etc. Often, such procedures build a list of the labels encountered as they go. The list is *in-order* if the labels from the left branch of a node precede the label of the node and the labels of the right branch follow the node label. The list is *prefix-order* if the node label comes first, then the labels from the left branch, followed by the labels from the right branch.

a Define a predicate in_order/2 whose first argument is a binary search tree and whose second argument is the in-order list of nodes accumulated by a left-to-right depth-first traversal of the tree.

b Define a predicate prefix_order/2 whose first argument is a binary search tree and whose second argument is the prefix-order list of nodes accumulated by a left-to-right depth-first traversal of the tree.

6-10 Define a predicate delete/3, which is specified as follows:

delete(InTree, Label, OutTree) holds *if and only if*

OutTree is the binary search tree resulting from the deletion of the node containing Label from InTree while keeping all the remaining nodes of InTree.

6-11 Modify the path-finding programs for Exercises 5-1–5-6 in the style of smart_path/3 of Section 6.5 to avoid looping; extend the modifications in the style of path/4 to return the path found.

6-12 Continuing Exercise 5-9, define a predicate propagate/2 that, when coupled with a circuit represented as in Section 1.2, will determine the propagation of signals through the circuit. Specifically:

propagate(In, Out) holds *if and only if*
- In is a list of terms of the form v(I, Val), where I is an input wire and Val is either *on* or *off*; for example, In might be [v(a,on),v(b,off),...]
- Out is a list of terms of the form v(O, Val), where O is an output wire and Val is either *on* or *off*; for example, Out might be [v(h,off)]
- The values listed on the list Out are the result of propagating the values listed on In through the circuit.

6-13 a Modify the state representation of the eight puzzle in the style used for the Russian farmer problem in Section 6.5 (i.e., using a list of terms to represent the state). Create representations for both of the *squares* styles of representation and for both of the *tiles* approaches.

b Create clauses for move/2 as described in Exercises 5-10 and 5-11. Compare these clauses with those from Exercises 5-10 and 5-11 with regard to clarity and compactness.

c Following the style of the approach to the Russian farmer problem, develop a predicate solve/2 for the eight puzzle which acts as follows:

solve(Start, MoveList) holds *if and only if*

Start is a configuration of the 8 puzzle and MoveList is a list of legal moves beginning with configuration Start and terminating in the goal configuration.

6-14 Continuing Exercise 5-9, create a predicate depends_on_via/3 that is a variant of depends_on/2 and that returns a list consisting of the sequence of tasks leading from Activity_1 to Activity_2 in its third argument.

6-15 Continuing Exercise 5-12, modify the predicate connected/2 to have three arguments such that the third argument returns a list of sections connecting the first and second arguments.

6-16 Continuing Exercise 5-2, create a predicate leads_to_via/3 that returns the sequence of compounds produced in passing from the first argument compound to the second argument compound. Create a variant of this in which the list returned in the third argument consists of pairs a(E,C), where E is the enzyme that produced C from the preceding compound in the list. Make similar extensions to affects/2.

6-17 Modify the path-finding predicates of Exercises 5-14 and 5-15 to avoid loops in paths and to return the computed paths.

CHAPTER 7

PRAGMATICS

In Chapters 1–6, we studied the pure core of the Prolog language, touching only briefly on the built-in procedures. In this chapter, we will introduce all of the major groups of built-in predicates, together with the additional control facilities. For each group, we present a basic description together with some simple examples. All of the groups are used in significant ways in Part II. Readers should read through this chapter once, and then proceed to Part II, returning to the appropriate sections in this chapter as various built-ins and control primitives are utilized in Part II.

7.1 CONTROL: DISJUNCTION, CUT, NEGATION AND RELATIVES

We have already seen the importance of the ordering of the rules of a Prolog program in affecting the control of the search for solutions. Other control mechanisms are available as built-in primitives. They allow users to add expressibility and power to their programs and to improve their efficiency.

The search space that Prolog must examine when looking for a solution can be greatly reduced in certain cases, through the judicious use of control primitives. The cut (!) primitive is one such example. Without it, Prolog must exhaustively search the space of all potential solutions.

The control primitives are built-in predicates that are hardwired in the Prolog compiler. In the following subsections, we will describe their form and use. The primitives we will introduce are available with any Prolog compiler.

7.1.1 Disjunction (;)

Disjunction takes the form:

First Goal ; Second Goal

This expression may appear as a goal in the body of a rule. It succeeds if either *First Goal* or *Second Goal* succeeds. Prolog initially attempts to solve *First Goal*. If First Goal succeeds, the complete disjunction succeeds. If, later, Prolog backtracks to this disjunction, *Second Goal* will be called. The following example shows the use of disjunction as the boolean or connective. Suppose the following program is consulted:

language (postscript).
language (pascal).
food (burrito).
food (crab).
food (steak).

Assume we submit the following goal:

```
?-language(postscript) ; food(postscript).
yes.
```

Note that although postscript is not a food, the goal succeeds. This is because only one of the two subgoals has to succeed for ";" to succeed. Similarly, the goal

```
?-language(steak) ; food(steak).
yes.
```

succeeds because *food (steak)* succeeds.

In the next example, we will add a few more facts to the database we just consulted. This example shows that disjunction (;) also succeeds if both of its arguments can succeed. Add these two facts to the previous program:

food (prolog).
language (prolog).

and submit the goal:

```
?-language(prolog) ; food(burrito).
yes.
```

Note that the subgoal *food (burrito)* is never run, even though it is true. That is because *language (prolog)* succeeds and that is enough for the disjunction (;) to succeed.

This example shows that ";" will fail if neither of the subgoals succeeds.

```
?-language(fortran); food(fortran).
no.
```

The next example illustrates the behavior of *;* upon backtracking.

```
?-language(X) ; food(X).
X = postscript  ;
X = pascal  ;
X = burrito  ;
X = crab  ;
X = steak  ;
X = prolog  ;
X = prolog  ;
no.
```

We are asking about all objects X that are either a language or a food. The answer $X = prolog$ appears twice since we have added the two facts *food (prolog)* and *language (prolog)*. Hence, upon backtracking in the search for more solutions, *prolog* appears twice: once as a language and once as a food.

Disjunction may also be used in defining rules. For example, a parent can be a mother or a father. Therefore the parent relationship can be expressed as the following rule:

```
parent (Parent, Child)
      : -
      mother (Parent, Child) ;
      father (Parent, Child).
```

This rule is equivalent to the following two-clause definition:

```
parent (Parent, Child)
      : -
      mother (Parent, Child).
parent (Parent, Child)
      :-
      father (Parent, Child).
```

7.1.2   If-then and If-then-else (->)

These control primitives have the following forms:

Condition -> TrueGoal.
Condition -> TrueGoal ; FalseGoal.

In the first case, if *Condition* succeeds, *True Goal* will be executed. If *Condition* fails, nothing more is attempted and the if-then construct fails. For example, suppose we consult the program consisting of the following rule and facts:

```
salary (X,Salary)
      : -
      employee (X) -> rank (X, Rank),
      wages (Rank,Salary).
```

```
employee (keith).
employee (harry).
rank (keith, 1).
rank (harry, 2).
wages (1, 3000).
wages (2, 2000).
```

The goal

```
?-salary(janet, Salary).
no.
```

fails because *employee (janet)* fails. But the following goal succeeds:

```
?-salary(harry, Salary).
Salary = 2000,
yes.
```

In the if-then-else construct, *TrueGoal* will be executed if *Condition* succeeds. If the *Condition* fails, *FalseGoal* will be executed. Assume we replace the salary rule above with the following:

salary (X, Salary)

: -

employee (X) -> (rank (X,Rank), wages (Rank, Salary)) ; salary = 0.

This means that to compute someone's salary, check first whether that person is an employee. If that succeeds, solve the salary goal by finding that person's rank and the salary attached to that rank. If that person is not an employee, the salary is $0. Using the new rule for salary together with the previous facts, the goal

```
?-salary (janet, Salary).
Salary = 0
yes.
```

will succeed.

Hence, *Condition -> TrueGoal* can be read as

If *Condition* then *TrueGoal*

and *Condition -> TrueGoal ; FalseGoal* can be read as

If *Condition* then *TrueGoal* else *FalseGoal*

7.1.3 Cut (!)

This built-in is denoted by an exclamation point (!) and called *cut*. When encountered, (!) effectively cuts the solution search space by discarding all choices made since the parent goal started execution, including the choices, if any, created by calling the parent call. The parent goal of a cut is the goal matching the head of the rule in whose body the particular cut (!) occurs.

When properly used, (!) can dramatically enhance the efficiency of a program. On the other hand, if not properly used, it can also introduce serious problems. Cut can be used in one of the following forms:

First Goal, !, Second Goal
First Goal, !; Second Goal

Assume we consult the following program:

eats (chris, pizza): - !.
eats (mick, Anything).

Let's see what happens when we submit the goal

```
?-eats(Person, pizza).
```

The answer returned will be

```
Person = chris ;
no.
```

When solving this goal, Prolog tries the first rule, which succeeds but causes a cut to be executed. Hence, *Person = chris* is returned as a first solution. But when we ask for more solutions the answer is no. When the cut was executed, the choice point for the goal *eats/2* was removed. As a result, the solution *Person = mick* is not found even though *mick* eats *Anything*. To say that the choice point for *eats/2* is removed means that Prolog cannot backtrack and try other rules for *eats/2*.

The next example is slightly more complex. Consider the program

```
cool (X)
      :- X = peewee, !, fail.
cool (X).
```

This says that if *X = peewee*, then fail the goal *cool (X)*. But if *X* is anyone else, then *X* is cool. Submit the elementary goal

```
?-cool(peewee).
no.
```

This goal fails. Here is how it works. *X = peewee* succeeds in the first rule and the cut is executed, thus preventing any backtracking. The construct [*X = peewee, !*] has succeeded, therefore Prolog attempts to solve *fail*. That goal will fail and since backtracking has been blocked by the cut (!), the goal *cool (peewee)* fails. On the other hand, submit the goal

```
?-cool(mickeymouse).
yes.
```

This goal succeeds. The initial subgoal of the first rule fails since *mickeymouse = peewee* fails. Hence, Prolog moves to the second rule, which solves the goal.

7.1.4 Fail

Fail is a built-in that always fails, thus causing the current goal in which it appears to fail. It is often used in conjunction with cut (!) to control the execution of goals and the search for solutions.

Assume that Harriet is writing a program to remind her which foods cause allergic reactions, and therefore are not safe for her to eat.

```
safe (X) :- allergen (X), !, fail.

safe (X) :- fruit (X); vegetable (X).

safe (X) :- meat (X).

allergen (eggs).
allergen (strawberries).
allergen (peanuts).
fruit (strawberries).
fruit (apricots).
```

The goal

```
?-safe(strawberries).
no.
```

would fail even though the fact *fruit(strawberries)* succeeds using the second rule. What happens is that in solving *safe(strawberries)*, the first rule is tried first. Hence, Prolog attempts to solve

allergen (strawberries), !, fail.

Since *allergen (strawberries)* succeeds and (!) succeeds, Prolog now reaches *fail,* which fails. But because of the cut (!), Prolog cannot backtrack to the choice point for safe/1, hence the second rule cannot be tried, and thus the goal fails.

Another example:

```
?-fail -> write(a).
no.
?-fail -> write(a); write(b).
b
yes.
```

The first goal fails since it is an if-then construct and the condition fails. The second goal succeeds since it is an if-then-else construct, and although the condition fails, the else part (the subgoal *write (b)*) succeeds.

It is interesting to note that if-then and if-then-else can be defined in terms of cut. For example, a particular if-then construct

Cond -> Goals

could be replaced by the call

myTest($V_1, \ldots, V_n$)

where $V_1, \ldots, V_n$ are all the variables occurring in Cond or Goals, and myTest/n is defined by

myTest($V_1, \ldots, V_n$)
    :-
    Cond, !, Goals

If $V_1, \ldots, V_n$ are all the variables occurring in Cond, IfGoals, or ThenGoals, a particular if-then-else construct

Cond -> IfGoals; ThenGoals

could be replaced by the call

yourTest ($V_1, \ldots, V_n$)

where yourTest/n is defined by

yourTest ($V_1, \ldots, V_n$)
    :-
    Cond, !, IfGoals

yourTest (V_1, . . . , V_n)

:-

ElseGoals.

7.1.5 Negation (not)

The forms in which negation can be introduced are

not (Goal)
not Goal
\+ Goal
\+ (Goal)

If the *Goal* fails, then *not (Goal)* succeeds. If *Goal* succeeds, then *not (Goal)* fails. This is the reason why negation in Prolog is called *negation by failure*. When *not (Goal)* succeeds, it doesn't bind any variables in *Goal*. For example:

edible (X)

:-

food (X), not (poisonous (X)).

food (mushrooms).
food (apples).
poisonous (mushrooms).

Then

```
?-edible (X).
X = apples;
no
```

Only *X = apples* is returned as a solution. Since *food (apples)* succeeds and *poisonous (apples)* fails, then *not (poisonous (apples))* succeeds and hence *X = apples* is a solution for edible(X). But since *poisonous (mushrooms)* succeeds, *edible (mushrooms)* fails.

7.2 LOOKING AT THE PROGRAM

After a program has been consulted, the user can ask to see what clauses constitute the program or a particular procedure in the program. The predicate *listing* with no arguments prints all the clauses in the program, whereas the predicate *listing* with one argument prints all the clauses for all predicates matching the specified argument. The forms are

listing
listing(Predicate)
listing(Predicate/Arity)
listing(Module:Predicate/Arity)

If *Predicate* is the name of a predicate, all the clauses of any arity are listed by *listing(Predicate)*. If the *Arity* is specified, only the clauses for *Predicate/Arity* are listed. For example, assume the program is

```
sales (larry, manager, senior).
sales (janet, clerk).
sales (X, Position)
    :-
    works (X,sales-dept),
    employee (X, Position).
```

Listing will behave as follows:

```
?-listing(sales/3).
sales(larry, manager, senior).
yes.
?-listing(sales).
sales(larry, manager, senior).
sales(janet, clerk).
sales(_1200, _396):-
    works(_1200, sales_dept),
    employee(_1200, _396).
yes.
```

Note that the clauses are listed in the order in which they appear in the program, and that all variables are replaced by their internal representations.

7.3 BUILTINS AFFECTING THE PROGRAM

Some Prolog predicates can directly affect the program, adding or removing facts and rules while the program is running. The set of facts and rules pertaining to a predicate with a given arity is called a *procedure*. For instance, in the program

```
parent (Parent, Child)
    :-
    mother (Parent, Child);
    father (Parent, Child).
parent (joe, suzy).
parent (lillian).
parent (harry).
```

The first two clauses pertain to the predicate *parent* of arity 2 (since it has two arguments), denoted by *parent/2*. The last two clauses pertain to *parent/1*. Hence, this program has two procedures: *Parent/2,* consisting of the first two clauses, and *parent/1,* consisting of the last two clauses. We will later see how to add or remove clauses from these procedures.

7.3.1 Assertions

Assertions allow the user to add to the basic knowledge incorporated in a program by adding clauses to the program. There are three forms of assertions:

assert (Clause)	adds *Clause* to a procedure, with no specification of order;
asserta (Clause)	adds *Clause* at the beginning of a procedure;
assertz (Clause)	adds *Clause* at the end of a procedure.

The *Clause* is added to the procedure in the program with the same name and arity as the *Clause* being asserted. All uninstantiated variables occurring in *Clause* are re-quantified before *Clause* is added to the database. In essence, a copy of *Clause* is made, and all the uninstantiated variables occurring in this copy of *Clause* are replaced by completely new variables that have no connection to the originals occurring in *Clause;* this copy of *Clause* is what is added to the database.

Because of this behavior, the order of calls invoking assert is important. For example, assuming no clauses already exist for *p/1,* the first of the following goals will fail, while the second succeeds.

```
?-X = a, assert(p(X)), p(b).
no.
?-assert(p(X)), X = a, p(b).
X = a,
yes.
```

What happens in the first goal is that the fact *p(a)* is added to the program, so *p(b)* fails, since there is no matching fact in the database when it runs. In the second goal, the fact *p(SomeVar)* is added to the program, *X* = *a* succeeds since it only needs to instantiate the variable *X* to the atom *a* (note that the *X* in the goal no longer has any connection to the variable *SomeVar* in the copy of *p(X)* that was added to the program), and now *p(b)* succeeds since the matching fact *p(SomeVar)* occurs in the program.

The following example shows how the different forms of *assert* work:

```
?-assert (p(a)), asserta (p(c)), assertz (p(b)).
yes.
?-listing (p/1).
p(c).
p(a).
p(b).
yes.
```

The first subgoal, *assert (p(a)),* adds *p(a)* to the program. The placement of a clause by *assert/1* is defined by the implementation, so you can't assume that it goes at the beginning, middle, or end of the procedure. The second subgoal, *asserta (p(c)),* adds the clause *p(c)* at the beginning of the procedure *p/1,* hence before *p(a).* The last subgoal adds *p(b)* at the end of *p/1.*

Calls to assert (or asserta or assertz) can also occur in the bodies of rules. Moreover, assert (as well as asserta and assertz) can be applied to rules. Such calls should be of the form

assert((Head :- Body)).

Notice the extra parentheses to keep the Prolog reader from becoming confused.

7.3.2   Retractions

Retractions allow the user to remove clauses from the program. The form is *retract (Clause).*

A call *retract(Clause)* causes the first clause for the given procedure whose head matches (unifies) with *Clause* to be removed from the program. Note that in this context, we interpret facts as degenerate rules having heads but no bodies. The following example shows how *retract/1* can be used to get rid of comic book heroes in a program. Assume the program is

```
hero (spiderman).
hero (superman).
hero (batman).
```

We submit the goals

```
?-retract(hero(superman)).
yes.
?-listing(hero).
hero(spiderman).
hero(batman).
yes.
```

We see that *hero (superman)* is no longer in the program after the first goal succeeds. We submit the goals

```
?-retract(hero (X)).
X = spiderman ;
X = batman ;
no.
?-listing(hero).
yes.
```

The first goal removed the clause *hero (spiderman)* and, upon backtracking, also removed *hero(batman)*. Upon backtracking once more, no clauses for *hero/1* are left to be removed, so the last goal (invoked by the last semi-colon typed) fails. *listing(hero)* now returns no clauses for hero since none are left.

Like assert, calls to retract can occur in the bodies of rules and can also be applied directly to rules. The call should be of the form

```
retract( (Head:-Body) ).
```

Notice the extra parentheses to keep the Prolog reader from being confused.

7.3.3   Removing a Procedure

To remove an entire procedure from a program, the *abolish/2* builtin works faster than retracting all the clauses of the procedure one at a time. The form is

abolish (Name, Arity).

All the clauses for the specified procedure *Name/Arity* are removed from the database. Suppose we return to the program

hero (spiderman).
hero (superman).
hero (batman).

The goal

```
?-abolish(hero,1).
yes.
```

will remove all the clauses for *hero/1*.

7.3.4   Directly Accessing Clauses of a Procedure

Sometimes it is necessary to directly obtain one or more clauses for a procedure without actually executing or running a goal corresponding to the head. The clause/2 built-in predicate supplies the means of doing this. The general form is

clause(Head, Body).

Head is a term that can possibly match against the head of some clause in the program, and *Body* is an expression (often a variable) that can match against the body of the clause whose head matched Head. For example, consider the small parent program from Section 7.3:

Parent (Parent, Child)
  :-
  mother (Parent, Child);
  father (Parent, Child).
parent (joe, suzy).
parent (lillian).
parent (harry).

Consider the following calls to clause/2:

```
?-  clause(parent(P,C), Body).
P = _12345
C = _12347
Body = (mother(_12345, _12347);father(_12345, _12347))   ;
P = joe
C = suzy
Body = true
```

As this example shows, when *Head* matches against a fact, *Body* is matched against the atom "true". This corresponds to the interpretation of facts as unconditional rules. Like assert and retract, calls to clause/2 can occur in the bodies of rules.

7.4   COMPARING TERMS AND SORTING LISTS

Next, we take a look at builtins for comparing terms. The following builtins take two terms as arguments and check whether or not their internal representations are identical. Their forms are

Term1 == *Term2*
Term1 \== *Term2*

Term1 is identical to *Term2* if they can be unified *and* variables occupying equivalent positions in both terms are absolutely identical. No variables are bound inside a call to either ==/2 or \==/2. The following examples illustrate the action of these two builtins:

```
?- bar \= = foo.
yes.
?- f(b) = = f(b).
yes.
?- X = = Y.
no.
?- f(X) \= = f(X).
no.
?- (a,b,c) \= = (a,b,c).
no.
```

The next two builtins check whether two terms are unifiable or not. Their forms are

Arg1 = *Arg2*
Arg1 \= *Arg2*

The Prolog unifier is called to unify *Arg1* and *Arg2*, binding variables if necessary. If the two terms can be unified, = succeeds while \= fails. The procedure \= succeeds if the two terms cannot be unified. This is different from the \== procedure, as shown in one of the following examples.

```
?-f(A,A) = f(a,B).
A = a
B = a
yes.
?-f(A,A) = f(a,b).
no.
?-X = f(X).
X = f(f(f(f(f(f(f(f(f(f(f(...)))))))))))
yes.
?-X\=1.
no.
?-X \= =1.
X = _32164
yes.
```

In various applications it is useful to order Prolog terms and to sort lists of terms according to this order. Prolog provides a standard ordering that is related to the usual *lexicographic* or *dictionary* order of words. The lexicographic ordering of words is informally defined as follows:

> Word1 lexically precedes Word2 *if and only if*
> given that N is the number of the first letter (from left to right) at which Word1 differs from Word2, letter number N of Word1 precedes letter number N of Word2.

Normally, the upper and lowercase versions of a letter are taken to be the same. However, Prolog distinguishes them, so that, for example, the atoms "ab" and "aB" are different. Consequently, it must also distinguish them for ordering purposes. To this end, it orders characters according to their ASCII codes:

> Character C1 precedes character C2 if the ASCII code of C1 is less than the ASCII code of C2.

Prolog uses this ordering in defining its standard order for atoms, which is denoted by @<. That is, if A1 and A2 are atoms, then

> A1 @< A2 *if and only if* (*)
> given that N is the first character position at which A1 and A2 differ, character number N of A1 precedes character number N of A2 in the sense of the ASCII ordering.

Prolog extends ordering to all terms by first grouping the terms for ordering purposes:

> *Variables @< Numbers @< Atoms @< Compound Terms*

Within the groups, the elements are ordered as follows:

Variables
    Ordering of variables is implementation dependent and often reflects the relative age of the variable in the sense of its creation in an internal data area.

Numbers
    Numbers are ordered according to their standard (signed) magnitude.

Atoms
    Atoms are ordered as defined by (*) above.

Compound terms
    Compound terms are ordered by an extension of the @< for atoms, numbers, and variables as follows. Let T1 and T2 be compound terms. Then

> T1 @< T2 *if and only if*
> *Either* the functor of T1 precedes the functor of T2 in the sense of @<, *or*
> The functors of T1 and T2 are identical, and if N is the first argument position in which an argument S1 of T1 differs from the corresponding argument S2 of T2, then S1 @< S2, *or*
> The functors of T1 and T2 are identical, and every argument of T1 is identical with the corresponding argument of T2, but T2 has additional arguments.

Consequently, if BYE is an uninstantiated variable, the following will hold:

> BYE @< 34.5 @< 'JACK' @< bill @< ff(ab) @< j(a,b,c) @< j(a,b,a,b).

The comparison operators @=<, @>, and @>= have the obvious meanings relative to @<. The builtin compare/3 is also based on the standard order. The general form of a call to compare/3 is

compare(Relation, Term1, Term2)

where *Relation* is one of "=", "<", or ">". Compare is defined as

compare(Relation, Term1, Term2) *if and only if*
        Relation is "=" and Term1 is identical with Term2 (Term1 = = Term2), *or*
        Relation is "<" and Term1 @< Term2, *or*
        Relation is ">" and Term1 @> Term2.

In particular, if Relation is an uninstatiated variable, it is unified with the appropriate value. Thus, for example,

```
?-Left = foo(bar), Right = 'ABC', compare(Rel, Left, Right).
Left = foo(bar)
Right = 'ABC'
Rel = >
yes.
```

Prolog supplies a builtin-sorting predicate that will sort lists according to the standard order. Not surprisingly, it is called *sort/2*. The general form of calls to it is

    sort(Unsorted, Sorted).

Thus, for example:

```
?- sort( [ j(a,b,a,b), 'JACK', ff(ab), 34.5, j(a,b,c), bill],
Sorted).
Sorted = [34.5, 'JACK', bill , ff(ab), j(a,b,c), j(a,b,a,b)]
yes.
```

7.5 COLLECTING INFORMATION

Suppose you want to collect all the solutions to some goal together in a list. The builtins *setof/3* and *bagof/3* will do just that. The forms are

    setof (Template, Goal, Collection)
    bagof (Template, Goal, Collection)

These predicates collect together in the list, *Collection,* all the instances of *Template* such that *Goal* is provable. *Template* is a term that usually shares variables with *Goal*.

Calls to bagof/3 produce a *Collection* whose instances of *Template* occur in the order corresponding to the successful solutions of Goal. This order is the same as if one submitted *Goal* as a top-level goal and repeatedly hit semi-colon to backtrack through all the possible ways of solving Goal. If there are no ways to solve *Goal,* the call to bagof fails. Consider the following program:

```
likes (kev,running).
likes (kev,lifting).
likes (keith,running).
likes (keith,lifting).
likes (ken,swimming).
likes (johanna,swimming).
likes (andy,bicycling).
likes (chris,lifting).
likes (chris,running).
```

The following goals illustrate the behavior of bagof/3:

```
?-bagof(Person, likes(Person, running), Runners).
Person = _123
Runners = [kev, keith, chris]
yes.
?-bagof(kev_sport(Sport), likes(kev, Sport), KevSports).
Sport = _123
KevSports = [kev_sport(running), kev_sport(lifting)].
yes.
?-bagof(Sport, likes(bill, Sport), BillSports).
no.
```

Setof/3 produces a *Collection* that is sorted according to the standard order (see Section 7.4) with all duplicate elements removed. For all practical purposes, setof is defined in terms of bagof:

> setof(Template, Goal, List)
>
> :-
>
> bagof(Template, Goal, Bag),
> sort(Bag, List).

If we replace the calls to bagof in the example above by setof, we obtain the following behaviors:

```
?-setof(Person, likes(Person, running), Runners).
Person = _123
Runners = [chris, keith, kev]
yes.
?-setof(kev_sport(Sport), likes(kev, Sport), KevSports).
Sport = _123
KevSports = [kev_sport(lifting), kev_sport(running)].
yes.
?-setof(Sport, likes(bill, Sport), BillSports).
no.
```

Figure 7–1 suggests an intuition about the operation of bagof (and consequently setof also). In essence, bagof(Template, Goal, Result) sets up a subsidiary computation trying to repeatedly solve Goal, saving the instantiation of Template each time Goal is successfully solved, and then forcing a subsidiary failure (one that doesn't backtrack out into the computation before the bagof call). Each time this failure is forced, any variables in Template that were uninstantiated when the bagof call was first made are unbound again from any bindings that occurred during the call of Goal. This is necessary, of course, to be able to collect the possibly multiple instantiations of Template. Of course, variables occuring in Template generally also occur in Goal (the normal case).

Variables that occur in *Goal* and not in *Template* are known as *free variables*. As Figure 7–1 suggests, such free variables may have obtained values at earlier stages in computation before the bagof is invoked. On the other hand, they may be uninstantiated at the time the bagof is invoked. However, the process of running the *Goal* of the bagof may cause them to become instantiated. The question is, What happens to such variables when the bagof forces *Goal* to backtrack in looking for alternative solutions?

FIGURE 7–1
Computing a bagof subgoal.

Goal: G1,   G2, ...,   bagof(X, p(X,Y), L),   Gn, ...

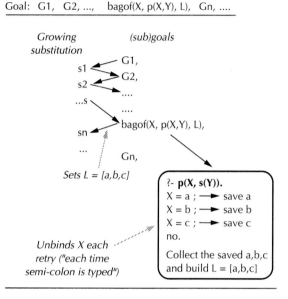

We know that those variables occurring in *Template* are reset (i.e., unbound) when the forced backtracking occurs. Are the free variables reset? The answer is no. Once a free variable is instantiated, it remains instantiated throughout the bagof computation. Note that if one forces the entire bagof computation to fail, and subsequently retry, then the free variables are reset. But this is failure from outside the bagof, rather than failure from inside the bagof. This is illustrated by:

```
?-setof(Sport, likes(Person, Sport), LikedSports).
Sport = _8
Person = kev
LikedSports = [lifting, running] ;
Sport = _8,
Person = keith
LikedSports = [lifting, running] ;
Sport = _8
Person = ken
LikedSports = [swimming]
... etc...
```

How do we describe the collection of all sports that are liked by someone? That is, the collection of all sports for which there is a person who likes that sport. The previous example shows that it will not do to simply place an uninstantiated variable in the Person position, since then all we get are the sports liked by kev, the sports liked by keith, etc., in succession. The key is in the phrase "There is a Person . . . ." Such a phrase is a *quantifier on* the variable Person. It attaches (or binds — unfortunately confusing terminology) any instances of the variable Person within its scope, which is simply the phrase following the quantifier phrase. Thus the scope of this quantifer is the phrase "who likes that sport." In this case, the word *who* is essentially equivalent to *Person*. Using the likes/2 predicate, this might be expressed

"there is a Person" such that likes(Person, Sport).

Prolog's notation for such (existential) quantifiers is

Person ^likes(Person, Sport).

Here is the important point of all this. The use of existential quantifiers inside a bagof/3 or setof/3 call forces Prolog to treat the quantified variable exactly the same way it treats variables that occur in the template. That is, when subsidiary backtracking is forced during the bagof computation, both the variables in the template and any existentially quantified variables are reset (i.e., unbound from any values). This enables us to directly use a bagof call to obtain the list of all sports that are liked by someone, as the following example shows:

```
?- setof(Sport, Person ^ likes(Person, Sport), LikedSports).
Sport = _8
Person = _10
LikedSports = [bicycling,lifting,running,swimming] ;
no.
```

If one has more than one variable to existentially quantify, two styles of expression are available:

bagof(T, V1 ^V2 ^V3 ^Goal, C)

or

bagof(T, [V1,V2,V3] ^Goal, C)

We now submit the following goals:

```
?- setof( [Sport,People],
setof(Person, likes (Person, Sport), People), Set).
Sport = _1
People = _2
Person = _4
Set = [bicycling,[andy]], [lifting,[chris,keith,kev]],
[running,[chris,keith,kev]],[swimming,[johanna,kev]]
yes.
?- setof(Person,  Sport ^ likes(Person, Sport), SetofPeople).
Person = _1
Sport = _2
SetofPeople = [andy,chris,johanna,keith,ken,kev]
yes.
?- bagof(Person,  Sport ^ likes(Person, Sport), BagofPeople).
Person = _1
Sport = _2
BagofPeople = [kev,keith,ken,johanna,andy,chris]
yes.
?- bagof(Sport,  Person ^ likes(Person, Sport), BagofSports).
Person = _1
```

```
Sport = _2
BagofSports = [running,lifting,running,lifting,swimming,swimming,
bicycling,lifting,running]
yes.
```

7.6 ANALYZING TERMS

A number of builtin predicates are available for breaking up terms into their components (functors and arguments), building up terms from given components, finding the arity of a term, deciding whether it is a variable, an atom, an integer, etc. These builtins are extremely useful in Prolog applications.

7.6.1 The Univ Builtin (=..)

This builtin translates between lists of components and the corresponding terms. Its forms are

> *Term* =.. *[Functor | Arguments]*
> *Term* =.. *List*

The univ (=..) builtin requires that its left side be a term (possibly a variable) and that its right side be a list, again possibly a variable. At least one of the two sides must be partially instantiated, otherwise an error occurs. The definition of univ runs as follows:

> T =.. [P | Args] holds *if and only if*
> T is a term whose principal functor is the atom P and whose arguments in order occur (in order) in the list Args.

This predicate can be used in one of two modes. If its left side is instantiated to a term (which may contain uninstantiated variables if it is a compound term), univ decomposes that term into the list on its right side. The list contains the functor of the term as its first element, followed by the arguments of the term, in order. Thus, for example,

```
?-my_pred(tom, A + B, f(X)) =.. [ Functor : Args ].
Functor = my_pred
Args = [tom, A + B, f(X)]
yes.
```

In the second mode, if the left side of the univ (=..) call is an uninstantiated variable X, while its right side is a list whose first element (at least) is a concrete atom P, univ binds the left-side variable (X) to a term whose principal functor is the atom P and whose arguments are those given by Args (which may be uninstantiated variables). In this mode, it operates as a constructor. For example,

```
?-X = .. [ zip, 4, h(VV), zap ].
X = zip(4, h(_23), zap)
VV = _23
yes.
?-X =.. [ +,3,1 ].
```

```
X = 3+1
yes.
?-1 =.. [ 1].
yes.
```

When *Term* is instantiated to a constant, *List* will be unified with the singleton list whose sole element is *Term*. If *Term* is a structured term, *List* will be unified with a list whose head is the principal functor of *Term* and whose tail is the list of arguments in *Term*. When *List* is instantiated to a singleton list whose element is an atom, *Term* will be unified with that element. If *List* has at least two elements, the first of which is an atom, *Term* will be unified with a term whose principal functor is the head of *List* and whose arguments are the remaining elements of *List* in order.

7.6.2   The Arg Builtin (arg/3)

This builtin accesses the arguments of a structured term. Its form is

> *arg (N, Structure, Argument)*

Argument will be unified with the *Nth* argument of *Structure*. *Nth* must be a positive integer. *Structure* should be a compound term whose arity is greater than or equal to *N*. When these conditions hold, *Argument* will be unified with the *Nth* argument of *Structure*. In all other cases, the call to arg will fail. The following examples illustrate the behavior of arg:

```
?-arg(2, stooges(larry, moe, curly),X).
X = moe.
yes.
?-arg(2, (a,b,c), X).
X = (b,c)
yes.
```

7.6.3   The Functor Builtin (functor/3)

This builtin creates skeletal compound terms or retrieves information about terms. Its form is

> *functor (Structure, Functor, Arity)*

The definition of functor is

> functor (*Structure, Functor, Arity*) holds *if and only if*
> > *Structure* is (bound to) a term whose principcal functor is *Functor* and whose arity is *Arity*.

The principal functor of the term *Structure* has the name *Functor* and the arity *Arity*, where *Functor* is an atom. Either *Structure* must be instantiated to a term or an atom, or *Functor* and *Arity* must be instantiated to an atom and a nonnegative integer, respectively. In the case where *Structure* is initially unbound, *functor/3* will unify *Structure* with a structured term of *Arity* arguments, where the principal functor of the term is *functor*. Each argument of the new structure will be a new uninstantiated variable. When *Structure* is instantiated to a structured term, *Functor* will be unified with the principal functor of *Structure* and *Arity* will be unified with the arity of the term. *functor/3* treats atoms as structured terms with arity 0. The principal functor of a list is "." with arity 2. Here are some examples:

```
?-functor(Structure,fish,2).
Structure = fish(_123,_124)
yes.
?-functor(city('Santa Monica','CA','USA'),Functor,Arity).
Functor = city
Arity = 3
yes.
```

7.6.4 Checking the Types of Terms

This group of builtins take a term as their argument and succeed only if that term is of a specific type. Their forms are

atom (Term)	*Term* is an atom.
atomic (Term)	*Term* is an atom or a number.
float (Term)	*Term* is a floating point number.
integer (Term)	*Term* is an integer.
number (Term)	*Term* is an integer or a floating point.
var (Term)	*Term* is an unbound variable.
nonvar (Term)	*Term* is an instantiated variable.

Each of these predicates will succeed when its argument is of the proper type and fail otherwise. *integer/1* and *float/1* examine only the internal representation of a number. For instance, the call *integer (2.0)* will succeed because *2.0* is represented internally as an integer. In addition, *float (4294967296)* will succeed because *4292967296* is represented by a floating point value because it is outside the range of the integer representation. The range for integer representation depends on particular implementations and machines. Often it is -2^{27} to $2^{27} - 1$. Here are several examples:

```
?-atom(apple).
yes.
?-integer(zool).
no.
?-float(cement).
no.
```

The following examples illustrate the range of integers:

```
?-integer(-134217728).
yes.
?-integer(-134217729).
no
?-integer(134217727).
yes.
?-integer(134217728).
no.
```

```
?-float(134217728).
yes.
```

var/1 succeeds if *Term* is an unbound variable and fails otherwise. *nonvar/1* succeeds when *Term* is a constant or structured term:

```
?-var(constant).
no.
?- nonvar(constant).
yes.
?-X = Y, Y = Z, Z = doughnut, var(X).
no.
?-var(X).
X = _25197
yes.
```

7.7   ARITHMETIC EXPRESSIONS

7.7.1   Evaluating Arithmetic Expressions (is/2)

The builtin for evaluating arithmetic expressions has the form

Result is Expression

Expression should be a ground term that can be evaluated. Numbers evaluate as themselves, and a list evaluates as the first element of the list. The operators listed in Figures 7–2 and 7–3 can also be evaluated when their arguments can be evaluated. If *Result* is an unbound variable, it will be bound to the numeric value of *Expression*. If *Result* is not unbound, it will be evaluated, and the value of the *Result* will be unified

---

FIGURE 7–2
Arithmetic operators for is/2.

Operator	Description
$-X$	unary minus
X div Y	integer division
X mod Y	X (integer) modulo Y
X xor Y	X exclusive or Y
X∗Y	multiplication
X+Y	addition
X−Y	subtraction
X/Y	division
X//Y	integer division
X∧Y	integer bitwise conjunction
X≪Y	integer bitwise left shift of X by Y places
X≫Y	integer bitwise right shift of X by Y places
X∨Y	integer bitwise disjunction
X^Y	X to the power of Y
[X] "X"	evaluates the character expression X
\X not(X)	integer bitwise negation
~Char	the ASCII code of Char

FIGURE 7–3
Arithmetic functions for is/2.

Operator	Description
abs(X)	absolute value
acos(X)	arc cosine
asin(X)	arc sine
atan(X)	arc tangent
cos(X)	cosine
cputime	CPU time in seconds since ALS Prolog started.
exp(X)	exponential function
floor(X)	the largest integer not greater than X
heapused	heap space in use, in bytes.
log(X)	natural logarithm
log10(X)	base 10 logarithm
random	returns a random real number between 0 and 1
round(X)	integer rounding of X
sin(X)	sine
sqrt(X)	square root
tan(X)	tangent
trunc(X)	the largest integer not greater than X

with the value of the *Expression*. Following are several simple examples illustrating the use of the arithmetic operators and functions.

```
?-1+1 is 3-1.
yes.
?-X is 6*7.
X = 42
yes.
?-X is 2.5 + 3.5.
X = 6
yes.
```

If is/2 attempts to evaluate an unknown operator, or if the expression being evaluated contains one or more uninstatiated variables, the call to is/2 will fail. Also, failure will occur if there are any arithmetic faults, such as overflow, underflow, or division by zero.

7.7.2 Comparing Arithmetic Expressions

Prolog provides several builtins for comparing arithmetic expressions. Their forms are

Expression 1	$<$	Expression 2	less than
Expression 1	$>$	Expression 2	greater than
Expression 1	$=:=$	Expression 2	equal
Expression 1	$= \backslash =$	Expression 2	not equal
Expression 1	$=<$	Expression 2	less than or equal
Expression 1	$>=$	Expression 2	greater than or equal

Both arguments to each relational operator should be instantiated to expressions that can be evaluated by is/2. The relational operator succeeds if the relation holds for the values of the two arguments and fails otherwise. A relational operator will fail if one or both of its arguments cannot be evaluated. The following examples illustrate the use of the arithmetic relational operators.

```
?-- 7*0 =< 1+1.
yes.
?- 1+1 =< 7*0.
no.
```

7.8 INPUT/OUTPUT

7.8.1 Writing Information

Like most programming languages, Prolog provides facilities for inputting and out-putting information. The builtins for writing and displaying information have the following formats:

> *write (Term)*   writes a term without quotes around quoted atoms
> *writeq (Term)*   writes a term using quotes around quoted atoms

Term is written to the current output stream. When Prolog is first started, the current output stream is set to the screen. In Section 7.8.3, we will see how to change the current output stream to other targets such as files. Uninstantiated variables are written as an underbar followed by a decimal number. These procedures do *not* place a full stop in the output stream after the term is written, as can be seen in the following examples.

```
?-write(Soysauce + 'chow mein').
_123 + chow mein
yes.
?-writeq(Soy sauce + 'chow mein').
_123 + 'chow mein'.
yes.
```

To leave a blank line in the current output stream, the builtin *nl/0* can be used. Its form is

> *nl.*

Here is an example:

```
?-write(start), nl, nl, nl, write(finish).
start


finish
yes.
```

On a more primitive level, the builtins *put/1, tab/1* will respectively write out a single character or print out a specified number of spaces:

> *put (CharCode)*
> *tab (N)*

If *Char* is bound to the ASCII code of a character (an integer within the range 0–255), *put/1* will write out the character whose ASCII code is *Char* to the current output stream, while *tab/1* will write out N space characters (ASCII 32) to the standard output stream, as is shown in the following:

```
?-put(65), tab(15), put(66) .
A               B
yes.
```

7.8.2 Reading Information

The Prolog builtin available for reading information from the current input stream is read/1:

> *read (Term)*

read (Term) reads the next term from the current input stream (see Section 7.8.3) and unifies it with *Term*. The term must be followed by a *full stop*. The current operator declarations are used to parse the term. If there are no more characters left on the standard input stream, *Term* will be unified with the atom *end-of-file*. The following examples illustrate the functionality of read/1:

```
?-write('hi>>'),read(Item).
hi>>hello(there).
Item = hello(there)
yes.
?-read(Item).
bye(Bill).
Bill = _8
Item = bye(_8)
yes.
```

The primitive builtins to use for reading character by character are *get/1* and *get0/1*. Their forms are

> *get (Char)*   read the next printable character
> *get0(Char)*   read the next character

get0/1 unifies *Char* with the ASCII code of the next character from the current input stream. If there are no more characters left, *Char* will be unified with −1. *get/1* discards all nonprinting characters from the current input stream. It unifies *Char* with the ASCII code of the first nonblank printable character. *Char* is unified with −1 on end-of-file. The following interaction illustrates the action of get/1 (as well as get0/1), assuming that the current input stream contains ABCDEFGHI (whether that stream is from a file or from the terminal):

```
?-get(First), get(Second), get(Third).
First = 65,
Second = 66,
Third = 67
yes.
```

7.8.3   Changing the Current I/O Stream

By default, the current input stream reads from the keyboard and the current output stream writes to the screen. The builtin predicates for changing the current input stream to a different source are the following:

see (File)	sets the current input stream
seeing (File)	returns the name of the current input stream
seen	closes the current input stream

see/1 sets the current input stream to the file named *File*. Input operations will start at the beginning of the file. By convention, *user* is the name of the keyboard (terminal), so that see(user) switches to reading from the keyboard. *seeing/1* unifies *File* with the name of the current input stream. If no stream has been explicitly opened by *see/1*, File will be unified with the atom *user* since it is the default. *seen/0* closes the current input stream if it is any stream other than *user*, and sets the current input stream to be *user*. If the current input stream is already *user,* seen/0 has no effect. Consider the following example:

firstTerm (File, Term)
:-
seeing (Current Input),
see (File),
read(Term),
seen,
see (Current Input).

A call to this predicate will have the following effects:

- The current input stream is saved in the variable *Current Input;*
- The file *File* is opened;
- A single term *Term* is read from the file;
- the file is closed;
- the previous input stream is restored.

Similarly, builtins exist for changing the current output stream:

tell (File)	sets the standard output stream
telling (File)	returns the name of the current output stream
told	closes the standard output stream

tell/1 sets the current output stream to the file named *File*. The previous contents of the file are discarded and output operations will start at the beginning of the file. By convention, the screen (terminal) is identified with the output file *user. telling/1* unifies *File* with the name of the current output stream. If no stream has been explicitly opened by *tell/1, File* will be unified with the atom *user,* since this is the default output stream. *told/0* closes the current output stream, setting the new output stream to be *user*. If the current output stream is already *user, told* has no effect. The following example is similar to the preceding input example:

```
firstTerm (File, Term)
   :-
   telling (Current Output),
   tell (File),
   write (Term),
   told,
   tell (Current Output).
```

This program will preserve the current output stream, open a File, write one Term to it, close the File and then restore the previous output stream.

7.8.4 Converting Between Atoms and Strings

Using get/1 and get0/1, we can input character streams and accumulate them as lists of the corresponding ASCII codes (as we will show in Section 7.8.5). However, we won't be able to do much of interest with such lists if we cannot connect them with the rest of Prolog, in particular with atoms. Fortunately, one of the builtins allows us to convert between an atom and the list of ASCII codes corresponding to the name of the atom. This builtin predicate is *name/2*, defined as

name(Atom, String) holds *if and only if*
    String is the list of ASCII codes making up the name of Atom.

Thus, for example, the following hold

name(abc, [97, 98, 99])
name('AB', [65, 66]).

To facilitate the use of such strings in programs, Prolog supports a convention that makes writing specific versions of such lists easier and more understandable. Suppose that one wants to write the list of ASCII codes corresponding to *abc* at some point in a program. Instead of having to write [97, 98, 99], we can simply write "abc". That is, an expression enclosed in a pair of double quotes is taken to denote the list of ASCII codes of the characters between the quotes. To include the double quote itself in such an expression, repeat it at the appropriate point. Thus, "a" "b" will denote [97, 34, 98].

7.8.5 Lexically Analyzing an Input Stream

If we wish to process a stream of characters according to the conventions of some language, whether a natural language like English or a formal language like Prolog, the first step is break up the undifferentiated stream of characters into lexical units, usually referred to as *words*. The basic machinery of Prolog, coupled with some of the builtins we have described so far, will enable us to construct programs that perform such lexical analysis. For our example, we will develop a small program that breaks up the input stream according to a simplified version of the conventions of English.

The program will assume that the input stream is intended to be one or more English sentences. Each time it is called, it will consume the characters starting with the current position and extending to the next full stop (.), exclamation point (!), or question mark (?). It will return a list of atoms corresponding to the way it breaks up the stream into words. Here is the top level of the program:

```
read_sentence(WordList)
    :-
    get(InitialChar),
    acceptable_in_word(InitialChar),!,
    read_words(InitialChar, [], BackwardsWordList),
    reverse(BackwardsWordList, WordList).
read_sentence([]).
```

The real workhorse of this level of the program is the predicate read_words/3. The first argument of read_words is the last character read before read_words/3 was invoked (we will see later why this a convenient approach). The second argument is an accumulator for the words of the sentence thus far read. We will see that it is quite natural to let these accumulate in reverse order. The third argument is the final list of words, which is simply the value of the accumulator when an end-of-sentence mark is encountered. Since the accumulator stores the words in reverse order, the last call in the body of read_sentence simply reverses this list to produce the output.

The first call in the body of read_sentence gets the next character from the input stream, while the second call tests whether this character is acceptable in an English word. These calls are present at this level simply because of the structure of read_words/3. The second clause for read_sentence handles exceptional situations such as trying to read a sentence from an empty stream (end_of_file has been reached). read_words/3 is defined in a mutually recursive way with continue_read_words/4. Together they implement the operation of the flow chart in Figure 7–4.

```
read_words(Char, CurrentList, FinalList)
    :-
    read_one_word(Char, Word, NextChar),
    continue_read_words(NextChar, [Word | CurrentList], FinalList).

continue_read_words(NextChar, CurrentList, FinalList)
    :-
    not(end_punctuation(NextChar)),
    get(NextNextChar),
    acceptable_in_word(NextNextChar),!,
    read_words(NextNextChar, CurrentList, FinalList).
continue_read_words(NextChar, CurrentList, CurrentList).
```

The second workhorse of this program is read_one_word/3. It is called with the last previous character read in its first argument. It tries to read one word from the input stream, returning that word in its second argument, and returning the first character following the word in its third argument. It calls read_word_chars/4 to get a reversed list of the characters making up the word. It then reverses this list and calls name/2 to obtain the atom corresponding to the characters in the list:

FIGURE 7–4
Control flow for reading sentences.

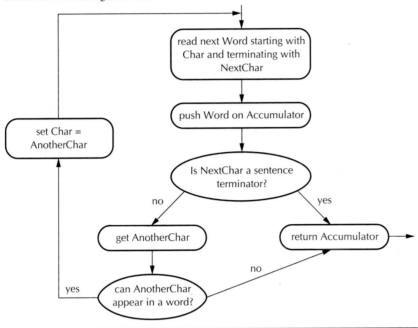

read_one_word(InitialChar, Word, FollowingChar)

   :-

read_word_chars(InitialChar, [], CharList, FollowingChar),
reverse(CharList, CorrectCharList),
name(Word, CorrectCharList).

The true heart of the program is read_word_chars/4. It is invoked with the most recently read character that can occur in a word in its first argument. Its second argument
is the list of previously read characters making up the current word, these characters
in reverse order. The third argument is used to return (pass out) the final list of characters, and the fourth argument returns the character immediately following the list being
read. read_word_chars/4 is defined mutually recursively with cont_read_word_chars/4.
Together they implement a loop similar to that shown above:

read_word_chars(CurrentChar, CurrentCharList, FinalCharList, FollowingChar)

   :-

get0(NextChar),
cont_read_word_chars(NextChar, [CurrentChar | CurrentCharList],
                          FinalCharList, | FollowingChar).

cont_read_word_chars(NextChar, CurrentCharList, FinalCharList, FollowingChar)

   :-

acceptable_in_word(NextChar),!,
read_word_chars(NextChar, CurrentCharList, FinalCharList, FollowingChar).

cont_read_word_chars(FollowingChar, FinalCharList, FinalCharList, FollowingChar).

Finally, there are the supporting predicates necessary for those defined above:

```
acceptable_in_word(Char)
    :-
    (~ a =< Char, Char =< ~ z) ;
    (~ A =< Char, Char =< ~ Z).

end_punctuation(~ .).
end_punctuation(~ !).
end_punctuation(~ ?).
end_punctuation(-1).

reverse(ListA, ListB)
    :-
    reverse(ListA, [], ListB).
reverse([], OutList, OutList).
reverse([Item | InTail], Stack, OutList)
    :-
    reverse(InTail, [Item | Stack], OutList).
```

Here is a simple test predicate with which to exercise the program:

```
run :-
    write('>>'),
    read_sentence(WordList),
    write(sent = WordList),nl.
```

The action of the program is illustrated by the following interaction:

```
?-run.
>> Hi  there, Ken!
sent=[Hi,there,Ken]
yes.
```

7.8.6 Printing Trees

In Section 6.4, we developed the concept of a binary tree together with predicates for manipulating such trees. At the end of that section, we created a sample program that generated a search tree whose entries were descriptors of the suitablility of various investments. Our goal here is to develop a program that can print out a humanly readable representation of such a tree. The sort of output we would like is illustrated in Figure 7–5.

In achieving this effect, the following considerations are important:

- We must traverse the input tree in right-to-left order;
- We must output the matter for the right-hand descendents of a node before outputting the label for the node;
- We must output the matter for the left-hand descendents of a node after outputting the label for the node;

FIGURE 7–5
A search tree printed in readable format.

```
                        stock(preferred)-medium
                stock(common)-low
                            savings_account(savings_and_loan)-low
                    savings_account(credit_union)-medium
            savings_account(commercial_bank)-medium
        savings_account(certificate_of_deposit)-high
                            retirement_plan(section_401k)-high
                    retirement_plan(keogh)-high
                retirement_plan(ira)-high
            retirement_plan(corporate)-high
                    mutual_fund(no_load)-high
                mutual_fund(load)-high
                    loans(treasury_bills)-high
        loans(commercial)-low
loans(bankers_acceptance)-low
                    limited_partnership(real_estate)-low
            limited_partnership(oil_and_gas)-low
                            life_insurance(whole_life)-high
                    life_insurance(term)-medium
                life_contract(single_payment)-high
            futures(silver)-low
        futures(gold)-low
                    bonds(us_government)-high
            bonds(state)-high
            bonds(municipal)-high
        bonds(corporate)-high
            annuity(single_premium)-high
```

- We must maintain a numeric argument representing the current indent level; this argument should be incremented by some fixed amount at every recursive call passing from a node to its descendents.

Suppose we name the desired predicate *show*. Then we know that *show* will have at least two arguments: the (sub)tree to be printed together with the indent level at which it should be printed. It turns out that these are the only arguments we need. Thus, we could set up our top-level goal as follows, where test/1 is as defined in Section 6.4:

```
testTreePrint :-
    test(Tree),
    show(Tree,0).
```

Our intent is that show/2 will print its first argument (Tree) in the desired form at an indent beginning as given by its second argument. We will assume that whenever show/2 is called, the cursor (or *printhead*) is at the left margin of the screen (or paper or window). In addition to handling the indenting, show/2 has three major tasks to accomplish:

- Printing the key and value of the immediate node;
- Getting the right subtree printed;
- Getting the left subtree printed.

Examination of Figure 7–5 shows that the right subtree is printed above the key and value of the node, while the left subtree is printed below the key and value. But since printing is carried out from the top to the bottom of the screen (window, page, etc.), we must consequently ensure that show/2 sets out to get the right subtree printed before it handles the printing of the immediate key and value, which in turn must happen before the printing of the left subtree. Finally, if the tree is empty (nil), there is clearly nothing to do. The code implementing these observations follows.

```
show(nil,_).

show(n(Left, Entry, Right), Indent)
    :-
    NewIndent is Indent + 4,      % calculate subtree indents
    show(Right, NewIndent),

    key_of(Entry, Key), value_of(Entry, Value),
    tab(Indent), write(Key),put(~ -),write(Value),nl,      % ~-= ASCII code

    show(Left, NewIndent).
```

7.9 OPERATOR DECLARATIONS

An operator is specified for the Prolog reader by declaring its position, precedence, and associativity, using the builtin *op/3*. For instance, a functor of the form

   functor (Argument1, Argument2)

can be declared in such a way as to allow the user to write

   Argument1 functor Argument2

One such example is the functor */2*, which allows the user to write 6*7 instead of *(6,7). An operator such as "*", which takes two arguments and is written between the two arguments, is called a *binary infix operator*. A functor with one argument can be declared as *prefix* or *postfix*, depending on whether we want the functor to appear before or after the argument. For example, *not* is a prefix operator since we can write it before its argument without any parentheses:

   not Goal.

The op/3 builtin has one of the following forms:

   op (Precedence, Type, Atom).
   op (Precedence, Type, [Atom | Atoms]).

The second form is equivalent to a sequence of declarations of the first form. Thus, for example,

```
:- op(234, fx, [hi,there,joe]).
```

is equivalent to the following three declarations:

```
:- op(234, fx, hi).
:- op(234, fx, there).
:- op(234, fx, joe).
```

Expressions containing multiple operators are potentially ambiguous. *Precedence* determines the interpretation of expressions involving multiple operators in the absence of parentheses. The operator with lower precedence applies to a smaller part of the expression. One way to think of this is with regard to adding parentheses back into the expression. Lower precedence operators have their associated parentheses added first. In all cases, the parentheses are added to surround the smallest possible part of the expression.

For example, "+" and "*" are declared as operators by the following:

```
:-op (500, yfx, '+').
:-op (400, yfx, '*').
```

Hence "*" has lower precedence than '+' . Therefore, the expression

$$1 + 4 * 3$$

is interpreted as

$$1 + (4 * 3).$$

The second argument of op/3 specifies the *type* of the operator. These types are summarized in Figure 7–6. The f symbol indicates the position of the operator. The x and y symbols indicate the positions of arguments to the operator. The fundamental rule for operators is that their arguments cannot have higher precedence than the operator itself. The y symbol indicates that an argument in that position can have precedence less than or equal to the precedence of the operator. The x symbol indicates that an argument in that position must have precedence strictly less than the precedence of the operator. (Operators of type *yfy* could lead to unresolvable ambiguity, and so are disallowed.)

FIGURE 7–6
Operator type descriptors.

Operator Type	Interpretation
xfy	infix
yfx	infix
xfx	infix
fy	prefix
fx	prefix
yf	postfix
xf	postfix

The *associativity* of a binary infix operator is determined by the type of the operator. For example, in principle, the expression 3/6/4 can be interpreted as (3/6)/4 (left associativity) or 3/(6/4) (right associativity). But since the slash (/) is declared as an operator by the declaration

    :-op(400, yfx, '/').

the slash is determined as a left associative operator, so 3/6/4 is interpreted as (3/6)/4. Here are some more examples illustrating operator declarations:

```
?-op(200, yfx,  [ to, on] ).
yes.
?-display(get to work on time).
on(to(get, work), time)
yes.
```

EXERCISES

7-1 a Given that X and Y are numbers, define max(X,Y,Z) and min(X,Y,Z).

   b Given that L is a list of numbers, define max(L, X) and min(L, X). (*Hint:* define lmax/3, which uses an extra argument to keep track of the largest number seen so far as you recursively scan L.)

   c Given that L is a list of numbers, define sum_of(L, S), which holds if and only if S is the sum of the numbers on L. (*Hint:* define sum_of/3, which uses an extra argument to accumulate the running total as you recursively scan L.)

7-2 Consider the version of the graph from Figure 5–7 seen in Figure 7–7, in which each edge is labeled with a value representing some notion of cost of traversing that edge (or perhaps the length of that edge).

   a Modify the database in Figure 5–7 to include this new information.

   b Modify the smart_path program in Section 6.5 to return the length or total cost of the path it found. (In the spirit of nonnaive reverse, use two additional arguments: one to accumulate a running sum of the length as the path is built and the other to return the final value).

7-3 Continuing Exercises 5-7 and 6-13 on project planning,

   a Define the following:

   • earliest_start(A, T) holds if and only if A is an activity in the project and the earliest time at which it can start is time T; (*Hint:* work recursively backwards through the

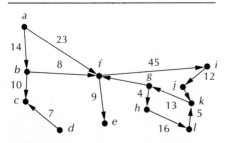

FIGURE 7–7

project tree from the final task; For each node, use setof/3 to collect the list of the node's immediate predecessors; calculate the earliest_start for each of them, and add the duration of each to compute the earliest time each will finish.)

- earliest_finish(A, T) holds if and only if A is an activity in the project and the earliest time at which it can be finished is T;
- min_project_time(T) holds if and only if T is the maximum of the earliest finish times for all the terminal activities of the project.

(*Note:* for some of these, you may want to make use techniques from Exercise 7-1.)

b Define a project activity to be *critical* if its earliest- and latest-start times coincide.

- Define the predicate critical(X), which holds if and only if X is a critical activity.
- Define the predicate partial_critical_path(L), which holds if and only if L is a list of critical activities listed in natural order of execution.
- Define the predicate critical_path(L), which holds if and only if L is a critical path through the project.

7-4 Recall that, for example, the call

functor(T, h, 4)

will cause T to be unified with the term h(A, B, C, D), where A, B, C, D are variables.

a Define a predicate copyTerm/2 such that copyTerm(T1, T2) holds if and only if T2 is a copy of T1. (Hint: use the observation above combined with use of arg/3.)

b Define a variant copyExcept/3 of copyTerm/2 specified as follows:

copyExcept(T1, Exceptions, T2) holds *if and only if*

Exceptions is a list of integers, T1 and T2 are terms with the same principal functors and arities, say = N, and for $i = 1 \ldots N$, if i is not a member of Exceptions, then the ith arguments of T1 and T2 are identical.

c Using the original *squares* representation of the eight puzzle (see Exercise 5-10), create new clauses for move/2 that make use of arg/3 and copyExcept/3 to relate the old and new states of the puzzle. You should be able to create a few clauses that handle all of the cases of move/2.

7-5 Continuing Exercise 4–7, use the tic-tac-toe representation constructed earlier to solve the following:

a Define the predicate

won(Who, Board)

which determines if either x or o has won the game.

b Define the predicate

makeMove(m(N,W), B1, B2)

which holds iff $1 <= N <= 9$, W is one of x or o, B1 is the representation of a board, and B2 is the board that results by putting W in the square N on B1 according to the following numbering of squares:

1	2	3
4	5	6
7	8	9

c Embed the machinery you have constructed for tic-tac-toe into a program that plays the game with a user. Build two versions:

1 A dumb version, which not only queries the user for the user's moves, but also asks the user where the machine should move.

2 A smart version, which chooses its own moves, trying to apply a few rules of thumb:
- Move to win if you have a winning position.
- Block the opponent if the opponent has a potential win (two in line with a blank).
- Occupy the center if you can.
- Occupy a corner if you can.

7-6 The IRS rules for who must file a return (contained in Appendix D) were encoded in a predicate must_file(Person) in Exercise 4-10. Use or modify this definition to prompt the user for appropriate information, if necessary, storing the information in the Prolog database using assert/1 (or asserta/1 or assertz/1), and print out a determination of whether the user must file a return.

7-7 **a** Modify the definition of testPrintTree/0 from Section 7.8.6 so that it writes the tree in a selected file (that can later be printed).

b Recall the definition of test/1 from Section 6.4:

> test(ResultTree)
>
> :-
>
> suitability_list(Items),
>
> do_inserts(Items, nil, ResultTree).

Modify this definition so that the suitability list (Items) is obtained by opening a selected file and reading a list term from that file. (Remember that items in the file must be terminated with a period.)

7-8 Using the enzyme database developed in Exercise 1-12 (see also Exercises 2-11, 3-7, 5-2, and 6-15), use setof/3 and length/1 to implement the following notions:

An enzyme is *focused* if it acts on only one compound and is *diffuse* if it acts on more than one compound.

7-9 Recall that the arithmetic predicate is/2 regards the presence of uninstantiated variables on the right side as an error. Use var/1 and/or nonvar/1 together with is/2 to define a predicate sum/3 that avoids this problem. Specifically,

sum(A,B,C) holds *if and only if* $C = A+B$, so long as *any two* of A, B, and C are instantiated.

Create a similar predicate prod/3 for multiplication. Use this to define a predicate ohm/3 encoding Ohm's law

$$E = I * R$$

in such a way that given any two parameters, one can obtain the value of the third.

7-10 Create a predicate show_tv/0 that prints a reasonable abstract representation of the TV schematic from Exercise 1-8 into a file.

7-11 Create a program that prints (into a file) the various rows of the IRS filing rules (see Appendix D), arranged in descending order of the gross income break point. The output should be arranged in neat columns, and the program should operate off the database created in Exercise 1-13. (Use name/2 and length/2 to determine the lengths of atoms; use functor/3 to obtain any functors, then use name/2 and length/2.)

7-12 Create a version of the must_file/1 program for children and other dependents, based on the rules in Chart B of Appendix D (see Exercise 4-10).

7-13 Modify the lexical analysis program in Section 7.8.5 to deal with intrasentence punctuation, such as commas, semi-colons, etc., as well as apostrophes. Modify the programs further to allow numbers to be present.

PART TWO

METALEVEL PROGRAMMING AND EXPERT SYSTEMS

CHAPTER 8

ELEMENTARY
EXPERT SYSTEMS

8.1 OBJECT-LEVEL EXPERT SYSTEMS

We will begin our study of expert systems programming in Prolog by looking at simple expert systems that can be expressed quite directly via Prolog rules. Just as with Prolog programming itself, the easiest way to learn to construct one of these systems is to build one. Lets start with a small medical advice-giving program based on the Drug database in Chapter 1. Figure 8–1 shows the database.

The advice-giving system we seek to construct will utilize the knowledge in this database to provide recommendations to the user as to what drugs to take, given information about the user's symptoms. Notice that the database can be said to embody considerable expertise just by itself. It contains substantial knowledge about the use of simple drugs. But it takes the form of a big table. A user would have to search through the table (by submitting queries) to determine the appropriate drug. Our problem is to figure out how to make that knowledge much more accessible, as if one were consulting an expert. (One would be very suspicious of an expert who had to spend a lot of time looking through large books in order to provide advice on what should be routine problems in her or his area of expertise.)

The assistance we would expect from a medical expert would be that he or she would tell us what drug we should take to treat the problem we are suffering from. The primary things the expert would consider would be that the drug would relieve the symptom without aggravating any other conditions that might be present. Thus, the expert would proceed to generate a recommendation as follows:

A person should take a given drug under the following circumstances:

- *The person complains of some symptom;*   (8.1)
- *The drug will suppress the symptom;*
- *The drug is not unsuitable for the person in the sense that it will not aggravate any other conditions from which the person is suffering.*

209

FIGURE 8–1

The basic drug database.

```
/*-------------------------------------------------------*
* Title: Lay Medicine                        *
*    (c) 1986 Applied Logic Systems, Inc.    *
* Author:  Kenneth A. Bowen                  *
*                                            *
* A database of over-the-counter U.S.        *
* medications, their uses and limitations.   *
*                                            *
*-------------------------------------------------------*/

/*    Predicate: relieves/2:
      relieves(DRUG, SYMPTOM).    */

relieves(aspirin, headache).
relieves(aspirin, moderate_pain).
relieves(aspirin, moderate_arthritis).
relieves(aspirin_codeine_combination, severe_pain).
relieves(cough_cure_xm, cough).
relieves(pain_gone, severe_pain).
relieves(ko_diarrhea, diarrhea).
relieves(de_congest, cough).
relieves(de_congest, nasal_congestion).
relieves(penicillin, pneumonia).
relieves(bis_cure, diarrhea).
relieves(bis_cure, nausea).
relieves(noasprinol, headache).
relieves(noasprinol, moderate_pain).
relieves(penicillin, pneumonia).
relieves(triple_tuss, nasal_congestion).

/*    Predicate: aggravates/2:
      aggravates(DRUG, CONDITION)

      CONDITION is a single disease process, or a collection of
      disease processes, sometimes called a syndrome. */

aggravates(aspirin, asthma).
aggravates(aspirin, peptic_ulcer).
aggravates(ko_diarrhea, fever).
aggravates(de_congest, high_blood_pressure).
aggravates(de_congest, heart_disease).
aggravates(de_congest, diabetes).
aggravates(de_congest, glaucoma).
aggravates(penicillin, asthma).
aggravates(bis_cure, diabetes).
aggravates(bis_cure, gout).
aggravates(bis_cure, fever).
```

If we choose to implement the top level of the advice-giving program using the predicate should_take(Person, Drug), an appropriate (though simple) definition might run

should_take(Person, Drug)
:-   (8.2)
complains_of(Person, Symptom),
suppresses(Drug, Symptom),
not(unsuitable_for(Person, Drug)).

The normal use of this predicate would be to submit a query with Person instantiated, but with Drug uninstantiated. Successful running of the query would cause Drug to become instantiated and its value to be typed out by the system:

```
?-  should_take( john,  Drug).
Drug = ......
```
(8.3)

To make this work, we must provide definitions for the predicates utilized in the body of the rule for should_take. First, there is complains_of. The role of this predicate is to gather the symptom(s) the user is encountering. We will defer its development briefly. Next is suppresses. One way that a drug can suppress a symptom is to relieve the symptom, so we can add the rule:

suppresses(Drug, Symptom) : _relieves(Drug, Symptom).   (8.4)

A drug might suppress symptoms in other ways, such as treating a disease that directly or indirectly causes the symptom. However, for the moment we will satisfy ourselves with this one rule for suppresses. Finally, we come to the last call in the body of the rule for should_take. First recall (see Section 7.1) that the meta-predicate *not* is very similar to logical negation:

- If P can be successfully solved, then not(P) will fail;
- If P cannot be successfully solved, then not(P) will succeed.   (8.5)

We are using a kind of double negation here:

not(unsuitable_for(Person, Drug)) will succeed if and only if *the system cannot prove, on the basis of the database and associated definitions, that Drug is unsuitable for Person.*   (8.6)

Our problem is to define what it means for a drug to be unsuitable for a person. In its greatest generality, a drug is unsuitable for a person if that drug aggravates some condition which the person suffers from. Thus, we can define

unsuitable_for(Person, Drug)
:-   (8.7)
aggravates(Drug, Condition),
suffers_from(Person, Condition).

Notice that, like the definition of should_take, the definition of unsuitable_for also depends directly on information that must be obtained from the user.

How should we go about obtaining the information we require from the user? The most primitive way imaginable is to require the user to edit the program database, adding assertions for complains_of and suffers_from that embody the user's medical state. If we add

complains_of(john, headache). (8.8)
suffers_from(john, peptic_ulcer).

we can run this query:

```
?-should_take( john, Drug ).
Drug = noasprinol;
no.
```

While this certainly enables the program to run, such an approach to obtaining information is ludicrous under most circumstances. Our ultimate goal is to produce expert systems programs that can be used by ordinary mortals, not just skilled programmers with knowledge of Prolog (in order to read the program and understand what it needs) and the ability to use arcane editors (perhaps the most difficult problem of all). Consequently, we want something better.

Let's tackle the problem of avoiding the editor first. To do this, we will need to invoke some input/output under program control (see Section 7.7). One approach would be to have complains_of present the user with all of the symptoms known in the database, asking the user to respond yes/no to each (and similarly for suffers_from). However, this is not a very good idea. In the first place, it would make for an awkward and clumsy program. But more importantly, if the collection of symptoms is large, this would be very tedious for the user who would have to consider a large number of symptoms that have no bearing on her or his problem. Since complains_of has nothing to go on but the user's name, it would be better to have the user tell the program what symptom is present. The first approach is to define complains_of:

complains_of(Person, Symptom)
  :- (8.9)
  write('What symptom are you bothered by?'),
  read(Symptom).

This will work, though it is not without problems. We will return to consider these problems later.

Let us move on to suffers_from. Imagine the system running the goal (8.3)—the suffering user is john. Successful running of the complains_of subproblem will instantiate Symptom (let's say to headache), and successful solution of the suppresses subproblem will instantiate Drug. (Initially, Drug will be instantiated to aspirin. However, if failure occurs, the system will backtrack and later instantiate Drug to noasprinol.) Thus, the last subproblem will be started with both Person and Drug instantiated. At that point, the current goal will be

?-not(unsuitable_for(john, aspirin)). (8.10)

In order to solve this last subproblem, the system will start up the subsidiary goal

?-unsuitable_for(john, aspirin). (8.11)

There is only one rule for unsuitable_for, and its head will match this goal. Consequently, the subsidiary goal will be transformed to

?-aggravates(aspirin, Condition), suffers_from(john, Condition). (8.12)

The first occurrence of aggravates in the database with aspirin in its first argument is

aggravates(aspirin, asthma). (8.13)

This matches the first subproblem, so the current subsidiary goal will be transformed to

?-suffers_from(john, asthma). (8.14)

At this point, we must decide how we are going to implement suffers_from. Since we see that its second argument—Condition—is instantiated when it is called, the most natural thing is to have suffers_from ask the user a yes/no question about Condition, as follows:

suffers_from(Person, Condition)
    :-
    write('Do you suffer from'), write(Condition), write('(yes/no) ?'), (8.15)
    read(Answer),
    Answer = yes.

So suppose we had added this definition, and that John responds *no*. Then the match

no = yes (8.16)

will fail, causing the suffers_from goal to fail. Prolog will backtrack and find a second solution to the aggravates(aspirin, Condition) subproblem, namely Condition = peptic_ulcer. Then it will attempt the goal

?-suffers_from(john, peptic_ulcer). (8.17)

Let us suppose that John answers *yes* when asked about this. The suffers_from subproblem will succeed, so that the subsidiary subproblem

?-unsuitable_for(john, aspirin). (8.18)

will succeed. Consequently, the original subproblem

?-not(unsuitable_for(john, aspirin)). (8.19)

will fail. This will cause Prolog to backtrack to the previous subproblem

?-suppresses(Drug, headache). (8.20)

It finds a second solution, namely Drug = noasprinol, and starts forward again, running the subproblem

?- not(unsuitable_for(john, noasprinol)). (8.21)

This causes Prolog to start the subsidiary subproblem

?- unsuitable_for(john, noasprinol). (8.22)

It matches this against the head of the only rule for unsuitable_for and transforms this current goal to

?- aggravates(noasprinol, Condition), suffers_from(john, Condition). (8.23)

However, there is no match in the database for the first subproblem of this goal, so the goal must fail. Consequently, the goal (8.22) fails, so the subproblem (8.21) succeeds. Thus, the original goal (8.3) will succeed, returning the answer

```
Drug = noasprinal.
```

Whew! It worked! But before we become too confident, let's look at some of the possible problems with the program, together with some suggested improvements. First, suppose that when he answered the suffers_from(john, peptic_ulcer) question, John had typed *y* or *yea* or *si* or *tak* or *hai,* all of which can mean yes. However, none of them will match *yes* in the equation Answer = yes. If we want our expert to be robust, it ought to understand at least some synonyms for yes. We could achieve this by taking the abstract datatype approach to such answers. We can do this by replacing the equation Answer = yes by a call on the predicate affirmative(Answer), and also adding facts asserting that various words constitute an affirmative answer. The result would look like this:

suffers_from(Person, Condition) (8.24)
    :-
    write('Do you suffer from'), write(Condition), write('(yes/no) ?'),
    read(Answer),
    affirmative(Answer).

affirmative(yes).

affirmative(y). (8.25)
affirmative(yea).
affirmative(si).
affirmative(tak).
affirmative(hai).
   ... etc ...

This is not the end of our problems with simple yes/no answers. Suppose that John intends to answer some question with *no,* but accidentally types *No.* We are using the Prolog reader (i.e., the read(__) predicate) to input the user's responses. But the Prolog reader tries to understand the input in terms of Prolog syntax. Thus, when the Prolog reader sees *No,* it sees an identifier beginning with an upper-case letter, so it believes that this is a variable. The system will create an uninstantiated variable to use for No and will bind the variable Answer to the variable No. In effect, the variable Answer will be replaced by the variable No in the body of (8.24). This will lead to the goal

?- affirmative(No).   (8.26)

being invoked. Since No is uninstantiated, this goal will match any of the facts in (8.25), leading to exactly the opposite of what ought to happen.

To solve this problem, we will combine use of another Prolog meta-level facility with a more thorough analysis of the yes/no question answering process. We could begin to cope with the problem above if we could recognize uninstantiated variables. Fortunately, one of Prolog's meta-level facilities allows us to do just that. Recall from Section 7.5 that Prolog provides a built-in one-place predicate *var*, which is used to determine whether or not its argument is an uninstantiated variable:

> *var(Expression) holds if and only if Expression is an uninstantiated Prolog variable.*

We can use var to recognize uninstantiated variables originating from improper input typing. But what should we do? When the user responds to a yes/no question from the program, we should take one of three possible actions:

1 Recognize the response as affirmative and proceed accordingly;
2 Recognize the response as negative and proceed accordingly;
3 If the response cannot be recognized as either affirmative or negative, explain the problem to the user and ask her or him to retype the answer correctly.

Because of the problem of Prolog variables, 3 really breaks down into two different actions:

3a If the user typed an atom that cannot be recognized as either affirmative or negative, so inform the user, possibly listing the acceptable positive and negative responses.
3b If the user typed an identifier beginning with an upper-case letter, explain that such inputs are improper and possibly list the acceptable responses.

In either case of 3, prompt the user for a new response, read it, and proceed. But note that we cannot assume that the user got the input correct, so we must re-check the new input just as before. Thus, after reading the user's input, we must submit it to a more general predicate act_on_yes_no, which acts according to this analysis. Here is how the new code will look:

suffers_from(Person, Condition)
 :-   (8.27)
 write('Do you suffer from'), write(Condition), write('(yes/no) ?'),
 read(Answer),
 act_on_yes_no(Answer).

act_on_yes_no(Answer)
 :-   (8.28)
 var(Answer), !,
 nl,
 write('You have typed an expression which I interpret as a Prolog variable.'),

```
        nl,
        write('This is probably because you began a word with an uppercase letter.'),
        nl, write('The list of acceptable positive responses is'),
        bagof(YesWord, affirmative(YesWord), Positives),
        write(Positives),
        nl, write('The list of acceptable negative responses is'),
        bagof(NoWord, negative(NoWord), Negatives),
        write(Negatives),
        nl, write('Please type a new (correct) response:'),
        read(NewAnswer),
        act_on_yes_no(NewAnswer).
act_on_yes_no(Answer) :- affirmative(Answer), !.
act_on_yes_no(Answer) :- negative(Answer), !, fail.
act_on_yes_no(Answer)
        :-
        nl, write('I can't understand your response.'),
        nl, write('The responses I can understand are these:'),
        bagof(YesWord, affirmative(YesWord), Positives),
        bagof(NoWord, negative(NoWord), Negatives),
        nl, write('Affirmative:'), write(Positives),
        nl, write('Negative:'), write(Negatives),
        nl, write('Please type a new (correct) response:'),
        read(NewAnswer),
        act_on_yes_no(NewAnswer).
```

```
affirmative(yes).
affirmative(y).                                                        (8.29)
affirmative(yea).
affirmative(si).
affirmative(tak).
affirmative(hai).
. . . etc . . .
```

```
negative(no).
negative(n).                                                          (8.30)
negative(ochi).
negative(nein).
. . . etc . . .
```

This provides a fairly robust treatment of yes/no question answering. Of course, we could have chosen to avoid using the Prolog reader, and instead performed character-level input (using get and get0—see Chapter 7), and sorted out what was happening more directly. However, there is a lot of detail in that approach. When it is reasonable to rely on the Prolog reader (as above), substantial programming effort can be saved. The use of operator declarations (Section 7.8) coupled with the error-handling types of clauses used above extends the range of usefulness of the Prolog reader substantially. However, there are circumstances in which this is difficult or impossible (e.g., providing serious natural language capabilities). In these circumstances, one combines lexical analyzers with parsers (which will be studied in Chapter 10).

There is yet another input problem lurking in the predicate complains_of. In its present form, complains_of assumes that the user understands the precise forms by which symptoms have been entered in the database. This is because complains_of simply accepts whatever the user types and hands that input directly to the predicate suppresses which heads off to the database. Thus complains_of is susceptible to the same sorts of problems we uncovered in suffers_from: The user might type a variable, or might type an expression close to one of the symptom names, but with a slight error. In either case, improper results are likely to follow. Moreover, the casual user cannot be expected to know anything about the forms in which the symptoms have been recorded. Even users familiar with the program's medical orientation might type shortened forms of symptoms (e.g., arthritis instead of moderate_arthritis) or common synonyms (e.g., stuffy_nose for nasal_congestion). Let's try to account for the use of synonyms since the techniques are interesting and instructive.

The best place to handle synonyms would seem to be within the complains_of predicate. After reading the user's typing, the predicate should examine it to determine whether or not the typed input is a variable (a no-no), and if it is not a variable, whether or not the input is a synonym for one of the recorded symptoms. But notice that the user might have in fact typed one of the recorded symptoms correctly. Thus, the logic of complains_of should have four major branches after it reads the user's input. These four branches will be implemented by four separate clauses. The four branches are

1 It should determine whether the input is a variable; if so, explain to the user and ask for retyping;
2 If the input is not a variable and is indeed identical to some recorded symptom (see below on how this is determined), complains_of should pass the input directly to suppresses;
3 If the input is not a variable and if the input is not identical to one of the recorded symptoms (see below) but is a synonym for a recorded symptom, complains_of should pass the synonymous recorded symptom to suppresses;
4 If the input is not a variable, is not a recorded symptom, and is not synonymous with any recorded symptom, complains_of should so inform the user and ask for a new try.

Here is one way to modify complains_of according to this prescription:

complains_of(Person, Symptom)
  :-   (8.31)
  write('What symptom are you bothered by?'),
  read(Answer),
  filter_symptom(Answer, Symptom).

filter_symptom(Answer, Symptom)
  :-   (8.32)

```
    var(Answer), !,                    % suppress other clauses if Answer is a variable
    nl, write('Your answer is a Prolog variable, most likely because' ),
    nl, write('you typed an identifier beginning with an upper-case letter.'),
    nl, write('Please try again, avoiding upper-case letters: '),

    read (NewAnswer),
    filter_symptom(NewAnswer, Symptom).
                        % passing the original variable Symptom to this recursive call
                        % on filter_symptom means that the original call on filter_symptom
                        % will get the result of filtering the NewAnswer


filter_symptom(Answer, Symptom)
    :-                                 % can assume Answer is non-variable
                                       % because of cut in first clause
    relieves(Anything, Answer), !,     % Is it a recorded symptom?
    Symptom = Answer.                  % Yes—return it.


filter_symptom(Answer, Symptom)
    :-                                 % can assume Answer is non-variable
    synonymous(Answer, Symptom),       % and that Answer is not a recorded
    ! .                                % symptom; suppress backtracking
                                       % to last (error) clause if synonym is found.


filter_symptom(Answer, Symptom)
    :-
    nl, write('I can't understand what you typed.'),
    nl, write('Please try again:'),
    read(NewAnswer),
    filter_symptom(NewAnswer, Symptom).


synonymous(Expression, Target)
    :-                                                              (8.33)
    synomym_for(Expression, FirstHit),
    !,                                 % simple case holds — ignore other cases
    check_ambiguity(Expression, Target).


synonymous(Expression, Target)
    :-
    . . . . . .                        % other more complex cases of synonymity may be possible
synonym_for(stuffy_nose, nasal_congestion).
synonym_for(pain, moderate_pain).
synonym_for(pain, severe_pain).
. . . . . .
synonym_for(Anything, Anything)                                    (8.34)
    :-                                 % Anything is a synonym for itself if
    relieves(SomeDrug, Anything).      % it has been recorded in the database
```

```
check_ambiguity(Expression, FinalSynonym)
    :-                                                                      (8.35)
    setof(Hit, distinct_synonym_for(Expression, Hit), Synonyms),
    decide_ambiguity(Synonyms, FinalSynonym).


distinct_synonym_for(Expression, Hit)
    :-
    synonym_for(Expression, Hit),
    Expression \== Hit.
decide_ambiguity([FinalSynonym], FinalSynonym)
    :- !.                                                        % No ambiguity.
decide_ambiguity(Synonyms, FinalSynonym)
    :-                              % ambiguous: more than one hit because
                                   % first clause failed to match
    select_one([nl, 'Your response is ambiguous',nl,
        'Please select a synonym - type corresponding number',nl],
        Synonyms, FinalSynonym).


select_one(Message, ChoiceList, Choice)
    :-                                                                      (8.36)
    write_list(Message,),
    get_choice(Choice_List, Choice).


get_choice(Choice_List, Choice)
    :-                                                                      (8.37)
    write_numbered_list(ChoiceList, 1, Length),
    nl, write('Choice  = '),
    read(Number),
    ((integer(Number), 1  =< Number, Number  =< Length) →
        nth_element(ChoiceList, Number, Choice) ;
        nl, write('Improper entry or number out of range . . . please try again'),
        nl,
        get_choice(ChoiceList, Choice) ).


write_list([]).                                                             (8.38)
write_list( [Item | Items ] )
    :-
    write_out( Item ),
    write_list( Items ).


write_numbered_list( [ Im ], CurCount, Length) :- Length is CurCount -1.    (8.39)
write_numbered_list( [ Item | Items ], CurCount, Length)
    :-
    write(CurCount), write(':'), write(Item), nl,
    NextCount is CurCount + 1,
    write_numbered_list( Items, NextCount, Length).
```

nth_element([Choice | _], 1, Choice) :- !.   (8.40)
nth_element([_ | Tail], CurCountDown, Choice)
    :-
    CurCountDown > 1,
    NextCountDown is CurCountDown − 1,
    nth_element(Tail, NextCountDown, Choice).

write_out(nl) :- !, nl.
write_out(Item) :-
    write(Item).

Wow! That's the biggest program we've built so far! Notice the use of cut(!), disjunction(;), and if-then-else; (→ __ ; __). Reread Section 7.1 if they mystify you. Most of this code is straightforward, based on simple and direct recursions. You should study it all carefully. The definition of filter_symptom (8.32) is explained by the attached comments.

Let's examine the really interesting points in this. First, there is the logic of the first clause (8.33) of the predicate *synonymous*. It assumes that the user's input might be ambiguous—that it might be synonymous with more than one recorded symptom. So check_ambiguity is called to handle this determination. Its approach is straightforward. By using *setof* (see Section 6.2), it collects together the list of all recorded symptoms that are synonymous with the user's input, but that are distinct from that input. If this list has only one element, the user's input was not ambiguous, so the desired recorded symptom is the sole element of that list. On the other hand, if the list has length greater than 1, the user's input was ambiguous and so choose_one is called to assist the user in choosing the desired recorded symptom. The latter predicate prints out the message contained in its first argument, then calls get_choice to perform the actual choosing. The predicate get_choice acts according to the following procedure:

Step 1   It prints out a numbered form of the list of choices, calculating the numbering of the list as it goes;
Step 2   It prompts the user to type a number and reads what the user types;
Step 3   It checks that what the user typed is an integer in the proper range;
Step 4a If the input was a number in the proper range, it calls nth_element to extract the corresponding element of the choice list, and exits;
Step 4b If the input either was not an integer, or was an integer, but was out of range, it so informs the user, and then calls itself again, effectively cycling back to Step 1.

Thus choose_one effectively presents the user with a menu of choices from which to select the desired synonym. In Prolog systems that provide windows and menu facilities (such as ALS Prolog), this can be carried out much more compactly and elegantly. Even the simple teletype kind of output used above is reasonably congenial. We coded these predicates in the manner shown in order to make them general purpose. By breaking out the choice operations into separate predicates, and by passing to these predicates the messages to be printed (instead of coding the messages directly in the predicate bodies), we have made it possible to reuse these predicates in other settings in this program and other programs. No matter how good the basic programming language tools one is using, coding substantial programs is a painfully tedious task. (How many times have you risen from a long coding session with neck stiff, back aching, and head thumping?) Systematically attempting to produce your own general reusable predicates is one way to lessen the pain. We will encounter another such general and reusable construction in the next section.

Two sample interactions with the program follow.

```
?-should_take(ken, What).
What symptom are you bothered by? headache.
Do you suffer from asthma (yes/no) ? y.
What = noasprinol
yes.
?-should_take(ken, What).
What symptom are you bothered by?  pain.
Your response is ambiguous
Please select a synonym - type corresponding number
1:  moderate_pain
2:  severe_pain
Choice =  2.
What = aspirin_codeine_combination
yes.
```

There are many more improvements we can and should make in this program. We will consider one of them in Section 8.3; others will develop in the remainder of the book. But next, we will consider the general structure of many expert systems.

8.2 GENERATE AND TEST

The program we developed in the last section exhibits a classic organization common in many artificial intelligence programs. This structure is called *generate and test*. Conceptually, it is very simple, as illustrated in Figure 8–2. One thinks of the generator as producing a stream of candidate solutions or hypotheses that are sent, one by one, to the tester, which checks each candidate, filtering out those that are not in fact solutions, and passing on the correct solutions.[1] This organization can be utilized in cases where all of possibly many solutions are desired, as well in cases where only one solution is desired. In the latter case, one simply turns off the process after the first correct solution is emitted.

---

[1] This appears to be an almost universal approach to problems of diagnosis and treatment, whether the subject is living (medicine) or electro-mechanical (engineering). It is generally extremely difficult to positively prove that a proposed "fix" is genuinely suitable for the subject mechanism. Instead, we try to convince ourselves that the proposed "fix" will not introduce any new problems. Moreover, the use of Prolog's negation-by-failure seems to correspond to everyday human reasoning. When trying to convince ourselves that no new problems will be introduced, we do not logically prove that no new problems will be introduced. Instead, we examine all the ways we can think of by which a new problem might be introduced and convince ourselves that they are not applicable to the case at hand. The nearest thing to positive proof is appeals to experience: "I've done this many times before, and no problems arose." But this is just a disguised form of negation by failure, it is not positive proof that problems won't be introduced. Appeals to experience only indicate that no cases in which problems were introduced have been encountered, not that the introduction of new problems is impossible.

FIGURE 8–2
The Structure of generate and test programs.

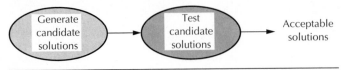

The operation of such programs can take one of several possible approaches. The two extreme forms are

- The generator and tester operate independently, each at their own pace. As the generator produces solutions, they queue up in the connecting pipeline (a buffer), and the tester checks each at its leisure;
- The generator and tester operate synchronously, taking turns. The generator first produces a candidate, passes it to the tester, and goes to sleep. The tester processes the candidate, then goes to sleep, waking up the generator as it does so. The generator produces another candidate, passing it to the tester, going to sleep again; the tester processes the next candidate and goes to sleep again, reawakening the generator as it does so, etc.

In either case, the action of the system continues until the system's termination criterion is met: production of a single solution, production of a specified number of solutions, or examination of all candidates and production of all solutions.[2]

Prolog's backtracking facilities make it very easy to implement generate and test programs operating in the second mode. Schematically, the structure of such programs appears as follows:

generate_and_test(Solution)

:-

generate(Solution),
test(Solution).

Given the goal

?-generate_and_test(Solution).

such a program will operate as follows. First, the initial goal will be transformed to

?- generate(Solution), test(Solution).

The first subgoal will be chosen and will run until it successfully produces a candidate, binding the variable Solution to a representation of the candidate solution. Then the

---

[2] When individual solutions are large, another organization which is compatible with either mode of operation — can be adopted: The generator only partially produces a candidate solution and the tester begins work on such partial solutions. The motivation for this is that the tester can often eliminate candidates based on only a partial description of the candidate. When feasible, this can save substantial computational effort. However, this organization requires careful co-ordination between generator and tester, as well as sophisticated control facilities, which can either be provided by the underlying programming language or implemented by the programmer.

second subgoal will start running. If the candidate contained in Solution is in fact a correct solution, *test* will succeed, and so the original goal will succeed, yielding:

```
?- generate_and_test( Solution).
 Solution = first solution
```

However, if the first candidate, contained in Solution, is not in fact a correct solution, the subgoal test(Solution) will fail. Then the program will backtrack to the generate subgoal, trying to find another method of successfully running that subgoal. If another means of solving the first subgoal can be found, generate will succeed again, binding Solution to the second candidate. The test subgoal will run again with Solution bound to this second candidate, etc. All solutions can be found by repeatedly typing a semicolon:

```
?-generate_and_test(Solution).
 Solution = first solution ;
 Solution = second solution ;
. . . . . .
 Solution = last solution ;

 no.
```

The simple medical advisor of the last section exhibits this structure. The predicate suppresses constitutes the generator portion, while the subgoal not(unsuitable_for(___)) constitutes the tester portion. As the details of the medical advisor suggest, the complete structure of such programs often takes the following form:

expert

    :-   ($$)

    obtain(ProblemDescription),
    generate(ProblemDescription, Solution),
    test(ProblemDescription, Solution),
    report(ProblemDescription, Solution).

Sometimes it is desirable to compute the entire list of solutions and pass the solution list on to another predicate for further processing (e.g., ranking of solutions, etc.). One simple way to achieve this is to use *bagof* or *setof*:

expert

    :-   (##)

    obtain(ProblemDescription),
    setof(Solution,
        (generate(ProblemDescription, Solution),
        test(ProblemDescription, Solution)),
        Solutions),
    process(ProblemDescription, Solutions),

    . . . .

As the skeleton ($$) suggests, the problem description can be stored in a variable, which is then passed to the successive portions of the program. This is certainly the approved method of communication between procedures. However, the logical purity of such communication is not without its cost. There are two major expenses:

- It tends to distort the natural expression of domain expertise in the program— we will observe this in some detail later;
- Whatever is learned during the test phase is forgotten when the system back-tracks.

The second problem is especially vexing. For example, any information that the predicate unsuitable_for obtains from the user (John) will be forgotten when the program backtracks to suppresses in order to generate another candidate. Also, sometimes the test phase of the program draws intermediate conclusions about the problem that would be useful both to generate and to test during later stages. But they too will be forgotten. Can we overcome this? The answer is yes. But like most good things, solving this problem is not without its costs. One method is to use Prolog to construct a higher-level logic system that interprets the rules of expertise and that also provides more powerful facilities that will cope with these and other difficulties. The cost here is decreased performance efficiency and more programming. The second method is to risk abandoning the logical soundness of pure Prolog programming by dynamically recording the newly acquired information in the program database. That is, use assert to add information, and retract to remove it as necessary.

Let us put these facilities to work, constructing a general scheme for simple generate and test-based diagnostic systems. This example presents what probably should be regarded as a shell schemata, rather than a single shell proper. It is also of the diagnostic/classificatory type, but in this case it will be applied to the identification of hickory trees. This shell assumes that the domain knowledge consists of a collection of symptoms or characteristics that are associated with various members of a collection of diagnoses or identifications. The symptoms or characteristics are referred to as traits of the diagnoses or identifications. The collection of all characteristics that are *traits* of a given identification is taken as the characterization of the (presence of) the identification. (We will comment below regarding a more sophisticated approach.) The action of the shell we will construct breaks into four phases:

1 Obtain initial information on the traits present from the user;
2 Conjecture plausible diagnoses or identifications consistent with the initial information.
3 Remove unsuitable candidates from the conjecture list, interacting with the user as necessary to obtain additional information.
4 Report the final conclusions to the user.

The shell we will construct will make use of the database manipulation facilities to record the information it obtains from the user, as well as additional conclusions that it draws from that data. The top level of the shell appears as follows:

```
identify
    :-
    obtain_description,
    entertain_hypothesis(Identification),        % these 2 goals are a generate
```

```
        validate(Identification),                        % and test loop
        report(Identification).
```

The four phases of the shell action listed above correspond to the first four procedure calls in the body of *identify*. The second and third calls constitute a simple generate-and-test loop, conjecturing a single hypothesis and attempting to validate the conjecture. If the attempted validation fails, Prolog's chronological backtracking returns to generate another conjecture, which is then subjected to validations, etc. Obtaining the initial information from the user and recording it in the database is performed as follows. Note that the asserta builtin is used to ensure that the data obtained from the user is recorded before any pre-existing clauses that might have been entered to serve as defaults.

```
    obtain_description
        :-
        write('Observation:'),
        read(Observer),
        dispatch(Observer).
```

```
    dispatch(done).                                      % if the user wants to quit,
    dispatch(quit) :- abort.                             % let her or him, otherwise:
    dispatch(Observation)
        :-
        asserta(observed(Observation)),                 % record the observation &
        obtain_description.                              % get another one
```

Now we must turn to the generation of hypotheses for testing. We begin with a very simpleminded approach that we will later refine. Simply, we conjecture an Identification if there is some Characteristic, which the user has observed and conveyed to us, that is also a trait of the Identification. This is done by the first clause for entertain_hypothesis below. In order to cater to the situation in which the user ventures no information at all, the second clause simply guesses wildly. However, after making such a wild guess, later interaction with the user will presumably generate information, though that first wild guess may be incorrect. Since Prolog's chronological backtracking will not get back to using the first clause for entertain_hypothesis, we replicate it as the third clause. Finally, the last clause deals with the case that no conjectures can be validated to conform to the symptoms or characteristics presented by the user. Here is the code:

```
    entertain_hypothesis(Identification)
        :-
        observed(Characteristic),
        trait(Characteristic, Identification).
```

```
    entertain_hypothesis(Identification)
        :-
        not(observed(_)),
        trait(_, Identification).
```

```
entertain_hypothesis(Identification)
    :-
    observed(Characteristic),
    trait(Characteristic, Identification).

entertain_hypothesis(_)
    :-
    write('I have no item in my database with those characteristics.'),nl,
    abolish(observed,1),
    abolish(does_not_hold,1),!,fail.
```

Validation of a hypothesis in this setting means verification that all the descriptors or characteristics attached to the hypothesis as traits by the database have or can be observed by the user. In our simple approach here, we have assumed that the knowledge of traits is encoded by a two-place predicate *trait* whose first argument is a Characteristic and whose second argument is an Identification. To validate a conjectured Identification, we must collect together the list (called the Characterization) of all Characteristics that are traits of the given Identification. We use the Prolog builtin bagof for this below. (Another approach would be to maintain this list precomputed.) Having obtained the Characterization list, we must verify that each Characteristic on it has been, or can be, observed by the user. Thus, we must simply recurse down this list, attempting to check off each item on the list. This portion of the work is encoded in the predicates validate and verify below.

```
validate(Identification)
    :-
    bagof(Attribute, trait(Attribute,Identification), Characterization),
    verify(Characterization),!.

verify([ ]).
verify([Attribute | Rest_of_Attributes])
    :-
    check(Attribute),
    verify(Rest_of_Attributes).
```

As can be seen, in order for verify to succeed, check must succeed on each element of the list. One way to check off an element is to see from the database that it has been observed (the first clause for check below). On the other hand, various circumstances can have led us to conclude that a certain Characteristic is not present. We record this using the predicate does_not_hold. Thus, assuming the Characteristic in question has not been recorded in the database as being observed, the second clause for check attempts to determine whether it has been concluded that the given Characteristic does not obtain; in this case, the cut-fail combination (. . . , !, fail.) at the end of the clause guarantees that the given call to check will fail, and consequently that the parent call to verify will also fail. Finally, if the given Characteristic has not already been recorded as being observed, and we have not concluded that Characteristic cannot obtain, we fall back on asking the user about it in the third clause for check. The clauses for ask_about are similar to those presented earlier for suffers_from in Section 8.1. Here is the code:

```
check(Attribute)
    :-
    observed(Attribute),!.
check(Attribute)
    :-
    does_not_hold(Attribute)!,fail.

check(Attribute)
    :-
    ask_about(Attribute).

ask_about(Attribute)
    :-
    write('Is it true that'), write(Attribute), write('?'),
    read(Answer),
    act_on(Answer, Attribute).

act_on(yes, Attribute)
    :- !,
    asserta(observed(Attribute)).

act_on(Other, Attribute)
    :-
    asserta(does_not_hold(Attribute)),!,fail.
```

The cuts are used in check since we want exactly one of the clauses to be executed exactly once: the cuts commit us to the respective choices. As with check, we use cuts in act_on since we want exactly one of the clauses for act_on to be executed. We use asserta for reasons similar to those regarding dispatch above. Also, when we have queried the user as to whether a certain characteristic has been observed, instead of immediately failing (in order to make the invoking check fail), we first record that the queried Characteristic does_not_hold so that work with later conjectures will not have to query the user again concerning this Characteristic. Lastly, reporting the result to the user is simple:

```
report(Identification)
    :-
    write('The item appears to be a'),
    write(Identification), nl,
    bagof(Characteristic, trait(Characteristic, Identification), Traits),
    write('The traits were:'),
    write(Traits), nl.
```

The code thus far forms a complete simple shell. It can be run with a variety of knowledge presented in the appropriate format. For example, consider the knowledge concerning the classification of hickory trees from Chapter 1:

```
trait(bud_scales(valvate),bitternut_hickory).
trait(buds(yellow),bitternut_hickory).
trait(bud_scales(valvate),pecan_hickory).
trait(buds(brownish),pecan_hickory).
trait(bud_scales(imbricate),pignut_hickory).
trait(terminal_buds(short),pignut_hickory).
trait(bud_scales(imbricate),mockernut_hickory).
trait(terminal_buds(large),mockernut_hickory).
trait(outer_scales(deciduous),mockernut_hickory).
trait(bud_scales(imbricate),shellbark_hickory).
trait(terminal_buds(large),shellbark_hickory).
trait(outer_scales(persistent),shellbark_hickory).
trait(twigs(orange_brown),shellbark_hickory).
trait(bud_scales(imbricate),shagbark_hickory).
trait(terminal_buds(large),shagbark_hickory).
trait(outer_scales(persistent),shagbark_hickory).
trait(twigs(reddish_brown),shagbark_hickory).
```

In this knowledge base, some traits, e.g., short versus large, are opposites. If the user tells us that the terminal buds are not large, we should be able to conclude that they are short. The following clauses, called by check, carry out shallow reasoning to accomplish this. These rules function as defaults for observed; hence the use of asserta in dispatch and act_on, which places the new information above these defaults.

```
observed(outer_scales(X))
    :-
    opposite(X,Y),
        does_not_hold(outer_scales(Y)).

observed(terminal_buds(X))
    :-
    opposite(X,Y),
    does_not_hold(terminal_buds(Y)).

observed(bud_scales(X))
    :-
    opposite(X,Y),
    does_not_hold(bud_scales(Y)).

opposite(short,large).
opposite(large,short).
opposite(deciduous,persistent).
```

opposite(persistent,deciduous).
opposite(valvate,imbricate).
opposite(imbricate,valvate).

The following clauses for observed, similar to those above, carry out shallow reasoning to allow users to make use of synonyms for the descriptors entered in the basic database.

observed(outer_scales(X))
    :-
    synonymous(X,Y),
    observed(outer_scales(Y)).

observed(terminal_buds(X))
    :-
    synonymous(X,Y),
    observed(terminal_buds(Y)).

observed(bud_scales(X))
    :-
    synonymous(X,Y),
    observed(bud_scales(Y)).

synonymous(valvate,nonoverlapping).
synonymous(imbricate,overlapping).
synonymous(short,stout).

Let us next consider modifications that will provide for more focused generation of hypotheses, and consequently reduce the need for user interaction to a near minimum. In the code above, we conjectured an Identification if just one of the observed Characteristics was a trait of the Identification. What we will now do is change this so that we only conjecture an Identification if it is consistent with all the recorded observations from the user. Our revised top level of the system would appear

identify
    :-
    obtain_description,
    collect(Hypotheses),   *% get all consistent identifications*
    filter(Hypotheses, Identification),   *% & filter out failures*
    report(Identification).

    . . . obtain_description . . . as before

entertain_hypothesis(Identification)
    :-
    observed(Characteristic),
    trait(Characteristic, Identification).

```
collect(Hypotheses)
    :-                                        % gets the "reasonable" candidates
    setof(H, entertain_hypothesis(H), Hypotheses).
```

Our initial criteria for reasonable hypotheses is just as before, namely, possessing one of the observed traits as a characteristic. But then we filter the list of reasonable hypotheses. The predicate filter(Hypotheses, Identification) filters the list of reasonable Hypotheses down to the Identification(s) in two steps. It first removes conjectures inconsistent with already observed data, then attempts to validate each of the remaining conjectures. The code runs as follows:

```
filter(Hypotheses, Identification)
    :-
    setof(A, observed(A), Observations),
    filter_consistency(Hypotheses, Observations, Possible_Ids),
    validate_filter(Possible_Ids, Identification).

filter_consistency([], _, []).

filter_consistency([Hyp | Hyps], Observations, [Hyp | Ids])
    :-
    consistent(Hyp, Observations), !,
    filter_consistency(Hyps, Observations, Ids).

filter_consistency([_ | Hyps], Observations, Ids)
    :-
    filter_consistency(Hyps, Observations, Ids).
```

The predicate

```
filter_consistency(Hyps, Obs, Result)
```

holds if Result is the list of all elements of the list Hyps that are consistent with every observation on the list Obs. Moreover, a hypothesis is consistent with all the elements of the list Observations if it is not inconsistent with any element of Observations. Finally, p(A) and p(B) are inconsistent if A and B are opposite characteristics. Here is the code:

```
consistent(Hyp, []).

consistent(Hyp, [Observation | Observations])
    :-
    not(inconsistent(Hyp, Observation)),
    consistent(Hyp, Observations).

inconsistent(Hypothesis, Observation)
    :-
    Hypothesis =.. [Predicate, Hypothesis_Argument],
    Observation =.. [Predicate, Observation_Argument],
    opposite(Hypothesis_Argument, Observation_Argument).
```

The final filtering out of unreasonable hypotheses is under the control of the predicate

validate_filter(Hyps, Idents)

which holds if Idents consists of all elements of Hyps that can be validated by the same methods as used earlier.

validate_filter([], []) :- !.

validate_filter([Identification], [Identification]) :- !.

validate_filter([Hyp | Hyps], [Hyp | Ids])
   :-
   validate(Hyp), !,
   validate_filter(Hyps, Ids).

validate_filter([_ | Hyps], Ids)
   :-
   validate_filter(Hyps, Ids).

8.3 QUERY-THE-USER

We devoted considerable attention in Section 8.1 to the problem of interaction with the user because this is an extremely important consideration for most expert systems, especially those intended to offer advice to human beings. Some of the users of expert systems will be experts in the domain of the system's knowledge (or at least quite familiar with the area) but will not in general be skilled programmers. Even more will not be at all familiar with the area of the system's expertise. Consequently, most advice-giving systems should be as *user friendly* as possible. There are many aspects to being a *friendly* program. They include

- The program should make no assumptions about the user's programming knowledge or skills;
- Programs intended for wide use should minimize assumptions about the user's knowledge about the program's domain of expertise;
- It should be easy for the user to recover from input mistakes;
- Unnecessary questions and interaction should be avoided;
- The program should be able, when requested, to explain the reasoning leading to its conclusions or recommendations, to explain why it is asking certain questions, etc.
- When appropriate, the program should be able to store the information and conclusions generated between different sessions with the same user.

The first two items concern the overall design and conceptual organization of the program. The latter four items are within the province of the implementer of the program (who may or may not be the same as the designer). We explored some aspects of the third item (recovery from input mistakes) in Section 8.1, and developed some methods (use of assert) to minimize unnecessary questions (the fourth item above) in Section 8.2. We will examine some approaches to the last two items in the next chapter. In this section, we will further explore interaction with the user, studying a technique that can improve program organization and ease the program development burden.

Let's return to the medicine program. In Section 8.1, we gradually developed some interesting techniques for dealing with the input required for the predicates suffers_from/2 and complains_of/2. The code developed appeared to be specific to each predicate—it certainly was only accessible through calls to the respective predicates. If one continued to develop this program, presumably there would be an increasing number of predicates that required similar code handling interaction with the user. Consequently, it is worth attempting to abstract what we did in Section 8.1 to create some general facilities that can be utilized for a wide range of predicates requiring interaction with the user.

If we examine the two situations, we find that in both cases, we have a predicate call containing a variable of particular interest (among the other variables in the call). In one case (calls to suffers_from/2), the variable is instantiated at the time of the call, and we want to ask the user whether the predicate holds of the given value (e.g., 'Do you suffer from . . . ?'). In the other case, the variable is uninstantiated at the time of the call, and we want to request a value for the variable from the user (e.g., 'What SYMPTOM are you complaining of?'). Our goal is to build a general mechanism that can be used to handle such situations for a variety of predicates. Let's call the predicate implementing this general mechanism ask_about. Thus, it would seem that that we must supply ask_about with information about the call together with information about the variable in question. One way to supply information about the call is to simply provide a complete copy of the call. And information about the variable in question can be transmitted by simply supplying the variable. Thus, ask_about will have two arguments. The new definitions of complains_of/2 and suffers_from/2 might now appear as follows:

```
suffers_from(Person, Condition) :-
    ask_about(suffers_from(Person, Condition),Condition).
```

```
complains_of(Person, Symptom) :-
    ask_about(complains_of(Person, Symptom),Symptom).
```

It is clear that ask_about/2 must behave differently in the two cases depending on whether or not the variable of interest (the second argument of ask_about/2) is instantiated or not. Thus, ask_about/2 will have two clauses beginning as shown below:

```
ask_about(PredicateCall, InfoVar)
    :-
    var(InfoVar),!,                          % get value for InfoVar from user
    .....
```

```
ask_about(PredicateCall, InfoVar)
    :-
```

```
    nonvar(InfoVar),!,                    % ask user question about (value of) InfoVar
    .....
```

To continue the development, consider the second case: InfoVar is instantiated, so we need to ask the user whether or not the fact embodied in PredicateCall is true. We could, of course, print something as simple as "Does <PredicateCall> hold?" . For example,

    Does suffers_from(john, peptic_ulcer) hold ?

However, since we are trying to provide reasonably high-quality user interactions, we can improve on this by supplying information on how to ask questions about the given predicate. Thus, let's add the following to the program:

```
ask_confirm(suffers_from(Patient, Condition),
    ['Do you suffer from ', Condition, ' (yes/no) ?'], Condition).
```

The general form for these facts is

    ask_confirm(PREDICATE_CALL, QUESTION_LIST, VARIABLE).

Here, QUESTION_LIST is a list made up of atoms and variables from the predicate call (which will be instantiated by the time ask_confirm is run). Note that another version of this question might be

```
ask_confirm(suffers_from(Patient, Condition),
    ['Does',Patient, 'suffer from ', Condition, ' (yes/no) ?'], Condition).
```

Assume that such facts have been added to the program for each predicate for which we will be asking a confirmatory question. Then we can complete the second clause for ask_about/2 as follows, making use of some of the predicates developed in Section 8.1:

```
ask_about(PredicateCall, InfoVar)
    :-
    nonvar(InfoVar),!,                    % ask user question about (value of) InfoVar
    ask_confirm(PredicateCall, Question, InfoVar),
    write_list(Question),
    read(Answer),
    act_on_yes_no(Answer).
```

The clause uses the interaction predicates we developed in Section 8.1 for dealing with yes/no answers.

To develop the first clause for ask_about, we must similarly add information to the program to handle requests when InfoVar is not instantiated. Let's add the following:

```
ask_info(complains_of(Patient, Symptom),
    [ 'What symptom are you bothered by?' ], Symptom).
```

As above, another version might be

```
ask_info(complains_of(Patient, Symptom),
    [ 'What symptom does ',Patient, ' present?' ], Symptom).
```

The general form of these facts will be

ask_info(PREDICATE_CALL, QUESTION_LIST, VARIABLE).

where QUESTION_LIST is a list made up of atoms and variables from the predicate call (which will be instantiated by the time ask_confirm is run). Now we can develop the first clause for ask_about/2 as follows:

```
ask_about(PredicateCall, InfoVar)
    :-
    var(InfoVar),!,                                  % get value for InfoVar from user
    ask_info(PredicateCall, Question, InfoVar),
    write_list(Question),
    read(Answer),
    check_response(PredicateCall, Answer, InfoVar).
```

The role of check_response/3 will be similar to the role of filter_symptom/2 in Section 8.1: To check whether or not the user's input is acceptable. With this in mind, we can immediately adapt the first and fourth clauses of filter_symptom as follows:

```
check_response(PredicateCall, Answer, InfoVar)
    :-
    var(Answer), !,                       % skip other clauses if Answer is variable
    nl, write('Your answer is a Prolog variable, most likely because'),
    nl, write('you typed an identifier beginning with an uppercase letter.'),
    nl, write('Please try again, avoiding uppercase letters: '),
    read(NewAnswer),
    check_response(PredicateCall, NewAnswer, InfoVar).
                    % passing the original variable InfoVar to this recursive call
                    % on check_response means that the original call to check_response
                    % will get the ultimate result of checking the NewAnswer
```

Additional clauses for check_response(Predicate, Answer, InfoVar) to be developed

. . .

```
check_response(PredicateCall, Answer, InfoVar)
    :-
    nl, write('I can''t understand what you typed.'),
    nl, write('Please try again: '),
    read(NewAnswer),
    check_response(PredicateCall, NewAnswer, InfoVar).
```

What remains for us to do is to develop clauses for check_response that will fit between the two above, and that will provide means of checking that the user's response is clearly acceptable to the program, or that it is synonymous with an acceptable response, or is acceptable for some other reason, etc. In the case of filter_symptom/2 in Section 8.1, a response was directly acceptable if it occurred as the second argument of a *relieves* fact in the database. Thus, there was a test to perform to determine direct acceptability, namely run relieves/2 with the user's response in the second argument and any variable in the first argument position:

?-relieves(Anything, UsersAnswer).

Just as we told ask_about/2 how to ask particular questions via ask_info and ask_confirm facts, we can tell check_response/3 how to test responses via facts we will add to the database. Suppose, for example, we add the following:

ask_acceptability(complains_of(_,_), Answer, relieves(_, Answer)).

The general form of these facts will be

ask_acceptability(PREDICATE_CALL, TESTVAR, TEST).

Here, TESTVAR occurs in the expression TEST, where the latter is of the form to match against heads of various facts or rules in the program that will directly or indirectly perform the required test on the (value of) TESTVAR. Assuming that such facts have been added to the program, the second clause for check_response, analogous to the second clause of filter_symptom, can now be written as follows:

```
check_response(Predicate, Answer, InfoVar)
    :-                                    % can assume Answer is non-variable
                                          % because of cut in first clause
    ask_acceptability(Predicate, Answer, Test),
    Test, !,                              % Is it acceptable?
    InfoVar = Answer.                     % Yes - return it.
```

These three clauses for check_response/3 would be perfectly adequate. If we want increase the program's flexibility, we can add treatment of synonyms as follows, imitating our approach in Section 8.1:

```
check_response(PredicateCall, Answer, InfoVar)
    :-                                    % can assume Answer is non-variable
                                          % and is not basically acceptable;
    synonymous(PredicateCall, Answer, InfoVar),
    ! .                                   % suppress backtracking to final
                                          % (error)clause if synonym is found

synonymous(PredicateCall, Expression, Target)
    :-
    synonym_for(PredicateCall, Expression, FirstHit),
    !,                                    % at least one synonym exists
                                          % - avoid error case
    check_ambiguity(Predicate, Expression, Target).
```

%synonymous(PredicateCall, Expression, Target)
% :-
% . . . . . .
% other more complex cases of synonymity may be possible

synonym_for(_, stuffy_nose, nasal_congestion).
synonym_for(complains_of(_,_), zip, cough).
synonym_for(complains_of(_,_), zip, nasal_congestion).

The predicate check_ambiguity/3 is implemented just as in Section 8.1, with the sole modification of adding the additional argument PredicateCall as necessary. Obviously, other clauses may be added, extending further the flexibility of the user interface.

8.4 ACCUMULATING PROOFS FOR EXPLANATIONS

Advice-givers (consultants, lawyers, doctors, stock brokers) are often asked the reasons for the advice they offer. Few of us are prepared to deal blindly with the advice we receive, no matter how dearly we have paid for it. This applies even more so to expert programs, since most people will regard advice from programs even more suspiciously than advice from humans. Thus, we must consider methods for allowing our programs to present reasons for their advice—better reasons than "Because I say so"! The most direct reason a program could present would be a compressed version of its deduction or line of reasoning leading to the advice. Since the reasons will be presented at the end of the program's run, it must have some means of accumulating and saving the significant elements of its deduction as it proceeds. One way to do this would be to accumulate the steps as a list that is held in a variable. To do this, of course, various of the predicates in the program must have a variable used for this purpose. This variable will be above and beyond those used for the basic manipulation of knowledge.

Let's consider the last form of the medic advice-giving program. The principal predicate is should_take/2, which is invoked by a goal of the form

?- should_take(Person, Drug).

The variable Person is usually instantiated when this goal is submitted, while the variable Drug is uninstantiated and receives a value during execution of the goal. Our earlier observations suggest that should_take/2 must be changed to should_take/3, which will be invoked by a goal of the form

?- should_take(Person, Drug, Reason).

When the goal is submitted, Person will be instantiated, while Drug and Reason will be uninstantiated. To enable us to make the interactions more pleasant, let's first wrap a simple layer of code around this goal, as follows:

```
run
    :-
    write('Name  ='), read(Person),
    should_take(Person, Drug, Reason),
    write_list(['Recommend taking ', Drug, nl]),
    write('Explanation:'),nl,
    write_nl_list(Reason).
```

run

    :-

    write('I don''t know how to help you.'),nl.

The second clause for run deals with any situations in which should_take/3 fails. The predicate write_nl_list/1 is similar to write_list/1, except that it starts a new line after each item on the list is printed. Here is its definition:

write_nl_list([]).
write_nl_list([Item | Items])

    :-

    write(Item),nl,
    write_nl_list(Items).

Let's tackle should_take/3. Recall the definition of should_take/2:

should_take(Person, Drug)

    :-

    complains_of(Person, Symptom),
    suppresses(Drug, Symptom),
    not(unsuitable_for(Person, Drug)).

Since the new third argument of should_take/3, Reason, is intended to contain the list of reasons for the resulting advice, it is natural to add a similar argument to the calls in the body of the rule, and combine the various subsidiary lists of reasons at the end. The code will look like this:

should_take(Person, Drug, Reason)

    :-

    complains_of(Person, Symptom, ComplainsReason),
    suppresses(Drug, Symptom, SuppressesReason),
    not(unsuitable_for(Person, Drug, UnsuitReason)),
    append(SuppressesReason, UnsuitReason, InterReason),
    append(ComplainsReason, InterReason, Reason).

The two calls to append at the end combine the three subsidiary lists into the final list reason. We will see that there is a difficulty with the third call involving not. However, let's first consider complains_of and suppresses. The latter is dealt with quite easily:

suppresses(Drug, Symptom, [relieves(Drug, Symptom)])

    :-

    relieves(Drug, Symptom).

On the other hand, complains_of/3 will require us to modify ask_about:

complains_of(Person, Symptom, ComplainsReason)

    :-

    ask_about(complains_of(Person,Symptom), Symptom, ComplainsReason).

To extend ask_about/2, we proceed in a similar manner:

```
ask_about(Predicate, InfoVar, Reason)
    :-
    var(InfoVar),!,                          % get value for InfoVar from user
    ask_info(Predicate, Question, InfoVar),
    write_list(Question),
    read(Answer),
    check_response(Predicate, Answer, InfoVar, Reason).


ask_about(Predicate, InfoVar, [userinfo-Predicate])
    :-
    nonvar(InfoVar),!,                       % ask user question about (value of) InfoVar
    ask_confirm(Predicate, Question, InfoVar),
    write_list(Question),
    read(Answer),
    act_on_yes_no(Answer).
```

The first clause passes the (uninstantiated) variable Reason down to check_response/4 to generate the reason. On the other hand, the second clause directly presents a Reason for its conclusion. Continuing, we define check_response/4 as follows:

```
check_response(Predicate, Answer, InfoVar, Reason)
    :-
    var(Answer), !,            % suppress other clauses if Answer is a variable
    nl, write('Your answer is a Prolog variable, most likely because '),
    nl, write('you typed an identifier beginning with an upper-case letter.'),
    nl, write('Please try again, avoiding upper-case letters: '),
    read(NewAnswer),

    check_response(Predicate, NewAnswer, InfoVar, Reason).
                    % passing the original variable InfoVar to this recursive call
            % on check_response means that the original call to check_response
                    % will get the ultimate result of checking the NewAnswer


check_response(Predicate, Answer, InfoVar, [userinfo-Predicate])
    :-                                       % can assume Answer is non-variable
                                             % because of cut in first clause
    ask_acceptability(Predicate, Answer, Test),
    Test, !,                                 % Is it acceptable?
    InfoVar = Answer.                        % Yes - return it.


check_response(Predicate, Answer, InfoVar, userinfo-Predicate])
                    [synonymous(Answer, InfoVar),
    :-                                       % can assume Answer is non-variable and
    synonymous(Predicate, Answer, InfoVar),   % that Answer is not a basic
    ! .                                      % acceptable response; suppress
```

% backtracking to final (error) clause
% if synonym is found.

check_response(Predicate, Answer, InfoVar, Reason)
:-
nl, write('I can''t understand what you typed.'),
nl, write('Please try again: '),
read(NewAnswer),
check_response(Predicate, NewAnswer, InfoVar, Reason).

In the first and fourth clauses, the variable Reason is passed unchanged to the recursive call on check_response/4 since no conclusion has been reached. In the second clause, the user's response is found acceptable, so the reason is created. Similarly, the user's response is also found acceptable in clause three, but here the reason created includes the synonym relation that was used.

We'll turn to the third call in the body of the rule for should_take/3. Intuitively, it appears correct: We prove that unsuitable_for(Person, Drug, UnsuitReason) is false with reason UnsuitReason. However, the difficulty lies in the fact that Prolog's builtin *not* is only an approximation of real logical negation. Recall that *not* is actually *negation by failure*. To solve the goal not(G), Prolog tries to solve the subsidiary goal G. Things work like this:

If G succeeds, then not(G) fails.
If G fails, then not(G) succeeds.

This is a reasonable approximation of negation (reread Sections 2.2 and 3.4). However, our difficulty is of an operational nature. Recall that when Prolog fails to solve a goal G, it backtracks to an earlier choice point. Not only does it return computational control to that earlier point, but it returns the environment to the state at that earlier point. The latter means that it *undoes* all the variable bindings made since it passed that choice point. Thus, no information can be passed out of a failed computation for later use. But this means that even if not(G) succeeds, because this depends on G failing, no information can be passed out of the goal not(G) via variable bindings. Thus, even if

not(unsuitable_for(Person, Drug, UnsuitReason))

succeeds, the variable UnsuitReason will be unbound! We cannot obtain reasons for proofs of negative goals, at least by the naive direct approach we have tried to take.

What is our problem, really? It is twofold:

- We want to prove a negative assertion;
- We want to extract information from a successful proof of the negative assertion.

Thus, we might solve our problem by one of the following two approaches:

1 Find a method of proving the desired negative assertion that allows us to pass out information using variable binding;
2 Find a different method of passing information out of the present approach to proving negative assertions.

There is a solution to 2, namely to add asserts to the body of unsuitable_for/2, which record the required information, then make calls on these asserted facts after not(unsuitable_for . . .) has finished to obtain the information. However, this has several negative features. First, adding these asserts complicates the body of unsuitable_for/2 which should be a domain knowledge rule only. Secondly, the recorded information would clutter the program and possibly conflict with other calls on unsuitable_for/2: managing this problem would definitely complicate the program.

Fortunately, there is a solution to 1 that is more appealing, though it is not without impact. The builtin *not* provides a uniform method of dealing with negations of goals. Our alternative method will be to take a nonuniform approach, to explicitly define what it means for a drug not to be unsuitable for a person. If we can define such a notion by more or less ordinary Prolog clauses, we will be able to pass information out using variable bindings. Let's try to define a predicate not_unsuitable_for/3. The specification for the predicate is this:

> not_unsuitable_for(Person, Drug, Reason) holds *if and only if*
> Reason = no_aggravated_conditions *and*
> *there is* no Condition which Person suffers from such that Drug aggravates Condition.

This leads to the following:

- If there exists a Condition such that suffers_from(Person, Condition) holds and aggravates(Drug, Condition), then not_unsuitable_for(Person,Drug, Reason) should fail;
- Otherwise, not_unsuitable_for(Person, Drug, no_aggravated_conditions) should succeed.

Consequently, we can use the following Prolog definition:

```
not_unsuitable_for(Person, Drug, _)
    :-
    aggravates(Drug, Condition),
    suffers_from(Person, Condition,_),
    !, fail.

not_unsuitable_for(Person, Drug, [no_aggravated_conditions]).
```

This completes the modifications to the program. Some examples of its action are shown here.

```
?- run.
Name = ken.
What symptom are you bothered by?  headache.
Do you suffer from asthma (yes/no) ? n.
Do you suffer from peptic_ulcer (yes/no) ? n.
Recommend taking aspirin
Explanation:
userinfo-complains_of(ken,headache)
relieves(aspirin,headache)
```

```
no_aggravated_conditions
yes.

?- run.
Name = ken.
What symptom are you bothered by? pain.
Your response is ambiguous
Please select a synonym - type corresponding number
1:  moderate_pain
2:  severe_pain
Choice = 2.
Do you suffer from asthma (yes/no) ? y.
Recommend taking pain_gone
Explanation:
synonymous(pain,severe_pain)
userinfo-complains_of(ken,severe_pain)
relieves(pain_gone,severe_pain)
no_aggravated_conditions
yes.
```

EXERCISES

8-1 Develop a simple consultant system in the spirit of should_take/2 from Section 8.1 that will assist with TV problems based on the database developed in Exercise 1-9.

8-2 Using the photography fault database developed in Exercise 1-14, develop a core photography expert system around a predicate

should_apply(Remedy)

similar in spirit to the lay medicine system predicate should_take/2 initially developed in Section 8.1. Extend this using the tools developed in Section 8.1. Also, extend the database to cover the entire table in Appendix E.

8-3 If necessary, reorganize the IRS filing rule databases (see Appendix D) developed in Exercises 1-13, 2-12, 3-10, 4-10, 7-6, 7-11, and 12 to develop an expert consultation system based on the must-file/1 predicate in the style of the should_take/2 predicate of the lay medicine example of Section 8-1.

8-4 Modify the obtain_description/0 predicate used in Section 8.2 so that the user does not have to type a Prolog term. That is, instead of typing

bud_scales(imbricate).

the user could type

bud_scales imbricate.

Use the lexical analysis tools developed in Section 7.8.5 to accomplish this.

8-5 Following the spirit of the Hickory tree identification system developed in Section 8.2, use the clouds databases (see Appendix C) developed in Exercises 1-10–11, 2-10, 3-6, and 5-13 to produce a generate-and-test style expert system for classifying and identifying clouds. The system should make maximal use of query-the-user facilities, should support use of synonyms, etc., and should provide explanations to the user.

8-6 Develop a generate-and-test style expert system for dealing with automobile fuel system problems (see Appendix F), based on the database developed in Exercise 3-11. (If necessary, reorganize that database). Extend this expert system to cover both fuel system and engine problems as presented in Appendix F. The system should make maximal use of query-the-user facilities, should support use of synonyms, etc., and should provide explanations to the user.

CHAPTER **9**

METALEVEL SHELLS

9.1 A PROLOG INTERPRETER IN PROLOG

First, let us consider the basic structure of a Prolog interpreter. The typical Prolog interpreter (or compiler) is prepared to accept a database of Prolog clauses (facts and rules) representing its knowledge. It accepts from the user a (simple or compound) goal and attempts to solve that goal in a backward-chaining, depth-first manner. We can declaratively describe such a clause interpreter as

Goal is solvable
  if Goal is empty.

Goal is solvable
  if SubGoal is selected from Goal with Remaining left over, *and*
  Rule is a rule in the database, *and*
  Rule has parts Head and Body, *and*
  Head matches SubGoal via substitution S, *and*
  NewGoalSkeleton is obtained by combining Remaining with Body, *and*
  NewGoal is obtained by applying substitution S to NewGoalSkeleton, *and*
  NewGoal is solvable.

The *structure-sharing* approach to Prolog implementation obviates the necessity to ever actually apply a substitution in the interpreter. Instead of maintaining *concrete* formulas, such systems maintain *virtual* formulas, which can be thought of as skeletons containing variables, paired with a substitution that, if actually applied, would produce the desired concrete formula. At all times, there is one global substitution used in the system: All the virtual formulas and terms consist of skeletons paired with this global substitution. The process of matching or unifying two such virtual formulas or terms is quite like the naive unification algorithm, with the following addition: whenever

242

in the process of unification a variable is encountered in either term (or formula) being matched, one is required to *de-reference* the variable relative to the global substitution. That is, one *applies* the substitution to the variable (this amounts to a table lookup) and continues the matching process with the value obtained in place of the variable. This process is recursive: If the value *looked up* is again a variable, one applies the substitution again, etc. Since substitutions are finite objects, one must eventually terminate in a concrete object or in a variable that has no value in the substitution. In the latter case, the last obtained variable is set to have its companion matching term as its value in the substitution. Thus, in this setting, the unification algorithm computes an extension of the input global substitution, provided the concrete terms underlying the virtual terms are in fact unifiable. Thus, we can ignore the handling of substitutions, assuming it is taken care of by the matching process.

With this background, let us write, in Prolog, an interpreter for pure Prolog clauses. The top level of the interpreter appears as follows:

```
solvable(Goal)
    :-
    empty(Goal).

solvable(Goal)
    :-
    select(Goal, SubGoal, Remaining),
    in_database(Rule),
    parts(Rule, Head, Body),
    match(SubGoal, Head),
    combine(Remaining, Body, NewGoal),
    solvable(NewGoal).
```

Here we assume that select/3 cannot hold if Goal is in fact an empty goal.

To this pure Horn clause interpreter, Prolog adds a procedurally oriented aspect. It assumes that

- The clauses inhabiting the database are in fact linearly ordered;
- The subgoals in both rule bodies and goals are linearly ordered (from left to right);
- *in_database* chooses Rules in accordance with the database order;
- *select* chooses the first subgoal from the Goal;
- *combine* places the elements of the rule Body, in order, before the elements of Remaining.

Finally, the overall control of Prolog is governed by chronological backtracking. If, in its work, Prolog encounters a step that cannot succeed, Prolog retreats to the chronologically most recent point of the computation at which a choice was made. This must be a point where the selection of the next rule from the database was made. Prolog undoes the effects (on the substitution) of having matched the head of this rule against the selected subgoal and chooses to select the next rule in the database following the previously selected rule. Then it proceeds in its basic forward direction.

We must define the supporting predicates for the interpreter. Let us first consider the predicate *match*. It is defined by the builtin "=":

match(X, Y) :- X = Y.

The definition of *select* trades on a clever design decision in Prolog implementation, that there is ultimately only a contextual distinction between clauses and terms: clauses are really terms in disguise. Thus, the comma that functions as conjunction in the construction of rules is really on the same footing as the plus (+) used in constructing arithmetic terms. Consequently, Prolog allows us the following definition of *select*:

select((SubGoal, Remaining), SubGoal, Remaining)
    :- !.

select(SubGoal, SubGoal, true).

The constant *true* is used to represent the empty goal. The first clause defines selection from a compound goal, while the second defines selection from a goal consisting of one subgoal alone. As one might expect, *combine* can be defined similarly:

combine((A, B), Remaining, (A, Rest))
    :- !
    combine(B, Remaining, Rest).

combine(A, Remaining, (A, Remaining)).

Many will recognize this as a disguised version of appending lists together. Even *parts* can be given a Prolog definition, specifically,

parts((Head :- Body), Head, Body)
    :- !.

parts(Fact, Fact, true).

The second clause reflects the interpetation of a fact as a rule with an empty body. The first clause depends on the design decision mentioned above: the implication connective (:-) is regarded as a term construction operator just as comma or plus.

To define *in-database*, we must make recourse to an extralogical feature of Prolog: explicit access to the database. This is the built-in predicate called *clause*, which is defined as

clause(A, B) holds *if and only if*
there is a clause C in the database such that the head of C matches (unifies with) A and the body of C matches B. If C is a fact, the body of C is taken to be "true".

With this in hand, we can define in-database as

in_database((Head :- Body))
    :- !,
    clause(Head, Body).

```
in_database(Fact)
    :-
    clause(Fact, true).
```

9.2 INTERPRETERS FOR RULE-BASED SYSTEMS

Consider a simplified version of the original medical advice system developed in Section 8.1:

```
should_take(Person, Drug) :-
    complains_of(Person, Symptom),
    suppresses(Drug, Symptom),
    not( unsuitable_for(Person, Drug) ).

unsuitable_for(Person, Drug) :-
    aggravates(Drug, Condition),
    suffers_from(Person, Condition).

suppresses(Drug, Symptom)
    :-
    relieves(Drug, Symptom).

relieves(aspirin, headache).
        :
relieves(bis_cure, nausea).

aggravates(aspirin, peptic_ulcer).
        :
aggravates(bis_cure, gout).

suffers_from(Person, Condition) :-
    ask_about(suffers_from(Person, Condition),Condition).

complains_of(Person, Symptom) :-
    ask_about(complains_of(Person, Symptom),Symptom).

ask_about(Question,Argument) :-
    nonvar(Argument),!,
    write('Does'),write(Question),write('?'),
    read(Answer),
    act_on(Answer).

ask_about(Question,Argument) :-
```

```
        var(Argument),!,
        write('What does'),write(Question),write('?'),
        read(Argument).

    act_on(yes).
    act_on(y).
```

This simple program is invoked by submitting a goal such as

    ?- should_take(bob, What).

It already illustrates substantial use of metaprogramming techniques in its definitions of the predicates ask_about, suffers_from, and complains_of. The definitions of the latter three predicates make use of the identification of formulas with terms, so that the formula that occurs as the head of the rule for suffers_from is identified with the term that is the first argument of ask_about in the body of the rule for suffers_from, while the second argument of ask_about is identified with the second argument of that term, which in turn is identical with the head of the rule. The definition of ask_about uses the built-in var predicate to test whether that variable—which is the second argument of the invoking call to suffers_from—is bound or unbound and performs different acts accordingly.

Let us assume that we wish to incorporate both a facility to treat confidence factors and to accumulate deductions to provide for explanations to the user. In Section 8.4, we accumulated deductions by adding an extra argument to certain predicates. If we followed this line, we would add two extra arguments to all of the appropriate predicates in which the confidence factors and proofs are recorded and transmitted. The disadvantage of this approach is that it complicates the preparation and presentation of the knowledge of the system. One of the arguments set forth for the rule-based approach to expert systems development is the modularity and clarity of rule-based presentations of domain knowledge. However, the addition of extra arguments to record and transmit confidence factors and proofs substantially reduces this modularity and clarity. Not only do the rules become more complicated to read, but new rules must not only express domain knowledge but must also contain code reflecting the handling of the confidence factors and proofs.

A preferable approach would be to leave the rules (nearly) unchanged, to create some method of attaching confidence factors to the facts and rules, and to write an interpreter (and ultimately compiler) that could manipulate the rules, confidence factors, and proofs. All of the information necessary for calculating confidence factors and proofs would be hidden inside this interpreter or *shell*. The metaprogramming facilities of Prolog make this an easy task.

Let us attach confidence factors to knowledge by the simple expedient of writing them into files along with the knowledge. We'll define "::" as a binary infix operator for this purpose:

    :-op(1200, yfx, '::').

This declaration will be placed in the main file defining our shell. Assuming that it is in force, we can express one possible version of the system knowledge in another file ('medicknw.k'), as follows:

    should_take;(Person, Drug) :-
        complains_of(Person, Symptom),
        suppresses(Drug, Symptom),
        not(unsuitable_for(Person, Drug)) :: 0.9.

    unsuitable_for(Person, Drug) :-
        aggravates(Drug, Condition),
        suffers_from(Person, Condition) :: 0.8.

    suppresses(Drug, Symptom)
        :-
        relieves(Drug, Symptom)   :: 0.85.

    relieves(aspirin, headache)   :: 0.96.
    relieves(bis_cure, nausea)   :: 0.93.

    aggravates(aspirin, peptic_ulcer)   :: 0.92.
    aggravates(bis_cure, gout)   :: 0.77.

Besides building facilities for confidence factors and proof accumulation into our shell, we will also use the consolidated *query-the-user* facility (developed in Section 8.3) in the shell. Thus, we will add the following assertions to our knowledge file:

    ask_info(complains_of(Person,Symptom),
                    ['What symptom are you bothered by?'], Symptom).

    ask_confirm(complains_of(Person,Symptom),
                    ['Are you bothered by ', Symptom, ' (yes/no) ?'], Symp-
                    tom).

    ask_acceptability(complains_of(Person,Answer), Answer, relieves(_, Answer)).

    ask_info(suffers_from(Person, Condition),
                    ['What condition do you suffer from?'], Condition).

    ask_confirm(suffers_from(Person, Condition),
                    ['Do you suffer from ', Condition, ' (yes/no) ?'], Con-
                    dition).

    ask_acceptability(suffers_from(Person, Answer), Answer, aggravates(_, Answer)).

This completes the organization of the domain knowledge our system is to possess. We are now faced with two tasks:

1 Creating Prolog clauses that represent this knowledge, and
2 Using those clauses.

To handle the first problem, we must create a customized version of Prologs built-in *consult* predicate, which we have whimsically named *sweep_in*. Its definition runs

```
sweep_in;(File)
    :-
    see(File),
    process_file,
    seen,
    write(ok).

process_file
    :-
    read(Clause),
    dispatch(Clause).

dispatch(end_of_file) :- !.

dispatch(QualifiedClause)
    :-
    QualifiedClause = (Clause :: Confidence),!,
    assertz(Clause),
    Clause = .. [Op, Head, Body],
    work_on(Op, Head, Body, Clause, Confidence),
    process_file.

dispatch(UnQualifiedClause)
    :-
    assertz(UnQualifiedClause).

work_on(':-', Head, Body, Clause, Confidence)
    :-
    clause(Head, Body, Ptr),
    assertz(conf(Ptr, Confidence)).

work_on(Op, Head, Body, Clause, Confidence)
    :-
    clause(Clause, true, Ptr),
    assertz(conf(Ptr, Confidence)).
```

This definition makes full use of the various database access and modification facilities described in Section 7.3. The main loop of *sweep_in* is the mutually recursive pair of procedures process_file and dispatch. The first successively reads terms from the file, while the second determines whether or not the end of the file has been reached. In the latter case, dispatch determines whether the term is of the form

(Clause :: Confidence)

or not. If not, it simply asserts the term as an ordinary clause. But in the former case, it extracts Clause from the term and asserts it, retaining a database pointer *Ptr* for the newly asserted clause. It then asserts an auxilliary fact

conf(Ptr, Confidence).

to record the user's confidence in that Clause.

Finally, we must construct a shell that can utilize the information that sweep_in has recorded, including the confidence factors, as well as maintain traces of its proofs, etc. The shell we will present is simply an emendation on the basic Prolog interpreter presented in the last section. The shell's primary predicate, called solve/3, is defined as

```
:-op(1200, yfx, '::').
:-op(700, yfx, if).


solve(true, 1.0, []) :-!.


solve( (A,B), Conf, Proof)
        :-
        solve(A, C1, P1),
        solve(B, C2, P2),
        conj_conf(C1, C2, Conf),            % confidence calculation
        append(P1, P2, Proof).


solve(A, C, [(A if B) | P2])
        :-
        clause(A, B, Ptr),
        conf(Ptr, C1),
        solve(B, C2, P2),
        rule_conf(C1, C2, C).               % confidence calculation


solve(A, C, [asked(A)])
        :-
        ask_about(A),
        obtain_conf(C).                      % determine confidence


solve(not(A), C, [negate(A,P1)] )
        :-
        solve(A, C1, P1),
        !,
        C1 < 0.3,
        neg_conf(C1, C).                     % confidence calculation


solve(not(A), 1.0, [not(A)-exhaustion]) :-!.
```

```
solve(A, 1.0, [A-builtin])
    :-
    clause(A, B, Ptr),
    not(conf(Ptr, C1)),
    A.
```

The second argument to solve/3 is its Certainty in the solution to the Goal in its first argument, and the third argument is the Proof generated in the course of obtaining the solution. Apart from these additional arguments and a few extra calls in the bodies of the clauses (to deal with the certainty factors), the first three clauses are just a variation on the Prolog interpreter in Section 9.1. The binary infix operator *if* is used to construct terms representing rules. Fleshing this out to a full program requires little more than a few additional definitions. The confidence calculation predicates can be defined according to the knowledge engineer's needs. We supply one simple set of predicates for this:

```
conj_conf(X, Y, Z)
    :-
    min(X, Y, Z).

rule_conf(X, Y, Z)
    :-
    max(X, Y, Z).

neg_conf(X, Y)
    :-
    Y is 1.0 - X.

min(X, Y, X)
    :-
    X =< Y.

min(X, Y, Y)
    :-
    X > Y.

max(X, Y, X)
    :-
    Y =< X.

max(X, Y, Y)
    :-
    Y > X.

act_on(yes).
act_on(y).
```

Note also that nothing in this overall approach requires us to use real numbers for our confidence values. We could just have well have used the three atoms *certain*, *possible*, and *impossible*, together with appropriate definitions of the confidence calculation predicates. The ask_about predicates are those developed in Section 8.3. The definition of obtain_confidence is given:

obtain_conf(C)
>   :-
>   write('What is your confidence in that answer?'),
>   read(C).

We can organize use of the advisor system in this setting with these predicates:

loadmedic
>   :-
>   sweep_in('medicknw.k').

medic
>   :-
>   write('Name = '), read(Person),
>   solve(should_take(Person, Drug), Conf, Proof),
>   write(Person),write(' should take '),write(Drug),nl,
>   write(confidence = Conf),nl,
>   write('Explanation:'),nl,
>   write(Proof),nl.

Using these top-level predicates, we can observe the following interactions:

```
?- loadmedic.
Swept in medicknw.k
yes.
?- medic.
Name = ken.
What symptom are you bothered by? headache.
What is your confidence in that answer? 0.8.
Do you suffer from asthma (yes/no) ? y.
What is your confidence in that answer? 0.7.
ken should take noasprinol
confidence=0.9
Explanation:
[should_take(ken,noasprinol) if(complains_of(ken,headache),
suppresses(noasprinol,headache), not unsuitable_for(ken,
noasprinol)), asked(complains_of(ken,headache)),
suppresses(noasprinol,headache) if relieves(noasprinol,
headache),relieves(noasprinol,headache) if true,(not
unsuitable_for(ken,noasprinol))-exhaustion]
yes.
```

Everything about this is reasonable except the presentation of the explanation—it is almost indecipherable! To render this more civilized, first modify the last call of medic/0:

```
medic :-
      write('Name = '), read(Person),
      solve(should_take(Person, Drug), Conf, Proof),
      write(Person),write(' should take '),write(Drug),nl,
      write(confidence = Conf),nl,
      write('Explanation:'),nl,
      write_nl_list(Proof),nl.
```

Define write_nl_list/1 as

```
write_nl_list([]).

write_nl_list([Item | Items])
      :-
      print(Item),nl,
      write_nl_list(Items).

print((Conclusion if true))
      :-!,
      print(Conclusion).
print((Conclusion if Premises))
      :-!,
      print(Conclusion),write('if '),
      nl,tab(3),
      print(Premises).
print(asked(What))
      :-!,
      print(What),write(' – asked').
print((A,B))
      :-!,
      print(A), write(' & '),
      nl,tab(3),
      print(B).
print(Item)
      :-
      write(Item).
```

With these modifications, the interaction now appears as

```
?- medic.
Name =  ken.
What symptom are you bothered by? headache.
What is your confidence in that answer? 0.8.
Do you suffer from asthma (yes/no)  ?y.
What is your confidence in that answer? 0.7.
ken should take noasprinol
confidence=0.9
```

```
Explanation:
should_take(ken,noasprinol)if
   complains_of(ken,headache) &
   suppresses(noasprinol,headache) &
   not unsuitable_for(ken,noasprinol)
complains_of(ken,headache) -- asked
suppresses(noasprinol,headache)if
   relieves(noasprinol,headache)
relieves(noasprinol,headache)
(not unsuitable_for(ken,noasprinol))-exhaustion
yes.
```

If we examine the code for the second clause of solve/3, we can see one disturbing element (even though it operates perfectly correctly):

> solve((A,B), Conf, Proof)
>
>   :-
>
>   solve(A, C1, P1),
>   solve(B, C2, P2),
>   conj_conf(C1, C2, Conf),   % *confidence calculation*
>   append(P1, P2, Proof).

This disturbing element is the use of append/3 to patch the subproofs together. If the reasoning carried out by the expert system is at all deep and complex, it is quite possible that the subproofs P1 will get quite long. Thus, the system will spend lots of time appending proofs together. Let us explore a technique that can avoid this inefficiency.

Our problem is that we are generating a list (the proof) in the normal list order, and we don't know how long it will be (which is why we are using the list *datatype*). What we would like to be able to do is to hold onto one list and gradually add each element at the end as it is generated, just as one does with a pencil-and-paper list on a clip board. What we need is an extensible version of a list, rather than the fixed lists we have worked with so far. To understand the technique to be introduced, consider the following list:

> L = [a, b, U, d].

The first, second, and fourth elements of L are determined, but the third element U is an uninstantiated variable. Thus we can say we are dealing with a four element list whose third element is unknown but may receive a value at a later time. This is illustrated in the following interaction:

```
?-L = [a, b, U, d], write(L), nl, U is 3 + 5, write(L), nl.
[a, b, _12554, d]
[a, b, 8, d]
yes.
```

We have actually seen this sort of behavior before: A complex term is constructed with some of its components being uninstantiated variables that receive values at a later time. In general, such an expression is called a *partially-instantiated term*.

In this example, one of the elements of the list was an uninstantiated variable. However, suppose we describe a list as follows:

M = [p,q |TM].

In this case, all of the individual elements we are aware of are specific. However, the tail of the list M is uninstantiated! That is, we know that M is a list beginning with p and q, and followed by some unknown further elements—maybe three more elements, maybe 425 more, or maybe even no more—but at the moment, we don't know anything about the tail TM. We will learn about it later when TM receives a value. If TM is unified with [r, s, t], M will become the list [p, q, r, s, t]. If TM is unified with [], then M will become the list [p,q]. And if TM is unified with [r, s |TM2], M will become the list

M = [p, q, r, s | TM2].

So then we know that M has at least four elements, but we won't know any more about M until TM2 receives a value.

This is the key to the notion of an extensible list. We keep steadily instantiating the previous tail variables to a list containing the newly generated item followed by a new uninstantiated tail variable. For example, if we are generating the sequence p, q, r, s, . . . , the behavior would look like the table in Figure 9–1. Obviously, the trick is that at each step, the current tail variable must be made available to the procedure charged with putting the newly generated element onto the end of the list.

Let's first build a small program to read items from the keyboard until it sees the atom *done* and accumulates the list of the items read using this technique. The simple top level is

```
test :-
      readList(L),
      write(list = L),nl.
```

To define readList/1, proceed as follows:

```
readList(CurrentTail)
      :-
      write('>>'),
      read(Item),
      decide(Item, CurrentTail).

decide(done, CurrentTail)
      :-
      CurrentTail = [].
decide(OtherItem, CurrentTail)
      :-
      CurrentTail = [ OtherItem | NextTail],
      readList(NextTail).
```

FIGURE 9–1

Successive extentions of a list.

Step	Current M	Tail variable	Action
start	M	M	noaction
gen. p	M	TM1	M = [p | TM1]
gen. q	M = [p | TM1]	TM2	TM1 = [q | TM2]
gen. r	M = [p,q | TM2]	TM3	TM2 = [r | TM3]
gen. s	M = [p,q,r | TM3]	TM4	TM3 = [s | TM4]
. . . .	. . . .	. . . .	. . . .

Running this test program, we observe this interaction:

```
?-test.
>> hi.
>> everyone.
>> good(day).
>> 23.4.
>> done.
list=[hi,everyone,good(day),23.4]
yes.
```

In order to observe the internal behavior as the list is built, let's modify the program to print out the growing extensible list at each step of the way:

```
test :-
    readList(L, L),
    write(list-L),nl.

readList(CurrentTail, OrigList)
    :-
    write(OrigList),
    write('>>'),
    read(Item),
    decide(Item, CurrentTail, OrigList).

decide(done, CurrentTail, OrigList)
    :-
    CurrentTail = [].
decide(OtherItem, CurrentTail, OrigList)
    :-
    CurrentTail = [ OtherItem | NextTail],
    readList(NextTail, OrigList).
```

With this version of the program, the interaction appears as

```
?-test.
_12345>>hi.
[hi | _12347]>> everyone.
```

```
[hi,everyone | _12349]>> good(day).
[hi,everyone,good(day) | _12351]>> 23.4.
[hi,everyone,good(day),23.4 | _12353]>> done.
list=[hi,everyone,good(day),23.4]
yes.
```

Thus, the extensible list technique works to grow a list in the order of the generation of its elements. We need simply adapt solve/3 to utilize extensible lists to manage its accumulation of proofs. The original version of solve used only one argument for proofs. However, in the new version, a particular invocation of solve must receive a *current proof tail* as input when invoked and must return a *new proof tail* when it finishes. It will unify the current proof tail with a list expression involving the new proof tail. Here is the revised code, defining solve/4:

solve(true, 1.0, InPrfTail, InPrfTail) :-!.

solve((A,B), Conf, InPrfTail, OutPrfTail)
    :-
    solve(A, C1, InPrfTail, InterPrfTail),
    solve(B, C2, InterPrfTail, OutPrfTail),
    conj_conf(C1, C2, Conf).   *% confidence calculation*

solve(A, C, [(A if B) | InterPrfTail], OutPrfTail)
    :-
    clause(A, B, Ptr),
    conf(Ptr, C1),
    solve(B, C2, InterPrfTail, OutPrfTail),
    rule_conf(C1, C2, C).   *% confidence calculation*

solve(A, C, [asked(A) | OutPrfTail], OutPrfTail)
    :-
    ask_about(A),
    obtain_conf(C).   *% determine confidence*

solve(not(A), C, [negate(A, SubProof) | OutPrfTail], OutPrfTail)
    :-
    solve(A, C1, SubProof, []),
    !,
    C1 < 0.3,
    neg_conf(C1, C).   *% confidence calculation*

solve(not(A), 1.0, [not(A)-exhaustion | OutPrfTail], OutPrfTail):-!.

solve(A, 1.0, [A-builtin | OutPrfTail], OutPrfTail)
    :-
    clause(A, B, Ptr),
    not(conf(Ptr, C1)),
    A.

To run this, we need only change the definition of medic/0 to call solve/4 (instead of solve/3) with the fourth argument set to [ ], since at the top level, the extensible list should be terminated

```
medic :-
    write('Name = '), read(Person),
    solve(should_take(Person, Drug), Conf, Proof, [] ),
    write(Person),write(' should take '),write(Drug),nl,
    write(confidence = Conf),nl,
    write('Explanation:'),nl,
    write_nl_list(Proof),nl.
```

9.3 SOLVING CONSTRAINTS

The final example in this chapter is a shell oriented toward the solution of constraints. It was designed in the course of producing a solution to the "Jobs" puzzle.[1] The puzzle runs as follows: There are four people and eight jobs, as indicated in the table in Figure 9–2. Each person is to hold exactly two jobs. The constraints of the problem are

- Each person holds exactly two jobs
- The job of nurse is held by a male
- The husband of the chef is the telephone operator
- Roberta is not a boxer
- Pete is not college educated
- Roberta, the chef, and the police officer went golfing together

From ordinary use of language and common sense, we can set down some immediate relevant knowledge:

- Roberta and Thelma are females
- Steve and Pete are males

---

[1] In Wos et al., *Automated Reasoning, Introduction and Applications*, Prentice-Hall.1984, p.55.

FIGURE 9–2
People and jobs

Person	Jobs
Roberta	chef
Thelma	guard
Steve	nurse
Pete	telephone operator
	police officer (no gender implied)
	teacher
	actor
	boxer

- Actors are male
- Roberta, the chef, and the police officer are all distinct
- Husbands are male
- The nurse, teacher, and police officer are all college educated

Let us express some aspects of the problem in Prolog, starting with the ultimate goal or solution. We can describe the assignment of a job to a person with a two-place term

has_job(Person, Job)

for example,

has_job(steve, nurse).

Thus, one approach is to express the problem as a collection of eight such terms:

has_job(roberta,	R_Job1)	has_job(roberta,	R_job2)
has_job(thelma,	T_Job1)	has_job(thelma,	T_job2)
has_job(steve,	S_Job1)	has_job(steve,	S_job2)
has_job(pete,	P_Job1)	has_job(pete,	P_job2)

If we collect these terms into a list, we can set our sights on defining a predicate solve/2 that expresses the action of our interpreter or shell:

```
:- solve(
[has_job(roberta,    R_Job1),    has_job(roberta,    R_job2),
   has_job(thelma,    T_Job1),    has_job(thelma,    T_job2),
   has_job(steve,     S_Job1),    has_job(steve,     S_job2),
   has_job(pete,      P_Job1),    has_job(pete,      P_job2)],
                      Result).
```

The general form of our shell call is

solve(Goal, Result)

The Goals argument is a list of subproblems—in our case, the has_job subproblems. Each of these subproblems contains uninstantiated variables at the outset. Solving a subproblem amounts to choosing values for its uninstantiated variables. Working through such a sequence of choices can always be organized as using three lists:

| To_Be_Done_List, | Completed_List, | Final_Result_List |

Since at the outset, the Completed_List is empty, we can define our basic *solve* predicate (that has only two arguments) in terms of another solve predicate that has three arguments, taking the Initial_Goals to be the To_Be_Done_List:

```
solve(Initial_Goals, Final_Result)
    :-
    solve(Initial_Goals, [ ], Final_Result)
```

We begin to approach the meat of our general problem. We must define the action of the three-argument solve predicate. It splits into two cases:

1 There is more work to do;
2 It believes the work is over,

The first case is covered by one clause:

solve([SubGoal | OtherSubGoals], Established, FinalResult)
> :-
> conjecture(SubGoal, Established),
> satisfy_local_constraints([SubGoal | Established]),
> solve(OtherSubGoals, [SubGoal | Established], FinalResult).

Notice that we can read this as

In order to solve a list consisting of a SubGoal and some OtherSubGoals,
relative to what has already been Established, *proceed as follows:*
- Conjecture a solution to SubGoal relative to what has been Established;
- Check that this conjecture, together with what has already been Established, satisfies all local problem constraints;
- Add the solved SubGoal to what has been Established; and
- Go on to solve the OtherSubGoals.

The second case is also covered by one clause:

solve([ ], Established, FinalResult)
> :-
> satisfy_global_constraints(Established),
> FinalResult = Established.

This clause can be read

When there are no more subgoals to be solved,
- Check that what you have Established satisfies any global constraints, then
- Return what you have Established as the FinalResult.

Before we elaborate on what it means to satisfy local or global constraints, let's jump to expressing some of the knowledge together with some of the constraints of our particular problem in Prolog. The jobs, the people, and the gender of the people are easily expressed with one-place predicates:

job(guard).	person(roberta).	female(roberta).
job(nurse).	person(thelma).	female(thelma).
job(teacher).	person(steve).	male(steve).
job(actor).	person(pete).	male(pete).
job(boxer).		
job(chef).		
job(telephone_operator).		
job(police_officer).		

Some of the elementary knowledge appears as

not_college_educated(pete).

at_most_2(A, B, C)
>
> :-
>
> A = B; A = C; B = C.

can_be_husband(X, Y)
>
> :-
>
> male(X), female(Y).

college_educated(X)
>
> :-
>
> not(not_college_educated(X)).

can_golf_together(roberta, Person2, Person3)
>
> :-
>
> diff(roberta, Person2),
> diff(roberta, Person3),
> diff(Person2, Person3).

Let us look at the problem of expressing some of the more substantive constraints that we have to maintain in the search for a solution to the puzzle. Two of the necessary constraints are specified by

male(Person)
>
> :-
>
> has_job(Person, nurse).

diff(Job1,Job2)
>
> :-
>
> has_job(Person1, Job1),
> has_job(Person2, Job2),
> diff(Person1,Person2).

Though we have first expressed these constraints as simple Prolog clauses, it turns out to be convenient to separate them from the rest of the program's clauses. Since ordinary Prolog does not allow us to split up the database, we do this by turning these clauses into terms and wrapping a *local_constraint* assertion around them, as follows:[2]

local_constraint((male(Person) :- has_job(Person, nurse))).

local_constraint((diff(Job1,Job2) :-
>
> has_job(Person1, Job1),
> has_job(Person2, Job2),

---

[2] In Prolog systems, such as ALS Prolog, that support a module system, this separation can be effected much more naturally.

diff(Person1,Person2)
)).

Our particular problem has only one global constraint:

global_constraint((has_job(Person, Position) :- job(Position)))

We have the heart of solve/3 to complete. First, we must have a method for conjecturing solutions:

conjecture(has_job(X, Y), Established).
    :-
    person(X),
    job(Y),
    not(member(has_job(X, Y), Established)).

To test whether all local constraints are satisfied, we simply check that it is not the case that there exist any failed local constraints:

satisfy_local_constraints(Established).
    :-
    not(exist_failed_local_constraint_for(Established)).

Checking whether there exist failed local constraints means repeatedly finding a local constraint and testing whether or not it has been satisfied:

exist_failed_local_constraint_for(Established).
    :-
    local_constraint((Constraint_Head :- Constraint_Body)),
    satisfy(Constraint_Body, Established),
    not(satisfy(Constraint_Head, Established)).

This states that

In order to determine whether there exists a failed local constraint, find a local constraint

- Whose Body is satisfied by the Established facts, and
- Whose Head is not satisfied by the Established facts.

Finally, to test whether a constraint is satisfied, we proceed as follows:

satisfy(true, Established).

satisfy((Condition, Rest), Established)
    :-
    member(Condition, Established),
    satisfy(Rest, Established).

satisfy((Condition, Rest), Established)
    :-

```
    call(Condition),
    satisfy(Rest, Established).

satisfy(Condition, Established)
    :-
    not( Condition = (_,_) ),
    member(Condition, Established).

satisfy(Condition, Established)
    :-
    not( Condition = (_,_) ),
    call(Condition).
```

The global constraints are dealt with similarly:

```
satisfy_global_constraints( Established )
    :-
    not( exist_failed_global_constraint_for( Established ) ).

exist_failed_global_constraint_for( Established )
    :-
    global_constraint( ( Constraint_Head :- Constraint_Body ) ),
    satisfy( Constraint_Body, Established ),
    not( satisfy( Constraint_Head, Established ) ).
```

The program is easily run with the test predicate:

```
jobs :- jobs(L), write(L), nl.
```

Running it produces this interaction:

```
?-jobs.
[has_job(steve,nurse),has_job(steve,police_officer),
has_job(thelma,boxer),has_job(thelma,chef),
has_job(pete,actor),has_job(pete,telephone_operator),
has_job(roberta,teacher),has_job(roberta,guard)]
yes.
```

One could use write_nl_list/1 from the previous section to produce the more readable output:

```
has_job(steve,nurse)
has_job(steve,police_officer)
has_job(thelma,boxer)
has_job(thelma,chef)
has_job(pete,actor)
has_job(pete,telephone_operator)
has_job(roberta,teacher)
has_job(roberta,guard)
```

EXERCISES

9-1 Revise the simple TV consultant system developed in Exercise 8-1 by adding (arbitrary) confidence factors and fitting the knowedge within the framework of solve/3 as developed in Section 9.2.

9-2 Continuing with the photography fault database developed in Exercise 1-14, revise the photography expert system developed in Exercise 8-2 by adding (arbitrary) confidence factors and fitting the knowedge within the framework of solve/3 as developed in Section 9.2.

9-3 Continue the work with the IRS filing rule databases developed in Exercises 1-13, 2-12, 3-10, 4-10, 7-6, 7-11–12, and 8-3 to develop an expert consultation system based on the must-file/1 predicate in the style of the solve/nnn predicates developed in this chapter.

9-4 Use the clouds databases developed in Exercises 1-10–11, 2-10, 3-6, and 5-13 together with the system developed in Exercise 8-5 to produce an expert system for classifying and identifiing clouds based on the approaches of Section 9.2, utilizing confidence factors and providing explanations, etc.

9-5 Use the work of Exercise 8-6 as a basis for creating an automobile repair consultant system using the approaches of Section 9.2, using (arbitrary) confidence factors, providing explanations, etc.

9-6 Make the necessary changes to solve/? and supporting predicates in Section 9.2 to replace the use of real numbers as confidence factors by the use of the atoms:

true, likely, unknown, unlikely, false.

9-7 Use the contraints approach of Section 9.3 to solve the following puzzle: [3]

Murder occurred one evening in the home of a married couple and their son and daughter. One member of the family murdered another member, the third member witnessed the crime, and the fourth member was an accessory after the fact.

1 The accessory and the witness were of opposite sex.

2 The oldest member and the witness were of opposite sex.

3 The youngest member and the victim were of opposite sex.

4 The accessory was older than the victim.

5 The father was the oldest member.

6 The killer was not the youngest member.

Who was the killer?

9-8 Use the contraints approach of Section 9.3 to solve the following puzzle: [4]

In the town of Arlington the supermarket, the department store, and the bank are open together on one day each week.

1 Each of the three places is open four days a week.

2 On Sunday all three places are closed.

3 None of the three places is open on three consecutive days.

4 On six consecutive days:

- the department store was closed on the first day
- the supermarket was closed on the second day
- the bank was closed on the third day
- the supermarket was closed on the fourth day

---

[3] From George J. Summers, *New Puzzles in Logical Deduction*, Dover, NY, 1968.
[4] From George J. Summers, *New Puzzles in Logical Deduction*, Dover, NY, 1968.

- the department store was closed on the fifth day
- the bank was closed on the sixth day

On which one of the seven days are all three places in Arlington open?

9-9 The N queens problem is to find a way of placing N queens on an N×N chessboard so that none of the queens is attacking any other. (A variation is to find all such solutions.) Explore using the methods of Section 9.3 to solve this problem.

9-10 Develop a notation for attaching brief names to rules to be used with solve/??, such as

> r23 #- suppresses(Drug, Symptom)
>
> :-
>
> relieves(Drug, Symptom) :: 0.85.

a Modify sweep_in/1 to handle these names: not only should it correctly read the expressions, extracting the rule and confidence factor as before, but it should associate the name with the rule in a manner similar to the association of the confidence factor with the rule.

b Modify the explanation facility developed in Section 9.4 so that it refers to rules by name rather than printing out the rule,

c Add a facility to the shell so that after the explanation is presented using rule names, the user can selectively ask for the rules to be displayed.

CHAPTER **10**

PARSING AND DEFINITE CLAUSE GRAMMARS

10.1 STEPPING-STONE PARSING AND LIST REPRESENTATION

The input a program receives, whether from a terminal or from a file, is generally a stream of characters. The program's task is to process and react to this stream of characters in an appropriate manner. Sometimes the stream is short and easy to handle, as in the case of simple interactive responses from the user. For example, the affirmative/negative responses in some of our consultation programs are relatively short and easy to handle. We have already seen examples where the input may be more complex. For example, in the Hickory tree identification program, the user types in compound Prolog terms for the program to process. Successful processing of the user's input involves breaking the undifferentiated stream of characters into subunits, then determining how or whether these combined subunits can be construed as a Prolog term. Thus, if the user types in

buds(yellow),

the program initially sees this list of ASCII codes:

[98,117,100,115,40,121,101,108,108,111,119,41].

To successfully construe this list as the intended Prolog term, the program must first break up the list, as follows:

[98,117,100, 115],   [40],   [121,101,108,108,111,119],   [41].

The next step is to see this as a list of corresponding atoms:

[buds, '(', yellow, ')'].

265

Finally, the program must process this list to recognize the term: buds(yellow). The middle step in this process, passing from short lists of ASCII codes to corresponding atoms, is easily accomplished using the Prolog builtin name/2 (see Chapter 7). For example, the following are all true:

name(buds, [98,117,100, 115]).

name('(', [40]).

name(yellow, [121,101,108,108,111,119]).

name(')', [41]).

Consequently, we can view the character stream processing problem as a two-step process:

1 Turning the initial stream of ASCII codes into an appropriate list of atoms. This step is called *tokenization* or *lexical analysis*. The atoms in the list are called *tokens*.
2 Processing the list of tokens to recognize the desired input. This step is called *parsing*.

This view is useful for processing almost any type of character-stream input, not just input intended to represent Prolog terms. It is useful (and standard) for processing character-stream input representing other computer languages (e.g., FORTRAN, LISP, Ada), as well as natural languages such as English.

The lexical analysis step is not usually very difficult (though one usually wants it to be accomplished fairly efficiently). For example, in Section 7.7.5, we developed a lexical analysis program for simple English sentences. The parsing problem is generally much more difficult, and there is a large and continually growing literature concerning it. We will examine a useful set of tools that Prolog provides for handling many parsing problems. As it is often useful for expert systems to provide input/output that at least has the feel of natural language, if not real natural language understanding, we will examine the problem of parsing elementary English.

Parsing begins with a sequence of tokens—we will assume the tokens are all Prolog atoms, though one might represent tokens by complex Prolog terms in some parsing problems. Consider the simple English sentence that has been tokenized to yield the following list of atoms:

[the, new, student, expertly, designed, an, efficient, program].

Intuitively, we can view this sentence as a set of stepping stones in a brook and the parsing problem as the task of stepping from one stone to the next, under certain rules, to get from one side of the brook to the other:

We will have successfully stepped from stone to stone across the brook if we can do it in such a way that by the end, we can recognize the entire sequence as a sentence:

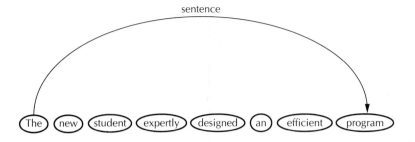

What will enable us to view the entire seqence as a sentence is a rule that allows us to view sentences as composed of parts, and to recognize that our particular sequence of tokens can be seen in the form(s) of those parts. Thus, one of the standard rules of grammar is that a sentence is composed of a noun phrase followed by a verb phrase:

> sentence → noun_phrase, verb_phrase.

Consequently, we can see our particular sequence of tokens as a sentence if we can see it as a noun phrase followed by a verb phrase:

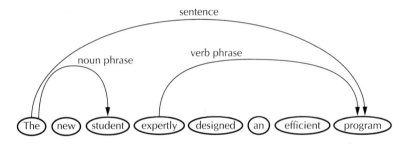

This reduces the problem of hopping from the first to the last stone to the shorter hops indicated. However, we must reduce these smaller hops even further, since we can in fact only step from one stone to the next at a time. This restriction reflects the computer's (program's) basic processing limitations: It must process one token at a time, in the order they are received. Thus, we must find some further grammar rules that will enable us to cross the gaps that remain. Three such are the following:

> noun_phrase → adjective, noun.
> noun_phrase → determiner, noun_phrase.
> verb_phrase → adverb, verb, noun_phrase.

Using these together with the grammatical roles of the individual words (stepping stones), we can complete the parsing process as shown in Figure 10–1.

Of course, our programs don't have stepping stones to work with, but they do have lists of atoms to process. In moving towards real programs that will accomplish the required parsing, it will be useful to slightly modify our intuitive pictures above. We drew the pictures with the arrows for phrases starting and terminating directly on the stepping stones. However, it turns out to be closer to the real intuition to make the arrows start and terminate between the stepping stones, as shown in Figure 10–2.

FIGURE 10–1

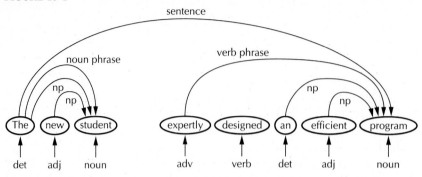

This suggests that the various grammatical components correspond to subsequences of the stepping-stone words or to sublists of the complete token list. The arrows in Figure 10–3 suggest that the various components (e.g., a particular noun phrase or a particular verb phrase, etc.) extend from one point in the total list to another point. For example, we might say that there is a verb phrase extending from the point before the atom *expertly* to the end of the list, or that there is a noun phrase extending from the point before the atom *new* to the point before the atom *expertly*. Suppose that we adopt the convention that a place in a list can be specified as the tail of the list from the point on. Thus, the "point before the atom *expertly*" would be denoted by the sublist

[expertly, designed, an, efficient, program].

Using this convention, this grammatical analysis can be expressed by the table in Figure 10–4.

One important point to note is that in each case in this table, the *Extends To* list is a tail of the *Extends From* list. Moreover, the sublist of atoms corresponding to the grammatical unit is in fact the difference between the *Extends From* list and the *Extends To* list.

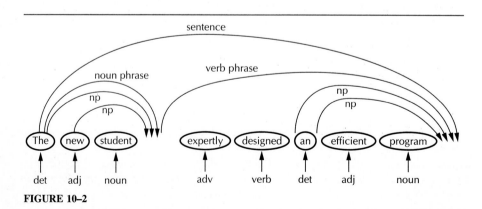

FIGURE 10–2

FIGURE 10–3

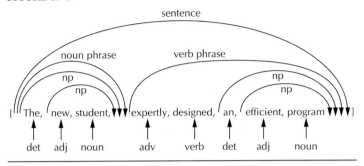

Our problem is to put these various observations together in such a way as to be able to utilize the grammar rules for recognizing whether or not the given list of atoms is an English sentence. Consider one of the rules for noun phrases:

noun_phrase → adjective, noun.

This is the rule used to recognize that the sublist [new, student] is a noun phrase. The statement that this rule applies in the table above could be phrased as

> If
>> List = [new,student,expertly,designed,an,efficient,program]
>
> and
>> Tail = [expertly,designed,an,efficient,program],

FIGURE 10–4

Grammatical unit	Extends from	Extends to	Difference
np	[the,new,student,expertly,designed,an,efficient,program] [expertly,designed,an,efficient,program]		[the,new,student]
np	[new,student,expertly,designed,an,efficient,program] [expertly,designed,an,efficient,program]		[new,student]
vp	[expertly,designed,an,efficient,program] []		[expertly,designed,an,efficient,program]
np	[an,efficient,program] []		[an,efficient,program]
np	[efficient,program] []		[efficient,program]

then there is a noun phrase extending from List to Tail because *new* is an adjective and *student* is a noun.

But notice that the applicability of this rule has no concern with the actual content of Tail, just that Tail is in fact a tail of List. Consequently, we could rephrase this rule as

> If
>   List = [new, student | Tail],
> then there is a noun phrase extending from List to Tail because *new* is an adjective and *student* is a noun.

Let's abstract from the particular words new and student, as follows:

> If
>   List = [Token1, Token2 | Tail]
> and if Token1 is an adjective and if Token2 is a noun, then there is a noun phrase extending from List to Tail.

For our next step, write

> np(List, Tail)

to mean *there is a noun phrase extending from List to Tail*; write adjective(T) to mean that token T is an adjective; and write noun(T) to mean that token T is a noun. We can then rephrase our rule as follows:

> np(List, Tail) holds if
>   List = [Token1, Token2 | Tail] and adjective(Token1) and noun(Token2).

Finally, if we utilize Prolog pattern matching, we can write this as

> np([Token1, Token2 | Tail], Tail) if
>   adjective(Token1) and noun(Token2).

However, we can recognize that this is in the form of a Prolog rule, namely:

> np([Token1, Token2 | Tail], Tail)
>   :-
>   adjective(Token1), noun(Token2).

Let's compare this with the original grammar rule:

noun_phrase	$\rightarrow$	adjective,	noun
np([T1, T2 | Tail], Tail)	:-	adjective(T1),	noun(T2)

Finally, let us compare the original reading of the grammar rule with the problem-solving reading of the corresponding Prolog rule:

> A noun phrase consists of an adjective followed by a noun.

> In order to show that there is a noun phrase extending from [T1, T2 | Tail] to Tail, it suffices to show that T1 is an adjective and that T2 is a noun.

Consider another grammar rule, the one describing sentences:

sentence → noun_phrase, verb_phrase.

From our example, it is tempting to say that a sentence must extend from the beginning of the token list to the end. But what if our stream of input consists of several sentences, and we must parse each of them? Thus, we must phrase the required rule for sentence in the same spirit as the one for noun phrase above:

> There is a sentence extending from List to Tail if
>> there is a noun phrase extending from List to InterTail and
>> there is a verb phrase extending from InterTail to Tail.

The intermediate point InterTail is a tail of List, while on the other hand, Tail is a tail of Intertail:

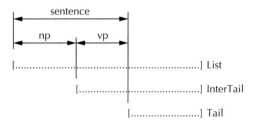

Thus, the corresponding Prolog version of the rule can be phrased

```
sentence(List, Tail)
    :-
    noun_phrase(List, InterTail),
    verb_phrase(InterTail, Tail).
```

We can apply similar analyses to the remaining grammar rules. The complete collection of grammar rules and their Prolog correspondents will now appear as follows:

```
sentence → noun_phrase, verb_phrase.

noun_phrase → adjective, noun.

noun_phrase → determiner, noun_phrase.

verb_phrase → adverb, verb, noun_phrase
```

```
sentence(List, Tail)
    :-
    noun_phrase(List, Intertail),
    verb_phrase(InterTail, Tail).

noun_phrase([Token1, Token2 | Tail], Tail)
    :-
    adjective(Token1), noun(Token2).
```

```
noun_phrase([Token1 | InterTail], Tail)
    :-
    determiner(Token1),
    noun_phrase(InterTail, Tail).

verb_phrase([Token1, Token2 | InterTail], Tail)
    :-
    adverb(Token1),
    verb(Token2),
    noun_phrase(InterTail, Tail).
```

To enable us to run these rules, we simply need definitions for the basic categorization predicates such as adjective/1. A small subset of such definitions adequate for our example sentence would be the following:

```
determiner(the).
determiner(an).
noun(student).
noun(program).
adjective(new).
adjective(efficient).
adverb(expertly).
verb(designed).
```

We can run this simple parser by submitting the following goal:

```
?- sentence([the,new,student,expertly,designed,
                        an,efficient,program],Left).
Left = []
yes.
```

It is instructive to run the goal with some additional (irrelevant) words at the end of the input list:

```
?- sentence([the,new,student,expertly,designed,
                        an,efficient,program,some,stuff],Left).
Left = [some,stuff]
yes.
```

10.2 PARAMETER-FREE DEFINITE CLAUSE GRAMMARS

The high degree of structural similarity between the various grammar rules and their Prolog correspondents suggests that we might be able to systematically transform the grammar rules into the corresponding Prolog rules. On the surface, it looks like a simple matter of converting "→" and adding some arguments to expressions such as noun_phrase. However, note that in some cases we added two arguments (e.g., occurrences of noun_phrase), while in others we added only one (e.g., occurrences of adjective). So it would seem that the transformation is not so simple. Or, it could be that while our analysis in the last section is very appealing, it could be revised to produce slightly different versions of the rules, which make this conversion easier.

In line with the latter possibility, suppose we attempt to arrange that the conversion would add two arguments to each element in the grammar rule. Thus, the basic grammatical category predicates such as adjective, adverb, etc., would have to be construed in such as way as to make this possible. Suppose we treat these category primitives in the same spirit as the *phrase* predicates such as noun_phrase. That is, let us think of an adjective as being a short primitive adjective phrase. In particular then, such an adjective phrase would have to extend from one point in a list to another. We could make a new definition of adjective:

```
adjective([new | Tail], Tail).
adjective([efficient | Tail], Tail).
```

Similarly,

```
determiner([the | Tail], Tail).
determiner([an | Tail], Tail).
noun([student | Tail], Tail).
noun([program | Tail], Tail).
adverb([expertly | Tail], Tail).
verb([designed | Tail], Tail).
```

Then we would revise the other rules:

```
sentence(List, Tail)
    :-
    noun_phrase(List, InterTail),
    verb_phrase(InterTail, Tail).


noun_phrase(List, Tail)
    :-
    adjective(List, InterTail),
    noun(InterTail, Tail).


noun_phrase(List, Tail)
    :-
    determiner(List, InterTail),
    noun_phrase(InterTail, Tail).


verb_phrase(List, Tail)
    :-
    adverb(List, InterTail1),
    verb(InterTail1, InterTail2),
    noun_phrase(InterTail2, Tail).
```

This version runs with the same results as the earlier version. And now we observe a very high degree of uniformity in the correspondence between original grammar rules and their Prolog versions. Not only does every element of an original grammar rule receive two arguments, but we can observe the following:

- The first argument of the head of the Prolog rule is the first argument of the first goal in the body;
- The second argument of the head of the Prolog rule is the second argument of the last goal in the body;
- The second argument of every goal in the body (except the last goal) is the first argument of the next goal in the body; moreover, these are the only two occurrences of this variable in the entire rule.

This all suggests that we should be able to define a two-place predicate that will convert grammar rules to the corresponding Prolog rules:

expand_grammar_rule(GrammarRule, PrologRule).

Since both $\rightarrow$ and :- are normally defined to be binary infix operators in Prolog, we can make the following top-level definition:

expand_grammar_rule((Left $\rightarrow$ Right) , (Head :- Body))
    :-
    expand_single(Left, Head, First, Second),
    expand_sequence(Right, Body, First, Second).

The definition of expand_single/4 is simple: It assumes that its first argument is an atom and that its third and fourth arguments are variables (they could be terms), and it unifies its second argument (which should be a variable used for output) with the term whose functor is the first argument and whose two arguments are the original third and fourth arguments:

expand_single(Atom, Result, Arg1, Arg2)
    :-
    Result =.. [Atom, Arg1, Arg2].

There are two primary cases in the definition of expand_sequence/4, depending on whether or not its first argument is a compound of the form (A , B). Thus, we can begin building this definition:

expand_sequence((Atom, Rest), ??, InVar, OutVar)
    :-!,
    ???.

expand_sequence(Atom, ??, InVar, OutVar)
    :-
    ???.

Roughly, what expand_sequence must do is (recursively) work its way through the sequence making up the right side of the grammar rule, applying expand_single to each element and making sure that it patches together the (new) second arguments of each call with the (new) first argument of the next call. At the end of the list, it simply applies expand_single to the last element of the right side of the grammar rule. At each step, it receives an input variable that was the output variable of the preceding step. It should use this input variable as the first argument of the current call to be created. It should also create a new variable to use as the second argument and return this new variable (which is the second argument of the current call) when it finishes the current call—this will make the variable available as the input variable for the next call. Figure 10–5 suggests the process.

Let's try developing the definition of expand_sequence/4:

```
expand_sequence( ( Atom, Rest), (Exp_Atom, Exp_Rest), InVar, OutVar)
    :-!,
    expand_single(Atom, Exp_Atom, InVar, InterVar),
    expand_sequence( Rest, Exp_Rest, InterVar, OutVar).


expand_sequence( Atom, Exp_Atom, InVar, OutVar)
    :-
    expand_single(Atom, Exp_Atom, InVar, OutVar).
```

We can test our expansion program with the following simple goal:

```
run(PrologRule)
    :-
    expand_grammar_rule( (verb_phrase → adverb, verb, noun_phrase), Prolog-
Rule).
```

```
?run(R).
R = (verb_phrase(_17,_15):-adverb(_17,_27),verb(_27,_39),
noun_phrase(_39,_15))
yes.
```

10.3 BUILDING AN INTERNAL REPRESENTATION

We have shown how to recognize sentences in the previous sections, which is all very good. However, for these techniques to really be useful, we must extend them so that we not only recognize sentences, but also obtain some sort of internal representation of the sentence to use for various purposes, such as question-answering, recording information, etc. One of the standard items to obtain is a representation of the parse tree for the sentence. Figure 10–6 illustrates the parse tree for our sample sentence according to the grammar rules we have been using. The Prolog term shown in Figure 10–7 is a reasonable representation of this parse tree.

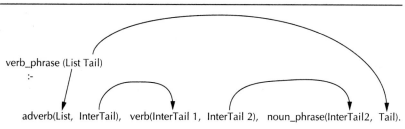

verb_phrase (List Tail)
    :-
adverb(List, InterTail), verb(InterTail 1, InterTail 2), noun_phrase(InterTail2, Tail).

FIGURE 10–5

FIGURE 10–6

A parse tree for a sentence.

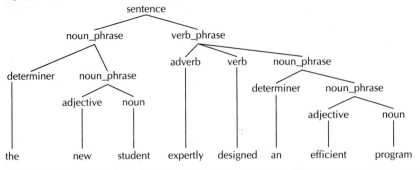

The problem of accumulating such a term as we execute the Prolog forms of the grammar rules is similar to the problem of accumulating proofs, which we considered in Section 8.4. As in that case, the basic technique is to use an extra argument to accumulate the tree, just as we previously used an extra argument to accumulate a proof. In fact, it is natural to think of the parse tree as a proof of the parse of the sentence. With this in mind, we can revise the grammar rules from the previous section as follows:

sentence(sent(NP, VP), List, Tail)
    :-
    noun_phrase(NP, List, InterTail),
    verb_phrase(VP, InterTail, Tail).

noun_phrase(np(ADJ, NOUN), List, Tail)
    :-
    adjective(ADJ, List, InterTail),
    noun(NOUN, InterTail, Tail).

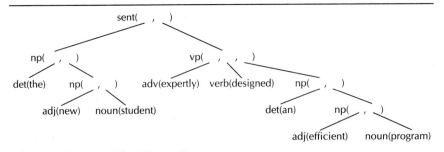

sent(np(det(the),np(adj(new),noun(student))),
            vp(adv(expertly),verb(designed),np(det(an),np(adj(efficient),noun(program)))))

FIGURE 10–7

A prolog term representing a parse tree.

CHAPTER 10: PARSING AND DEFINITE CLAUSE GRAMMARS **277**

```
noun_phrase( np(DET, NP), List, Tail)
    :-
    determiner(DET, List, InterTail),
    noun_phrase(NP, InterTail, Tail).

verb_phrase( vp(ADV, VERB, NP), List, Tail)
    :-
    adverb(ADV, List, InterTail1),
    verb(VERB, InterTail1, InterTail2),
    noun_phrase(NP, InterTail2, Tail).

determiner( det(the), [the | Tail], Tail).
determiner( det(an), [an | Tail], Tail ).
adjective( adj(new), [new | Tail], Tail ).
adjective( adj(efficient), [efficient | Tail], Tail ).
noun( noun(student), [student | Tail], Tail ).
noun( noun(program) , [program | Tail], Tail).
adverb( adv(expertly), [expertly | Tail], Tail ).
verb( verb(designed), [designed | Tail], Tail ).
```

We can revise one of our previous test predicates as follows:

```
run2(Tree, Left)
    :-
    sentence( Tree, [the,new,student,expertly,designed,an,efficient, program,
                some,stuff,here],Left).
```

Here is the result of running a call on run2:

```
?-run2(T, L).
T =sent(np(det(the),np(adj(new),noun(student))),
vp(adv(expertly),verb(designed),np(det(an),
np(adj(efficient),noun(program))))))
L = [some,stuff,here]
yes.
```

Thus, we can extract information from the parsing process just as we extracted information from the proof process. Consider the following extended versions of the original grammar rules:

```
sentence(sent(NP, VP)) → noun_phrase(NP), verb_phrase(VP).
noun_phrase(np(ADJ, NOUN)) → adjective(ADJ), noun(NOUN).
noun_phrase(np(DET, NP)) → determiner(DET), noun_phrase(NP).
verb_phrase(VP) → adverb(ADV), verb(VERB), noun_phrase(NP).
```

Comparing these versions with the *extra-argument* versions of the Prolog rules, it is clear that the arguments in these grammar rules correspond one-for-one with the extra arguments in the Prolog rules. Consequently, it ought to be possible to extend our earlier program expand_grammar_rule to convert such extended rules to their Prolog correspondents. Let's recall the assumptions made by the earlier expansion program:

- Every element of an original grammar rule receives two arguments;
- The first argument of the head of the Prolog rule is the first argument of the first goal in the body;
- The second argument of the head of the Prolog rule is the second argument of the last goal in the body;
- The second argument of every goal in the body (except the last goal) is the first argument of the next goal in the body; moreover, these are the only two occurrences of this variable in the entire rule.

A little reflection shows that these assumptions are still correct, provided that we interpret the phrase "receives two arguments" generously as "receives two *additional* arguments." In particular then, we can no longer assume that all the elements of the original grammar rules are atoms. Some may be compound terms. Moreover, we shouldn't assume that all of the compound terms will have just one argument: We had better attempt to assume that each element of a grammar rule is a compound term with an unspecified number of arguments. Examination of the program reveals that only one subsidiary predicate actually deals directly with the terms occurring in the grammar rule: expand_single/4. Instead of its previous simple definition, it must now break apart the incoming term (using =..), append the two added arguments to the list of the incoming term's arguments, and build the resulting term using =.. . Here is the revised program:

```
expand_grammar_rule( (Left → Right) , ( Head :- Body ) )
    :-
    expand_single(Left, Head, First, Second),
    expand_sequence(Right, Body, First, Second).

expand_single( Term, Result, Arg1, Arg2)
    :-
    Term =.. [Functor | Term_Args],
    append(Term_Args, [Arg1, Arg2], New_Term_Args),
    Result =.. [Functor | New_Term_Args].

expand_sequence( ( Term, Rest), (Exp_Term, Exp_Rest), InVar, OutVar)
    :-!,
    expand_single(Term, Exp_Term, InVar, InterVar),
    expand_sequence( Rest, Exp_Rest, InterVar, OutVar).

expand_sequence( Term, Exp_Term, InVar, OutVar)
    :-
    expand_single(Term, Exp_Term, InVar, OutVar).

append([], Right, Right).
append([Head | Tail], Right, [Head | Result_Tail])
    :-
    append(Tail, Right, Result_Tail).
```

It is easy to revise our previous test predicate:

    run(PrologRule)
        :-
        expand_grammar_rule(
        (verb_phrase(vp(A,V,NP)) →
            adverb(A), verb(V), noun_phrase(NP)), PrologRule).

Finally, here is the resulting interaction:

```
?- run(R).
R = (verb_phrase(vp(_11,_6,_4),_33,_31):-
adverb(_11,_33,_50),verb(_6,_50,_69),
noun_phrase(_4,_69,_31))
yes.
```

10.4 USING DCGs WITH EXPERT SYSTEMS

Definite Clause Grammars (DCGs) have been used extensively for the development of complex natural language understanding programs. But they are also easy to use for less ambitious tasks, such as providing simple program input that has a "natural" feel, even though the program is not really attempting to understand the language in the sense of more complex approaches. As an example, consider the hickory tree identification program. The user must supply descriptions of observed traits to the program, such as bud_color(yellow). The program would have a more friendly feel to it if the user could type either yellow bud_color. or bud_color yellow. to the program instead of the Prolog term. Without significantly revising the identification program, we must interpose a parser between the program and the user. The parser will accept the user's input, parse it, and pass the accumulated internal representation (which should be 'bud_color(yellow)') on to the identification program.

Here is the collection of all the terms representing traits that the program expects to receive, together with the atom *done*.

    bud_color(yellow)
    bud_color(brownish)
    bud_scales(valvate)
    bud_scales(imbricate)
    terminal_bud_size(short)
    terminal_bud_size(large)
    outer_scales(persistent)
    twig_color(orange_brown)
    twig_color(reddish_brown)
    done

In each case (except, of course, for *done*), we would like to be able to accept input consisting of the functor followed by the argument, or the argument followed by the functor, with no parentheses present. Thus, a simple pair of rules to recognize these forms would be

    descriptor → trait, value.
    descriptor → value, trait.

We can obtain an internal form as follows:

    descriptor(desc(T, V)) → trait(T), value(V).
    descriptor(desc(T, V)) → value(V), trait(T).

We also need a rule to recognize the atom *done*:

    descriptor(done) → finished.

The expansion of these grammar rules will lead to the following Prolog rules:

    descriptor(desc(T, V), List, Tail)
        :-
        trait(T, List, InterTail), value(V, InterTail, Tail).

    descriptor(desc(T, V), List, Tail)
        :-
        value(V, List, InterTail),
        trait(T, InterTail, Tail).

    descriptor(done, List, Tail)
        :-
        finished(List, Tail).

Thus, we need only supply definitions for the category predicates trait/3, value/3, and finished/2. Here they are:

    trait(bud_color, [bud_color | Tail], Tail).
    trait(bud_scales, [bud_scales | Tail], Tail).
    trait(terminal_bud_size, [terminal_bud_size | Tail], Tail).
    trait(outer_scales, [outer_scales | Tail], Tail).
    trait(twig_color, [outer_scales | Tail], Tail).

    value(yellow, [yellow | Tail], Tail).
    value(brownish, [brownish | Tail], Tail).
    value(valvate, [valvate | Tail], Tail).
    value(imbricate, [imbricate | Tail], Tail).
    value(short, [short | Tail], Tail).
    value(persistent, [persistent | Tail], Tail).
    value(orange_brown, [orange_brown | Tail], Tail).
    value(reddish_brown, [reddish_brown | Tail], Tail).

    finished([done | Tail], Tail).

We can carry out initial testing with the test predicates

    run1(D) :-
        descriptor(D, [bud_color,yellow],_).

```
run2(D) :-
     descriptor(D, [yellow, bud_color],_).
```

Using these, we obtain the following interactions:

```
?- run1(D).
D = desc(bud_color,yellow)
yes.
?- run2(D).
D = desc(bud_color,yellow)
yes.
```

To get the desired front-end behavior, we must couple these parsing predicates with the lexical analysis predicates for English, which we developed in Section 7.7.5. However, we need to make one small change in that program. Namely, we must slightly extend the allowable characters for words since we are using the underbar character (_) in the words of our current input. Recall the original definition handling acceptable characters:

```
acceptable_in_word(Char)
     :-
     (~ a =< Char, Char =<~ z) ;
     (~ A =< Char, Char =<~ Z).
```

We need only add one more disjunction to this clause:

```
acceptable_in_word(Char)
     :-
     (~ a =< Char, Char =<~ z) ;
     (~ A =< Char, Char =<~ Z);
     Char =~ _.
```

We can now construct a test predicate coupling this lexical analysis with the desired parsing:

```
run3(D) :-
     write('Description:'),
     read_sentence(WordList),
     descriptor(D, WordList,_).
```

Using this, we obtain the following interactions:

```
?- run3(D).
Description: bud_color yellow.
D = desc(bud_color,yellow)
yes.
?- run3(D).
Description: yellow bud_color.
D = desc(bud_color,yellow)
yes.
?- run3(D).
Description: done.
D = done
```

```
yes.
?- run3(D).
Description: large terminal_bud_size.
D = desc(terminal_bud_size,large)
yes.
```

Finally, we turn to coupling all this with our the Hickory tree identification program. The predicate concerned with getting user input was

```
obtain_description
    :-
    write('Observation: '),
    read(Observer),
    dispatch(Observer).
```

Essentially, we simply have to replace the call on read/1 by the combination of read_sentence/1 and descriptor/3. However, we still have one small problem, namely that the internal form produced by descriptor/3 in its first argument is not the kind of term that dispatch/1 expects (except for the atom *done*). For example, descriptor/3 will produce the term

```
desc(bud_color, yellow),
```

where dispatch/1 (and the rest of the identification program) expects the term

```
bud_color(yellow).
```

However, it is easy to create the latter term from the former using the builtin univ predicate, as follows:

```
fixup(desc(Trait, Value), Fixed)
    :-
    Fixed = .. [ Trait, Value ].


fixup(Anything, Anything).
```

We can now revise obtain_description/0:

```
obtain_description
    :-
    write('Observation: '),
    read_sentence(WordList),
    descriptor(D, WordList,_),
    fixup(D, Observer),
    dispatch(Observer).
```

Revising obtain_description/0 as indicated, and consulting read_sent.pro along with hick_id.pro, we obtain the following interaction:

```
?- identify.
Observation:  bud_color yellow.
Observation:  done.
Is it true that bud_scales(valvate)? yes.
```

```
The item appears to be a bitternut_hickory
The traits were: [bud_scales(valvate),bud_color(yellow)]
yes.
?- identify.
Observation:  persistent outer_scales.
Observation:  terminal_bud_size short.
Observation:  done.
Is it true that bud_scales(imbricate)? yes.
The item appears to be a pignut_hickory
The traits were:
[bud_scales(imbricate),terminal_bud_size(short)]
yes.
```

EXERCISES

10-1 In *Mathematical Logic*,[1] A. Church defines the notion of a *well-formed formula (wff)* of the propositional calculus as follows:
- Any propositional variable standing alone is a wff;
- If **A** and **B** are wffs, then so is (**A** ⊃ **B**);
- If **A** is a wff, then so is (∼ **A**).

Propositional variables were p, q, r, p_1, q_1, r_1, p_2, ..., etc.

As a concession to the paucity of most computer keyboards, let us revise this specification as follows:

A propositional variable is any identifier beginning with p, q, or r, and followed by zero or more digits (e.g., p, q23, r042).
- Any propositional variable standing alone is a wff;
- If **A** and **B** are wffs, then so is (**A** imp **B**);
- If **A** is a wff, then so is (neg **A**) .

    a Develop a lexical reader suitable for wffs;
    b Develop a DCG for wffs that accepts input from the lexical reader of **a** and that produces a suitable internal form for the formulas.

10-2 Continue Exercise 10-1 by combining the wff reader with a program that checks whether or not the formula read is a tautology, a contradiction, or neither, and reports the result to the user.

10-3 The phrase-structure rules for English shown in Figure 10–8 are from *Syntax*, by P. W. Culicover, (Academic Press, 1976, p.59). Items in parentheses are optional. Items in

---

[1] A. Church, *Mathematical Logic*, v. I, Princeton University Press, Princeton, NJ, 1956, p.119.

PSR1:	S	→	NP AUX VP
PSR2:	AUX	→	TENSE (M) (have en)(be ing)
PSR3:	VP	→	V (NP)
PSR4:	NP	→	{ ART (ADJ) N / PN }

M = *modal*	ART = *article*	N = *noun*
V = *verb*	ADJ = *adjective*	PN = *proper noun*

FIGURE 10–8

braces indicate disunctive rules, i.e., two rules, etc. The *marker* TENSE takes **present**, **future**, **past**, etc., as values. It does not actually occur in surface utterances, but combines at the deep level to produce the surface value. For example, John + **past** + write become John wrote, etc. Explore the extent to which these rules can be encoded as DCGs.

10-4 The phrase-structure rules for English shown in Figure 10–9 are from *Modern English Linguistics*, by J. P. Broderick, (Thomas Crowell Co., NY, 1975, pp.243–244). The

---

FIGURE 10–9

$$S \rightarrow (\left\{ \begin{array}{c} Q \\ IMP \end{array} \right\}) + (not) + NP + AUX + VP + (ADVM) + (AADVP) + (ADVT) + (ADVR) + \ldots$$

$$VP \rightarrow \left\{ \begin{array}{c} V + (NP) + (PP) + (PP) \\ be + (\{ \begin{array}{c} ADJP \\ NP \end{array} \}) \end{array} \right\}$$

$$\left\{ \begin{array}{c} ADVM \\ ADVP \\ ADVT \\ ADVR \end{array} \right\} \rightarrow \left\{ \begin{array}{c} PP \\ ADV \end{array} \right\}$$

ADJP $\rightarrow$ ADJ + (PP)

PP $\rightarrow$ P + NP

$$NP \rightarrow \left\{ \begin{array}{c} (DET) + N \\ NP + S \\ it + S \end{array} \right\}$$

AUX $\rightarrow$ TNS + (M) + (PERF) + (PROG)

$$TNS \rightarrow \left\{ \begin{array}{c} \text{-prs} \\ \text{-pst} \end{array} \right\}$$

M $\rightarrow$ {can, may, will, shall, should, must, ...}

PERF $\rightarrow$ have-en

PROG $\rightarrow$ be-ing

V $\rightarrow$ {build, work, write, ...}

$$ADV \rightarrow \left\{ \begin{array}{l} \text{enthusiastically, there, then, deliberately, ...} \\ \text{how, where, when, why, ...} \end{array} \right\}$$

ADJ $\rightarrow$ {dilligent, fond, happy, ...}

P $\rightarrow$ {with, at, in, for, ...}

DET $\rightarrow$ {a, the, this, that, ...}

$$N \rightarrow \left\{ \begin{array}{l} \text{woman, leader, car, William, play, ...} \\ \text{who(m), what, ...} \end{array} \right\}$$

TNS marker behaves similarly to the TENSE marker in Exercise 10-3. Devise a DCG that captures this set of rules as closely as possible.

10-5 In his book, *Symbolic Logic*,[2] Lewis Carroll treats many topics, among them syllogisms. In Book VIII, Chapter I, Section 9, he presents a number of collections of premises from which one is to draw a conclusion. Here are some of them, with the conclusion to be drawn from each appearing in italic:

1

(1) Babies are illogical;
(2) Nobody is despised who can manage a crocodile;
(3) Illogical persons are despised.
Babies cannot manage crocodiles.

5

(1) No ducks waltz;
(2) No officers ever decline to waltz;
(3) All my poultry are ducks.
My poultry are not officers.

6

(1) Every one who is sane can do Logic;
(2) No lunatics are fit to serve on a jury;
(3) None of *your* sons can do Logic.
None of your sons are fit to serve on a jury.

34

(1) The only books in this library that I do *not* recommend for reading are unhealthy in tone;
(2) The bound books are all well-written;
(3) All the romances are healthy in tone;
(4) I do not recommend you to read any of the unbound books.
All the romances in this library are well-written.

40

(1) No kitten that loves fish is unteachable;
(2) No kitten without a tail will play with a gorilla;
(3) Kittens with whiskers always love fish;
(4) No teachable kitten has green eyes;
(5) No kittens have tails unless they have whiskers.
No kitten with green eyes will play with a gorilla.

a Develop a DCG that will accept each of the assertions of syllogisms of these sorts (utilize the result of Exercise 7-13); the DCG rules should yield a reasonable internal form for the assertions.

b Explore developing a program that will test whether or not a given conclusion syllogistically follows from a collection of premises. (*Hint*: Develop a program that first transforms the internal forms generated by the DCG into a useful standard format; Carroll has much useful material on this in his book.)

c Explore developing a program that will syllogistically draw the sorts of conclusions presented by Carroll.

---

[2] *Lewis Carroll's Symbolic Logic*, Clarkson N. Potter, Inc., NY, 1977.

10-6 In his landmark paper,"The Concept of Truth in Formalized Languages," [3] Alfred Tarski
utilized a formal language specified in a manner similar to the following:

1 The logical constants are **N**, **A**, **P**, and **I**;

2 The variables are any identifier beginning with "x" and followed by one or more vertical
bars "|", e.g., x|, x||||, . . . , etc.

3 If **U** and **V** are variables, then **IUV** is an expression;

4 If **E** is an expression, the **NE** is an expression;

5 If **E** and **F** are expressions, then **AEF** is an expression;

6 If **E** is an expression and **V** is a variable, then **PVE** is an expression.

a Create a lexical reader suitable for reading in expressions.

b Create a DCG that accepts expressions and creates an internal form from them.

---

[3] Reprinted in Alfred Tarski, *Logic, Semantics, Metamathematics*, Clarendon Press, Oxford, 1956,
pp.170–171.

CHAPTER 11

COMPILING KNOWLEDGE

The ruled-based shells we developed in Chapter 9 are interpreters: They perform their action by interpreting each significant linguistic item from the source at run time. The interpreters are written in Prolog to interpret another language (which we defined and whose expressions only happen to be acceptable Prolog terms—we could relax this by writing an appropriate parser as we did for fragments of English in Chapter 10.) This provides considerable flexibility and compactness. However, for large or complex programs, there can be a noticeable cost in slower performance. We could improve that performance if we could, once and for all, translate the source for the rule-based expert system into a set of Prolog clauses that provided exactly the same performance as occurs when the rule-based expert system source is interpreted by a particular interpreter, such as those developed in Chapter 9. The process is one of compilation or source-to-source transformation—whatever the name, it amounts to a translation of code in one language to code in another. In this case, the translation is from the rule-based language to ordinary Prolog. In this chapter, we will develop a translation technique corresponding to the *solve* interpreter of Section 9.3.

First, recall the domain knowledge for the simple medical expert system shown in Figure 11–1. This domain knowledge was accompanied by some metalevel knowledge, as shown in Figure 11–2.

These two collections of clauses constitute the input to our knowledge compiler. The output will be a third collection of clauses, which combines this information with the knowledge embedded in the solve/3 or solve/4 shell developed in Chapter 9. Our first step is to develop a strategy for carrying out this compilation. To this end, recall that in Section 8.1 we developed the first object-level expert system for giving lay medical advice. In Section 8.4, we extended this simple system to provide explanations of its advice. The technique we used was to add extra arguments to the domain predicates to accumulate the proofs during computation. In essence, when we constructed the shell(s) solve/3 and solve/4 in Chapter 9, we moved these extra arguments out of the domain predicates into the solve predicate and its support predicates. Our strategy for knowledge compilation will be to reverse this process. That is, our knowledge compiler

FIGURE 11–1
Domain knowledge for lay medicine advisor.

relieves(aspirin,headache)	:: 0.96.
relieves(aspirin,moderate_pain)	:: 0.8.
relieves(aspirin,moderate_arthritis)	:: 0.87.
relieves(aspirin_codeine_combination,severe_pain)	:: 0.45.
relieves(cough_cure_xm,cough)	:: 0.85.
relieves(pain_gone,severe_pain)	:: 0.88.
relieves(ko_diarrhea,diarrhea)	:: 0.75.
relieves(de_congest,cough)	:: 0.85.
relieves(de_congest,nasal_congestion)	:: 0.85.
relieves(penicillin,pneumonia)	:: 0.9.
relieves(bis_cure,diarrhea)	:: 0.7.
relieves(bis_cure,nausea)	:: 0.93.
relieves(noasprinol,headache)	:: 0.93.
relieves(noasprinol,moderate_pain)	:: 0.84.
relieves(triple_tuss,nasal_congestion)	:: 0.85.
aggravates(aspirin,asthma)	:: 0.89.
aggravates(aspirin,peptice_ulcer)	:: 0.92.
aggravates(ko_diarrhea,fever)	:: 0.75.
aggravates(de_congest,high_blood_pressure)	:: 0.83.
aggravates(de_congest,heart_disease)	:: 0.81.
aggravates(de_congest,diabetes)	:: 0.74.
aggravates(de_congest,glaucoma)	:: 0.91.
aggravates(penicillin,asthma)	:: 0.82.
aggravates(bis_cure,diabetes)	:: 0.88.
aggravates(bis_cure,gout)	:: 0.77.
aggravates(bis_cure,fever)	:: 0.98.

```
aggravates(Drug,Condition)
    :-
    compound(Drug,Components),
    member(OtherDrug,Components),
    aggravates(OtherDrug,Condition)                    ::1.0.

compound(aspirin_codeine_combination,[codeine,aspirin]) ::1.0.

should_take(Person,Drug)
    :-
    complains_of(Person,Symptom),
    suppresses(Drug,Symptom),
    not(unsuitable_for(Person,Drug))                   :: 0.9.

suppresses(Drug,Symptom)
    :-
    relieves(Drug,Symptom)                             :: 0.85.

unsuitable_for(Person,Drug)
    :-
    aggravates(Drug,Condition),
    sufffers_from(Person,Condition)                    :: 0.7.
```

FIGURE 11–2
Metalevel knowledge for lay medicine advisor.

```
ask_info(complains_of(Person,Symptom),
                    ['What symptom are you bothered by?'],Symptom).
ask_confirm(complains_of(Person,Symptom),
                    ['Are you bothered by',Symptom,'(yes/no)?'],Symptom).
ask_acceptability(complains_of(Person,Answer),Answer,relieves(_,Answer)).
ask_info(suffers_from(Person,Condition),
                    ['What condition do you suffer from?'],condition).
ask_confirm(suffers_from(Person,Condition),
                    ['Do you suffer from',Condition,'(yes/no)?'],Condition).
ask_acceptability(suffers_from(Person,Answer),Answer,aggravates(_,Answer)).
requires_files([-confcalc]).
main(should_take(input(Person,['Name = ']),output(Drug,
                    [Person,'should take',Drug]))).
knowledge_preds([k(relieves/2),k(aggravates/2),k(compound/2),k(should_take/2),
                    k(suppresses/2),k(unsuitable_for/2)]).
```

will generate the target set of clauses by moving the necessary extra arguments back into the domain clauses and will modify the calls in the bodies of the domain clauses to support this.

One question should immediately arise: Why doesn't this violate the doctrine, advanced in Chapter 9 as the rational for shells, that the domain knowledge should be left pure? The answer is that by constructing a tool that transforms the domain knowledge, we can have our cake and eat it too! The original source domain knowledge (and metaknowledge) is left unchanged. The tool uses this knowledge to generate a separate version of the domain knowledge, which is encumbered with additional computational information. This generated version executes more quickly than the pure version can under the shell, yet provides all the additional facilities the shell provides (e.g., proofs for explanations, confidence factors, etc.) If use and testing suggest modifications that should be made, either or both of the domain or metaknowledge sources are modified, and the knowledge compiler is run again to produce a new "encumbered" version of the knowledge, as suggested in Figure 11–3. Thus, the domain and metaknowledge are kept pure and separate but are used to generate a more efficient encumbered version, just as, for example, a C compiler transforms C code into assembly code, which is then further processed by an assembler.

Recall the definition of solve/4 from Section 9.2:

```
solve(true, 1.0,InPrTail, InPrfTail):-!.

solve((A,B),Conf, InPrfTail,OutPrfTail)
        :-
        solve(A,C1,InPrfTail, InterPrfTail),
        solve(B,C2,InterPrfTail,OutPrfTail),
        conj_conf(C1,C2,Conf).          % confidence calculation
```

FIGURE 11–3
Overall action of the knowledge compiler.

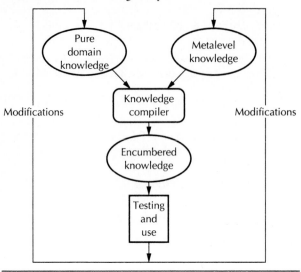

solve(A,C,[(A if B) | InterPrfTail],OutPrfTail)
    :-
    clause(A,B,Ptr),
    conf(Ptr,C1),
    solve(B,C2,InterPrfTail,OutPrfTail),
    rule_conf(C1,C2,C).

% confidence calculation

solve(A,C,[asked(A) | OutPrfTail],OutPrfTail)
    :-
    ask_about(A),
    obtain_conf(C).

% determine confidence

solve(not(A),C,[negate(A,SubProof) | OutPrfTail],OutPrfTail)
    :-
    solve(A,C1,SubProof,[]),
    !,
    C1<0.3,
    neg_conf(C1,C).

% confidence calculation

solve(not(A),1.0, [not(A)-exhaustion | OutPrfTail],OutPrfTail):-!.

solve(A,1.0,[A-builtin | OutPrfTail],OutPrfTail)
    :-
    clause(A,B,Ptr),
    not(conf(Ptr,C1)),
    A.

The arguments of solve/4 take the following roles:

1st argument	the current goal being interpreted
2nd argument	returns the confidence in the current goal solution
3rd and 4th arguments	used to accumulate the proof

Thus, it would appear likely that we will have to add extra arguments corresponding to arguments 2–4 to the domain predicates during the compilation process. In addition, we will certainly need to add extra calls into the bodies to perform confidence calculations, as well as perhaps other "housekeeping" work.

Let us assume that the domain knowledge is stored in one file, called *medicknw.k*, and the metalevel knowledge is in another file, called *medicknw.mta*. Moreover, suppose that we want the compiled knowledge to be stored in the file *xmedic.pro*. This suggests that the topmost predicate of knowledge compiler or expander will be organized as follows:

```
xpand_file(KnowFile,MetaFile,TargetFile)
    :-
    initialization and other special tasks, including opening input and output files,
    loopAndExpand(arguments),

    any final tasks & cleanup,
    told,
    seen.


xpand_file(_,_,_)
    :-
    told,seen.
```

The overall structure of loopAndExpand/? will be

```
loopAndExpand(arguments)
    :-
    read(Item),
    dispatchXpand(Item, arguments).


dispatchXpand(end_of_file, arguments)          % No more clauses
    :-!.


dispatchXpand((X :: C), arguments)             % Clause with
    :-!,                                       % confidence factor
    xpand_know( (X :: C), XRule, arguments),
    write_out (XRule),nl,
    loopAndExpand(arguments).


dispatchXpand(X, arguments)                    % Clause without
    :-                                         % confidence factor
    write_out (X),nl,
    loopAndExpand(arguments).
```

The schematic predicate *write_out* (X) is used to write X to the target file. We could simply use write/1. However, there are two reasons to use a predicate that at least partially *pretty prints* X:

1 You may want to examine the generated code: Using plain write/1 makes the output very hard to read.
2 Some operating systems and/or editors get unhappy if a file contains lines that are too long: pretty printing avoids this.

One version of such a pretty printing predicate in ALS Prolog is write_out/1 contained in the builtins file. It is invoked by the call

builtins:write_out(X).

We will use this in the program we develop.

Note that our configuration of dispatchXpand/? makes the assumption that all domain knowledge will carry an explicit confidence factor. Any clauses not carrying a confidence factor will be regarded as supporting Prolog clauses and simply copied over into the target file.

As the structure of dispatchXpand/? indicates, the principal predicate of the knowledge compiler proper will be

xpand_know((X :: C), XRule, *arguments*),

which takes a qualified clause (i.e., a clause with a confidence factor) as its input and produces the expanded version of that clause as its second argument. As the schema indicates, we will discover that additional arguments for xpand_know will be necessary. Since the original solve/4 has separate clauses for facts and for rules proper (i.e., possessing bodies), we would expect the same for xpand_know:

```
xpand_know( ( (Head :- Body) :: RuleConfid ), (XHead :- XBody), arguments )
    :-!,
    xpand_head(Head, XHead, Confid, ProofIn, ProofOut),
    ProofIn = [(Head if Body) | InterPrfTail],
    xpand_body(Body, XBody, InterPrfTail, ProofOut, RuleConfid, ConfidAccum,
        ConfidAccum, Confid, arguments ).
```

```
xpand_know((Fact :: Confid), XFact, arguments )
    :-
    Fact = ..[Pred | FactArgs],
    append(FactArgs, [Confid, [Fact | PrfTail], PrfTail ], XFactArgs),
    XFact = ..[Pred | XFactArgs].
```

Let's examine the second clause for xpand_know. This handles the case of a qualified fact. As we indicated earlier, we are assuming that the expansion of the domain knowledge clauses will add three additional arguments corresponding to the second, third, and fourth arguments of solve/4. This is just what this clause for xpand_know does. For example, consider the following domain fact:

relieves(aspirin, headache)   :: 0.96.

The result of running xpand_know on this would produce the following ordinary Prolog fact as the expansion:

relieves(aspirin, headache, 0.96, [relieves(aspirin, headache) | PrfTail], PrfTail).

Turning to the first clause for xpand_know, the definition of xpand_head is similar to what xpand_know did for facts:

xpand_head(Head, XHead, Confid, ProofIn, ProofOut)

    :-

    Head = ..[Pred | HeadArgs],
    append(HeadArgs, [Confid, ProofIn, ProofOut], XHeadArgs),
    XHead = ..[Pred | XHeadArgs].

As one might expect, the definition of xpand_body is a bit more complex:

xpand_body((Goal, Goals), (XGoal, XGoals), ProofIn, ProofOut, RuleConfid,
              Confids, ConfidsTail, FinalConfid, *arguments*)

    :-!,

    xpand_goal(Goal,XGoal, ProofIn,InterProofTail,GoalConfid, *arguments*),
    ConfidsTail = [GoalConfid | NextConfidsTail],
    xpand_body(Goals, XGoals, InterProofTail, ProofOut, RuleCo.ifid, Confids,
              NextConfidsTail, FinalConfid, *arguments*).

xpand_body(Goal, (XGoal, ConfiCalc), ProofIn, ProofOut, RuleConfid, Confids,
              ConfidsTail, FinalConfid, *arguments*)

    :-

    xpand_goal(Goal, XGoal, ProofIn, ProofOut, GoalConfid, *arguments*),
    ConfidsTail = [GoalConfid],
    setupConfid(Confids, RuleConfid, FinalConfid, ConfiCalc).

xpand_body works its way recursively through the body of the clause, successively expanding each (sub)goal, and after it has finished expanding the last subgoal, it adds on computation of the confidence factor for the rule. Schematically, the expanded rule will look like Figure 11–4.

In this figure, the goals *x_complains_of*, etc., are only schematic—we will see their proper forms later. However, this schema shows us that xpand_body must account for two features:

1 The confidence factors for the subgoals must accumulated in a list that is passed to the final confidence calculation; also, the final confidence calculation must have the rule's own confidence factor available, as well as the head variable Confid in which the calculated confidence factor is to be placed.

2 The original input proof variable for the head is matched against an extensible list of the form

    [(Head if Body) | InterPrfTail],

by expand_know; InterPrfTail is passed to expand_body, which must make sure it is passed to the first subgoal as its input proof argument; then for each subgoal,

FIGURE 11–4
Schematic form of an expanded rule.

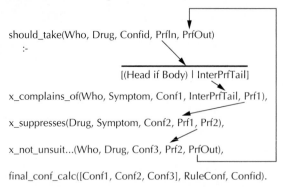

expand_body must make sure that the output proof argument is passed as the input proof argument to the next subgoal; finally, the output proof argument of the last subgoal must be matched against the output proof argument of the head.

Thus, the primary arguments of xpand_body are

xpand_body(
    Goal,   the goal or body to be expanded
    XGoal,   the expanded goal or body
    ProofIn,   the current input proof variable (for Goal)
    ProofOut,   the output proof variable for the head
    RuleConfid, the confidence factor for the rule
    Confids,   the head of extensible-list accumulating confidence factors
    ConfidsTail, the current tail of extensible-list accumulating confidence factors
    FinalConfid, the result of the final confidence calculation (= Confid from head)
arguments)

Examination of the first clause for xpand_body (which is the recursive clause) shows that it straightforwardly performs the tasks required by 1 and 2. The second clause for xpand_body deals with the situation when xpand_body has reached the last subgoal in the body. This is expanded to the combination of the direct expansion of the subgoal, together with the final confidence calculation created by setupConfid/4. Also, this clause terminates the extensible list used to accumulate the confidence factor arguments from each subgoal and also matches the output proof argument of the last subgoal against the output proof variable for the expanded clause head.

We can now examine xpand_goal. We will see shortly that there are several special cases that xpand_goal must handle. However, let's first consider its general case:

xpand_goal(Goal, XGoal, ProofIn, ProofOut, GoalConfid, *arguments*)
    :-
    Goal =.. [Pred | Args],
    append(Args, [GoalConfid, ProofIn, ProofOut], XGoalArgs),
    XGoal =.. [Pred | XGoalArgs].

For this case, the action of xpand_goal is quite like xpand_head and the case of xpand_know for facts: It simply adds on the appropriate three arguments to create XGoal. At this point, we have defined enough of xpand_know, regardless of how we handle *arguments,* to process simple facts and rules. For example, given the input

(relieves(aspirin, headache) :: 0.96),

xpand_know will produce the output

relieves(aspirin,headache,0.96,
    [relieves(aspirin,headache) | _438],_438).

Given the input

(suppresses(Drug, Symptom)
    :-
    relieves(Drug, Symptom) :: 0.85),

expand_know will produce this output:

suppresses(_1932,_1933,_1958,
    [suppresses(_1932,_1933) if relieves(_1932,_1933) | _1976], _1954)
    :-
    relieves(_1932,_1933,_1991,_1976,_1954),
    confidence_calculation .

Continuing with the definition of xpand_goal, there are several special cases that xpand_goal must handle:

- The goal is of the form not(Goal)
- The goal is an askable goal

In addition, xpand_goal must be able to distinguish between goals corresponding to qualified facts from the domain knowledge base and goals corresponding to unqualified supporting Prolog predicates. We will call the latter *builtins,* whether they are Prolog builtins or are supporting Prolog predicates programmed by the user. xpand_goal can recognize negations simply by the form of the argument: not(Something). However, to make the remaining distinctions, we must supply it with more information. This is the role of *arguments,* which we have carried along thus far in our development. We will break arguments into two separate arguments:

arguments = Know, MetaInfo

We can determine the askable predicates by using information from the metalevel knowledge file. Thus, we will use MetaInfo to store this information. The simplest way is to let MetaInfo be a list consisting of all the assertions found in the meta-level information file (MetaFile in xpand_file). First, we can refine our definition of xpand_file to set up MetaInfo as follows:

xpand_file(KnowFile, MetaFile, TargetFile)
    :-
    get_metaK(MetaFile,KnowPreds,MetaInfo),

initialization & other special tasks,

loopAndExpand(*arguments*),

any final tasks & cleanup,
told,
seen.

xpand_file(_,_,_)
  :-
  told,seen.

get_metaK(MetaFile,KnowPreds,MetaInfo)
  :-
  see(MetaFile),
  readList(MetaInfo),
  seen,
  member(knowledge_preds(KnowPreds), MetaInfo).

readList(List)
  :-
  read(Item),
  disp_readList(Item, List).

disp_readList(end_of_file, []).
disp_readList(Item, [Item | ListTail])
  :-
  readList(ListTail).

As can be seen, get_metaK/3 sets up both MetaInfo and Know, the two components of *arguments*. MetaInfo becomes just the list of items that can be read from the MetaFile. To assign a value to Know ($=$ KnowPreds), get_metaK simply looks for an expression of the form

knowledge_preds(KnowPreds)   (11.1)

on the list it constructed. This is equivalent to saying that it finds an expression of that form in the MetaFile. What we have done is establish a convention: The metalevel knowledge file must contain an expression of the form (11.1), where the argument KnowPreds must be a list of elements of the form k(Pred/Arity) for each predicate that is a qualified knowledge predicate in the domain knowledge file. Thus, for example, our lay medicine metalevel knowledge file medicknw.mta contains the assertion

knowledge_preds([k(relieves/2),k(aggravates/2),k(compound/2),k(should_take/2),
                  k(suppresses/2),k(unsuitable_for/2)]).

The case of askable predicates is recognized by determining whether the metalevel knowledge contains an *ask-info* assertion concerning the goal or an *ask-confirm* assertion, as follows:

```
xpand_goal(Goal, XGoal, ProofIn, ProofOut, GoalConfid, Know, MetaInfo)
    :-
    (member( ask_info(Goal, _, _), MetaInfo);
                        member( ask_confirm(Goal, _, _), MetaInfo) ),
    !,
    XGoal = (ask_about(Goal), obtain_conf(GoalConfid)),
    ProofIn = [asked(Goal) | ProofOut].
```

In this case, we simply include the same code in the body of the expanded clause as occurred in the body of solve/4 for the case of askable predicates.

We can recognize a generalized builtin predicate by determining that it is not recorded on Know, the list of knowledge predicates, thus:

```
xpand_goal(Goal, Goal, ProofIn, ProofOut, 1.0, Know, MetaInfo)
    :-
    is_builtin(Goal, Know, MetaInfo),
    !,
    ProofIn = [Goal-builtin | ProofOut].

is_builtin(Goal, Know, MetaInfo)
    :-
    functor(Goal, Pred, Arity),
    not(member( k(Pred/Arity), Know) ).
```

In this case, the expanded goal is identical with the original goal.

Finally, we must handle the case in which the subgoal in the body is of the form not(Goal). The simplest approach would be to apply xpand_goal recursively to Goal to produce XGoal, then to insert not(XGoal) in the appropriate place in the expanded body. However, as we have previously observed, we cannot extract any information from not(XGoal). In particular, we can't extract any confidence or (sub)proof information. But solve/4 does produce some (limited) information of this type. That original shell, solve/4, has two clauses to deal with this case:

```
solve(not(A), C, [negate(A, SubProof) | OutPrfTail], OutPrfTail)
    :-
    solve(A, C1, SubProof, []),
    !,
    C1 < 0.3,
    neg_conf(C1, C).                              % confidence calculation

solve(not(A), 1.0, [not(A)-exhaustion | OutPrfTail], OutPrfTail) :-!.
```

When solve/4 succeeds on not(Goal), one or the other of these two clauses has to succeed. Thus, intuitively, it would seem reasonable to create two fragments of code corresponding to these two clauses, connect them with a disjunction, and put the whole mess at the appropriate point, as is suggested in Figure 11–5.

However, examination of the clauses for solve/4 shows that cuts are positioned so that no more than one of the clauses can succeed. That is, if the first clause succeeds,

FIGURE 11–5
A possible expansion of a not(...) subgoal.

Head :- *Subgoals, not (Goal), MoreSubgoals.*

XHead :- *XSubgoals, (Part_1 ; Part_2), XMoreSubgoals.*

---

the cut will prevent the second clause from being used if backtracking forces a return to that point in the computation. But that would seem to be easy to take care of: just add a cut after Part_1 in the schema of Figure 11–5, as shown in Figure 11–6. This is quite appealing intuitively. Unfortunately, it has a fatal flaw. The flaw is due to the presence of the cut. Recall that the presence of a cut eliminates the consideration, on backtracking, of any alternative clauses for subgoals occurring to the left of the cut in the body of the clause in which the cut occurs. In the schema of Figure 11–6, this means that backtracking could not try alternative clauses for any calls occurring in *XSubgoals*. But this might eliminate finding a correct solution to a goal matching *XHead*. Why doesn't solve/4 encounter this problem? Because the cut occurs in the body of solve/4 but isn't mixed in with the body of any domain knowledge clause. Taking this as a cue, we could package up the code we have generated—that is, the expression (*Part_1* , ! ; *Part_2*)—using a fixed predicate, such as *xsnot/1*, which might be roughly defined as follows:

xsnot(XGoal, *other_args*)

:-

XGoal ,
confidence_calculation.

xsnot(XGoal, *other_args*).

Our schematic expansion would then appear as shown in Figure 11–7.

Since xsnot is supposed to capture the action of solve/4 in the case of negative subgoals, we would expect it to have two clauses corresponding to the two clauses of solve/4 in the negative case. The three additional arguments allow us to extract the necessary information:

xsnot(XGoal, GoalConfid, NegConfid, SubProof)

:-

XGoal ,

!,

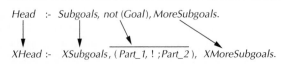

Head :- *Subgoals, not (Goal), MoreSubgoals.*

XHead :- *XSubgoals, (Part_1, ! ;Part_2), XMoreSubgoals.*

FIGURE 11–6
Refinement of the possible expansion of not(...) subgoals.

FIGURE 11–7
Expansion of not(...) using xsnot(...).

$Head$:- $Subgoals, not (Goal), MoreSubgoals.$

$XHead$:- $XSubgoals, xsnot(XGoal, ...), XMoreSubgoals.$

        GoalConfid < 0.3,
        neg_confid(GoalConfid, NegConfid).

    xsnot(XGoal, GoalConfid, 1.0, exhaustion).

Finally, we must show how xpand_body will create the confidence calculation code at the end of the expanded body. First examine the code for solve/4 in the case of a conjunctive subgoal:

    solve((A,B), Conf, InPrfTail, OutPrfTail)
      :-
      solve(A, CA, InPrfTail, InterPrfTail),
      solve(B, CB, InterPrfTail, OutPrfTail),
      conj_conf(CA, CB, Conf).   *% confidence calculation*

Let's see what happens if we have three goals to solve:

    solve((A,(B,C)), Conf, InPrfTail, OutPrfTail)
      :-
      solve(A, CA, InPrfTail, InterPrfTail),
      solve((B,C), CB_C, InterPrfTail, OutPrfTail),
      conj_conf(CA, CB_C, Conf).   *% confidence calculation*

But using the basic clause on the second call in the body, this becomes

    solve((A,(B,C)), Conf, InPrfTail, OutPrfTail)
      :-
      solve(A, CA, InPrfTail, InterPrfTail_1),
      solve(B, CB, InPrfTail_1, InterPrfTail_2),
      solve(C, CC, InterPrfTail_2, OutPrfTail),
      conj_conf(CB, CC, CB_C).   *% confidence calculation*
      conj_conf(CA, CB_C, Conf).   *% confidence calculation*

Our definition of conj_conf/3 is associative in the following sense. Let c_c be a function such that for any X, Y, and Z,

    conj_conf(X, Y, Z) holds if and only if Z = X c_c Y.

Then, for any X, Y, and W, it is true that

    (X c_c (Y c_c W)) = ((X c_c Y) c_c W).

Because of this associativity, we can reorder the confidence calculation at the end of the clause above as follows:

```
solve( ( A,(B,C) ), Conf, InPrfTail, OutPrfTail)
    :-
    solve(A, CA, InPrfTail, InterPrfTail_1),
    solve(B, CB, InPrfTail_1, InterPrfTail_2),
    solve(C, CC, InterPrfTail_2, OutPrfTail),
    conj_conf(CA, CB, CA_B).              % confidence calculation
    conj_conf(CA_B, CC, Conf).           % confidence calculation
```

When xpand_body reaches the last subgoal in the body of the clause being expanded, it has accumulated a list (Confids) of all the confidences associated with all of the subgoals in the body. It passes this together with the rule's confidence factor to setupConfid/4.

```
xpand_body(Goal, (XGoal, ConfiCalc), ProofIn, ProofOut, RuleConfid, Confids,
    ConfidsTail, FinalConfid, Know, MetaInfo)
    :-
    xpand_goal(Goal, XGoal, ProofIn, ProofOut, GoalConfid, Know, MetaInfo),
    ConfidsTail = [GoalConfid],
    setupConfid(Confids, RuleConfid, FinalConfid, ConfiCalc).
```

What setupConfid must do is recurse down the list Confids, creating the equivalent of the sequence of confidence calculations in the example above. At the end, it must combine the last (conjunctive) confidence value with the rule confidence value. Here is the code:

```
setupConfid(Confids, RuleConfid, FinalConfid, ConfiCalc)
    :-
    Confids = [C1 | RestConfids],
    conjoinConf(RestConfids, C1, ConjConfid, ConjCalc),
    ConfiCalc = (ConjCalc, rule_conf(ConjConfid,RuleConfid,FinalConfid) ).

conjoinConf([C | Confids], LastC, ConjConfid,
                    (conj_conf(LastC, C, NextC), RestConjCalc) )
    :-
    conjoinConf(Confids, NextC, ConjConfid, RestConjCalc).

conjoinConf([C], LastC, ConjConfid, conj_conf(LastC, C, ConjConfid) ).
conjoinConf([], LastC, LastC, true).
```

At this point, xpand_know can generate code for all of the clauses in our domain knowledge file. For example, given the input

```
( should_take(Person, Drug)
    :-
    complains_of(Person, Symptom),
    suppresses(Drug, Symptom),
    not(unsuitable_for(Person, Drug)) :: 0.9 ),
```

xpand_know would generate the following output:

```
should_take(_26,_1730,_1770,
        [should_take(_26,_1730) if (complains_of(_26,_27),
            suppresses(_1730,_27),
            not unsuitable_for(_26,_1730)),
            asked(complains_of(_26,_27)) | _1817],
        _1766)
    :-
    ask_about(complains_of(_26,_27)),
    obtain_conf(_1808),
    suppresses(_1730,_27,_1833,_1817,_1829),
    xsnot(unsuitable_for(_26,_1730,_1862,_1860,[]),_1862,_1887,_1860),
    _1829 = [neg(unsuitable_for(_26,_1730),_1860) | _1766],
    conj_conf(_1808,_1833,_1902),
    conj_conf(_1902,_1887,_1909),
    true,
    rule_conf(_1909,0.9,_1770).
```

There are a few remaining considerations to complete the code for xpand_file. First, since the expanded clauses may utilize the operators "if" and "::" , we must ensure that the appropriate operator declarations are included in the TargetFile. So we refine the first clause of the definition of xpand_file further:

```
xpand_file(KnowFile, MetaFile, TargetFile)
    :-
    get_metaK(MetaFile,KnowPreds,MetaInfo),
    tell(TargetFile),
    write(':-op(1200, yfx, ''::'').'),nl,
    write(':-op(700, yfx, if).'),nl,
    initialization & other special tasks,
    loopAndExpand(KnowPreds,MetaInfo),
    any final tasks & cleanup,
    told,
    seen.
```

We must also make sure that the file *asking.pro* is loaded when the TargetFile is loaded. Also, there may be other files developed that will be required. To deal with this possibility, we will adopt the convention that all these files will be specified by the following sort of declaration in the MetaFile:

```
requires_files([-confcalc]).
```

We further refine the first clause of xpand_file/3:

```
xpand_file(KnowFile, MetaFile, TargetFile)
    :-
    get_metaK(MetaFile,KnowPreds,MetaInfo),
    tell(TargetFile),
    write(':-op(1200, yfx, "::").'),nl,
```

```
write(':-op(700, yfx, if).'),nl,
write(':-[-asking].'),nl,
write(':-[-'),writeq(MetaFile),write('].'),nl,
(member(requires_files(FileList), MetaInfo),
      write(':-'),writeq(FileList),write('.'),nl; true),
nl,
```

initialization & other special tasks,

```
loopAndExpand(KnowPreds,MetaInfo),
```

any final tasks & cleanup,
```
told,
seen.
```

Recall that xpand_goal replaced an askable Goal with an expression involving ask_about(Goal). ask_about calls check_response, which eventually calls ask_acceptability. So this predicate, which appears in the MetaFile, must be loaded when the TargetFile is loaded. Since other metalevel predicates might also be needed, we simply caused the entire MetaFile to be loaded in the code above.

But consider the clause of check_response in which the call to ask_acceptability occurs:

```
check_response(Predicate, Answer, InfoVar, [userinfo-Predicate])
     :-                          % can assume Answer is nonvariable
                                 % because of cut in first clause
     ask_acceptability(Predicate, Answer, Test),
     Test, !,                    % Is it acceptable?
     InfoVar = Answer.           % Yes - return it.
```

After the call to ask_acceptability succeeds, the term appearing in the third argument is called as a goal. For example, here are the two ask_acceptability assertions in our example MetaFile (medicknw.mta):

```
ask_acceptability(complains_of(Person,Answer), Answer, relieves(_, Answer)).
ask_acceptability(suffers_from(Person,Answer),Answer, aggravates(_, Answer)).
```

Thus, successful execution of check_response (and ultimately ask_about) will require us to run relieves/2 or aggravates/2 successfully. But these original versions of the knowledge predicates won't be loaded with TargetFile. Instead, the expanded versions relieves/5 and aggravates/5 will be loaded. Of course, we could simply load all of the original knowledge together with the expanded forms. However, when the domain knowledge base is large, this would impose a heavy load on the system. Fortunately, the expanded forms contain all the information check_response requires. All we need do is define the original versions in terms of the expanded-argument versions, as follows:

```
relieves(Drug, Symptom)
     :-
     relieves(Drug, Symptom, _, _, _).
```

```
aggravates(Drug, Condition)
    :-
    aggravates(Drug, Condition, _, _, _).
```

We used anonymous variables for the extra arguments since we don't care about their values.

The only remaining question is for which domain knowledge predicates we should add such definitions. We could analyze the metalevel knowledge to determine this precisely. However, we'll use a simpler (but cruder) approach: add them for all the domain knowledge predicates. First, we further refine the first clause for xpand_file:

```
xpand_file(KnowFile, MetaFile, TargetFile)
    :-
    get_metaK(MetaFile,KnowPreds,MetaInfo),
    tell(TargetFile),
    write(':-op(1200, yfx, "::").'),nl,
    write(':-op(700, yfx, if).'),nl,
    write(':-[-asking].'),nl,
    write(':-['),writeq(MetaFile),write('].'),nl,
    (member(requires_files(FileList), MetaInfo),
        write(':-'),writeq(FileList),write('.'),nl; true),
    nl,
    initialization & other special tasks,
    loopAndExpand(KnowPreds,MetaInfo),
    setupKnowConnects(KnowPreds),
    told,
    seen.
```

We then add the following definitions:

```
setupKnowConnects([]).
setupKnowConnects([k(Pred/Arity) | RestKnowPreds])
    :-
    XArity is Arity + 3,
    functor(Original, Pred, Arity),
    functor(XOriginal, Pred, XArity),
    Original =.. [_ | OrigArgs],
    XOriginal =.. [_ | XOrigArgs],
    identifyElts(OrigArgs, XOrigArgs),
    Clause = (Original :- XOriginal),
    builtins:write_out(Clause),
    setupKnowConnects(RestKnowPreds).

identifyElts([], _).
identifyElts([Var | RestOrigArgs], [Var |RestXOrigArgs])
    :-
    identifyElts(RestOrigArgs, RestXOrigArgs).
```

There is one final consideration that is not absolutely essential, but that will make the TargetFile generated by our knowledge compiler easier to use. This is the problem of invoking the expert system using the expanded code. In this case of our example, we would start the system with the following type of top-level goal:

:- should_take(bill, Drug, Confidence, Proof, []).

However, it would be nice to package this up so that the system would ask us for the name of the Person being considered and would print a readable representation of the Proof. Of course, we could program that part by hand. However, we can make a simple declaration in the MetaFile describing the top-level goal, then teach our knowledge compiler to create appropriate code in the TargetFile.

Consider the following declaration:

main(should_take(input(Person,['Name =']),
                    output(Drug,[Person,' should take ', Drug]))).

The conventions for this declaration are

- main(...) is wrapped around the original top-level call;
- The arguments of the call are instantiated to descriptors;
- Descriptors come in one of the following two forms:
  input(*Variable, PromptList*)   output(*Variable, PromptList*)
- *PromptList* consists of atoms or the *Variable* in the descriptor.

The intent is that our knowledge compiler should use such a declaration to generate a definition of the following schematic form:

start
      :-
      interact with the user to instantiate all input variables;
      make the appropriate call to run the system;
      report the values of all output variables;
      report the confidence;
      provide an explanation.

For example, given the sample declaration above, our knowledge compiler will produce the following:

start :-
      write_list(['Name =']),
      read(_172),
      true,
      should_take(_172,_182,_351,_349,[]),
      write_list([_172,' should take ',_182]),
      nl,
      true,
      write('Confidence ='_351),
      nl,
      write('Explanation:'),
      nl,

```
        write_nl_list(_349),
        nl.
```

First, we make our final refinement of the first clause of xpand_file:

```
xpand_file(KnowFile, MetaFile, TargetFile)
        :-
        get_metaK(MetaFile,KnowPreds,MetaInfo),
        tell(TargetFile),
        write(':-op(1200, yfx, "::").'),nl,
        write(':-op(700, yfx, if).'),nl,
        write(':-[-asking].'),nl,
        write(':-['),writeq(MetaFile),write('].'),nl,
        (member(requires_files(FileList), MetaInfo),
            write(':-'),writeq(FileList),write('.'),nl; true),
        nl,
        (member(main(MainDecl), MetaInfo),
            process_main(MainDecl); true),
        nl,
        see(KnowFile),
        loopAndExpand(KnowPreds,MetaInfo),
        setupKnowConnects(KnowPreds),
        told,
        seen.
```

Define process_main/1 as follows:

```
process_main(MainDecl)
        :-
        put(~ %),write(main = MainDecl),nl,
        MainDecl  = .. [Pred | ArgsDescs],
        splitUp(ArgsDescs, Vars, Inputs, Outputs),
        makeInputCode(Inputs, InputCode),
        makeOutputCode(Outputs, ReportCode),
        append(Vars, [Confid, Proof, [] ], XMainArgs),
        XMain  = .. [Pred | XMainArgs],
        MainClause = (start :- InputCode, XMain, ReportCode,
            write('Confidence' = Confid),nl,
            write('Explanation:'),nl,
            write_nl_list(Proof),nl ),
        builtins:write_out(MainClause).
```

```
splitUp([], [], [], []).
```

```
splitUp([input(Var, IOList) | RestArgsDescs], [Var | RestVars],
                        [i(Var, IOList) | RestInputs], Outputs)
        :-
        splitUp(RestArgsDescs, RestVars, RestInputs, Outputs).
```

```
splitUp([output(Var, IOList) | RestArgsDescs], [Var | RestVars],
                                Inputs, [o(Var, IOList | RestOutputs])
    :-
    splitUp(RestArgsDescs, RestVars, Inputs, RestOutputs).

makeInputCode([], true).

makeInputCode([i(Var, IOList) | RestInputs], InputCode)
    :-
    InputCode = (write_list(IOList), read(Var), RestInputCode),
    makeInputCode(RestInputs, RestInputCode).

makeOutputCode([], true).

makeOutputCode([o(Var, IOList) | RestOutputs], OutputCode)
    :-
    OutputCode = (write_list(IOList), nl, RestOutputCode),
    makeOutputCode(RestOutputs, RestOutputCode).
```

To invoke our knowledge compiler on our sample files, we submit the following goal:

```
:-xpand_file('medicknw.k', 'medicknw.mta','xmedic.pro').
yes.
```

Here is the file *xmedic.pro* generated by this goal:

```
:-op(1200, yfx, '::').
:-op(700, yfx, if).
:-[-asking].
:-[-'medicknw.mta'].
:-[-confcalc].

start :-
    write_list(['Name  =']),
    read(_172),
    true,
    should_take(_172,_182,_351,_349,[]),
    write_list([_172,' should take ',_182]),
    nl,
    true,
    write('Confidence  ='_351),
    nl,
    write('Explanation:'),
    nl,
    write_nl_list(_349),
    nl.
```

relieves(aspirin,headache,0.96,
        [relieves(aspirin,headache) | _438],_438).
relieves(aspirin,moderate_pain,0.8,
        [relieves(aspirin,moderate_pain) | _480],_480).
relieves(aspirin,moderate_arthritis,0.87,
        [relieves(aspirin,moderate_arthritis) | _522],_522).
relieves(aspirin_codeine_combination,severe_pain,0.45,
        [relieves(aspirin_codeine_combination,severe_pain) | _564],_564).
relieves(cough_cure_xm,cough,0.85,
        [relieves(cough_cure_xm,cough) | _606],_606).
relieves(pain_gone,severe_pain,0.88,
        [relieves(pain_gone,severe_pain) | _648],_648).
relieves(ko_diarrhea,diarrhea,0.75,
        [relieves(ko_diarrhea,diarrhea) | _690],_690).
relieves(de_congest,cough,0.85,
        [relieves(de_congest,cough) | _732],_732).
relieves(de_congest,nasal_congestion,0.85,
        [relieves(de_congest,nasal_congestion) | _774],_774).
relieves(penicillin,pneumonia,0.9,
        [relieves(penicillin,pneumonia) | _816],_816).
relieves(bis_cure,diarrhea,0.7,
        [relieves(bis_cure,diarrhea) | _858],_858).
relieves(bis_cure,nausea,0.93,
        [relieves(bis_cure,nausea) | _900],_900).
relieves(noasprinol,headache,0.93,
        [relieves(noasprinol,headache) | _942],_942).
relieves(noasprinol,moderate_pain,0.84,
        [relieves(noasprinol,moderate_pain) | _984],_984).
relieves(triple_tuss,nasal_congestion,0.85,
        [relieves(triple_tuss,nasal_congestion) | _1026],_1026).
aggravates(aspirin,asthma,0.89,
        [aggravates(aspirin,asthma) | _1068],_1068).
aggravates(aspirin,peptic_ulcer,0.92,
        [aggravates(aspirin,peptic_ulcer) | _1110],_1110).
aggravates(ko_diarrhea,fever,0.75,
        [aggravates(ko_diarrhea,fever) | _1152],_1152).
aggravates(de_congest,high_blood_pressure,0.83,
        [aggravates(de_congest,high_blood_pressure) | _1194],_1194).
aggravates(de_congest,heart_disease,0.81,
        [aggravates(de_congest,heart_disease) | _1236],_1236).
aggravates(de_congest,diabetes,0.74,
        [aggravates(de_congest,diabetes) | _1278],_1278).
aggravates(de_congest,glaucoma,0.91,
        [aggravates(de_congest,glaucoma) | _1320],_1320).
aggravates(penicillin,asthma,0.82,

```
                    [aggravates(penicillin,asthma) | _1362],_1362).
aggravates(bis_cure,diabetes,0.88,
                    [aggravates(bis_cure,diabetes) | _1404],_1404).
aggravates(bis_cure,gout,0.77,
                    [aggravates(bis_cure,gout) | _1446],_1446).
aggravates(bis_cure,fever,0.98,
                    [aggravates(bis_cure,fever) | _1488],_1488).
aggravates(_1519,_1520,_1554,
                    [aggravates(_1519,_1520)
                    if (compound(_1519,_1527),
                    member(_1534,_1527),
                    aggravates(_1534,_1520)) | _1572],_1550)
                    :-
        compound(_1519,_1527,_1587,_1572,
                    [member(_1534,_1527)-builtin | _1618]),
        member(_1534,_1527),
        aggravates(_1534,_1520,_1634,_1618,_1550),
        conj_conf(_1587,1,_1658),
        conj_conf(_1658,_1634,_1665),
        true,
        rule_conf(_1665,1,_1554).


compound(aspirin_codeine_combination,
                    [codeine,aspirin],1,
                    [compound(aspirin_codeine_combination,
                        [codeine,aspirin])
                    | _1698],
                    _1698).


should_take(_26,_1730,_1770,
                    [should_take(_26,_1730)
                    if (complains_of(_26,_27),
                    suppresses(_1730,_27),
                    not unsuitable_for(_26,_1730)),
                    asked(complains_of(_26,_27)) | _1817],
                    _1766)
                    :-
        ask_about(complains_of(_26,_27)),
        obtain_conf(_1808),
        suppresses(_1730,_27,_1833,_1817,_1829),
        xsnot(unsuitable_for(_26,_1730,_1862,_1860,[]),_1862,_1887,_1860),
        _1829 = [neg(unsuitable_for(_26,_1730),_1860) | _1766],
        conj_conf(_1808,_1833,_1902),
        conj_conf(_1902,_1887,_1909),
        true,
        rule_conf(_1909,0.9,_1770).
```

```
suppresses(_1932,_1933,_1958,
        [suppresses(_1932,_1933)
        if relieves(_1932,_1933) | _1976],_1954)
        :-
    relieves(_1932,_1933,_1991,_1976,_1954),
    true,
    rule_conf(_1991,0.85,_1958).


unsuitable_for(_95,_2032,_2064,
        [unsuitable_for(_95,_2032)
        if (aggravates(_2032,_96),
        suffers_from(_95,_96)) | _2082],_2060)
        :-
    aggravates(_2032,_96,_2097,_2082,
        [asked(suffers_from(_95,_96)) | _2060]),
    ask_about(suffers_from(_95,_96)),
    obtain_conf(_2131),
    conj_conf(_2097,_2131,_2151),
    true,
    rule_conf(_2151,0.7,_2064).


relieves(_2166,_2167) :-
    relieves(_2166,_2167,_2171,_2172,_2173).
aggravates(_2202,_2203) :-
    aggravates(_2202,_2203,_2207,_2208,_2209).
compound(_2238,_2239) :-
    compound(_2238,_2239,_2243,_2244,_2245).
should_take(_2274,_2275) :-
    should_take(_2274,_2275,_2279,_2280,_2281).
suppresses(_2310,_2311) :-
    suppresses(_2310,_2311,_2315,_2316,_2317).
unsuitable_for(_2346,_2347) :-
    unsuitable_for(_2346,_2347,_2351,_2352,_2353).
```

Finally, here is an interaction illustrating the use of the expanded code:

```
?-[xmedic].
yes.
?-start.
Name = ken.
What symptom are you bothered by? pain.
Your response is ambiguous
Please select a synonym - type corresponding number
1:   moderate_pain
2:   severe_pain
Choice =  2.
What is your confidence in that answer? 1.
Do you suffer from asthma (yes/no) ? y.
What is your confidence in that answer? 1.
```

```
ken should take pain_gone
Confidence=0.9
Explanation:
should_take(ken,pain_gone)if
    complains_of(ken,severe_pain) &
    suppresses(pain_gone,severe_pain) &
    not unsuitable_for(ken,pain_gone)
complains_of(ken,severe_pain) -- asked
suppresses(pain_gone,severe_pain)if
    relieves(pain_gone,severe_pain)
relieves(pain_gone,severe_pain)
neg(unsuitable_for(ken,pain_gone),exhaustion)
yes.
```

EXERCISES

11-1 Apply xpand_file/3 to the solve-style expert systems developed in Exercises 9-1–9-5.

11-2 Explore the extent to which techniques in the spirit of xpand_file/3 can be applied to the constraint solution shell developed in Section 9.3.

CHAPTER **12**

MIXED FORWARD AND BACKWARD REASONING

Many expert systems shells base their search mechanisms on the forward-chained execution of rules—for example, most production rule systems. The methods we have developed in the preceding sections can be utilized to develop shells using these strategies. As an example, we will develop a small shell that implements the simple version of the EXPERT system, as described in Weiss and Kulikowski (1984). In this example, we adopt an interesting combination of forward and backward chaining. The simple example we consider is nicely constrained in that the rules (for car malfunction diagnosis) are of limited depth: no arbitrarily deep deduction branches can be created. This makes the construction of the inference engine especially simple. In essence, one simply wishes to draw all possible conclusions from the findings (i.e., user-reported facts) available to the system. These findings are acquired at the outset of the consultation session by a variety of types of questions. The types of questions, together with the internal forms of allowable answers, are declared by

```
findings([
     checklist('Type of problem:',
          [1(1, fews, 'Car Won't Start'),
          1(2, foth, 'Other Car Problems')]),
     multiple_choice('Odor of gasoline in carburetor:',
          [1(1, ngas, 'None'),
          1(2, mgas, 'Normal'),
          1(3, lgas, 'Very Strong')]),
     checklist('Simple checks:',
          [1(1, dim, 'Headlights are dim'),
          1(2,cfilt,'Fuel Filter Clogged'),
          1(3,lcab,'Battery Cables Loose or Corroded')]),
     checklist('Starter Data:',
          [1(1, ncmk, 'No Cranking'),
          1(2, scrnk, 'Slow Cranking'),
```

```
        1(3, ocrnk, 'Normal Cranking'),
        1(4, grind, 'Grinding Noise From Starter')]),
    numerical(temp, 'Outdoor Temperature (degrees F):'),
    yes_no(egas, 'Gas Gauge Reads Empty')
    ]).
```

In addition to this declaration, we also need the declarations of hypotheses, treatments, and domain-specific rules for establishing hypotheses and treatments. The declarations for hypotheses and treatments are

```
hyp(flood,'Car Flooded').
hyp(choke,'Choke Stuck').
hyp(empty,'No Fuel').
hyp(filt,'Fuel Filter Clogged').
hyp(cab,'Battery Cables Loose or Corroded').
hyp(batd,'Battery Discharged').
hyp(strtr,'Starter Malfunction').

treat(wait,'Wait 10 minutes or Depress Accelerator to Floor while Starting').
treat(open,'Remove Air Cleaner Assembly & Manually Open Choke with Pencil').
treat(gas,'Put More Gasoline into Tank').
treat(rfilt,'Replace Gas Filter').
treat(clean,'Clean and Tighten Battery Cables').
treat(gbatt,'Charge or Replace Battery').
treat(nstar,'Replace Starter').
```

Findings are recorded (using asserta) in the form

```
f(<finding identifier>,truth-value)
```

where the truth values are the atoms *true* and *false*. The rules for establishing treatments and diagnostic hypotheses are

```
h(wait, 0.9)
    :-
    f(fcws,true),h(flood,C), 0.2=<C,C=<1.0.
h(open, 0.5)
    :-
    f(fcws,true),h(choke,C), 0.2=<C,C=<1.0.
h(gas, 0.9)
    :-
    f(fcws,true),h(empty,C), 0.3=<C,C=<1.0.
h(rfilt, 0.8)
    :-
    f(fcws,true),h(filt,C), 0.4=<C,C=<1.0.
h(clean, 0.7)
    :-
    f(fcws,true),h(cab,C), 0.5=<C,C=<1.0.
```

```
h(gbatt, 0.8)
    :-
    f(fcws,true,h(batd,C), 0.4=<C,C=<1.0.
h(nstar,0.9)
    :-
    f(fcws,true),h(strtr,C), 0.4=<C,C=<1.0.
h(flood, 0.8)
    :-
    f(lgas,true).
h(choke, 0.6)
    :-
    f(temp,Temp), 0=<Temp,Temp=<50,
    some_of(1,[f(scrnk,true),f(ocrnk,true)]).
h(empty, 0.9)
    :-
    f(egas,true).
h(filt, 1.0)
    :-
    f(cfilt,true).
h(cab, 0.9)
    :-
    f(lcab,true).
h(batd, 0.7)
    :-
    f(scrnk,true),f(dim,true).
h(batd, 0.9)
    :-
    f(ncrnk,true),
    f(dim,true).
h(strtr, 0.7)
    :-
    f(ncrnk,true),
    f(dim,false).
h(strtr, 0.9)
    :-
    f(grind,true).

is_numeric(temp).

f(Anything,false)
    :-
    not(is_numeric(Anything)),
    not(f(Anything,true)).
```

Notice the last rule, which establishes a *negation by failure* interpretation for the falsity of nonnumeric findings. The code presented thus far constitutes the domain knowledge of automobile malfunction diagnosis. We must consider the shell that will utilize this knowledge. At the top level, it does not appear much different than our previous shells:

```
consultation:-
      sweep_in('car_rules.pro'),
      get_findings,
      draw_conclusions,
      rank(Diagnostic_Conclusions, Treatment_Recommendations),
      report(diagnostic_Conclusions, Treatment_Recommendations).

get_findings:-
      findings(Questions),
      ask(Questions).
```

Thus, to have a consultation, it suffices to load the rules for car diagnosis, get the appropriate findings from the user, draw conclusions from those findings, rank the conclusions and recommendations, and report them back to the user. To get the appropriate findings from the user, one need only ask the packaged questions that were declared in *car_rules.pro*. This is accomplished as follows:

```
ask([]).

ask ([Question | More_Questions])
      :-
      ask_specific(Question),
      ask(More_Questions).

ask_specific(multiple_choice(Heading,Options))
      :-
      write(Heading),nl,
      show_lines(Options),
      write('choose one:'),nl,
      read(Response),
      enter(Response,Options).

ask_specific(checklist(Heading,Options))
      :-
      write(Heading),nl,
      show_lines(Options),
      write('checklist:'),nl,
      read(Response),
      enter(Response,Options).

ask_specific(numerical(Finding_Id,Question))
      :-
      write(Question),write('(type number):'),
      read(Response),                              % should have type check
```

```
    asserta(f(Finding_Id, Response)).

ask_specific(yes_no(Finding_Id, Question))
    :-
    write(Question), write('(y n)?'),
    read(Response),
    act_on_yes_no(Response, Finding_Id).

act_on_yes_no(y, Finding_Id)
    :- !,
    asserta(f(Finding_Id, true)).

act_on_yes_no(AnythingElse, Finding_Id)
    :-
    asserta(f(Finding_Id, false)).

show_lines([]) :- nl.

show_lines([l(N, Id, Entry) | More_Lines])
    :-
    write('     '), write (N), write(') '), write(Entry), nl,
    show_lines(More_Lines).

enter([],_).

enter([Num|More_Nums],Option_List)
    :-
    single_entry(Num, Option_List),
    enter(More_Nums, Option_List).

enter(Num,Option_List)
    :-
    single_entry(Num,Option_List).

single_entry(Num, Option_List)
    :-
    look_up(Num, Option_List, Result),
    make_entry(Result).

look_up(Num,[l(Num,Finding_Id,_) | More_Options],Finding_Id)
    :- !.

look_up(Num,[_ | More_Options],Result)
    :-
    look_up(Num,More_Options,Result).
```

```
make_entry(Finding_Id)
    :-
    asserta(f(Finding_Id, true)).
```

Note that the entries made for the findings are entered using asserta, thus treating the rule for f(_,_) at the end of car_rules.pro as a default.

We must now consider the method of drawing conclusions from the recorded findings. Our method is as follows. We consider each finding in turn and draw whatever conclusion we can from that particular finding. Of course, the process of drawing a conclusion from one finding may require the checking of another finding. At the top level, we can express this using Prolog's chronological backtracking:

```
draw_conclusions
    :-
    f(Finding_Id, Value),
    pursue(f(Finding_Id, Value), Consequence),
    fail.

draw_conclusions.
```

The *fail* at the end of the first clause for *draw_conclusions* causes the system to iterate through all consequences of the selected finding, and, at the outer level, to iterate through all findings that have been recorded. Given that this is Prolog and that the process of backtracking undoes previously established bindings, all this iteration would be for naught if we did not record the consequences. As we will see later, we do this using assert. For the present, let us examine how pursue deduces consequences. Its code is organized thus:

```
pursue(Current_Assertion,Consequence)
    :-
    get_rule(Current_Assertion,Inter_Consequence,Body),
    matches(Current_Assertion,Body,Remaining_Body),!,
    call(Remaining_Body),
    check_asserta(Inter_Consequence),
    pursue(Inter_Consequence,Consequence).

pursue(h(ID, Value),h(ID, Value))
    :-
    (hyp(ID,_); treat(ID,Value)),!,
    asserta(h(ID,Value)).

pursue(Assertion,Assertion).
```

Given an Assertion, pursue attempts to find a recorded rule for which there is a call in its body that matches Assertion—the search is proceeding by forward chaining rather than backward chaining, which would attempt to match Assertion against the heads of rules. If Assertion indeed matches one of the calls in the body of the selected rule, the rest of the body of the rule is run in backward-chaining mode to see if it can be established. If this is the case, the head of the rule is a forward-chained consequence of the given Assertion. At that point, we record it in the database (if it hasn't previously been recorded) then transitively pursue the consequences of this new consequence of Assertion. The backtracking behavior of *draw_conclusions* causes *pursue* to iterate through all the rules that could be (forward chaining) applicable to the given Assertion. The code for *matches* and *check_asserta* is straightforward:

```
matches(Anything,true,true).

matches(Anything,Anything,true).

matches(Assertion,(Assertion,Rest_Body),Rest_Body).

matches(Assertion,(Literal,Rest_Body),(Literal,Remaining_Rest_Body))
    :-
    matches(Assertion,Rest_Body,Remaining_Rest_Body).

check_asserta(Assertion)
    :-
    Assertion, !.                                   % already recorded

check_asserta(Assertion)
    :-
    asserta(Assertion).
```

It would be possible to very simply define *get_rule* by the clause

```
get_rule(A,Head,Body)
    :-
    clause(Head,Body).
```

This approach would let get_rule blindly churn through the entire database, presenting *match* with all the recorded rules. Then match would filter out those that did not match Assertion in their bodies. However, this would be hideously inefficient. What would make it efficient would be an indexing mechanism that would allow get_rule to select only those rules that potentially match Assertion in their bodies; i.e., those rules whose bodies contain a call on the same predicate as appears in Assertion. We can do this as follows:

```
get_rule(Current_Assertion,h(Id,Value),Body)
    :-
    index(Current_Assertion,Ref),
    clause(h(Id,Value),Body,Ref).
```

Thus, the indexing mechanism relies on the database reference mechanism, just as the confidence factor mechanism did in earlier sections. It is the responsibility of the customized consult mechanism *sweep_in* to set up the indexing encoded in the predicate *index*. We will describe this below. First, let us finish off the predicates defining consultation. Note that in our definition of get_rule, we restrict ourselves to retrieving rules whose heads are of the form h(_,_), since this is all that is necessary for the simple example we are treating. More complex examples would need to relax this restriction by incorporating additional similar clauses for get_rule.

Having drawn all the conclusions we can from the findings, we must rank in order the conclusions and recommendations. This is easily done by collecting the conclusions and treatment recommendations into a list. By requiring that the elements of the list be terms with the confidence factor appearing first, we take advantage of the standard definition of setof, which sorts its elements lexicographically. Finally, report presents the results on the terminal. Here is the code:

```
rank(Diagnostic_Conclusions,Treatment_Recommendations)
    :-
    setof(h( HValue,HDescriptor ),
        HID^(h(HID,HValue),hyp(HID,HDescriptor)),
        Diagnostic_Conclusions),
    setof( h(TValue,TDescriptor ),
        TID^(h(TID,TValue),treat(TID,TDescriptor)),
        Treatment_Recommendations).


report(Diagnostic_Conclusions,Treatment_Recommendations)
    :-
    nl,write('INTERPRETIVE ANALYSIS'),nl,nl,
    write('Diagnostic Status'),nl,
    show_entries(Diagnostic_Conclusions),
    write('Treatment Recommendations'),nl,
    show_entries(Treatment_Recommendations).

show_entries([]) :- nl.

show_entries([h(Value,Descriptor) | Rest_Entries])
    :-
    write(' '),write(Value),write(' '),write(Descriptor),nl,
    show_entries(Rest_Entries)
```

It remains only to define the customized consult predicate sweep_in. Its structure is similar to the one we defined earlier. However, we are most interested in the indexing it must set up. Here is the top level:

```
sweep_in(File) :-
    see(File),
    process_file,
    seen,
    write(ok).


process_file :-
    read(Clause),!,
    dispatch(Clause).
```

```
dispatch(end_of_file).

dispatch(Clause):-
     assert(Clause,Ref),
     parts(Clause, Head, Body),
     insert_indexing(Head, Body, Ref),
     process.
```

The interesting work is done by insert_indexing, which sets up indices for those rules whose heads are of the form h(_,_) or f(_,_); it ignores any others. The indices it sets up are simple: It associates to each predicate call the database addresses of those clauses that have that predicate occurring in their bodies. Given the Body of the rule that was just asserted (together with its database Ref), *preds_in_body* extracts the list of predicates occurring in Body and assert_indices simply records an assertion

```
index(Pred, Ref).
```

for each predicate on that list. Here is the code:

```
insert_indexing(Head, Body, Ref)
     :-
     ( Head = f(_,_); Head = h(_,_) ),!,
     preds_in_body(Body, Pred_List),
     assert_indices(Pred_List, Ref).

insert_indexing(Head, Body, Ref).

assert_indices([],_).

assert_indices([Pred | More_Preds],Ref)
     :-
     assertz(index(Pred, Ref)),!,
     assert_indices(More_Preds, Ref).

preds_in_body(true,[]).

preds_in_body((A, B),[A | Rest_Preds])
     :-
     (A=f(_,_); A = h(_,_)),!,
     preds_in_body(B, Rest_Preds).

preds_in_body((A, B),Preds)
     :-
     preds_in_body(B, Preds).

preds_in_body(A,[A])
     :-
     (A = f(_,_); A = h(_,_)).
```

preds_in_body(_,[]).

parts((Head :- Body),Head, Body) :- !.

parts(Fact, Fact, true).

EXERCISES

12-1 Continuing with the photography fault database developed in Exercise 1-14, revise the photography expert system developed in Exercises 8-2 and 9-2 to fit within the framework of this chapter.

12-2 Revise the automobile repair consultant developed in Exercise 9-5 to fit within the framework of this chapter.

12-3 Explore the extent to which the transformation techniques (xpand_file/3) developed in Chapter 11 can be applied to the consultation system developed in this chapter.

APPENDIXES

APPENDIX A   TELEVISION SCHEMATIC AND REPAIR

Figure A–1 shows a block diagram of the black and white portion of a color TV receiver.

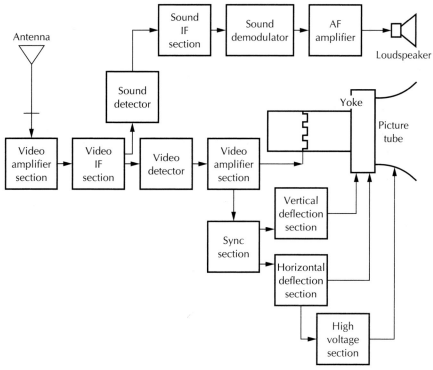

FIGURE A–1
Block diagram of a TV receiver.

Figure A–2 presents several problems that can occur with television receivers, together with some possible causes and possible remedies for the situation.

FIGURE A–2
Simple television troubleshooting.

Symptom	Possible cause	Possible remedy
Set seems dead	Power cord unplugged	Plug in cord
	Wall socket controlled by switch set at off	Turn switch on
	Circuit breaker or fuse for wall socket is tripped or blown	Reset circuit breaker or replace fuse
Set has picture but no sound on all channels	Volume is turned off	Turn up volume control
	Headphones are plugged into set	Unplug headphones
Set has picture and sound on all but one channel	Transmitting station has a problem	Call and complain
	Program is a silent movie	Turn on stereo and enjoy
Set has sound but black picture	Brightness control turned down	Turn up brightness control
Set has sound but gray, washed-out picture	Contrast control turned down	Adjust contrast control
Picture is too far to the left or right	Misadjusted horizontal control	Adjust horizontal control
Picture has diagonal black lines through is	Misadjusted horizontal control	Adjust horizontal control
Picture flips or rolls up and down	Misadjusted vertical control	Adjust vertical control

APPENDIX B   ENZYME SITES AND ACTIONS

Figure B–1 presents information on various human digestive enzymes, including the site of action, the food component acted upon, and the product(s) of the action.

FIGURE B–1
Functions of human digestive enzymes.

Enzyme	Site	Acts on	Products
amylase (saliva)	mouth	starch	sugars
pepsin	stomach	proteins	peptones
rennin	stomach	milk casein	paracasein
lactase	small intestine	sugars	monosaccharides
sucrase	small intestine	sugars	monosaccharides
maltase	small intestine	sugars	monosaccharides
peptidase	small intestine	peptones	amino acids
lipase	small intestine	fat	fatty acids
lipase	small intestine	fat	glycerol

APPENDIX C   CLOUD DESCRIPTIONS AND PROPERTIES[1]

FIGURE C-1
Classification of clouds.

Group		Tier or layer	
	Low (0–3 km)	Middle (3–7 km)	High (>7 km)
I Heap	Fair-weather cumulus	Swelling cumulus	Cumulonimbus
II Layer	Stratus	Altostratus	Cirrostratus
III Layers and Heaps	Stratocumulus	Altocumulus	Cirrocumulus
IV Precipitating	Nimbostratus Cirrus Cumulonimbus		
V Unusual	separate listing		

FIGURE C–2
Cloud group descriptions.

Cloud group	Description
Heap (cumulus family)	Flattish base; domed cauliflower top or anvil top; sharply defined edges; tower tops rise to differing heights; vertical and horizontal dimensions approximately the same; height ranges from < 300 m to > 20 km; horizontal diameter ranges from city block to 2 or 3 km; individual clouds well separated; color usually white, but can change to dark, heavy gray
Layer (stratus family)	Appear in layers; sheet-like; very short relative to horizontal extent; height typically 0.5–1 km; horizontal dimension ranges from 10km to 1,000km; (can cover 1,000,000 sq mi); poor distinction between individual clouds; color typically white to moderate gray
Heaps and layers	Appear as either heaps built in layers, with layers extending, or as moderately shallow layers of cumulus-appearing clouds; may appear curly or as large rounded lumps
Precipitating (nimbus family)	Usually associated with precipitation; may take variety or forms; typically moderate to dark, threatening gray

[1] The tables and drawings in this section are adapted from Vincent J. Schaefer and John A. Day, *A Field Guide to the Atmosphere*, copyright © 1981 by Vincent J. Schaefer and John A. Day. Reprinted by permission of Houghton Mifflin Co.

FIGURE C–3
Properties of types of clouds.

Cloud name	Description
Fair-weather cumulus	Flattish base with domed cauliflower tops; sharp edges; fairly short height (< 3 km); vertical and horizontal dimensions approximately the same
Swelling cumulus	Flattish base with domed cauliflower tops or domed tower tops; sharp edges; medium height (3–7 km); vertical and horizontal dimensions approximately the same
Cumulonimbus	Flattish base with domed cauliflower tops; sharp edges; very tall (> 7 km); vertical and horizontal dimensions approximately the same
Stratus	Sheet-like layers, very thin vertical dimension relative to horizontal dimension; ground level (fog) to 3 km height
Altostratus	Sheet-like layers, very thin vertical dimension relative to horizontal dimension; height ranges from 3–6 km; dull gray color or "ground-glass" appearance
Cirrostratus	Sheet-like layers, very thin vertical dimension relative to horizontal dimension; quite high (6–11 km); thin, wispy appearance
Stratocumulus	Mixture of layers and heaps; low (1–3 km); fuzzy edges, somewhat fluffy; sense of holes punched in clouds; generally flat bases
Altocumulus	Mixture of layers and heaps; height medium (3–7 km); fuzzy edges, some clouds blurring into others, generally flat bases; wrinkly
Cirronimbus	Mixture of layers and heaps or rolls; high (> 7 km); fuzzy edges, some clouds blurring into others, wispy
Nimbostratus	Low to middle height; darkish gray; ragged edges; precipitation falling from base
Cumulonimbus	Generally very tall, extending from lower (~ 3 km) levels to above 18 km; can be moderate diameter to huge (15–20 km); lid-like top, often extending as "anvil"; precipitation often falling from base
Cirrus	Very high (> 9 km), often wispy appearing, with trails and various strange shapes; produce precipitation (initially ice crystals, which may melt at lower levels)

FIGURE C–4

Illustrations of cumulus family clouds.

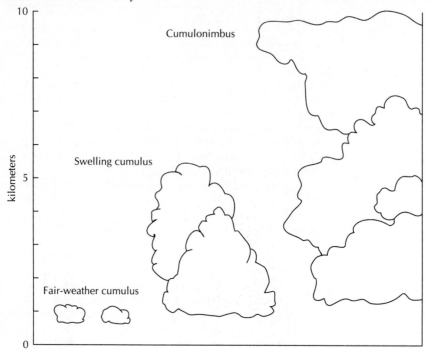

FIGURE C–5
Illustrations of stratus family clouds.

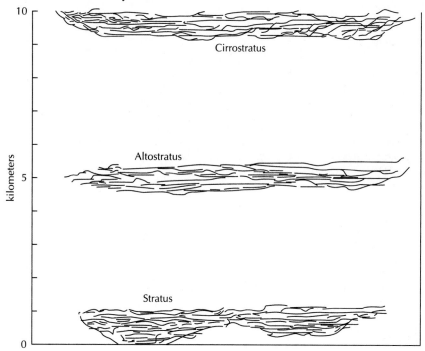

FIGURE C–6
Illustrations of layered heaps family clouds.

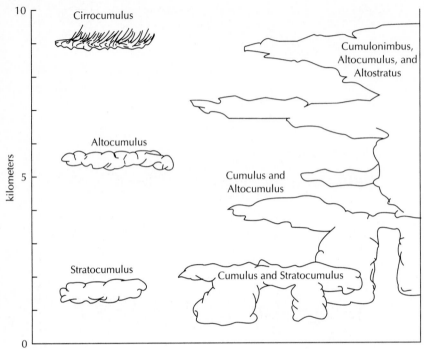

FIGURE C–7
Illustrations of nimbus family clouds.

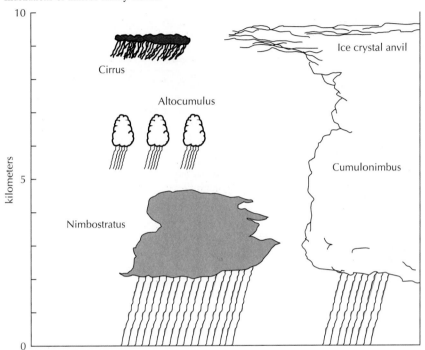

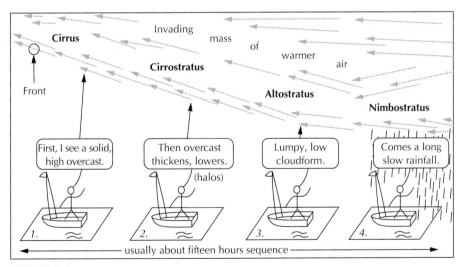

FIGURE C–8
The warm front's progress. (Adapted from Eric Sloane, *Eric Sloane's Weather Book*, Hawthorn Books, Inc., New York, 1952.)

APPENDIX D   IRS FILING RULES

Do I have to file?	Use **Chart A** to see if you must file a return. But, you must use **Chart B** if someone (such as your parent) can claim you as a dependent on his or her return. Also see **Other situations when you must file** on page 9.

Chart A—For most people

To use this chart, first find your marital status at the end of 1988. Then, read across to find your filing status and age at the end of 1988. You must file a return if your gross income* was at least the amount shown in the last column.

Marital status	Filing status	Age	Gross income
Single (including divorced and legally separated)	Single	under 65 65 or older	$4,950 $5,700
	Head of household	under 65 65 or older	$6,350 $7,100
Married with a child and living apart from your spouse during the last 6 months of 1988	Head of household (see Form 1040A, line 4 instructions)	under 65 65 or older	$6,350 $7,100
Married and living with spouse at end of 1988 (or on the date your spouse died)	Married, joint return	under 65 (both spouses) 65 or older (one spouse) 65 or older (both spouses)	$8,900 $9,500 $10,100
	Married, separate return	any age	$1,950
Married, not living with spouse at end of 1988 (or on the date your spouse died)	Married, joint or separate return	any age	$1,950
Widowed before 1988 and not remarried in 1988	Single	under 65 65 or older	$4,950 $5,700
	Head of household	under 65 65 or older	$6,350 $7,100
	Qualifying widow(er) with dependent child (see Form 1040A, line 5 instructions)	under 65 65 or older	$6,950 $7,550

*Gross income** usually means money, goods, and property you received on which you must pay tax. It does not include nontaxable income.

Chart B—For children and other dependents

If someone (such as your parent) can claim you as a dependent on his or her return and any of the following conditions apply to you, you must file a return. If your gross income was $1950 or more, you cannot be claimed as a dependent unless you were under age 19 at the end or 1988 or a full-time student and your parent(s) meet certain other tests. (See the instructions for line 6c of Form 1040A on page 17 for details.)

Unearned income includes taxable interest and dividends. Earned income included wages, tips, and taxable scholarships and fellowships.

1. Single dependents under 65
You must file a return if—

Your unearned income was:	and	the total of that income plus your earned income was:
$1 or more		more than $500
$0		more than $3000

2. Single dependents 65 or older or blind
You must file a return if—

• Your earned income was more than $3,750, or

• Your unearned income was more than $1,250 ($2,000 if 65 or older **and** blind), or

• Your gross income was more than the total of your earned income (up to $3,000) or $500, whichever is larger, plus $750 ($1,500 if 65 or older **and** blind.)

3. Married dependents under 65
You must file a return if—

• Your earned income was more than $2,500, or

• You had any unearned income and your gross income was more than $500, or

• Your gross income was at least $5 and your spouse files a separate return on Form 1040 and itemizes deductions.

4. Married dependents 65 or older or blind
You must file a return if—

• Your earned income was more than $3,100, or

• Your unearned income was more than $1,100 ($1,700 if 65 or older **and** blind), or

• Your gross income was more than the total of your earned income (up to $2,500) or $500, whichever is larger, plus $600 ($1,200 if 65 or older **and** blind), or

• Your gross income was at least $5 and your spouse files a separate return on Form 1040 and itemizes deductions.

Other situations when you must file

You must also file a return if you received any advance earned income credit (EIC) payments from your employer. You must file a return using Form 1040 if **any** of the following applied for 1988:

- You owe any special taxes, such as social security tax on tips you did not report to your employer, or

- You owe uncollected social security tax or RRTA tax on tips you reported to your employer, or

- You earned $400 or more from self-employment after you deduct your business expenses, or

- You earned wages or $100 or more from a church or a church-controlled organization that is exempt from employer social security taxes.

The rules apply to all U.S. citizens and resident aliens. They also apply to nonresident aliens and dual status aliens who were married to U.S. citizens or residents at the end of 1988 and who have elected to be treated as resident aliens. . . .

APPENDIX E   PHOTOGRAPHY TROUBLESHOOTING[2]

Negative and transparency faults		
Symptom	**Possible cause**	**Remedy**
Heavy negative or light positive image	Over-exposure	Check film speed setting, cell in meter, shutter speeds, automatic diaphragm in SLR lenses.
Light negative or heavy, dull positive image	Under-exposure	Check film speed setting. In very dull weather give extra exposure.
Branching, twig-like marks, dark on negatives	Static	Produced in hot, dry conditions. Rewind 35mm film slowly.
Tiny sharp-edged areas, clear on negatives, dark on transparencies	Dust on film during exposure	Remove dust from camera. Always clean camera, especially 35mm, inside and out before use.
Areas shaped like lens iris, dark on negatives, light on transparencies	Light reflections within lens	Try to avoid direct light hitting the lens.
Lines along length of film	Scratches	Check camera for rollers not freely rotating. Could be grit in 35mm cassette.
Fuzzy definition, some distances may be sharp	Out of focus	If this always happens have camera checked. Otherwise fault in setting camera.
All-over blurring, possibly with streaking of light parts	Camera shake	Squeeze release gently. Use faster shutter speed when possible. Hold camera correctly.
Blurred image in parts	Subject movement	Use faster shutter speed or avoid quick-moving subjects.
Overall mottle	Backing paper off-set	Occurs only with roll-film. Due to overlong storage or dampness.
Overlapping images	Incorrect winding	Check camera wind-on mechanism.

[2] Adapted from John Hedgecoe, *The Book of Photography*, copyright © 1976 Dorling Kindersley Ltd, published by Alfred A. Knopf, NY.

Processing faults

Symptom	Possible cause	Remedy
Dimple, or arc-shaped mark, sometimes accompanied by dent in film	Kink caused when loading film in tank	Occurs mostly with roll-film. No cure. Try to avoid.
Uneven diffused bands of light density	Wipe static	Caused by running fingers along film before loading.
Clear, or lighter area along length of negatives	Insufficient developer	Ensure film is completely covered in tank.
Round areas, lighter on negatives, darker on transparencies	Air bells	Tap tank on hard surface during first moments of processing.
Flat negatives, low density but ample shadow detail	Under development	Print on hard paper. Intensify only if unavoidable.
Contrasty negatives, fog level may be high, no over-exposure	Over-development	Print on soft paper. Reduce only if unavoidable.
Milky negatives	Incomplete fixation	Refix, preferable in fresh solution before exposing to bright light.
Short hair lines, parallel to edges of film	Cinch marks	Do not tighten rolled up film before processing.
Small, sharp areas with streamers	Chemical marks	Ensure all powder is dissolved before using solution.
Large spot of lighter density with greater density at edges	Drying mark	Use wetting agent in final rinse. Wipe down wet film.
Net-like cracks in gelatin	Reticulation	Avoid moving film from hot to cold.
Overall purple color with roll films	Regenerated backing dye	Rinse in sulfite solution or developer, wash and dry. Does not occur with all makes.

Paper faults

Symptom	Possible cause	Remedy
Gray veiling on margins	Fog	Unsafe safelight or old paper.
Overall yellow color	Staining	Over-long development. Old developer. Possible fixer no longer acidic.
Gray prints with no full black	Lack of contrast	If paper grade suits negative, insufficient development. Try giving 1 ½ to 2 minutes. Developer may be exhausted.
Poor image color	Contamination	If full time given to correct developer, suspect contamination of developer by fixer.
Black lines	Abrasion marks	May be caused by physical pressure before development. Sometimes caused by trimming before exposure. Can also result from prodding prints with sharp edged tongs during development.
Uneven density	Development marks	Usually caused by uneven development when prints have over-long exposure and are taken quickly from the developer in an attempt to compensate.

Color faults

Symptom	Possible cause	Remedy
Image much too orange/yellow	Daylight film used in artificial lighting or yellow filter accidentally left on lens	Use correct film and check for filters.
Image much too blue	Artificial light (type A or B) film used in daylight	Use correct film
Greenish image, with poor maximum density even in margins	Old film, outdated or stored badly. Could also be poor processing	Check film dates; try other processing services.
Pink lights in eyes with flash	Reflection from retinae	Move flashgun further from optical axis. With 110 camera use flash extender.
Bluish bias and poor contrast with flash	Smoky atmosphere	Take party pictures before too much cigarette smoke clouds the air.
Bluish landscapes, especially in distance	Haze recording as blue	Use UV or haze filter.
Reddish rendering, usually noticed with portraits	Picture taken at sunset or dawn	Change time of day, if desired.

APPENDIX F AUTOMOBILE ENGINE PROBLEMS[3]

FIGURE F–1
Troubleshooting basic engine performance.

Symptoms	Possible causes
Engine runs well, but it is hard to start when cold	• Wrong oil viscosity for prevailing temperature (see recommended viscosity chart in Section 8) • Stuck or improperly adjusted choke (Section 15) • Inadequate fuel pump volume, clogged fuel filter (Section 15) • Cracked distributor cap (Section 13) • Improper ignition timing/dwell angle (Section 13)
Engine idles poorly or stalls The engine runs rough; in extreme cases the whole car will shake. The engine may quit running while idling or driving.	• Idle speed/mixture improperly adjusted (Section 15) • Air leak at carbeurator base, intake manifold, or vacuum hoses (Section 15) • Clogged PVC valve/hose (Section 15) • Stuck or improperly adjusted choke (Section 15) • Incorrect timing/dwell; fouled spark plugs (Section 13) • Worn valves (Section 13)
Engine misfires at high speeds only	• Spark plug gaps too wide (Section 13) • Weak coil or spark plug wires; improper dwell angle (Section 13) • Inadequate fuel pump volume, clogged fuel filter (Section 15)
Engine misses at various speeds Steady jerking usually more pronounced as engine load increases. Exhaust has steady spitting sound at idle.	• Water/foreign matter in fuel • Insufficient dwell angle (Section 13) • Late ignition timing (Section 13) • Weak coil or condenser (Section 13)
Engine lacks power Engine delivers limited power under load or at high speed. Won't accelerate normally, loses power going up hills	• Wrong ignition timing (Section 13) • Fouled or improperly gapped spark plugs (Section 13) • Incorrect dwell angle, weak coil or condenser (Section 13) • Weak coil or condenser (Section 13) • Improperly adjusted valves (Section 8) • Worn piston rings, rings, valves (Section 8) • Inadequate fuel pump volume (Section 15)
Engine hesitates on acceleration Momentary lack or response as accelerator is depressed, most pronounced when pulling away from stop.	• Incorrect ignition timing (Section 13) • Inadequate fuel pump volume (Section 15)

[3] Material in this appendix is drawn, with permission, from *Chilton's Easy Car Care*, 2d ed., Kerry Freeman, Executive Editor, Chilton Book Company, Radnor, PA, 1985.

FIGURE F–1 (*continued*)

Symptoms	Possible causes
Engine detonates (pings) Detonation is a mild to severe ping, usually worse under acceleration. Engine makes a sharp metallic knock that sounds like a bolt rattling.	• Ignition timing over-advanced (Section 13) • Spark plug heat range too high (Section 13) • Stuck heat riser (Section 13) • Excessive carbon deposits in combustion chamber • Too low octane fuel (Section 5)
High oil consumption More than 1 quart every 500 miles	• Oil level too high (Section 8) • Oil of too light viscosity (Section 8) • External oil leaks (Section 4) • Worn cylinders or rings (Section 8)
Noisy valves	• Improperly adjusted valves (Section 8) • Incorrect engine oil level (Section 8) • Piece of carbon stuck underneath valve

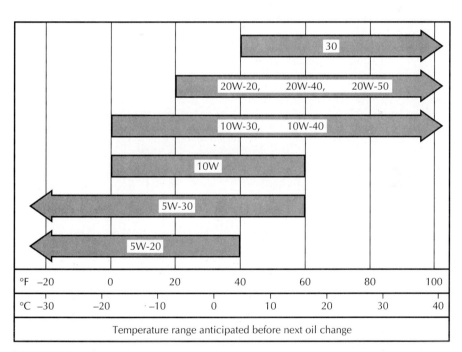

FIGURE F–2
Oil recommendations chart—gasoline engine.

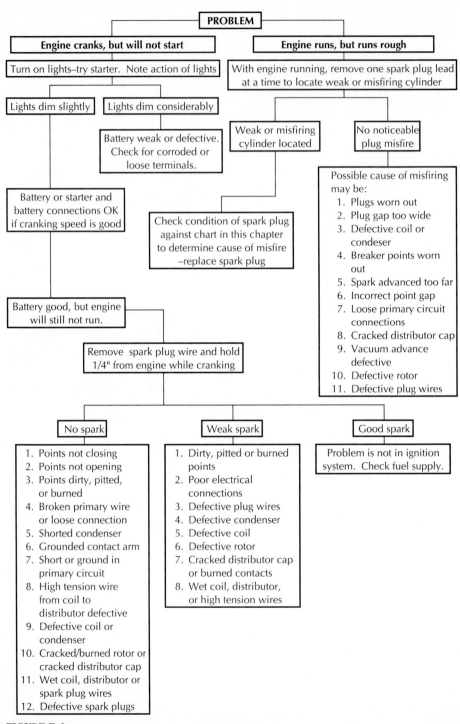

FIGURE F–3
Troubleshooting basic point-type ignition system problems.

FIGURE F–4

Troubleshooting basic fuel system problems.

Problem	Caused by	What to do
Engine cranks, but won't start (or is hard to start) when cold	• Empty fuel tank	• Check for fuel in tank
	• Incorrect starting procedure	• Follow correct procedure
	• Defective fuel pump	• Check pump output—see "Servicing the Fuel System"
	• No fuel in carburetor	• Check for fuel in the carburetor—see "Servicing the Fuel System"
	• Clogged fuel filter	• Replace fuel filter
	• Engine flooded	• Wait 15 minutes; try again—see "Servicing the Fuel System"
	• Defective choke	• Check choke plate—see "Servicing the Fuel System"
	• Water in fuel has frozen	• See "Servicing the Fuel System"
Engine cranks, but it is hard to start (or does not start) when hot—(presence of fuel is assumed)	• Defective choke	• Check choke plate—see "Servicing the Fuel System"
	• Vapor lock	• See "Servicing the Fuel System"
Rough idle or engine runs rough	• Dirt or moisture in fuel	• Replace fuel filter
	• Clogged air filter	• Replace air filter
	• Faulty fuel pump	• Check fuel pump output—see "Servicing the Fuel System"
Engine stalls or hesitates on acceleration	• Dirt or moisture in the fuel	• Replace fuel filter
	• Dirty carburetor	• Clean the carburetor—see "Servicing the Fuel System"
	• Defective fuel pump	• Check fuel pump output—see "Servicing the Fuel System"
	• Incorrect float level, defective accelerator pump	• Have carburetor checked

FIGURE F–4 (*continued*)

Troubleshooting basic fuel system problems.

Problem	Caused by	What to do
Poor gas mileage	• Clogged air filter	• Replace air filter
	• Dirty carburetor	• Clean carburetor—see "Servicing the Fuel System"
	• Defective choke, faulty carburetor adjustment	• Have carburetor checked
Engine is flooded (won't start, accompanied by smell of raw fuel)	• Improperly adjusted choke or carburetor	• Wait 15 minutes and try again, without pumping gas pedal. See "Servicing the Carburetor"
		• If won't start, have carburetor checked

FIGURE F–5

Symptoms of faulty emissions systems.

Symptom	Possible cause
Rough idle	Faulty PCV valve or clogged lines
	Faulty EGR valve
Hesitation on acceleration	Faulty PCV valve
Backfiring	Faulty air pump check valve
Overheating	Heater air cleaner defective

BIBLIOGRAPHY

PROLOG/LOGIC PROGRAMMING

Abramson, H., and Dahl, V., *Logic Grammars*, New York: Springer-Verlag, 1989.

Campbell, J., *Implementations of Prolog*, Chichester, West Sussex, England: Ellis Horwood Limited, 1984.

Clark, K., and McCabe, F., "Prolog as a language for implementing expert systems," in *Machine Intelligence 10*, eds. by Hayes, Michie, and Pao, New York: Wiley, 1982.

Clocksin, W., and Mellish, C., *Programming in Prolog*, New York: Springer-Verlag, 1981.

Coelho, H. and Cotta, J.C., (eds.), *Prolog by Example*, Berlin, Springer-Verlag, 1988.

Dahl, V., and Saint-Dizier, P., (eds.), *Natural Language Understanding and Logic Programming*, Amsterdam, The Netherlands: North Holland, 1985.

Dahl, V., and Saint-Dizier, P., (eds.), *Natural Language Understanding and Logic Programming II*, Amsterdam, The Netherlands: North Holland, 1988.

deGroot, D. and Lindstrom, G., *Logic Programming: Functions, Relations, and Equations*, Englewood Cliffs, N.J.: Prentice-Hall, 1986.

Gregory, S., *Parallel Logic Programming in PARLOG*, Reading, Mass.: Addison-Wesley, 1987.

Kowalski, R., *Logic for Problem Solving*, New York: North Holland, 1979.

Kowalski, R., and Bowen, K., (eds.), *Logic Programming; Proceedings of the Fifth International Converence and Symposium*, vols. I and II, Cambridge, Mass.: MIT Press, 1988.

Pereira, F., and Shieber, S., *Prolog and Natural-Language Analysis*, Stanford, Calif.: CSLI, 1987.

Merritt, D., *Building Expert Systems in Prolog*, New York: Springer-Verlag, 1989.

Lassez, J., (ed.), *Logic Programming; Proceedings of the Fourth International Conference*, Cambridge, Mass.: MIT Press, 1987.

Proceedings of the International Conference on Fifth Generation Computer Systems, 1984, Tokyo, Japan: ICOT, 1984.

Shapiro, E., (ed.), *Concurrent Prolog; Collected Papers*, vols. I and II, Cambridge, Mass.: MIT Press, 1987.

Tarnlund, S., (ed.), *Proceedings of the Second International Logic Programming Conference*, Uppsala, Sweden: Uppsala University, 1984.

van Caneghem, M., and Warren, D. H. D., (eds.), *Logic Programming and Its Applications*, Norwood, N.J.: Ablex Publishing Corp., 1986.

Weiss, S., and Kulikowski, C., *Designing Expert Systems*, Totowa, N.J.: Rowman & Allanheld, 1984.

Wos, L., Overbeek, R., Lusk, E., and Boyle, J., *Automated Reasoning, Introduction and Applications*, Englewood Cliffs, N.J.: Prentice-Hall, 1984.

INDEX